Macaronic Sermons

RECENTIORES: LATER LATIN TEXTS
AND CONTEXTS

Poetry and the Cult of the Martyrs: The Liber Peristephanon
of Prudentius
by Michael Roberts

Dante's Epistle to Cangrande
by Robert Hollander

*Macaronic Sermons: Bilingualism and Preaching in
Late-Medieval England*
by Siegfried Wenzel

MACARONIC SERMONS
Bilingualism and Preaching
in Late-Medieval England

Siegfried Wenzel

Ann Arbor

THE UNIVERSITY OF MICHIGAN PRESS

1997   1996   1995   1994   4   3   2   1

A CIP catalogue record for this book is available from the British Library.

Library of Congress Cataloging-in-Publication Data

Wenzel, Siegfried.
    Macaronic sermons : bilingualism and preaching in late–medieval
England / Siegfried Wenzel.
        p.   cm. — (Recentiores)
    Includes bibliographical references and index.
    ISBN 0-472-10521-3 (alk. paper)
    1. Christian literature, Latin (Medieval and modern)—England—
History and criticism. 2. Latin prose literature, Medieval and
modern—England—History and criticism. 3. English prose
literature—Middle English, 1100–1500—History and criticism.
4. Christian literature, English (Middle)—History and criticism.
5. Preaching—England—History—Middle Ages, 600–1500. 6. Sermons,
English (Middle)—History and criticism. 7. Sermons, Latin—
England—History and criticism. 8. Macaronic literature—History
and criticism. 9. Bilingualism—England—History. I. Title.
II. Series.
PA8045.E5W46   1994
878′.040809382—dc20   94-5120
                                                                CIP

Preface

This study has grown out of my previous work on English verses in medieval Latin sermons. When I examined sermon collections for the earlier project, I repeatedly came across linguistically mixed items where the English elements were not verses but prose inserts. I then planned to prepare a handlist of such macaronic sermons that might serve as a guide for other students. Over the years, however, starting with a paper in which I proposed a terminology that would distinguish different kinds of mixed sermons (1982), the handlist has grown into a full study, whose main purpose is not only to list but to analyze more closely a group of basically Latin sermons that include English prose elements in a way that mixes the two languages intimately within individual sentences.

Such macaronic prose texts from late-medieval England have never been the subject of detailed analysis, and the relevant sermons are largely unknown. Two exceptions are the work by Roy Haines on MS Bodley 649, presented in a series of articles (1972, 1975, 1976), and a dissertation by Patrick Horner on MS Laud misc. 706 in the Bodleian Library (1975, 1977, 1978, 1989). But Haines's interest was primarily that of a church historian, and Horner's dissertation focused on the purely English sermons in that collection. Neither scholar devoted much attention to the peculiar bilingual shape shown by many pieces in the two manuscripts. Yet these sermons form a linguistic, literary, and cultural phenomenon that demands closer investigation.

To describe and analyze the phenomenon, this book will study the manuscripts in which such macaronic sermons have been preserved and their authors, occasions, and audiences. It will then ask how one can explain the genesis of these linguistically mixed texts. Though this book was not undertaken to prove a thesis, in the course of writing it I have arrived at some definite views about the genesis and function of these sermons and their rhetorical effectiveness. I offer these views and my analysis as matters for discussion and further exploration.

The study of medieval sermons and preaching in England has in recent years benefited from a healthy revival of interest, and it has become clear that the work undertaken by Gerald Owst in the 1920s and 1930s, while retaining its value for the wealth of information it dug up and made available to historians and literary critics, stands in desperate need of updating and continuation. Fresh work needs to be done, beginning with the cataloging and analyzing of extant sermon collections—Owst's two volumes do not even contain an index of manuscripts quoted! At the same time, modern concerns redirect scholarly attention and pose a number of new questions that go far beyond what our forebears could have envisioned and that need to be answered if we want to understand the making of sermons, the practice of preaching, the prevailing attitudes toward texts, and similar solidly historical matters. To what extent, for example, do surviving sermons actually bear out the cliché that medieval preachers tritely repeated commonplaces cribbed from such handbooks as *Dormi secure*? How much variation is there among different copies of a sermon? Is it just as much as can be attributed to careless scribes who corrupted their models or, conversely, to intelligent ones who emended them; or do extant copies of the same sermon show, perhaps like versions of the same romance or tale, the result of deliberate variation effected in the course of oral performance (by a preacher) or of early editing (by a scribe)? And what can we possibly say about how close the preserved texts are to the form in which they were originally delivered?

These and similar questions require detailed examination of the texts. But these texts, for the most part, lie unedited in manuscripts whose decipherment requires uncommon linguistic and paleographical skills. Moreover, their existence and dissemination are very far from having been sufficiently charted. No inventory of medieval Latin sermons after 1350 parallels the existing *Index of Middle English Verse,* or the index of Middle English prose and the collection of records of the early English drama that are now in progress. The monumental *Repertorium* by Johannes Baptist Schneyer not only stops at the threshold of the period in which surviving sermons from England become more numerous and interesting but furnishes at best a preliminary guide whose details (attribution and authorship, variation between collections, dating, etc.) call for constant revision.[1]

The present book intends to make a contribution to the study of late-medieval preaching by examining a group of linguistically remarkable sermons, their macaronicity, and the manuscripts in which they have been preserved. Their linguistic form should prove of further interest to the study of multilingualism in England between approximately 1350 and 1450, the century that saw the rise of English as the preferred literary medium and its superseding of spoken French in more and more areas, both private and public. These changes from French to English are well known and have been documented in detail. But what about Latin? If, as many Chaucerians think, England's greatest poet of that century relied much on Latin sources but could read them only with some help in French, what are we to think of his contemporaries and their capacity to handle Latin? Was his friend John Gower a *rarissima avis* indeed in his ability not only to warble in English but to sing in French and to croak (?) in Latin? The use of literary Latin in Chaucer's age has been very little studied, and I hope that my examination of linguistically mixed texts may bring some discomfort and new life to current views about the general drift toward the vernacular and the linguistic competence among late fourteenth-century educated Englishmen. The connection of these texts with the name of Chaucer, incidentally, is not haphazard; as chapters 2 and 3 show, the majority of these texts seems to have originated in the generation between the rule of Richard II and the death of Henry V.

Most of the material used in this study is unpublished, and all quotations from medieval sermons are taken from the manuscripts. In citing the latter, I use the sigla and sermon numbers inventoried in appendix A. When the sermon number is followed by a slash and another number, the latter indicates the respective folio; thus, "W-070/131rb" refers to sermon 70 in Worcester Cathedral MS F.10, f. 131rb. When the manuscript text appears in one column, reference to the recto side of a folio

---

1. Johannes Baptist Schneyer, *Repertorium der lateinischen Sermones des Mittelalters für die Zeit von 1150–1350*, 11 vols., Beiträge zur Geschichte der Philosophie und Theologie des Mittelalters, vol. 43 (Münster, 1965–90). Some shortcomings have been pointed out by the directors of the team that is working on Schneyer's *Nachlaß* and that is planning to extend the *Repertorium* to 1500: L. Hödl and R. Hetzler, "Zum Stand der Erforschung der lateinischen Sermones des Mittelalters (für die Zeit von 1350–1500)," *Scriptorium* 46 (1992):129–35.

appears without the *r*. References to the three sermons edited in this book give their respective siglum and the line number as they appear in appendices B–D. In all quotations from macaronic sermons, English material is set in boldface. The original material quoted in the following chapters is taken from the manuscripts and presented in the original spelling; abbreviations have been silently expanded. I have silently accepted scribal corrections and have not emended the texts further except for an occasional added letter, enclosed in square brackets; and the notation [!], used for the more conventional [*sic*]. Marginalia are rendered in angle brackets, and interlinear material is reproduced between slashes. The editorial principles followed in editing the three sample sermons are set forth in the headnotes to appendices B and C.

In the research that lies behind these chapters, I have incurred many debts, which it is a pleasure to acknowledge with much gratitude. First and foremost, I thank the librarians and staffs who have given me courteous access to their collections and who in many cases provided microfilm copies. I am deeply grateful to them for permission to quote from the manuscripts in their possession. To the libraries mentioned in appendix A, I wish to add those of Jesus College (Cambridge), Merton College (Oxford), the University of Nottingham, and the cathedral libraries of Lincoln, Salisbury, and York. I am especially indebted to Canon Iain MacKenzie and Mr. Ronald Stratton of Worcester Cathedral for the privilege of working in the cathedral library at length; and to Dr. B. S. Benedikz of the University of Birmingham for depositing a Worcester Cathedral manuscript in the Bodleian Library. Travel grants from the American Philosophical Society (1972 and 1979), the American Council of Learned Societies (1987), and the National Endowment for the Humanities (1992) allowed me to visit and revisit libraries in England and France in search of sermon manuscripts. I am grateful to the libraries of the University of North Carolina at Chapel Hill and of the University of Pennsylvania for purchasing microfilms for my use. I also wish to thank the Master and Fellows of Balliol College, the Bodleian Library, and the Dean and Chapter of Worchester Cathedral, for permission to edit the three sermons in appendices B–D.

Alexandra Barratt, N. F. Blake, A. I. Doyle, Lawrence M. Eldredge, Patrick Horner, Sarah M. Horrall, Anne Hudson, Patricia Lehman, G. A. Lester, Robert E. Lewis, Derek Pearsall, Linda E. Voigts, and Christina Von Nolcken have given me various kinds of help, including responses to a questionnaire I sent out in 1984 about macaronic sermons.

Finally, a word of heartfelt thanks is due to my several "mistresses," currently a Dell 316SX, who have made recording these texts, reading them and distinguishing their linguistic components in different colors, and searching them for relevant material not only a less painful task than it would have been a generation ago but a genuine pleasure. I am deeply grateful to the University of Pennsylvania and my friend and former associate dean Stephen G. Nichols for providing me with these wonderful technological aids.

Contents

Abbreviations

The Bible is quoted according to the edition by Robert Weber, *Biblia sacra iuxta vulgatam versionem,* 3d ed., 2 vols. (Stuttgart, 1983). When referring to biblical books, I use the standard English names and abbreviations.

Bloomfield	Morton W. Bloomfield et al. *Incipits of Latin Works on the Virtues and Vices, 1100–1500* A.D. Cambridge, MA, 1979.
Caplan *Handlist*	Harry Caplan. *Mediaeval Artes Praedicandi: A Hand-List.* Ithaca, 1934.
Caplan *Suppl*	Harry Caplan. *Mediaeval Artes Praedicandi: A Supplementary Hand-List.* Ithaca, 1936.
CC	*Corpus Christianorum, series latina.* Various editors. Turnhout, 1954–.
Lombard *Sent*	Peter Lombard. *Sententiae.* Edited by Patres Collegii S. Bonaventurae Ad Claras Aquas. 3d ed., 2 vols. Grottaferrata, 1971. Quoted by book, distinction, and chapter; volume and page references added in parenthesis.
MED	*Middle English Dictionary.* Edited by Hans Kurath, Sherman Kuhn, and Robert E. Lewis. Ann Arbor, MI, 1954–.
OED	*New English Dictionary on Historical Principles.* Edited by J. A. H. Murray et al. Oxford, 1888–1928.
PL	*Patrologiae Cursus Completus: Series Latina.* Edited by J.-P. Migne. Paris, 1844–64.
Tubach	Frederic C. Tubach. *Index exemplorum: A Handbook of Medieval Religious Tales.* Helsinki, 1969.

CHAPTER 1

Macaronic Literature

Any society or social group in which at least some members are more or less fluent in more than one language tends to produce "texts," both oral and written, that mix languages in one form or another. Thus, when two of the heirs of Charlemagne's empire, after years of civil war, came to an agreement, they confirmed it with oaths spoken in the language of the other party, and these so-called Strasbourg Oaths of A.D. 842, in Romance and German, have found their way into the Latin of Nithard's *Histories*.[1] A formally very different sort of document that yet reflects precisely the same phenomenon is the famous Lindisfarne Gospels book, which presents the Latin Vulgate text of Scripture together with an interlinear gloss in Old English. Such bilingualism occurs in the societies of medieval Western Europe in many forms. It not only served preeminently practical purposes, as in the two examples cited or in later court records and biographies that tell us about bilingual proceedings and individuals, but was utilized for ultimately artistic aims.

Thus, in medieval England, poets frequently used Latin words, phrases, and even entire sentences in their vernacular compositions. The Anglo-Saxon poem *Phoenix*, after 666 alliterative lines in Old English, breaks into a bilingual coda.

Hafað us alyfed	*lucis auctor*
þæt we motun her	*mereri,*
goddædum begietan	*gaudia in celo.*

---

1. Nithardus 1907, 3.5, pp. 35–37.

(*The author of light* has granted us that we may here *merit,* obtain
with good deeds, *the joys in heaven.*)[2]

This bilingual pattern continues for a total of eleven lines. From the
thirteenth until the early sixteenth century, English poets produced hundreds of lyrics that similarly introduce Latin words or phrases into Anglo-
Norman or English stanzas, lyrics that are mostly religious but also
include an occasional drinking song, a political poem, or even humoristic
or satirical verses. The large corpus of over 500 carols of the late fourteenth and fifteenth centuries contains 210 items that show such a mixture, as for instance:

Atte domysday, when we haue nede,
   Tuis preclaris meritis
Then, we the pray, in worde and dede
   Succurre nobis miseris.
   O mater summi Iudicis,
   Succurre nobis miseris.[3]

This body of bilingual poetry even includes works by known authors:
Lydgate and Ryman in the fifteenth, Dunbar and Skelton in the early
sixteenth century.[4] Nor is such linguistic mixture in poetry limited to the
lyric. It occurs in *Piers Plowman* and was also used on the stage, both
in the Corpus Christi cycles[5] and in morality plays.[6]

For over a century, students of Middle English poetry have labeled
such linguistically mixed poems *macaronic.*[7] The word, originally in Latin, was evidently coined in the 1490s and referred to a kind of poetry fa-
vored by Italian humanists, predominantly in Padua, who mixed their
Latin hexameters with vernacular words and expressions, giving the latter

---

2. Blake 1964, ll. 667–69.
3. Greene 1977, 144.
4. The latter two have been recently analyzed by Archibald 1992.
5. Good examples occur in plays 21 ("Christ and the Doctors") and 22 ("The Baptism")
of the N-Town Cycle; see Spector 1991, 197–98, 203, 207–8.
6. Especially in *Mankind* (see note 12), but also in *Wisdom* and *The Castle of
Perseverance.*
7. The use of the term with special application to Middle English religious poetry from
1842 on has been critically surveyed by Wehrle (1933, xviii–xxxvii).

the correct Latin endings demanded by classical grammar.[8] The phenomenon has been much studied and has been linked to various medieval forerunners, especially the *latinus grossus* of fifteenth-century preachers who similarly produced what, to a humanist's eye, was a thoroughly debased Latin. Teofilo Folengo (d. 1544), who adopted this practice as a medium for wit, playfulness, and parody, defined his practice as follows.

> This poetic art is called "macaronic" from *macarones,* which are a certain dough made up of flour, cheese, and butter, thick, coarse, and rustic. Thus, macaronic poems must have nothing but fat, coarseness, and gross words in them.[9]

Based on Folengo's versifying practice, the *Oxford English Dictionary* defined macaronic primarily as "a burlesque form of verse in which vernacular words are introduced into a Latin context with Latin terminations and in Latin constructions." A fairly well-known example of this type of linguistic mixture is a jingle that has delighted generations of young scholars,

> Boyibus kissibus pretty girlorum
> Girlibus likibus, wanty somorum.

Here English words are provided with—in this case, syntactically incorrect—Latin endings. More truly in line with the quoted definition are the following macaronic verses from the pen of a German humanist.

> Illis sunt equidem, sunt, inquam, corpora *kleina,*
> Sed mille *erregunt Menschis Martrasque Plagasque,*
> Cum *steckunt Schnablum* in *Leibum Blutumque* rubentem
> Exsugunt.

---

8. This paragraph is indebted to the studies by Paoli 1959, Lazzerini 1971, Paccagnella 1973, and Torres-Alcalá 1984. See also Archibald 1992 for a parallel review.

9. "Ars ista poetica nuncupatur ars macaronica a macaronibus derivata, qui macarones sunt quoddam pulmentum farina, caseo, botiro compaginatum, grossum, rude et rusticanum; ideo macaronices nil nisi grassedinem, ruditatem et vocabulazzos debet in se continere." Cited by Paoli (1959, 5). Folengo's *Liber Macaronices* was published in 1517. Paoli makes the important clarification that in the early sixteenth century, *macaroni* probably referred to gnocchi (3–6).

(They [i.e., fleas] have, I say, *small* bodies, yet a thousand *cause
people tortures and pains* when *they put their beak* in *the body
and* suck red *blood*.)[10]

Here lexical elements from one language, in this case German, are cor-
rectly integrated into the grammatical structure of the other, Latin, thus
yielding German words with Latin endings.[11]

In Middle English this type of macaronic verse is quite rare. It makes
one of its few appearances in the morality play *Mankind,* where the
technique of providing English words with Latin endings serves to mock
or satirize the true Latin of the Vulgate Bible and thus forms one of
the play's various ways of characterizing good and evil figures by the
language they speak. While still in the state of grace, Mankind holds
on firmly to his spade and quotes Scripture.

Dauide seyth, "*Nec in hasta, nec in gladio, saluat Dominus.*"

But his moral seriousness is at once made fun of by Nought.

No, Mary, I beschrew yow, yt ys *in spadibus!*
Therfor Crystys curse cum on yowr *hedybus,*
     To sende you less myght![12]

Much more frequent in medieval English literature is the use of a
language mixture that combines not roots and terminations from different
languages but words, phrases, or entire sentences that follow completely
the grammatical rules of their respective tongue.[13] The quoted passage
from the Old English poem *Phoenix* provides a fine example of this

---

10. The hexameters were written by a German humanist under the pseudonym Gri-
phaldus Knicknackius ex Flohlandia and are quoted by Paoli (1959, 56). I have slightly
modernized the German words.

11. A parallel case in which modern English words are similarly inserted in a sentence
whose basic grammar is modern German would be: "Die cow ist über den fence gejumpt."

12. *Mankind,* ll. 397–400; in Eccles 1969, 166–67. I have italicized the Latin and
macaronic words and capitalized *Mary.*

13. The *OED* may recognize this sense of *macaronic* in its addition to the already
quoted definition: "Hence of language, style, etc.: Resembling the mixed jargon of macaronic poetry."

more prevalent type, as does a later, thirteenth-century Marian lyric that contains the lines

Al þis world was for-lore
   Eua peccatrice
Tyl our Lord was y-bore
   de te genetrice.

(All this world was lost *by sinful Eve* until our Lord was born *from you, his mother.*)[14]

In this wider sense of combining elements from two or more languages from the level of the word on up, the term *macaronic* has been adopted by modern English writers and is being applied to any kind of verse that mixes English and Latin (or French) in different structural forms and for a variety of rhetorical purposes.[15]

Such macaronic texts can be found not only in verse but in prose. There is probably no religious or devotional text in Middle English prose that does not include some Latin words, phrases, or sentences. The early thirteenth-century rule for nuns, *Ancrene Wisse,* contains hundreds of Latin quotations that furnish authoritative proof and compositional stepping stones in the development of the anonymous author's teaching.

Schirnesse of heorte is Godes luue ane. I þis is al þe strengðe of alle religiuns, þe ende of alle ordres. *Plenitudo legis est dilectio.* "Luue fulleð þe lahe," seið seinte Pawel. *Quicquid precipitur, in sola caritate solidatur.* "Alle Godes heastes," as sein Gregoire seið, "beoð i luue irotet."

(Cleanness of heart is the love of God alone. In this lies all the strength of all religious life, the purpose of all orders. *Love is the fulfilling of the law.* "Love fulfils the law," says St. Paul. *Whatever is com-*

---

14. Brown 1932, 26; I have introduced some capitalization.

15. Some examples are Pearsall 1970, 260, 273–74; Diehl 1985, 110–13; Swanton 1987, 137–38. Analyses of the various structural patterns in which Latin elements appear in vernacular poems can be found in Wehrle 1933; Diehl 1985, 111–12; and Archibald 1992. For the Latin tags and quotations in *Piers Plowman,* see especially Alford 1992 and Lindemann 1973.

manded is completed only with love. "All God's commandments,"
as St. Gregory says, "are rooted in love.")[16]

The mode illustrated here of integrating a Latin passage into an
English text—direct quotation followed or sometimes preceded by translation or paraphrase—and its rhetorical function are absolutely characteristic of Middle English sermons as well. In medieval vernacular
preaching, it was not only customary but evidently de rigueur to quote
authorities in their original Latin form, whether they were biblical, patristic, or pagan. Even the most rigorously English sermons have at least
one quotation in Latin, their thema[17]—even sermons produced by that
group of writers who were most strongly committed to presenting the
biblical text in the vernacular, the makers of the Wycliffite sermon cycle.
It is possible to claim that all Middle English sermons are macaronic.

Within this large territory of macaronic texts produced in late medieval
England, a number of sermons occupy a very special place. In contrast
to the just-quoted Middle English sermons, these texts use Latin as their
base language and mix some English elements into it. A longer passage
illustrates this kind of linguistic mixture and leads us to the questions
with which this book is primarily concerned.

Vt lego in sacra scriptura Mathei XVII et Marci IX, quando Christus
fuit hic in terris, **in releuynge and comfort of monkinde** operabatur
manu **wondirful miracles. He fedde ones** 5 milia hominum ex 5 panibus
et duobus piscibus, vt euangelium testatur. **He recured and halp mony
men** qui vexati a spiritibus immundis [MS mund'] fuerant. **He rerid
vp** Lazarum, Marie **and** Marthe broþer, **fro det to liue**, qui moriebatur
per IIII dies antea et fetebat **in his graue. þes wer gret** miracula. **And
alþowe þes schewid** aperte et approbabant quod fuerat verus Deus et
omnipotens, adhuc ad excludendum omnia dubia a suis discipulis [MS
diffi'lis] **and fullich settle hom** in fide, ascendit [MS asken it] in
montem excelsum et cepit tres ex discipulis suis secum, Petrum, Ia-
cobum, et Iohannem, et ibi transfigurauit se coram eis, **he turned him**

16. *Ancrene Wisse,* part 7. The text is from the edition by Tolkien (1962, 197), with
modern punctuation added. The translation is that of Salu (1955, 171), with some punctuation added.
17. This feature will be further analyzed below, in chapter 6.

extra similitudinem hominis in similitudinem deitatis, quia vt scriptura testatur, "vestes erant albe vt nix et facies eius resplenduit as **briȝt** sicut sol," et in illa gloriosa visione apparuerunt secum duo sancti prophete, Moises et Helias. Super istum textum dicunt doctores nostri in postillis et exposicionibus super hoc quod ille mons nichil aliud est nisi **heye monteyn** celi, in quo est eternalis gloria et gaudium. In illum **ioyful hil** Christus ascendit in nostra carne in die ascensionis et apparuit omnibus beatis spiritibus non [MS i'i] in similitudine sed in aperta claritate verissime deitatis. In istum montem nemo veniet nisi sit Petrus, Iacobus, et Iohannes. Quid est hoc dictum? **Scul no Robert ne Richard go to heuonn** sic? Absit, aliter. Sed si velint transire illuc, oportet vt sint spiritualiter Petrus. Petrus [MS *om.* = omitted] interpretatur agnoscens, **knowlichinge.** **þou most** fateri **þin offense and þi synne.** **þou schal now turne** extra pulcrum, **tel** vnam partem et dimittere alteram, sed plane vt offendisti referes **þi gostly fadur.** Et sicut Petrus fleuit amare quando negauit Christum, sic oportet te flere et habere **inward contricioun** pro peccato tuo. **þou most** eciam **be Iamis.** Iacobus interpretatur supplantator, **supplanting: þou most supplante and forsake al maner vices,** non ore sed corde. Non dimittes hodie et recurres cras, sed **þou schalt forsake hom and neuer haue wil to turne aȝayne** ad illa. Similiter **be Jonn.** Iohannes interpretatur gracia Dei, **grace of god. þis grace þou most nedeliche haue,** quia sine illa non potes actus interiores peragere nec transire ad gaudium celeste. **þorow** ista gracia **þou schalt rule þi liue in honeste and vertu, and so performe þin hynde.** Et si fatearis peccata tua isto modo et peniteas, inde **vtturlich forsake hom and continue þi liue in vertu,** et es habilis ascendere in montem cum Christo videre eius gloriosissimam transfiguracionem, **to beholdonn** super eius benedictam deitatem in eternum. Sed quid **betokon þe holi** prophete Moises **and** Helias qui apparuerunt cum Christo in monte? Per Moises, qui fuerat "mitissimus [MS *om.*] in terra," Numeri XII, possum bene intelligere **þe mekenes and þe godenes** quam Christus ostendit nobis dum sumus in hac terra, quia licet **we trespas aȝayns** him et offende him greouuslich sicut facimus omni die, **he takes no** subitam vindictam sed humiliter sustinet nos, **he sendus vs bodilich helthe** et quecumque necessaria. **And haue we** [MS *om.*] **neuer trespas so muche** contra ipsum, si velimus semel petere veniam, paratus est dare misericordiam. Sic quamdiu simus hic, apparet nobis Moises. Sed vere in proximo [MS *blank*] apparebit nobis Helias. Iste Helias fuit **þe sternest man and**

þe **most rigus** in antiqua lege. Per ipsum intelligitur þe **scharp
riȝtwisnes** que demonstratur in die iudicii peccatoribus. Illis Christus
solum apparebit Helias, quia vt Ieremias dicit, "Non parcet in illa
die Dominus nec miseretur," Ieremie XXI. **Kryþe neuer so sore** pro
adiutorio, **make neuer so muche mone,** non valebit tibi, Christus non
parcet in illa die, **he schal haue no ruth ne mercy** super te, **he nil bwe
þik time for no prayer,** sed **vtturliche** vult vindicare se de peccato tuo.
Omnes cautele **and sleȝtes** iuris non proficient tibi, non appellabis,
nec facies dilacionem cause tue. þer **schal no seriont of law** nec **prentise**
curie placitare pro te, sed tumet ibi respondebis et dabis compotum
quomodo expendisti vitam tuam. Et si [MS *blank*] de hoc mundo in
mortali peccato, sine aliqua gracia uel misericordia transibis ad ignem
inferni et dampnaberis sine fine. Et ideo sancta mater Ecclesia, que
figuratur per mulierem Cananeam de qua euangelium hodiernum fecit
mencionem, habens consideracionem illius asperi rigoris et tremendi
iudicii quod filia ipsius, quelibet anima Christiana que vexatur a [MS
om.] diabolo et vincitur catenis mortalis peccati, posset dum est hic
confiteri peccata sua et **repente her þrof** cum Petro, **fullich forsake
hom** cum Iacob, et graciose cum Iohanne **make** talem finem in hoc
seculo quod in tremendo iudicio Christus non appareat illi solum
Helias sed eciam Moises, non tantum demonstret ei **his vtmast rigur
but medle** [MS medie] **his mercy** cum iusticia, clamat sibi toto corde
et dicit, *Domine, adiuua me,* sicut **I tok to my prechynge.**

(As I read in Holy Scripture, Matthew 17 and Mark 9, when Christ
was here on earth, he worked wonderful miracles with his hand to
the relief and comfort of mankind. He once fed five thousand men
with five loaves and two fish, as the Gospel witnesses. He cured and
helped many men who had been tormented by impure spirits. He
raised up from death to life Lazarus, the brother of Mary and Martha,
who was lying dead for four days and stinking in his grave. Those
were great miracles. And although they showed openly and proved
that he was true and almighty God, still, to keep away any doubts
from his disciples and confirm them fully in their faith, he ascended
a high mountain and took three of his disciples with him: Peter,
James, and John. And there he became transfigured before them, he
changed himself from the likeness of man to the likeness of divinity,
because, as Scripture says, "his garments were white as the snow and
his face shone as bright as the sun." And in that glorious vision, two

holy prophets appeared with him, Moses and Elisha. On this text, our teachers say, in their postils and expositions on the text, that that mountain is nothing else than the high mountain of heaven, where there is eternal glory and joy. Christ climbed onto this joyful hill in our flesh on Ascension Day and appeared to all the blessed spirits, not in an image, but in the open clearness of his true godhead. To this mountain no one will come unless it be Peter, James, and John. What does this mean? Shall no Robert or Richard then go to heaven? Far from it, quite otherwise. But if they want to get there, they must be Peter in the spirit. "Peter" means "acknowledging." You must tell your offense and your sin. You must not turn outside what is fair, tell one part [of your sins] and leave the other, but you must report to your spiritual father plainly as you have offended. And as Peter wept bitterly when he denied Christ, so must you weep and have inward contrition for your sin. You must also be James. "James" means "supplanting." You must supplant and forsake every kind of vices, not with your mouth, but in your heart. You must not leave them today and return to them tomorrow, but you must forsake them and never have any desire to turn to them again. Likewise you must be John. "John" means "God's grace." This grace you must have of necessity, for without it you cannot perform those interior acts or pass on to the joy of heaven. Through this grace you must rule your life in honesty and virtue, and so perform your duty. And if you confess your sins in this way and are contrite, and then forsake them utterly and continue your life in virtue, you are able to ascend the mountain with Christ and see his most glorious transfiguration and behold his blessed godhead in eternity. But what do the holy prophets Moses and Elisha mean who appeared with Christ on the mountain? By Moses, who was "the meekest man on earth," Numbers 12, I can understand the meekness and goodness that Christ showed us while we are on this earth; for even if we trespass against him and offend him grievously, as we do every day, he takes no sudden revenge but sustains us humbly; he sends us health of body and whatever things we need. And however much we have trespassed against him, if we would once ask for forgiveness, he is ready to grant us mercy. Thus, however long we are here, he appears to us as Moses. But truly in the future he will appear to us as Elisha. Elisha was the sternest and most rigorous man in the Old Law. By him we understand the sharp justice that is shown to sinners on Judgment Day. To them, Christ will appear only as Elisha, for as Jeremiah says, "on that day the Lord will not spare or have mercy," Jeremiah 21. However much you may cry out for help, however much you may complain, it will not help you, Christ will not spare on that day, he will have no pity or mercy on you, he will not bend at that time to any prayer, but he will utterly take vengeance on your sin. All the ruses and tricks of the law will not help you; there will be no appeal for you or any postponement of your case. No attorney or barrister of the court will plead for you, but you yourself will give answer and render an account of how you have spent your life. And if [you depart] from this world in mortal sin, you will go to the fire of hell without any grace or mercy and will be damned forever. And thus, Holy Mother the Church, who is symbolized by the Canaanite woman of whom today's gospel spoke, considers the harsh rigor and fearful judgment, so that her daughter, that is, any Christian soul that is tormented by the devil and bound by the chains of mortal sin, might, while she is here, confess her sins and repent of them with Peter, forsake them entirely with James, and by grace come with John to such an end in this world that in his fearsome judgment Christ will appear to her not only as Elisha but as Moses, that he will not only show her his utmost rigor but mingle his justice with mercy; and she cries out to him with her whole heart and says, "Lord, help me," in the words I have taken for my sermon.)[18]

This lengthy paragraph comes from an early fifteenth-century sermon on the gospel of the daughter of the Canaanite woman healed by Jesus, where it forms the technical introduction to the thema *Domine, adiuva me* ("Lord, help me," Matt. 15:25). In it, Latin and English appear intimately mixed. Its matrix is Latin, but its texture frequently changes to English and then back again, with both languages preserving their characteristic syntactic patterns. Not uncommonly, a syntactic unit in one language, whether Latin or English, is interrupted by a single word from the other, as in "**þou most** fateri **þin offense**" or, conversely, in "sed **vtturliche** vult vindicare se." The English elements thus vary in length from single words to entire clauses. At several points they merely repeat the preceding Latin word: "agnoscens, **knowlichinge**"; "sup-

---

18. O–04/21r–v.

plantator, **supplanting**"; and "gracia Dei, **grace of god**." In these cases they constitute vernacular glosses; but elsewhere, in the vast majority of cases, they form indispensable parts of the text.

In contrast to the practice of Teofilo Folengo and his fellow humanists or to the debased Latin of Nought in *Mankind,* this sermon passage mixes English words and phrases into a Latin structure in such a way that each language preserves its own proper morphology and syntax.[19] At the same time, even a first glance reveals that the inserted English elements do not seem to occur simply because they were more immediately present to the mind of the speaker or writer of this text. In the two cases cited a few lines above, there is no reason why an English sentence should use *fateri* instead of **tell** or, conversely, why a Latin clause should use **vtterliche** instead of *complete* or a similar adverb. In neither case is the "foreign" word a rare or technical term; both words avoided in these examples can be found readily elsewhere in the same sermon.

The quoted passage already reveals how radically different these sermons are from the macaronic texts surveyed earlier in this chapter, not only in their linguistic structure, but even more so in the rhetorical function of their language mixture. The element of humor or burlesque that is characteristic of humanistic macaronic verses and of *Mankind* does not occur in these sermons at all; they are not *sermons joyeux* but instruments of serious moral exhortation.[20] They differ just as much from lyrical poems in which language mixture functions as a stylistic means for highly artistic and morally serious ends.[21] And they do not follow the practice of *Piers Plowman* and Middle English religious prose texts and sermons, which change languages for purposes of authoritative quotation. In the quoted example, neither language can be said to be privileged in such a way that it gives authority or produces a heightened rhetorical effect.

This macaronic phenomenon occurs in a number of sermons written in England between approximately 1350 and 1450. Does it deserve attention beyond being reported in a footnote to the history of the English

---

19. For the Latin lexicon, see chapters 5 and 6.

20. On *sermons joyeux,* see the fundamental study by Picot (1886–88) and the ongoing work by Koopmans. It should be stressed that modern authorities are very wary of seeing in *sermons joyeux* a parody of serious preaching; see Koopmans and Verhuyck 1986.

21. See Zumthor 1960.

language? Does it not, all too patently, reflect the transitional period
and state in which English came into its own as the preferred literary
vehicle? More particularly, does it not simply indicate that these writers
still clung to the traditional medium of theological discourse—clerical
Latin—while at the same time reaching out, however spottily, to the new
medium of the vernacular? Perhaps so, but several aspects make one
hesitate to accept what might seem so immediately obvious.

After 1350 and far into, if not beyond, the fifteenth century, Latin
remained what it had been throughout the preceding millennium: the
language in which theologians wrote. Whatever the reasons for this con-
tinuity may have been—whether force of habit or the availability of a
writing system with fixed abbreviations that allowed *reportatores* to take
notes quickly and helped scribes to save space—during the period with
which we are concerned, theological texts, including sermon collections,
not only continued to be copied in Latin but were freshly composed in
the learned language.[22] Why, then, do we have these strangely mixed
texts that linguistically are neither fish nor fowl? Did their authors or
copyists perhaps lack alertness or intellectual vigor to write well in one
or the other medium instead of slipping back and forth between them?
Or were the men who produced these sermons so thoroughly bilingual,
in both their written and spoken practice, that these mixed texts might
have formed a natural linguistic medium for them? And what about the
actual preaching? Were these sermons delivered in Latin, in English, or
in both languages at once?

The following chapters attempt to answer these questions. To do so,
we need, before all else, to establish a corpus of relevant macaronic
sermons. For this purpose, we must distinguish the kind of sermon that
is the concern of this study from others that also combine elements from
two different languages but do so in very different ways. Next, we must
describe the manuscripts that have preserved such sermons and analyze
the collections they contain. From that base, we can examine external
features of these macaronic sermons, such as their occasions, authorship,
contexts, and so on (chap. 4), and further analyze the peculiar grammatical structure of their linguistic texture (chap. 5). Finally, we can turn
to the major questions these sermons pose: what causes might explain
their genesis, and whether they were intended to be actually preached in
this bilingual form.

---

22. For example, the collections made by Ralph Atton (s. xiv), Thomas Brinton (d.
1389), and John Felton (1431); see below, chapter 3, note 93.

CHAPTER 2

Types of Bilingual Sermons

Such sermons as the one quoted in the previous chapter were only part of a larger field of sermons in which two languages—Latin and English, for our purposes—appear side by side. Of the sermons produced in England during the century from 1350 to 1450, a high percentage show some degree of such mixture. The amount of English in them may be extremely small—an English proverb, perhaps, or a couple of isolated English words embedded in many folios of Latin prose. An extreme case of such minimal English appears in a sermon that is identified by its rubric as having been "given at Northampton in the Provincial Chapter of the Black Monks."[1]

According to Benedictine constitutions of the fourteenth century, the provincial chapters, which were held triennially at Northampton, were to begin with a Latin sermon preached at the outset of the chapter on the first day and to end with an English sermon at a public mass two days later.[2] That this rule was followed is shown by several chronicle

---

1. "Sermo facta [!] apud Northamtoun in capitulo prouinciali nigrorum monachorum," written before the sermon in the text hand, a fifteenth-century Anglicana bookhand with Secretary features; London, British Library, MS Cotton Titus C.ix, f. 26. The manuscript contains monastic documents, including a cartulary of Darley Abbey, Derbyshire. Pantin thought the sermon might have been preached by William Waldene of Bury St. Edmunds at the provincial chapter of 1423; Pantin 1931, 2:135, 3:323.

2. According to the statutes for provincial chapters of 1343: "Primo autem die capituli, signo pulsato, et demum cessante, omnes prelati et procuratores absencium in choro conveniant usque ad finem misse de Sancto Spiritu celebrandi, cum collectis pro Romano pontifice, rege et regina ac liberis eorum, pace ecclesie statuque regni; Qua missa finita, signoque pulsato ad capitulum, procedant froccis induti, et statim fiat sermo, in cuius principio benefactores ordinis tam vivi, quam mortui commendentur; Quo finito, exeant seculares..." Pantin 1931, 2:58. This sermon was in Latin (cf. ibid., 1:88, 266; 2:7). On

entries.[3] The provincial chapter sermon I referred to, which has unfortunately not been preserved in its entirety, uses as its theme *Collegerunt pontifices concilium* ("The high priests convened a council," John 11:47). This thema and its development make it clear that the sermon was intended for the first occasion, that is, to be preached in Latin at the opening of the chapter. The text is entirely in Latin, with one minute exception: the unknown preacher says that in the same way that the Jews came to the raising of Lazarus not merely for Jesus' sake but to see Lazarus, many prelates have gathered not just for Jesus' sake, that is, for the benefit of their order,

> ymmo pocius, quod **parled** est, vt Lazarum intuerentur in antiquis amiciciis resuscitatum.

> (but rather, as it is said, to see Lazarus revived in old friendships.)[4]

To find a single English word in an otherwise Latin sermon is rare but not unique. However interesting, such cases pose a problem for this study: does one vernacular past participle make a sermon macaronic? According to the taxonomy I propose in the following paragraphs, it does. Yet this study focuses on texts such as the sample quoted and analyzed in chapter 1, texts in which a significant amount of English material is fully integrated into a basically Latin sermon. It is therefore necessary to survey the wider field of linguistically mixed sermons in some detail to distinguish among several classes and to define our subject more precisely.

Considering the relation that elements of the secondary language have to those of the primary language, I propose the following classification. At the simplest level, an English word may appear as a gloss that trans-

---

the third day of the provincial chapter, after the business of the chapter was concluded, "fiat ordinate processio, et missa pro pace, ac sermo / ad populum in lingua vulgari, et sic unusquique ad propria revertatur" (ibid., 2:60–61). Before these final ceremonies, the chapter would have assigned preachers for the next chapter (ibid., 2:12, 13, 15, 19–20, etc.). The practice involving at least the first sermon is attested for earlier chapters as well, both before and after the two English provinces were united in 1336 and met in Northampton.

3. For some examples, see Pantin 1931, 2:12–13, 15, 19–20, 23, 26, 97, etc.

4. F. 26. The exact flavor of the phrase "quod parled est" could be "as gossip has it." The secondary purposes for which those prelates have come together include "the tasting of Falernian cups" and other pleasures (ibid.).

lates the preceding Latin word, as in, "diffidencia, idest **wanhope**,"[5] or in "pedagium statuit, Anglice **tol**."[6] In a similar way, a Latin phrase may be glossed by an English one.

Puer quando percutit pomum suum, Anglice **knokeþ is happel**.[7]

Such vernacular glosses are frequently linked by connecting words, such as *idest* or *Anglice,* as in the quoted examples. Occasionally, however, they may appear in simple juxtaposition, as in,

habeatis internum dolorem, **an inderlych sorwe in herte**.[8]

Translation of elements from the Latin text can extend further to include entire sentences.

Ieronimus in quadam epistula: "O lacrima humilis, tua est potencia, tuum regnum. Tribunal iudicis non vereris, accusatoribus tuis inponis silencium. Non est qui neget ad Deum accedere, si solam [!] intres vacua non redibis, amplius cruciaris diabolum quam ignis infernalis. Quid plura? Sola vincis inuincibilem, ligas omnipotentem, inclinas filium virginis. **þou ter mylde, þyn is þe myth of þe kyngriche of heuene. þou doutest nouth þe dredful dom of þe last day. þou makest þi fomen, þe foule fendes of helle, stonde ful stille. þu deres more þe deuel þan doȝ þe hote feyer of helle. þe mai lette angle ne non creature to come tofor God boldelyche. Here þou biddist þi bone and passest nouth withouten spedygg.** Et quid plura . . . "[9]

Here the English translates and partially glosses a Latin source that has been quoted to prove the point that tears shed in penance and devotion

---

5. Cambridge, Jesus College MS 13, art. vi, f. 58v.

6. Holcot, sermon 34; Cambridge, Peterhouse MS 210, f. 43v.

7. A-15/71.

8. W-008/30ra.

9. A-28/93v, a sermon on *Lacrimis cepit rigare pedes eius*. The English was published by Erb (1971, 81).

have great power before God.[10] Such prooftexts could be drawn not only from the Church Fathers, as here, but similarly from Scripture or from any text deemed to have authoritative standing. In all these cases, the Latin quotation held an important function in the development of the sermon. Translating it into the vernacular would assure that during the delivery of the sermon, presumably in the vernacular, the preacher had the important passage ready at hand in the language of his preaching.

To this group of longer English elements in Latin sermons also belong translations of the sermon thema. A sermon preached in 1436 begins:

> *Que vtilitas in sanguine meo,* Psalmo 69. Karissimi, hec verba sic dici possunt: **Qwhat profyte is heere in myn blode?**[11]

It then continues in Latin without further English. Very many translations of themata and prooftexts of this kind—in fact, until well into the fifteenth century, most of them—appear in rhyme, a phenomenon I have studied at greater length elsewhere.[12]

To prove a point, preachers occasionally also used vernacular sayings, proverbs, and even parts of songs that had no counterpart in Latin. These consequently enter a sermon, as it were, on their own feet.

> Non erit tunc *tort et fort,* nec aliud breue, nec eciam, sicud iam dicitur, "þe riche hongeþ be þe pors, þe pore be þe þrote," sed fedus quod preuaricatus est, sicud propheta ait, in capud proprium retorquetur.

> (There will then [i.e., at the Last Judgment] be no "wrong and strong," nor another brief, nor even, as we now say, will "the rich hang by his purse, the poor by his throat," but the covenant that one has violated will, as the prophet says, fall on one's own head.)[13]

---

10. The quoted Latin sentences formed a commonplace in late medieval sermons and were attributed to various church writers. For other examples see *Fasciculus morum* V.x.5–11 (Wenzel 1989, 458, "Crisostomus"); Brinton, sermons 22 and 26 (1954, 1:89, 1:102, both "Bernardus"). A different English rendering appears in London, British Library, MS Harley 2250, f. 49v, attributed to "Johannes Crisostomus": "**O þu teer þat art mekely lettyn in oryson, þi myght ys so grete þat goys into heuen vp to Goddis trone . . .**"

11. Q-38/108.

12. Wenzel 1978 and 1986.

13. From X-23/248vb. For the English proverb, see Whiting and Whiting 1968, P302; for the biblical quotation, see Ezek. 17:19.

Though here the English saying is linked to its Latin context with a connecting phrase, it has no basis in Latin and is not subsequently translated into the sermon's dominant language. As was the case with simple glosses, longer English passages of this kind may, as here, be connected to the preceding Latin text by some linking word or phrase, or they may simply be juxtaposed.

The phenomenon of an English element that does not translate part of its Latin context can also appear in single words. These are usually technical terms, and their occurrence in English can most reasonably be explained by the writer's not having a Latin equivalent immediately available. A good example is

prudencia cuiusdam avis que vocatur **wodewale**.[14]

Such technical terms include names of animals and plants, of parts of military dress,[15] of various kinds of bread,[16] and much else. One favorite technical term among English preachers is **trewloue,** the quatrefoil or *amor fidelis*.[17]

All the English elements so far discussed—glosses, technical terms, translations of themes and of Latin authorities, and vernacular sayings[18]—I label *a* elements. They basically translate a part of the Latin discourse or are imported into it in the manner of quotations.

Very different in their function are what I call *b* elements. These are English words, phrases, clauses, periods, or paragraphs that serve as divisions, subdivisions, or distinctions in the sermon in which they appear. These functional elements are essential for the structure of scholastic sermons, a sermon form that is fully utilized in the macaronic texts that are studied here.[19] The main division unfolds the thema the preacher

---

14. Holcot, sermon 73; Cambridge, Peterhouse MS 210, f. 116v.

15. For example, in the edited sermon S-07, ll. 152–58.

16. Holcot, sermon 50; Cambridge, Peterhouse MS 210, f. 68r–v. This and the preceding example actually form distinctions, for which see below, p. 21.

17. For instance, in Z-05/16ra and Z-28/83ra as well as in edited S-07, l. 140; cf. Wenzel 1978, 159.

18. I also include in this category what I have called "message verses" in previous studies of verses in Latin sermons.

19. For the scholastic sermon, its structure, and the function and importance of the divisions, see Wenzel 1986, chapter 3. The relevance of this form to macaronic sermons will be further discussed below in chapter 4.

has chosen into a number of parts that subsequently furnish the material (*materia*) for the development (*processus*) of the sermon's major or principal members (*partes* or *principalia*). As was the case with the thema and with prooftexts, the division very often appears first in Latin and is then followed by an English translation. This frequently happens in sermons that are otherwise entirely in Latin, and the reason for adding an English rendering is undoubtedly its great structural importance for the entire sermon.

A fairly simple example may be quoted from a sermon by Robert Holcot, whose thema *In hiis que Patris mei sunt oportet me esse* ("I must be about my Father's business," Luke 2:49), is divided in the following way.

> In quibus verbis tria includuntur, scilicet:
>   ligamen obediencie, *oportet*;
>   conamen diligencie et sedulitatis, *me esse*;
>   solamen reverencie et magne dignitatis, quia *in*
>   *hiis que patris mei sunt.*
> In hiis, inquam, etc.
> Anglice:
>   **bond of buxumnesse,**
>   **lif of bysynesse,**
>   **stat of worthynesse.**

(In which words [i.e., of the thema] are three things included, namely: the bond of obedience, in *must;* the work of diligency and action, in *I* [must] *be*; the reward of reverence and great worth, in the words *about my Father's business.*)[20]

As in this case, the English form of the division is often linked to its Latin model by a connecting word, such as *anglice*. Whether such a linking word is present or not, when an English division is thus preceded by a Latin model, one could consider classifying the English as an *a* element that translates (or often paraphrases) part of the Latin context. I differentiate, however, between *a* and *b* elements, for several reasons. One reason is that next to sermons that present a Latin division followed

---

20. Cambridge, Peterhouse MS 210, f. 32ra.

by its English translation stand others, also essentially in Latin, whose division is given in English only, without a Latin model. Yet in both cases the English has a different and more significant function in the sermon than is the case with authoritative quotations, technical terms, and the like: the parts of the division structure the entire discourse. This function has a peculiar consequence, which is another reason for keeping *b* elements apart from *a* elements: the members of an English division tend to recur repeatedly in the course of the sermon that they help to structure.

Such repetition is well illustrated by a Good Friday sermon on *Percussa est tercia pars solis* ("The third part of the sun was smitten," Rev. 8:12). After an introductory section, the preacher divides his thema thus:

Hec verba signant—
quomodo Christus **wyrchit in hijs godhede,** sicut *sol*;
  hou he wonitȝ in hijs manhede, quia in *tercia parte*;
  and wat he suffrid for houre mysdede, quia *percussa est tercia pars solis.*

To this he immediately adds an alternate form of dividing the same thema (marked *Divisio secunda* in the margin).

Vel sic: In hijs verbis tangitur:
Cristis wyrchinge, que est ad modum *solis*;
et **Cristis cloþyng,** in *tercia parte,* que est corpus eius;
and Cristis suffryng, in *percussione.*

He expands the terms of the division into statements that will be used for the development.

**His worching hys endeles,
ys cloþyng hys wemles,
ys suffryg hys lekles.**

Then the development of the first principal begins at once. When the preacher arrives at the end of the first principal, he repeats the part of his main division that has been developed, quod fuit primum tactum in themate, scilicet **Cristis worching þat ys endeles,**

(which was the first thing touched upon in the thema, namely Christ's working that is endless,)

and then he moves directly into the development of the second principal.

Secundo principaliter dixi quod in verbis thematis tangitur **Cristis cloþing wemles.**

(For the second main part, I said that in the words of the thema, Christ's flawless clothing is touched on.)

The same procedure of repeating the respective members of the main division is again followed in the transition between the second and third principal parts.[21]

What has been said about English divisions applies also to subdivisions. These have the same form and function as a division, except that they structure the development of the principal parts rather than of the entire sermon. For example, a sermon on *Attulit alabastrum vnguenti* (Luke 7:37) divides its thema according to three persons who can be said to have brought a vessel of ointment: Mary Magdalene, the devout soul, and Christ. As the preacher begins the third principal part, he repeats the corresponding phrase from the main division, **salue for seke men bryngyng** (i.e., Christ brought a vessel by "bringing ointment for sick people"); and he at once gives the following subdivision:

Christus ... habuit se **os a leche or a fysiciane, os on hosteriche** et **a pellicane, and os a triaculour þat has triacle and bawme.**

(Christ acted like a leech or physician, like an ostrich or pelican, and like a healer that has treacle and balsam.)[22]

---

21. Oxford, Bodleian Library, MS Bodley 859, ff. 317–319v. The sermon text appears on ff. 314v–319v, 322–325v and ends incomplete. See also Wenzel 1986, 148–49.

22. Cambridge, Jesus College MS 13, art. vi, f. 67.

The three members of the subdivision are then developed in succession. Another English subdivision can be found in the first principal of edited sermon O-07; a rhymed one in the first division of edited sermon S-07.

The third structural feature of a sermon in which we find *b* elements, the distinction, similarly divides a term or object. But in contrast to the division and subdivisions, which are concerned with the thema or a part of the main division respectively, a distinction may appear at any point in the sermon as a device to dilate or amplify the current subject matter. Thus, it may list or enumerate the parts of a whole (such as a house, the year, or the sacrament of penance) or the properties of an object or concept (such as dawn or passionate love). For instance, a sermon for the Nativity of the Blessed Virgin, on *Multi in nativitate eius gaudebunt* ("Many will rejoice in his/her birth," Luke 1:14), develops its first principal, that we may rejoice in Mary's birth because she is a teacher for a good life, without a subdivision, but in the course of the development, it expands on three properties of light that are found in Mary as well: "Nam lux **meuyth lygthly, schewyth brygthly, and rewlyth rygthly**" ("For light moves lightly, shows brightly, and rules rightly").[23]

Though on the surface such *b* elements often resemble the English we found in the long paragraph cited in the preceding chapter—especially if, as is frequently the case, the phrases or lines of a division are themselves macaronic[24]—the differences are of major importance. To strengthen this point, I quote another macaronic passage of the kind that was discussed in the last chapter. It comes from a lengthy Good Friday sermon of the late fourteenth century, which presents a leisurely account of

---

23. Oxford, Bodleian Library, MS Barlow 24, f. 191r.

24. An example of a bilingual division is the following: "Dico pro processu quod [1] imperator omnipotens concessit cartam fidei, libertatis fidem, **to all seke and sory, to help hom** a demoniaca seruitute; [2] magister **ful wis** et valde bonus docuit leccionem eterne sapiencie fidei discipulis **vnwitty to knowen and louen** Deum suum in suo periculo viagio; [3] pater misericordie dedit þe **warant** regni celestis pueris mortalibus **to be seke[r]** in suo fine eterne hereditatis" ("For the development I say that [1] the almighty emperor granted a charter of faith, the faith of freedom, to all who were sick and miserable, to help them out of their servitude to the devil; [2] the very wise and good teacher gave a lesson of eternal wisdom [and] faith to his ignorant disciples, to know and love their God on their dangerous way; and [3] the father of mercy gave the guarantee of the heavenly kingdom to his mortal children, to be assured of their goal of eternal inheritance"), O-03/15. Such passages are genuinely macaronic, but because their English is part of *b* elements, I have not counted them in establishing the corpus of type C sermons.

Christ's passion. Judas's betrayal, especially his traitor's kiss, is likened to the faithlessness of the world.

> Et hic notandum quod illud factum signat bene tradicionem istius mundi, quia quando mundus dat homini diuicias **or ani ȝing to his liking,** tunc mundus ridet super hominem; et quando dat sibi solacia **and lustis an likingys,** tunc osculatur eum. Set quando dat sibi honores, **ȝen beginnis he to halssim and tak him in his armis,** et totum ad tradendum eum et decipiendum eum ad vltimum, quia quando habet eum in suis brachiis **and liftis him vp to ani hille of worchip,** tunc dabit sibi vnum **paschavme** et deiciet eum, et quanto ab alciori deicit eum, **ȝe sorrer he fallys,** et illud est suum intentum.

(And here we must note that that deed stands well for the betrayal of this world. For when the world gives a man riches or anything that is to his liking, the world laughs at him; and when the world gives him comfort and his desires and likings, it kisses him. But when it gives him honors, then it begins to embrace him and take him into its arms, and all this in order to betray and deceive him in the end, for when the world has him in its arms and lifts him up to any hill of honor, then it will give him a blow and throw him down, and the higher the place from which it flings him down, the more painfully he falls. And that is the world's intent.)[25]

The English elements in this Latin context, in contrast to *a* elements, do not gloss or translate Latin material; they are not technical terms, nor do they serve as vernacular prooftexts. Likewise, in contrast to *b* elements, they are not parts of a division, subdivision, or distinction. Instead, here the writer's thought moves forward without glossing, quoting, translating, or announcing a coming development, but it does so in a way that switches back and forth between Latin and English in the middle of the sentences. The English material in this passage thus forms syntactically integrated parts of bilingual prose sentences. I designate such elements as *c* elements.

These three groups into which English elements appearing in Latin sermons have been divided on the basis of their function also appear in

---

25. L-1/220.

reverse, so that the same classification can apply to Latin elements appearing in sermons whose dominant language is English. Thus, an English word or phrase might be provided with a Latin gloss.

> **And ȝit were þis peyn but in towchynge all-on,** in sensu tactus solum, **and bot a myle-vey.**[26]

A technical term might be introduced in Latin and at once translated into the vernacular.

> **Iff þer were had such a stone þat is called** lapis philosophorum, **elixer, such on** . . . [27]

A vernacular prooftext might be quoted and then translated into Latin.

> **As many fooles seyn, "When þat oþur do so, why may not I do so?—** quando alij transiunt ad diabolum, quare non ego?"[28]

Finally, entire divisions or distinctions may be given in Latin. For instance, an English sermon on *Si Filius Dei es, dic* ("If you are the Son of God, speak," Matt. 4:3) is built on the following division presented in Latin:

> Dic vt te pro peccatis dolentem Deus recipiat ad graciam; dic vt per te peccata confitentem mentis detergat maculam; et dic ut ad te pro peccatis satisfacientem remittat penam debitam. **First I sey, speke þat God resceyve þe to grace whils þat þou art for þi synnes sorowyng.**[29]

An example of a distinction that is cited in Latin is:

> **þis name Clement aftur þe exsposicion of þe *Catholicon*** est idem quam

---

26. Ross 1940, 240, ll. 17–19. Subsequent references to this volume are by page and line numbers (e.g., "Ross 1940, 240/17–19").
27. Ross 1940, 286/7–9.
28. Ross 1940, 68/28–31.
29. Ross 1940, 271/5–13.

nobilis, misericors, pius, et sanctus. **It is as muche to youre vndyr-
stondynge as noble, mercyfull, pitovous, and holy.**[30]

In the last two quotations, the Latin elements precede the English.
This order is the normal one for the two remaining situations in which
a Latin element of type *a* appears in an English context: themata and
the majority of prooftexts. English sermons written in the medieval
period normally begin with the thema announced in Latin, and many
of them further introduce their prooftexts in Latin that is subsequently
translated into the vernacular. Many examples for this general practice
can be found in the volume of Middle English sermons edited by Ross.[31]

The foregoing distinction based on different functions that elements
of the secondary language have within sermons in the primary language
allows us to classify bilingual sermons in a sequence of five types.[32] Type
A comprises sermons that contain one or several *a* elements. Type B
comprises sermons containing *b* elements. Some sermons of type B
contain only *b* elements, that is, vernacular divisions, subdivisions, or
distinctions (or parts thereof); those I call type B1. Others may show *a*
elements as well, such as English proverbs and common sayings and
translations of Latin authorities of various kinds; those I label B2.

Some B2 compositions are rich in English verses of all sorts and have
attracted the attention of a number of scholars.[33] A fine example is a
Good Friday sermon on *Quid fecit, quare morietur?* ("What has he
done, why shall he die?" 1 Sam. 20:32). This thema is at once—somewhat
feebly—translated into English rhyme.

What hath ys man do
þat he schal dyȝe ȝoo?

The next bit of English appears at the division, which consists of three

---

30. Ross 1940, 5/16–19.

31. For examples of a Latin thema followed by English translation, see Ross 1940,
3/19–23; 9/28–34; 46/15–17. For examples of Latin authorities followed by English translation, see Ross 1940, 3/5–7, 4/21–24, 8/15–17, 5/16–19 (quoted in the preceding text;
see n. 30).

32. In addition to letters A through E, I use 0 for Latin sermons without any English.
This classification is applied in the inventories found in appendix A.

33. Little 1943, 244–56; Pfander 1937; Erb 1971; Stemmler 1975; Wenzel 1978, 82–86.

rhyming lines in English. These are not repeated again, but the sermon eventually quotes seven stanzas translating the Improperia, *Popule meus, quid feci tibi?* Then it presents another seven English stanzas in which Christ speaks of the wounds he suffered as antidotes for the seven deadly sins. The following Latin story and moralization dealing with Christ as a lover-knight contains an English message verse of two lines. After several pages without any English comes a translation of a Psalm verse, and near the end of his sermon another prooftext, the meditative commonplace *Securum accessum habes, o homo, ad Deum,* is similarly rendered into three English couplets.[34]

Types A and B could logically be combined into a single type characterized by English elements that have structural functions (thema, division, prooftexts, and message verses), in contrast to the following type C. My reason for separating them into A and B, which also underlies my earlier explanation for placing *a* and *b* elements into separate categories, is the realization of the great, indeed crucial, importance that the division had in the structure of the scholastic sermon and, consequently, in the desire among medieval preachers to record it in English (and usually in rhyme) in their sermons that were written down in Latin.[35] In addition, as we saw in the earlier discussion, English words from the division or subdivision may recur throughout the development, creating a situation that is very similar to but not identical with type C, a situation that differs significantly from type A and therefore requires an intermediate class.

Type C sermons are texts that contain *c* elements, that is, English material that differs from *a* or *b* elements. The latter may of course also appear in type C sermons; but in such cases, what distinguishes a C sermon from a B sermon is the presence of English elements that do not have the structural functions of *a* or *b* elements. This sermon type, type C, which I consider to be genuinely macaronic, forms the subject of the present study.

Two more types reverse the relation of English to Latin and thereby form mirror images of A and B. Type D contains sermons that are

---

34. Cambridge, Jesus College 13, art. vi, ff. 83v–90v. The English pieces occur on ff. 83v (thema), 84v (division), 85–86v (Improperia), 86v–87 (seven wounds), 87 (message verse), 89 (psalm verse), and 90 (St. Bernard).

35. Wenzel 1986, 82–100. My study of macaronic sermons led me to realize the importance of the division.

basically in English but also have *b* elements in Latin, that is, Latin
divisions, subdivisions, or distinctions. Usually, such sermons in addition
quote their thema and perhaps some biblical and patristic prooftexts in
Latin. Type E sermons are, likewise, English texts that contain individual
Latin words and biblical quotations and other authorities, but no divisions, subdivisions, or distinctions. They further, and most commonly,
at least present in Latin the sermon thema or (in the case of homilies)
the biblical text on which the sermon is based; in fact, one hardly finds
any English sermons in the medieval period that do not give their thema
in Latin.[36]

The proposed classification is not without a number of problems,
especially with respect to the distinction between types B and C.[37] One
problem stems from the fact observed earlier that the English words of
a division or subdivision may be repeated in the following development.
When they do, the initial division is in some sermons given only in Latin,
while its repetition later on appears in English. In other sermons, the
initial division or subdivision is given in English, but when it reappears
in the development, it has undergone some verbal changes.[38] Another
kind of confusion arises when English words or phrases appear to be *c*
elements but really are parts of a distinction that is not clearly introduced
as such. For example, in one Christmas sermon, the preacher asks his
congregation to meditate on several properties of death. The last of these
is that death will touch them in diverse manners. The development of
this thought begins as follows:

Quarto dico quod vtinam cogitarent **how diuersliche deth towchyt**

---

36. If there are any, they would be the counterpart to sermons of type 0.

37. These problems would vanish if one were to consider only whether English elements
in Latin sermons were preceded by Latin equivalents or not, regardless of the function of
such English elements. But such an analysis would fudge the essential difference involved
in basically different kinds of language mixture and hence would lose the particular interest
that genuinely macaronic sermons have.

38. In B-127, for example, the second principal is originally announced as "þe **dome**
þat **demyth wyt-oute gyle**" (f. 220rb). But when the preacher gets to the development of
the second principal, he introduces it as "þe **dome** þat **demeth wyt-oute gyle** vel þe **dome**
þat **ys dredful**" (f. 221rb), and both **dred** and **-ful** continue to be used for verbal concordance. Similarly, the same principal part has a subdivision that includes, as one of its
four members, "To **fle** þe **dome we ben vn-my ȝthy**" (f. 221va). But in its development,
the line appears as, "þe **dome no man may fle**" (f. 222va)—not only is the wording
changed, but the rhyme scheme is altered, too. Another case appears in B-111 quoted in
chapter 4.

hem. Similis est mors **to a archer** tractanti et sagittanti ad vnam metam. Aliquando facit **a ouerschote** supra metam, et aliquando **a brodschote** a dextris et a sinistris, et aliquando sub meta **a schort schote**; aliquando **he truckyth to þe marke,** et tandem sine defectu vel **glyncchg** [?] percutit ipsam.[39]

The four "points" of the meditative simile "death is like an archer" are then developed in typical moral-allegorical fashion. The quoted English words and phrases "an overshot," "a broadshot," and so on, are not clearly announced as parts of a formal distinction and lack the most telling mark normally found—end-rhyme. But a reader familiar with the structure and wording of scholastic sermons will and must suspect that they belong to a distinction that can be formulated as follows:

In shooting at his mark, an archer can—
  make an overshot,
  make a broadshot,
  make a shortshot,
  hit the mark.

Such distinctions were readily available to medieval preachers and were employed everywhere.[40] In problematic cases of this kind, careful analysis of the sermon structure often tells us whether the given English material is part of a division, subdivision, or distinction, though some cases may remain questionable.

Another problem for accurate classification occurs as a result of what may be called "contextual attraction." Here the English material of a division leads the writer into continuing for several words to write English, thus creating a *c* element in a sermon that otherwise is of type B.

---

39. A-55/161.

40. See Powell and Fletcher 1981, p. 217, ll. 105–16. To the parallels cited in Powell and Fletcher's note on page 225 can be added another funeral sermon in Oxford, Bodleian Library, MS Barlow 24, f. 213 (death is like an archer "quia sicut ipse sagittat quandoque vltra signum et quandoque citra, etc."); a sermon for Rogation Days in Cambridge, Jesus College MS 13, part vi, f. 71 ("Mors enim assimilatur exili sagittario sagittanti ad metam et pluries deficienti. Vnde quando mors capit iuniorem te, tunc sagittat citra metum; quando capit seniorem te, tunc sagittat vltra metam; quando capit similem tibi, tunc sagittat a dextris vel a sinistris. Dico tibi, nunquam cessabit antequam percuciat te"); and Brinton's sermon 70 (1954, 2:324).

In the following example, after repeating the thema *Iesu, fili David, miserere mei* ("Jesus, son of David, have pity on me," Matt. 15:22) at the end of the introduction, the preacher at once presents the main division in English.

> **þe godenes of God in forgyvyng,**
> **þe bitternes of paynes o helle þat has non endyng,**
> **þe lythyrnes of syn and wykkyd lyvyng**
> **stires me to say on ilk synful mans behalf qwho-ere he be: Iesu,**
> **Dauides sonn, have mercy of me.**
> Primo dico quod þe **godenes of god,** etc.[41]

This sermon is generally of type B, using English only for its divisions and subdivisions. But the string of words "stires me ... he be" ("moves me to say on behalf of every sinful man, whoever he may be") is not part of the division; it was most probably generated by contextual attraction, thereby forming a bridge between the English division and the repetition of the thema. That the text then continues in Latin, "Primo dico quod," fully agrees with the normal patterns found in this sermon and the type to which it belongs. Contextual attraction may on occasion even produce a longer English passage caused by anticipating a vernacular *a* element. Thus, another sermon from the same manuscript begins as follows:

> *Scio hominem in Christo,* Corinthiorum 3. Reuerendi mei, **havyng reward to haly wryt and to þe techyng of owr doctour, ilk man in qwhat stat he be or in qwhat degre persavyng þe propyrtes of þe Trinite may wele say þe wordes þat I began: "In Crist I knawe a man."** Nam testante sacra scriptura ...

Here it would make best sense to think that the words "**havyng reward ... began**" appear in English because they anticipate the following rendering of the thema in English. Again, the sermon continues exclusively in Latin.[42]

The present study is concerned with texts of type C, whose language

---

41. Cambridge, Pembroke College, MS 199, ff. 89vb–90ra.
42. Ibid., f. 83vb.

continually moves back and forth between Latin and English within the boundaries of the sentence. What might account for such switching will have to be investigated further, but because of the classification I have established, we can already at this point say that, in contrast to type B sermons, it was not the preacher's need to have important structural elements before him in the language of his sermon delivery.

Discussing the phenomenon of such bilingualism requires a body of type C sermons in which the mixture appears to a significant degree. How much is that? One or two transitional passages of the kind just discussed, though potentially interesting, hardly make a genuinely macaronic sermon. Many linguistically mixed sermons contain occasional *c* elements but otherwise, and basically, belong to types A or B. For example, the first principal of a sermon on *Luna mutatur* ("The moon changes," Ecclus. 27:12) contains some *b* elements (the repeated part of the division), some *a* elements (two proverbs, an English saying quoted as part of a reported conversation, and two glosses of Latin phrases), and a single phrase of type *c* (the moon is said to be "cornuta **ase a rammes horn**").[43] Other sermons may contain an entire paragraph whose texture is characteristic of type C sermons, but the whole text certainly belongs to A or B. For the sake of taxonomic rigor, these cases must be classified as type C sermons, but they contain only a minimal amount of relevant material.

To focus on texts that show a significant amount of language mixture, I have limited my corpus of primary material to sermons that contain at least ten units of three or more successive words in English that are not a gloss, a quoted or translated authority, or part of a division, subdivision, or distinction. Ten units yield a significant amount of English material embedded in the Latin context; and the requirement of three or more English words per unit, which excludes single words and such minimal phrases as the marked infinitive (**to go**) and compound verb forms (**will see**), assures that the *c* elements required for a C sermon are of substantial length. In the following discussion, I remain aware of "minimal" and "marginal" sermons of type C and occasionally quote from them,[44] but in essence this study deals with fully macaronic sermons as just specified.

---

43. A-22/84.
44. There are thus three divisions of type C sermons:

My search through sermon manuscripts in the major collections has turned up forty-three separate fully macaronic sermons (type C), of which five occur in more than one manuscript.[45] As one might expect, the amount of English material in these sermons and the frequency with which their texts change from Latin to English and back vary greatly. In appendices B–D I have edited and translated three sample sermons of type C. These sermons illustrate, among other things, the wide spectrum of fully macaronic sermons, ranging from one sermon that barely qualifies for inclusion in type C (S-07) to one in which the number of c elements is relatively high (O-07). In appendix E I have tabulated the amount of English material of any kind (i.e., a, b, and c elements) in all fully macaronic sermons and have shown how often the language changes. To the forty-three sermons of type C can be added some forty sermons that can be classified as marginal or minimal C. Insofar as these occur in the major manuscripts analyzed in the following chapter, I have inventoried them in appendix A.

Minimal C: presence of single words or phrases of two words of type c.

Marginal C: beyond minimal C, presence of type c phrases of three or more words, but less than ten such.

[Full] C: beyond minimal and marginal, presence of ten or more type c phrases of three or more words.

45. It is not unlikely that systematic search or lucky discovery will add some further items to this list.

CHAPTER 3

The Manuscripts

The forty-three sermons I have classified as fully macaronic are found in thirteen separate manuscripts, which must now be examined in some detail. In this chapter I discuss the company the macaronic sermons keep, the kind of manuscripts that have preserved them, and the occasions, purposes, intended audiences, and authorship or at least affiliation of the sermons gathered in these codices. More detailed descriptions of the manuscripts and listings of their sermons can be found in appendix A.

These manuscripts can be assigned, at least roughly, to three different types: notebook, miscellany, and sermon collection.[1] Only one of them, manuscript T (Oxford, Magdalen College, MS 93), is a notebook. It is a paper manuscript, written by several hands of the late fifteenth century, and made up of several booklets that contain copies and excerpts of material relating predominantly to the spiritual life, including the apparently earliest extant copy of Thomas a Kempis's *De imitatione Christi*. Interspersed in this material appear ten sermons. That this volume represents a notebook is shown by the fact that many of its booklets have blank pages, evidently left so to receive further entries. In addition, in one booklet someone began an alphabetical collection of commonplaces headed by the letters *C* and *H*.[2] The booklets were bound together in the fifteenth century without any attempt to provide a continuous foliation

---

1. I have dealt further with the difficulty of labeling manuscripts that contain random sermon collections in a paper "Sermon Collections and Miscellaneous Manuscripts," read at a symposium on "The Taxonomy of Medieval Miscellaneous Manuscripts," University of Pennsylvania, Philadelphia, on March 26, 1993 (forthcoming).

2. Ff. 185–186.

or quire numbering. Instead, two medieval indices serve as guides to the collected material in the order in which the quires have been bound.

Of the ten sermons in this volume, five are entirely in Latin, four belong to types A or B, and one is fully macaronic. The latter is a Good Friday sermon on the thema *Amore langueo,* which has also been preserved in manuscripts B, D, and S. In T it is simply rubricated "de amore." Two other sermons are similarly topical (sermon 4 on penance, 7 on faith), whereas the others are, in no particular order, *de tempore* and *de sanctis,* including two sermons on the Annunciation. Of some interest is sermon 1, which was preached for the funeral of Isabel Fullthorp; her name is etymologized in a fashion that seems to have been especially dear to preachers of funeral sermons and recurs elsewhere in the manuscripts examined here.[3] None of these sermons reveals much about its intended audience. The occasional address "Karissimi" is faceless, and the texts contain no particular references that tell us whether they were directed to laypersons or the clergy.

Manuscript T is associated with John Dygoun, who graduated from Oxford in 1406 with a degree in both laws, held various appointments as a parish priest until 1435, and then was admitted as a recluse to the Carthusian priory of Sheen, Surrey, where he was still alive in 1445. He left several notebooks containing the fruits of his, and in T his fellow monks', labors of copying; these notebooks were eventually given to Magdalen College.[4] Three of Dygoun's contributions to Manuscript T bear the dates 1444 (f. 226v), 1439 (268v), and 1438 (275v). The macaronic sermon T-07 is in a different script from his.

Like notebooks, the two miscellanies to which we turn next, manuscripts D and L, collect works and treatises of various kinds, but in contrast to T, these codices are not made up of still partially blank booklets into which further material might have been copied. D (Dublin, Trinity College, MS 277) is a fifteenth-century paper manuscript into which one hand has collected a large number of treatises and excerpts that are fairly well grouped by major devotional topics or interests: the Blessed Virgin (pp. 1–120) and Christ's passion; the religious life, in-

---

3. In R-03, R-14, and W-108; the former two have been edited by Horner (1977, 1978). Similar name etymologies appear in Brinton's sermon 57, given at the funeral or anniversary of Sir John Colepeper (Brinton 1954, 2:264–65); and in sermon 62, at the funeral of Beatrice Grantson (ibid., 2:283).

4. Emden 1957–59, 1:615–16.

cluding part of David of Augsburg's *Formula novitiorum* and St. Brigid's *Revelations,* as well as Petrarch's answer to a letter by Sacramore de Pomeriis; penance and the vices and virtues, including a *Formula vite humane* attributed to "Martinus" and the *Conflictus vitiorum atque virtutum*; the Lord's Prayer, for which at least half a dozen expositions have been assembled, including one by the Dominican John Gray; the trials and tribulations of life; and finally the duties and neglect of the pastoral office, with a story of a pluralist, John Mauncell, who is condemned by Christ. Also noteworthy are copies of the Latin *Elucidarius,* Anselm's *Proslogium,* and the "Seven Penitential Psalms" by Petrarch.

In addition to three or four Latin sermons, the manuscript contains the macaronic Good Friday sermon *Amore langueo* already encountered in T. In D this sermon immediately follows a number of excerpts from meditative works that deal with Christ's passion, including the *Stimulus amoris,* the *Horologium sapientiae,* and a tract *De fletu et lacrimis*[5]; so it seems that the sermon found its way into this collection because of the interest it held for the collector as a prolonged meditation on Christ's suffering and death. The material assembled in this volume cannot be said to be distinctly intended for preaching.

In contrast, the other miscellany, L (London, Lambeth Palace, MS 352), contains some preaching materials, notably John Waldeby's exposition of the Pater Noster (some of whose parts have a sermonlike structure) and seventy-four paragraph-length summaries of sermons on the Sunday gospels, together with one fully macaronic sermon for Good Friday. The latter deals at length with Christ's passion and has a pronounced meditative character: the preacher narrates the events of the passion at some length and regularly draws moral lessons from them, a pattern very reminiscent of Ludolf of Saxony's *Vita Christi.*[6] Since this sermon (L-1) is preceded by several conventional meditations on Christ's passion, it is likely that it was copied into this book because of its thematic and functional interest.

Manuscript L, written on parchment by several hands of the late fourteenth and early fifteenth centuries, preserves a variety of treatises.

---

5. Colker 1991, 277.

6. See my discussion of the *sermo historialis* in Wenzel 1986, 148–52. A similar parallel to Ludolf of Saxony appears in another macaronic Good Friday sermon, S-07, which is edited in appendix B; notice especially the repeated questions "Why did Christ allow ..." at the end of subdivisions, followed by the answer "Surely, to give an example of ..."

Besides those already mentioned occurs a copy of Richard Rolle's Latin commentary on the Psalms. According to a note on the end flyleaf, the manuscript was a gift from Robert Norton, chaplain at the abbey of Benedictine nuns at Malling, Kent, to Master John May, rector of All Saints the Greater in London.

In the third category, which I have labeled sermon collections, fall manuscripts that essentially gather a larger number of sermons but no other treatises, or at best only a small amount of additional material that may have been useful in preaching.[7] To this category belong the remaining ten manuscripts that contain fully macaronic sermons, though one or two of them could arguably be classified as miscellanies or preacher's notebooks.[8] Manuscript B (Cambridge, University Library, MS Kk.4.24), a parchment codex of the first half of the fifteenth century, contains two separate sets of sermons written by the same hand.[9] A number of the volume's codicological features, such as rubrics, several medieval foliations, and several medieval quire signatures, allow us to reconstruct its composition with some certainty.

One scribe first wrote—or more precisely, copied[10]—two different sets of sermons into manuscript B, with six leaves between them left blank (i.e., the remainder of quire 15). Someone then foliated the first set in the upper right-hand corner of the rectos, to folio 115 (with one apparent jump in the numbering), leaving the blank folios unnumbered. The original folio numbers (1–115) and some other annotations were then

---

7. Books into which a scribe randomly collected sermons, short theological notes, distinctions, exempla, and the like, should therefore be considered preachers' notebooks. See Wenzel 1986, 5–6.

8. Especially A and Z.

9. It is possible to speak of the presence of two different scripts in this manuscript, the second being more emphatically Secretary than the main (first) in its angularity, tightness, and broken descender of lowercase p, and especially in its use of the crescent-with-dot mark for (usually) nasal abbreviation. The change from script 1 to 2 is sharply noticeable on ff. 19rb (to 22va) and 298vb. But it seems as if these characteristics of script 2 eventually and gradually subside back into script 1.

10. Evidence that the sermons in this manuscript (and in others) were copied rather than written out for the first time is (a) the fact that many of them are incomplete and (b) the presence of errors that are scribal and must have been caused by such common occurrences as misreading the exemplar, eyeskip, misunderstanding abbreviations, and the like. The text of manuscript B, specifically, is full of cases of dittography, of which some have been canceled, others not; of skipping one or more lines ahead, normally corrected; and of other scribal errors that have been corrected. Set 2 contains several sermons that are incomplete.

largely erased and replaced with rubrics that indicate instead the occasion of the respective sermon and its consecutive number (1–76), both items usually also appearing next to the beginning of the respective sermon. As this rubricator came to set 2, however, he changed his practice, and instead of the sermon numbers, he now placed the consecutive folio number (116–296) in the upper right-hand corner of the rectos. When this was done, he referred to these folio numbers in some of his rubrications in set 1. For example, the sermon *Extendit manum suam* in set 1 bears the rubric "In festo Corporis Christi" and the current sermon number 48 (modern f. 66). To the latter are added the numbers 150, 168, and 242. These refer to the medieval foliation of set 2 and to folios where three other sermons for the feast of Corpus Christi appear (i.e., modern ff. 155, 173, and 247). Moreover, the rubricator then filled the leaves that had been left blank (between medieval 115 and 116, modern 114va–120) with three indices for set 1. Two of these refer to the rubricator's sermon numbers, but the third utilizes the older, now largely erased foliation. After all this work, another, later hand foliated the entire volume consecutively, this time on the versos. This hand, in its turn, finally wrote a list of sermon themes for the church year at the very end of the codex, with references to the folios as he had numbered them throughout the codex. The extant manuscript is thus the result of copying sermons, of rubricating or foliating the volume, and finally of providing various indices that would allow a reader easy access to pertinent material for a given feast day or topic.[11]

What has been thus gathered and ordered in manuscript B is, however, of very diverse character. Set 1 presents itself as "Exhortations of Friar John of Bromyard, of the Order of Preachers," and the seventy-six sermons it contains for the Sundays, major feasts, and some saints' feasts from Advent through the twenty-fifth Sunday after Trinity neatly follow the order of the church year. The title seems to be authentic. Many cross-references in the body of these sermons refer to others in this collection as *exhortationes*.[12] That their author is the well-known

---

11. The sermons of set 1 are also divided into unequal sections marked by marginal letters (A–L in sermon B-007, for example); these are utilized in the second index, a "tabula realis," on ff. 115ra–120va, and in cross-references in other sermons of set 1.

12. Normally abbreviated as "ex." with number and alphabetical section reference, and often introduced with "vide supra" or "infra." All *exhortationes* of set 1 are divided into sections marked in the margins with letters in alphabetical order.

Dominican John Bromyard seems proven by the fact that sermon 48 refers twice to certain stories that can be found in a "summa pred'" with precise indication of their location.[13]

All the *exhortationes* have the same structure. They begin at once with a division of a word or concept contained in the announced thema and then develop it in an orderly fashion, with subdivisions, authorities, and some illustrative similes. In comparison with other sermons we shall examine, they are rather sparse: they give neither exempla nor moralized biblical figurae, and on the whole, they limit their range of authoritative quotations to Augustine, Gregory, and Chrysostom. In fact, the references to stories from the *Summa praedicantium* are a rarity and hence strengthen the possibility that here the author is quoting from an earlier work of his own.

In addition to this rhetorical sparseness, the *exhortationes* lack some of the major structural features of the scholastic sermon, such as protheme, prayer, closing formula, addresses, and what might be called a "preacher's voice": first person singular verb forms are practically non-existent, and the sermons' principal parts are usually introduced with a simple "Primo" and so on instead of the more customary "Primo dico" or "Sicut dixi."[14] Nonetheless, the *exhortationes* may be confidently regarded as being intended as sermons. Not only do the rubrics link them to specific occasions of the church year, but their text likewise refers to such occasions; sermon 59, for instance, alludes to the parable of the Pharisee and the publican with the remark "So did the Pharisee *today,* who attended to the sins of the publican and not to his own."[15] One

---

13. B-048 refers to E.6.x and E.6.25 (ff. 67ra and 68ra), that is, the article (E.6, "Eucharistia") and running section number of Bromyard's *Summa praedicantium* as they can be found in London, British Library, MS Royal 7.E.vi. Set 1 in MS B also contains at least two similar references to what may be Bromyard's sermons (on ff. 53vb and 60ra). In both cases the respective topic is treated in Bromyard's *Distinctiones* preserved in Oxford, Bodleian Library, MS Bodley 859 (ff. 116 and 201), but the sermon or distinctio numbers do not agree, nor do the *Distinctiones* use the specific English proverb and image used in MS B.

14. These remarks are generalizations, and exceptions can be found to many of them. For example, sermons 63, 72, and 74 end with a standard closing formula; 63 quotes several classical authorities; 66 contains a passage addressing the audience; and 6 begins its first principal with "Primo dico." But in general, standard features of the scholastic sermon appear only very sparsely here.

15. "Sicut Phariseus isto die qui ad peccata publicani et non ad sua respexit ..." (f. 87ra).

exhortation actually refers to itself as a *sermo*.[16] And finally, their inclusion in a volume that gathers fully scholastic sermons and, through its indices, makes all of them available to preachers should remove all doubt that these exhortations were deemed apt for use in the pulpit.

In contrast to this orderly sequence of structurally homogeneous sermons, set 2 is disorderly and variegated. It contains ninety-two sermons for all sorts of occasions. They are not arranged in any of the standard sequences used in *de tempore* or *de sanctis* sermon cycles. Many of them are incomplete and their texts are followed after the break-off point by blank spaces of different lengths. Their structures vary considerably, from fully scholastic sermons with prothemes and prayers, through pieces reminiscent of the exhortations of set 1, to items that develop the gospel lection in the manner of homilies (sermon 98, for instance). Most important for the purposes of this study is the number and variety of linguistically mixed sermons contained in this set. While the sermons of set 1 are entirely in Latin, with nine pieces containing only a rare English word or proverb (thus belonging to type A), the sermons of set 2 range over the entire linguistic spectrum, from pieces that are completely in Latin, through mixed sermons of various types (B, C with its various subgroups, and D), to items that are entirely in English (type E). Three sermons in this set are fully macaronic.

As far as they bear any indication of the occasion for which they were intended, the sermons of set 2 are, in no particular order, for selected Sundays and feasts of the church year, several saints (Stephen, John, Thomas of Canterbury, James, and the Blessed Virgin), and some of the special occasions recognized by major sermon cycles, such as a funeral or the dedication of a church. One sermon was to be preached *in tempore belli* (106). The *de tempore* sermons are heavily oriented toward Lent and Easter—thirty-eight of the ninety-two pieces. The pieces for special occasions include two marked to be preached to the clergy (80 and 89) and a third that was seemingly to be delivered at a visitation (81).

Ten further sermons are intended for a clerical audience, as is shown by their address form, "Reuerendi" or "Reuerendi domini." If we add to these a sermon that deals with the question "what a minister of God should be like" (154) and another that discusses pastoral duties (121),

---

16. "Ergo habeatis tercium punctum sermonis, idest fortitudinem et perseuerantiam in bono vsque illuc veniatis" (f. 72va).

we find that at least fifteen sermons in this set envision a clerical audience. The evidence for a lay audience of the other pieces is perhaps not as strong, but the catechetical nature of some of them and the concern of others (116-18) with explaining the threat of excommunication, which parish priests were required to preach about once or several times a year, make a lay audience for at least those sermons likely. Of some interest, in this as well as other respects, is sermon 129, in which at some point the preacher addresses his audience with an imaginary objection: "But you say: 'Frater, my enemy says against me, and without cause, that I cannot for the whole world please him.' Truly, my beloved, . . . "[17] The address *frater,* "brother," may indicate that a clergyman or member of a religious order is speaking to another of his kind, or it could stand for "friar" and hence signal that the objection is spoken by a layperson. Given the nature of the imaginary objection, the latter situation is more likely.

If this reading is correct, the quoted sentence can be added to other indications that connect these sermons with the mendicants. One sermon mentions St. Francis (113), another refers to "what the friar preaches" (116), and a third explicitly identifies Nicholas de Lyra as a Friar Minor, which I take to be an expression of communal pride that is rare in the frequent citations of the well-known biblical commentator (130).[18] Possible further evidence for specifically Franciscan authorship lies in the fact that several sermons utilize material from the Franciscan handbook *Fasciculus morum* (109, 134, and perhaps 111). Given this much, one is all the more startled to come across one sermon that is outspokenly antifraternal (158). Intended for the First Sunday of Lent and preparing its audience for their Easter obligation, it eventually discusses where and to whom they should make their confession. The preacher's stand in these controversial matters is unequivocal: go to your parish church and avoid the *oratorium fratrum*; the privileges of hearing confession that the mendicants have received are quite inappropriate—no holy order of possessioners has ever asked for such, and even St. Francis, in his last will, spoke against them (f. 288r-v)! This is, of course, a copy of a sermon by the fourteenth-century champion of antifraternalism, Richard

---

17. "Set dicis: 'Frater, et sine causa dicit inimicus meus contra me quod non possum pro toto mundo indulgere sibi.' Vere, karissime . . . " (f. 229rb).

18. "Narrat et dicit Nicholas de Lira, Frater Minor et magister Parisiensis" (f. 230vb).

Fitzralph, preached at St. Paul's Cross, London, on 26 February 1367.[19] Unless these sermons in set 2 are by an author who was closely linked to the Franciscans yet highly critical of their privileges, the discrepancy in this set must be explained by suggesting that it gathers sermons from different hands—a situation that occurs several times again in other sermon collections. This suggestion can be further supported by the fact that four sermons in set 2 contain cross-references to other sermons, of which two are not found in this manuscript.[20] In other words, set 2 is not a complete copy of a single set of sermons but rather a selection, possibly made from several sets or cycles.

The codex holds some more information that furnishes a rare insight into the use of its sermons. On at least twenty-three pages, English names appear in abbreviated form in the top margins of the manuscript, nineteen in the first set of sermons and four in the second.[21] Except for four instances,[22] the names have been erased but are legible under ultraviolet light. They evidently refer to about twenty villages and hamlets in southwestern Bedfordshire and eastern Buckinghamshire, with a heavy concentration in the hundred of Manshead and particularly on Leighton (modern Leighton Buzzard), which appears in more than half of these annotations.[23] Again with four exceptions, the names appear in series from two to eight, with the order of the villages named varying from instance to instance. For example, one series lists Billington, Leighton, Stanbridge, Eggington, and Eyton (modern Eaton Bray)— all villages in the neighborhood of Leighton Buzzard (f. 5v); another lists Eggington, Westoning, Ge' (Gre? Gro?), Slapton, Leighton, "Lyn" (possibly Linslade, across the Ouzel from Leighton), Toddington, and "Tyn" (Tingrith)—once again all villages in Bedfordshire, with the

---

19. Fitzralph's sermon 67. See Gwynn 1937, 55; Walsh 1981, 416.

20. The cross-references are B-128/224ra to B-108; B-128/226rb to B-130; B-129/227vb to B-128; B-129/228va to B-130; B-145/262va to B-090; B-129/228ra to *Domine quo vadis*, not here; B-148/268vb to *Surrexi ut apparerem dilecto*, not here.

21. Ff. 1, 2v, 4, 5v, 9, 29, 31, 34, 35, 37, 39, 41v, 54, 62 74v, 76v, 77, 102v, 104, 143, 215, 217, 296.

22. Ff. 34, 143, 215, 217.

23. Modern Chalgrave, Wingfield (?), Eaton Bray, Eversholt, Harlington, Leighton (Buzzard), Billington, Eggington, Stanbridge, Clipston, Milton (Bryan), Tingrith, Toddington, and Westoning—all in Manshead Hundred; perhaps Edlesborough (which formerly belonged to Manshead Hundred), Flitwick (Redbornestoke Hundred), Linslade and Slapton (Bucks.), and two more whose abbreviations remain cryptic: Ge' or Gre' or Gro (perhaps Grove?) and Tei' (?).

exception of Slapton and Linslade, which lie just across the border
in modern Buckinghamshire. As I cannot detect any element these
places had in common other than geographic proximity, it would seem
that the annotations preserve a record of the churches where a given
sermon was preached.[24] Because it is unlikely that the same sermon
was preached in four or eight different churches on the same day, we
may be permitted to think that the annotations record the efforts of
one or more preachers over a period of years. As most of the twenty
named places formed separate parishes, it is most likely that they were
thus served by a member of a religious order. What that order might
have been must remain speculative.[25] The true significance of these
annotations, if my reading is correct, is that they show us the use
made of a composite sermon collection for preaching in relative small
villages and country parishes.

The next manuscript to be discussed, Q (Oxford, Bodleian Library,
MS Lat.th.d.1), is the most personal sermon collection under consideration. Many of its sermons bear the name of Nicholas Philip, who
tells us in a musical cipher that he owned this book, belonged to the
[Franciscan] custody of Cambridge and the convent of Lynn, and wrote
the book at Lichfield in 1436.[26] An earlier quire declares that it belonged
to Nicholas Philip and was written in 1432 at Lynne. Other mentions
of his name, usually at the end of sermons, begin with "quod," which
would indicate that Philip was the scribe.[27] In addition to Philip's name,
the manuscript records a number of dates between 1430 and 1436 and
place names (Newcastle, Oxford, Lichfield, and Lynn), which suggests
that Friar Nicholas not only copied these sermons but may have preached
them himself. Whether he is also their author is less certain. Four successive sermons are connected with the name Melton written in rubrics

---

24. The sermons thus annotated would be 1–4, 6, 23–24, 26–29, 31, 39, 45, 52, 53
(perhaps twice), 68 or 69, 70, 87, 124–25, 165.

25. The nearest houses of the Franciscans would have been in Aylesbury and Bedford;
of the Dominicans, in Dunstable.

26. "Liber fratris Nicholai Phillip de custodia Cantebrigie et conventus Lennie, script'
lichefelde 1436." The words from *Liber* to *Lennie* are in a musical cipher. I fail to understand
Fletcher's puzzlement about the cipher (1986, 202 n. 34), since its meaning is patently
clear from the clue that precedes it; see Stainer and Stainer 1901, 2:65, and the facsimile
in 1: plate 29.

27. To the mentions of Philip's name set out by Fletcher can be added a reference
within a sermon, at the beginning of the first principal: "Nota bene Phelyp" (133v).

that normally appear in the top margin (61–64),[28] and it is likely that this annotation indicates Melton's authorship of these pieces. This is probably William Melton, a famous Franciscan preacher traceable in other records.[29] Fletcher has suggested that a third name, Helbeche or Holbeche, which occurs twice in similar rubrics (51 and 68), is that of yet another, unknown preacher and author.[30] That the collection is a product of Franciscan preaching is beyond doubt: apart from the personal names, sermons 36 and 37 speak of the order and mention its founder, four are intended for visitation of friars (34–37), and sermon 59 is for the profession of a Franciscan novice. It is no surprise that in the sixteenth century the book belonged to a Friar Thomas Goddard and was to go to the Franciscan house at Babwell after his death.

Manuscript Q is a paper codex, made up of several booklets and written in a single hand that is dateable to the mid-fifteenth century.[31] It has suffered much from damp and the general brittleness of its paper and has lost a good deal of material, especially on its first thirty folios. Despite its physical deterioration, which makes an even perfunctory collation hazardous, the volume still shows a medieval foliation and two catchwords.[32] The booklets are of distinctly varying sizes, and it has been suggested that at least six such booklets were gathered before foliation.[33] At the end of the volume occurs a table, written in the late fifteenth century, which lists the themata and occasions of the sermons together with folio references. With the table's help, the manuscript has been analyzed and discussed by Alan J. Fletcher,[34] who suggests that it is similar to a preacher's sermon diary, though it must be said that the collection lacks some essential features of a diary.[35]

---

28. All bear the date 1431, and sermon 63 also has the name "Phelypp" at its end.

29. For the identity of Melton and possible relationships between him and Philip, see Little 1943, 245–46, and Fletcher 1986, passim.

30. Fletcher 1986, 192.

31. If it is Nicholas Philip's hand, its date would be in the 1430s, at the latest 1436. The text contains a number of dittographies and an occasional minor error (such as *fudicia* for *fiducia*, Q-24/79), but as far as the sorry state of the codex allows us to tell, it does not show the kind of scribal errors that would place it at one or more removes from the original (unless Friar Nicholas was an unusually accurate scribe), nor is its text much corrected.

32. At ff. 74v, 81v.

33. See Fletcher 1986, 199 n. 2.

34. Fletcher 1986.

35. The sermons in Q are not entered in their chronological sequence, and they lack

In addition to notes, tales, and a list of sermon themata, the codex contains about fifty-seven full sermons.[36] Some of these are entirely in Latin; a large number of others belong to types A, B, and minimal and marginal C; and seven sermons are fully macaronic.[37] None of the latter— in fact, none of the volume's sermons—recur in the other manuscripts that are here described. In most cases, the occasion for a given sermon is specified in the top margins, usually written across an opening, though here and there this information also appears marginally next to the sermon's beginning. Such rubrication tells us that most sermons are for selected Sundays and major feasts from Advent through the post-Pentecostal season, with the same concentration on Lent that can be found in other collections. Except for a sermon on the Blessed Virgin, there are none for other saints. Several sermons are for special occasions, such as visitation (34–37, the first three are in addition assigned to a specific Sunday), a synod (27), and the profession of a novice (59). Together with these, which would have been preached before a clerical audience, at least half a dozen further sermons use the address form "Reuerendi." Sermons 17 and 27 deal specifically with the pastoral office. The sermons do not follow any overall liturgical order, but one can notice a certain grouping: several sermons for Easter (22–26), on the passion (38–43), and for the visitation of friars (34–37) occur together, as do sermons on the same thema (e.g., 29–31, 45, and 47–48) or topic (*sanguis* in 38–40), those assigned to "Melton" (61–64), and the fully macaronic ones (19–25). It is therefore likely that they were collected according to thematic concerns.

This thematic concern also appears in another feature of the collection. Several times, a full sermon is surrounded either by further themata for

---

the personal format ("There I said"; "first the prayer was made"; "then it was shown"; "then a story was told"; and so forth) that characterizes the sermon diary of Richard Fitzralph. For the latter, see Gwynn 1937.

36. Fletcher lists seventy items, counting the list of themata, stories, and other pieces as separate items. I follow his numbering here and in appendix A. Sometimes a story that Fletcher analyzes as a separate item is explicitly intended to be included in the sermon next to it; thus, item 46 is introduced with "Nota hanc historiam quia concludit predicta" (135r). As the colophon makes clear, it is not about the sacrament but about man's three enemies, the main topic of sermon 45. Similarly, 49 is an additional *auctoritas* expanding the biblical quotation with which 48 ends.

37. I consider Q-24 the protheme for Q-23 and consequently count the two items as one sermon (Q-24). There is also much overlap between Q-25 and Q-22, but I count these two separately.

which this sermon could be used or by entire introductions that could be used with it for occasions different from the one specified in the main rubric. For example, item 23 is the main body of a sermon on grace for Lent. At its end the writer has added three more biblical themata for which the sermon could be used; they all contain the word *gracia*. The following item, 24, forms the antethema and introduction (thus marked in the margin) for any sermon that contains the word *gracia* in its thema. Similarly, sermon 53, with the key term *sanguis,* is followed by at least two more optional introductions (ff. 149v and 150), both of which refer back to 53. Often the full sermons contain not one but two, and in one instance even three (53), introductions after the formal protheme, all of them clearly marked as such in the margins. Finally, two sermons on the key term *dii* (22 and 25) share a good deal of the same substance, though they are written for different themata. This indicates that the collector's aim was to gather material that could be used on different occasions—macroformulas, as I have called them elsewhere.[38] A similar process was used in the sermons of manuscript O (discussed below), except there the macroformulas have become part and parcel of the written-out sermons, similar to Q's 22 and 25.

The four manuscripts to which I turn next lack the distinct personality of Q. They are essentially sermon collections, but they also contain other preaching material or even entire treatises that must have been deemed useful to preachers. Moreover, in contrast to Q and B, they share a number of sermons among themselves and with other manuscripts yet to be discussed. S (Oxford, Balliol College, MS 149) is a fourteenth-century parchment codex made up of two parts that were bound together and provided with signatures in the fifteenth century. No medieval foliation is visible, but in the first part of the codex, a current hand has written the themata of the respective sermons in the upper right corners of the rectos and has added other annotations.[39] Part 2, dating from the middle of the fourteenth century, forms a miscellany and contains one sermon. In contrast, part 1 is basically a sermon collection with a treatise by Uhtred of Boldon, a popular exposition of the Decalogue (here also called *sermo*), and some other miscellaneous matter. The collection contains twenty-three sermons, of which twenty-one are written in one hand

---

38. Wenzel 1986, 206–7.
39. The manuscript is described in Mynors 1963, 130–35.

of the late fourteenth century (post 1381) and two (sermons 18–19) in one or possibly two different, more cursive hands, which are much like the one that has corrected and annotated the other sermons. The main hand is an awkward Anglicana trying to imitate *textualis*; in copying the sermons, it has introduced many scribal errors, and the text is heavily corrected.

This collection preserves the names of two preachers. Sermon 15 is ascribed to a Iohannes de Scrata of the Friars Minor, whom I cannot identify. The same is the case with a Master Henry Chambron, to whom sermons 20 and 23 in this manuscript are ascribed, and whose name appears a third time in the text of sermon 1.[40] Sermon 20 is a shorter, somewhat defective, and heavily corrected variant of S-19 (a lengthy and tedious discourse), and the latter is also preserved in A-35, Z-20, and Cambridge University Library Ee.6.27. This is not the only sermon that S shares with other manuscripts that contain macaronic sermons. Of its twenty-three pieces, seven, including the Good Friday sermon *Amore langueo,* occur also in A, B (two), D, H, T, W (four), Z (two), and Cambridge University Library Ee.6.27. It appears that the sermons collected in S enjoyed a fair degree of popularity.

The sermons are *de tempore* and follow no particular order. Two are explicitly addressed to the clergy (13 and 15). Sermon 11 refers to "us religious" and "us curates and rectors of the Church,"[41] which would suggest that both speaker and audience were members of a religious order exercising the cure of souls. Several other sermons speak of clerical duties (1 and 8),[42] while sermon 16 was given at a university. Of these twenty-three sermons, two are fully macaronic; the others are in Latin or are of types B and marginal C.

Similar to S, manuscript A (Cambridge, University Library, MS Ii.3.8)

---

40. The reading "Chambron" is clear at S-20 and S-23; the form of the name in the text of S-01 is somewhat questionable: "Chamber*noun*"? (f. 6v). The other copies of sermon S-01 have: "Chab'" (H-25/88v), "Chauymon" (W-006/21v), and "Cha*m*born*n*" (Z-19/55vb).

41. "Quid enim prodest nobis religiosis voce habitu [!] mundum plus diligere quam laici vel mercatores. . . . Quid enim prodest nobis curatis et rectoribus ecclesie" (f. 49v).

42. My usage of *addressed* differs from Sir Roger Mynors's descriptive phrases "addressed to 'predicatores'" and others, in that I so designate only sermons whose explicit address form suggests the clergy ("Reuerendi patres," "Magistri," and so on). That a sermon speaks about the duties of a preacher in its protheme may not necessarily mean that it was addressed to a clerical audience, as Mynors seems to imply.

contains one sermon (35) that occurs in three other manuscripts (S, Z, and Cambridge University Library Ee.6.27); two further sermons appear also in H (36 and 48), and one each in O (26), U (15), W (47), and Brinton's sermon collection (57). The paper volume was written by several hands that range in date from the early to the very late fifteenth century. It bears a medieval foliation in the upper right-hand corner of the rectos, with some disturbance in the numbering (see appendix A), the significance of which is not clear. On the front flyleaves, a late-medieval hand has indexed the sermons by thema and folio; the list gives a total of fifty-eight sermons. The book bears a note according to which Johannes Metton (Merton? Morton?) bought it from William Denham (?).

Besides these sermons, the volume contains three different treatises on the Ten Commandments, an *ars praedicandi,* and—interspersed with the sermons—other material for preachers, such as exempla, commonplaces with English translations, expanded distinctions, and skeleton sermons. It is not always easy to distinguish between a full sermon and an extended distinction; fortunately, the medieval index provides some help to decide between them. Many sermons are incomplete, ending with the marginal note "vacat" (f. 53) or "non plus in copia" (ff. 76, 78, 89v), and the scribes have frequently left blank spaces.

Except for one sermon for the feast of St. Thomas the Apostle, the sermons—so far as they bear any indications—are *de tempore,* but they do not follow any liturgical order. As is the case in other collections, sermons for Lent and Easter predominate (there are over twenty). One sermon (42) explicitly addresses "You who have the cure of souls, priests and pastors, to whom in particular the present collation is directed"[43] and discusses the priestly office and its duties, though, curiously enough, it uses as its formal address "Karissimi" and not the expected "Reuerendi." The latter or a variant form appears in nine other sermons, which may therefore be thought of as being intended for a clerical audience. This is clearly the case in sermon 49, which discusses how and what a pastor or preacher should teach the people. Sermon 29 refers to another sermon not included here. It also distinguishes itself by recommending that its audience make their confession to their parish priest or his vicar or substitute, a recommendation that silently excludes visiting

---

43. "Vos autem animarum curatores, sacerdotes, et pastores, quibus specialiter presens collacio dirigitur" (f. CXXVIII).

friars. Another sermon (50) is even more noteworthy for its outspoken sympathy for the Lollards. Its thema, "How shall the realm stand firm?" and its introduction give it a certain nationalistic tone, leading to a lament at the moral decadence of England. Part of the decay stems from the scorn and abuse that many churchmen heap on their neighbors:

> In this high and venerable place you can very often hear that the one who stands here to preach God's word—or who ought to do so— through his entire sermon or at least through a large part of it, does nothing else but despise his neighbors. Here he reproaches simple people who labor to learn God's law and to live by it; there he despises faithful priests who preach Christ's doctrine without flattering and respecting persons; and in his animosity, he calls such men miserable heretics and Lollards and reports of them many lies and made-up stories that the latter never dreamed of. And thus, where the church-man ought to preach Christ, who is Truth, he preaches himself and the teaching of his father, the devil, namely, slander and lies.[44]

The same sermon also contains a reference to the papal schism under Boniface, which would date it to 1389–1404.[45] Another sermon (57) yields an even more specific date: it was preached on a fourth Sunday of Lent that coincided with the feast of St. Gregory the Great (12 March). This occurred in 1374, 1385, 1396, and 1458, so that the sermon was probably preached in 1396.

Fewer than half of the fifty-eight sermons are entirely in Latin; the others belong to types A, B, and minimal and marginal C; and two sermons are fully macaronic. The B sermons in particular are rich in English verses, which have attracted attention previously.[46]

---

44. "Potestis enim nimis sepe audire in isto alto et venerabili loco quod ipse qui hic stat vel stare deberet ad predicandum verbum Dei per totum sermonem suum vel saltem per magnam partem nichil aliud facit quam despicit proximos suos. Ibi reprobat simplices viros qui laborant vt addiscant legem Dei et viuant secundum eam, ibi despicit fideles sacerdotes qui absque adulacione et personarum accepcione doctrinam Christi predicant, vocando tales cum magno spiritu hereticos miseros et lollardos, et narrat de ipsis multa mendacia ficta que nunquam cogitabantur. Et sic vbi deberet predicare Christum, qui est veritas, predicat seipsum et doctrinam patris sui diaboli, scilicet detracciones et mendacia" (f. 148).

45. "Et iam videmus et vidimus quanta fuit dissencio ab eo in principio istius scismatis, scilicet in creacione pape Vrbani sexti, quando scilicet magna pars Ecclesie occidentalis dimisit ipsum. Et in tempore istius pape est adhuc maior dissencio facta" (f. 149).

46. See Erb 1971; Stemmler 1975; Wenzel 1978, 1986.

Manuscript Z (Arras, Bibliothèque Municipale, MS 184 [254]) also contains a variety of treatises and excerpts interspersed among its fifty-seven sermons: theological notes, stories and fables, two Wycliffite tracts in English, a short *ars praedicandi,* Origen's Latin homily on St. Mary Magdalene, miracles of the Blessed Virgin, Nicholas de Hanapis's *Liber de exemplis sacre scripture,* Odo of Cheriton's *Fabulae,* a treatise on confession by William of Auvergne, and other pieces conceivably of use for preachers or curates. In some cases, it appears that the material is united by a common topic; for example, the first Wycliffite tract, on the Lord's Prayer, follows a Latin sermon on the Pater Noster and may have been intended as part of the otherwise incomplete sermon Z-04. The shorter notes and extracts are not entered simply to fill existing blank spaces between the sermons; and many times, an item that begins as a full sermon eventually turns into a series of notes, so that the whole volume resembles a preacher's notebook. It was written in England, in the fifteenth century, by one hand. Its medieval foliation and rubrication (sermon themata in upper right of rectos) indicate that when the volume was bound, two bifolia were misplaced, and that after the binding, one entire quire and a number of leaves were lost. There is some evidence to think that these sections may have been excised by an orthodox reader.[47]

The sermons have some interesting peculiarities. As in other collections, six of them use the address "Reuerendi," presumably envisioning a clerical audience. But one sermon (44) contains a clear statement that it was preached to, or intended for, a mixed audience: after inviting his congregation to say a prayer, the preacher leads to the main division by saying:

When I see my audience, it seems to me there are two kinds of people here, namely, clerics and layfolk. And so I propose to direct my sermon to each of these, and first to the clerics, because according to Ezechiel, "you must begin from my sanctuary."[48]

---

47. In contrast to the original folios i and 1, which probably were cut out to destroy evidence of the volume's ownership.

48. "Viso auditorio videntur michi esse hic duo genera hominum, scilicet clerici et seculares, et ideo propono ad vtrum sermonem meum dirigere, et primo clericis, quia 'a sanctuario meo incipite,' Ezechielis" (f. 133va).

A few lines later, he begins part 1 with: "At the beginning all clerics, from the pope to the most simple priest, are exhorted to exhort, admonish, and preach . . . "[49]

Sermon 3 mentions "our blessed father Francis," and the implied Franciscan connection of this and other pieces is supported by the use of material from the *Fasciculus morum* in five sermons.[50] Sermon 3 is the same as H-04, and about a dozen sermons in this manuscript occur also in other collections that are here analyzed: four or five in H,[51] two in S, and one each in A, W, Oxford Trinity College 42, and Cambridge University Library Ee.6.27. Three further sermons have also been preserved in Cambridge Jesus College MS 13, article vi, which is an interesting collection of sermons with many bilingual items but none of type C. Clearly, the collector of Z cast his net widely, and he caught some rather strange fish. It is not surprising that one sermon (1), according to its headnote, was preached at Oxford in 1382 by Master Henry Chambron, whose name we met earlier in manuscript S, or that a second piece in Z also refers to "this university," though without further details (10). But it is strange, from a chronological point of view, that the manuscript also contains one of Robert Grosseteste's sermons delivered at Lyons a century and a half earlier (i.e., in 1250, sermon Z-22). And peculiarity turns into outright oddity when one finds that next to what seems to be solid orthodoxy appears a sermon that was "preached by Robert Lychelade, Bachelor of Arts at Oxford, which he wrote and said that every word in it is true; for which he was banished by the monks on October 1 (?), 1315 [!]."[52] The sermon is heavily critical of the shortcomings of priests and monks, an aspect that is shared by yet another piece, sermon 49, though this again is anonymous. Yet this seeming disparateness among manuscript Z's members is counterbalanced by an element of internal coherence: eleven of the fifty-three sermons contain references to other sermons in the collection, which in all but one case are correct.[53]

---

49. "In principio hortantur omnes clerici, a papa vsque ad simplicissimum sacerdototem [!] hortari, monere, et predicare" (f. 133va).

50. They are sermons 16, 24, 30, 37, and 40.

51. Though essentially the same sermons, their texts differ here and there.

52. "Iste sermo fuit predicatus a domino Roberto Lychelade bacalaurio in artibus Oxon', quem scripsit et dixit quod omnia verba in eo scripta sunt vera, pro quo fuit bannitus per monachos i'us [i'o, i.e., primo?] die mensis octobr' anno Domini MCCCxv⁽ᵗᵒ⁾ [!]" (f. 38rb). On Lychlade and this sermon, see Catto and Evans 1992, 226, 233, 238.

53. The odd piece is sermon 26; it refers "de 7 donis Spiritus Sancti, sicut patet supra

Of the fifty-three sermons two thirds are entirely in Latin (36). The others range from types A, B, and minimal and marginal C to D. One sermon, *Christus passus est,* is fully macaronic and has also been preserved in three other manuscripts (H, S, and W).

Four sermons in Z are shared by manuscript H (London, British Library, MS Harley 331), which like Z has suffered some material loss. A paper manuscript of ninety-nine leaves, written by several hands of the second half of the fifteenth century, it was formerly part of a larger codex, of which, according to the preserved medieval foliation, it formed quires VIII–XIII or folios 89–167. Extant are twenty-five complete sermons and some miscellaneous theological material that was evidently added in the process of copying or binding. The sermons are for various Sundays of the church year and for saints' feasts, in no regular order. An unusually large percentage—nine out of twenty-five—also appear elsewhere. They include not only its one fully macaronic piece (*Christus passus est pro nobis,* sermon 25, also in S, W, Z) and a sermon that refers to "beatus pater noster Franciscus" and the four topics of preaching that the saint enjoined in his rule (f. 1, already mentioned in the discussion of Z), but also a hitherto unnoticed copy of the Latin version of Thomas Wimbledon's *Redde rationem villicationis tuae*[54] and other sermons shared with A, B, and W. The sermons in H contain five cross-references to other sermons, of which two are extant; the others may have been in the lost portion of this manuscript. Two of the sermons that H shares with Z have, in Z, similar cross-references; these references are omitted in the versions preserved in H. Besides the one macaronic piece, the sermons in this manuscript are either entirely in Latin or belong to type B or (one) to marginal C.

The remaining manuscripts lead us into a somewhat different world. All four are more purely sermon collections than the preceding four volumes. But more importantly, they are all connected with monastic, specifically Benedictine, preaching. Manuscript O (Oxford, Bodleian Library,

---

in sermone dominice 2ᵉ quadragesime" (f. 79ra). There is such a sermon, 38, but it occurs infra and has nothing on the seven gifts; the latter are treated in 29, which again occurs infra (not supra) and is for Pentecost. The reference may reflect a different order in the exemplar.

54. Not noted in Knight 1967, 18–20; or in Owen 1966, 176 n. 3. Another version is A-48. A further copy of the Latin version occurs in Oxford, Trinity College MS 42, ff. 47–56.

MS Bodley 649), a parchment codex written by one hand in the first half of the fifteenth century, is the most notable of all the manuscripts discussed here, because it holds the largest number of fully macaronic sermons in a single manuscript, twenty-two out of a total of forty-five. The codex has a medieval foliation, which lacks folios 133–145 in the very middle of the present volume. This suggests that a quire of twelve, the usual quiring of the volume, has either been lost since the fifteenth century or was actually never included; it is possible that this quire was intended to hold an index to the sermons. This gap in the quiring separates two distinct sermon sets, which must be described individually.

Set 1 has deservedly received attention from church historians for its remarkable references to and concern about contemporary events. The sermons here collected persistently attack the Lollards as the "poison-mongers" responsible for so much decadence in the realm and the English church.[55] In addition, several of them praise King Henry V for his glorious championship of church and state and allude to his recent victory, presumably at Agincourt.[56] Because the king is spoken of as still living, these sermons would have been composed between 1415 and 1421. On internal evidence, they can be attributed to a single author.[57] Though his identity is not revealed,[58] we can be certain that he was a Benedictine: he speaks of himself as a *possessionatus*[59] and praises

---

55. All sermons in set 1 except O-04 refer to Lollards or Lollardry; none in set 2 do. For a detailed study of their attacks, see Haines 1972, 1975, 1976, 1978, 1989; Hudson 1988, 436–37.

56. See especially Haines 1976 and Horner 1989.

57. Such evidence is the repeated use of the same topics and major images, characteristic phrasing, favorite quotations, and blocks of identical verbal material. Such features also appear, for instance, in the sermons by Fitzralph and Brinton.

58. The manuscript contained a note, now no longer readable, which linked the sermons or manuscript with a John Swetstock, about whom nothing else is known and who probably was only the scribe of the volume. As for the possible authorship of John Paunteley, see the discussion of manuscript R later in this chapter.

59. The Lollards "**castonn a myn** ad columpnam pocess' [= possessionatorum], profunde foderunt pro thesauro Ecclesie, fecerunt media ad temporalem manum ad capiendum nostras possessiones. Ultra vires laborabant ad rapiendum nostrum victum" (f. 35). Similarly in O-24, the Lollards "**cast a myne** ad turrim possessionatorum, foderunt alte pro thesauro Ecclesie, fecerunt media ad dominos temporales ad auferendum nostrum victum, vltra vires laborabant ad rapiendum nostras possessiones" (f. 125). In O-15, the Lollards are said to have advised "dominos temporales spoliare templum, **to takonn away** suas possessiones, **to benym hom** suum victum" (f. 94; the same in R-12/66v).

the Benedictine order.[60] He also refers to Oxford as his place of study.[61]

This set contains twenty-five sermons, of which one is minimal C, two are entirely in Latin, and an astonishingly large proportion—twenty-two—are fully macaronic. A number of these sermons are for the Lenten season and call their audiences to penitence. The first thirteen occur in correct chronological order but are then followed randomly by sermons for some other Sundays, for Sts. Mark and Birinus, for the Assumption, and for a funeral. Some of them, especially 20 and 21, deal specifically with the duties of the clergy and the pastoral office and are addressed to a clerical audience. At least one sermon specifies a university audience at Oxford (8). A large number use such forms of address as "Reuerendi domini," "Venerandi domini," "Domini mei," or plain "Domini," forms that might point to a clerical audience. However, this presumptive correlation does not hold for this collection, because in several cases the addressees, "reuerendi domini," are asked to "go to your curate in this holy season" and make their confession (for example, 5 and 9). The injunction to turn to one's curate who "is ready to receive you into the ship" of holy church (10) recurs in a number of sermons and, if my reading is correct, tags these pieces as addressed to the laity.

The most striking feature of the sermons in this collection in respect to their audience is that several sermons contain evidence of being directed to both clerics and laity at once. Sermon 10, from which I have just quoted the injunction to turn to one's curate, addresses, two pages earlier, "you masters of the vessel, who have the cure of souls."[62] Similar

---

60. In past ages, people who lived a perfect life could be found in all religious orders, "sed multitudo sanctorum qui vixerunt et moriebantur sub vexillo sancti Benedicti enarrant aperte ad oculum quanta virtus et perfeccio fuit olim in nostra veteri oppressata religione" (O-25/132v). But notice that sermon 24 includes in its lengthy invitation to prayer the "venerabile collegium et capitulum sancti Francisci" (O-24/124v). It could have been preached by a Benedictine monk at a Franciscan chapter meeting or in the Franciscan house at Oxford.

61. O-08 begins by likening Oxford University to the woman clothed with the sun of Rev. 12:1. Later, the preacher laments the university's current decadence and speaks of Fortune's wheel, of which his master had spoken the previous Sunday: "Super istam rotam **clymbeth mony man, boþe of þe clergi and of the laife, both seculeres and** regulares **gape ful fast vpward**, vt honorabilis meus magister **told ȝow on Sonday last was fuld sadlich**" (f. 49v).

62. "Vos magistri nauis, qui habetis curam animarum" (f. 64v). But soon thereafter: "**þi curate** ... Vestri curati parati sunt recipere vos in nauem" (f. 65), and later, "Refer tuo curato" (f. 66v).

verbal evidence appears in other sermons, which therefore must have been addressed to, or at least intended for, a mixed audience of clergy and laypersons.[63] We should probably think of the sermons in set 1 as omnibus sermons that give general spiritual exhortation to all estates.

At least one sermon contains a cross-reference to another piece in this set (24 to 22). More importantly, four of its macaronic sermons also occur in manuscript R.[64] Other features that connect set 1 with R are further discussed below.

Set 2 in manuscript O contains twenty sermons, but in contrast to set 1, these are mostly in Latin, except for one each of types A, B, and marginal C. Some are for Sundays in different parts of the church year, at least eight for saints, and one for the dead; they do not follow any patent liturgical order. Nor do they bear clear indications of their intended audience; where addresses are used, these tend to be "Karissimi,"[65] with only sermon 43 using "Reuerendi" (together with "Karissimi"). Apart from lacking fully macaronic sermons, this set also differs from set 1 in stylistic aspects, notably its predilection for such typically popular elements as stories, fables, and moralized pictures. But at least one piece in set 2 speaks to *vobis viris ecclesiasticis et literatis* (O-44/218v), and others are larded with learned literary and even scientific references (especially 37). Another difference is that many sermons in set 2 lack the formal polish and firm structure that characterize set 1; several tend to ramble (e.g., 34–35) or peter out (e.g., 39). That these sermons were copied and stand at least at one remove from the original is shown by the many blank spaces left for names that evidently were not understood by the scribe.[66] None of these pieces share the anti-Lollard and nation-

---

63. Two more cases: sermon 10 invites its mixed audience to prayer with the words "Temporalis et spiritualis quilibet vir et mulier, leuate seu extollite ad Deum manus et corda" (f. 2v); sermon 2 addresses first "tu sacerdos" (f. 11) but later seemingly speaks to laypersons: "Cape exemplum ergo de curato tuo" (f. 11v). Both parts of the audience are addressed in successive sentences: "Ideo qui figuramini per Moisen, indulgete cure vestre, date vos deuotis precibus, cognicioni et contemplacioni diuine. Et vos qui estis de laife, tak þi Pater Noster and þi Credo, et non vlterius ascendas" (O-13/80v).

64. Sermons 5, 12, 15, and 19. Notice that one (nonmacaronic) sermon in set 2 (39) also occurs in manuscript A.

65. Thus sermons 29, 31–32, 34–35, 38, 40–45.

66. E.g., O-39 leaves a blank for "Furseus" (f. 192); compare with A-26/91v. Further evidence comes from a note in O-39 that directs the reader/preacher to "develop as you have it elsewhere in this and the other quire" (f. 192v), but the passage referred to seems to be lacking in O.

alistic tone of set 1 or give evidence of Benedictine authorship; to the contrary, sermon 44 speaks against churchmen who criticize the poor Friars Minor (f. 220), though these remarks need not necessarily indicate mendicant provenance.

As already mentioned, set 1 of O shares four of its sermons as well as other distinctive features with manuscript R (Oxford, Bodleian Library, MS Laud misc. 706). This parchment codex, written by several hands in the first half of the fifteenth century, is made up of several booklets and was bound at St. Peter's Abbey, Gloucester, in the late fifteenth or early sixteenth century, when some loss and wrong ordering occurred.[67] It belonged to John Paunteley, a Benedictine monk from St. Peter's Abbey and "sacre pagine professor" at Oxford around 1410, who is mentioned as preaching the funeral sermon for Abbot Walter Froucetur on 3 May 1412. Given Paunteley's ownership of this volume and his preaching activity, it is possible that the sermons in R come from his pen, including the distinctive macaronic ones; and given a number of similarities between R and O, he might also be the author of the macaronic sermons in set 1 of O.[68]

Besides some scientific material at the end, R contains a total of thirty-three sermons, a prayer destined for a sermon (Horner 1989, no. 8, probably intended for sermon 7), and a translation of a thema (Horner 1989, 19).[69] Four sermons are fully macaronic, of which three also appear in O.[70] The others are entirely in Latin or belong to types A, B, minimal and marginal C, and E. The sermons are for a variety of Sundays, feast days, and saints' feasts and appear in no regular liturgical order. Several throughout the collection are for the Lenten season, especially the third Sunday in Lent. Of note are two funeral sermons (sermon 3 for Abbot Walter Froucetur and 14 for Thomas Beauchamp, Earl of Warwick).[71] The collection includes a number of sermons that were certainly given at a monastery or before monastic audiences: sermon 5 on the Assumption

---

67. See especially Horner 1975.

68. See most recently Horner 1989 and Haines 1989, 203.

69. The contents of R are listed in Horner 1989, 329–32. My list in appendix A gives only the full sermons, and to facilitate use of the manuscript, I refer to the modern foliation, even though it is partially erroneous.

70. R-02, 12, and 13; the fourth, R-14, is unique to R. Another sermon shared between the two manuscripts, R-28 and O-19, is only minimal C.

71. Both edited by Horner (1977, 1978). I preserve the spelling "Froucetur" of the manuscript.

with a lament at modern Benedictine decadence, 6 for a general chapter of the Cistercians,[72] 18 for the visitation of a Benedictine house, 29 to a monastic audience on Christmas Eve, and 31 delivered at St. Albans. Sermon 30, in English, speaks of "owr gloryous patroun synt Albone" (f. 149v) and hence may also have been given at the monastery dedicated to the saint. Another sermon, in English with some Latin authorities and scraps (20), was similarly given at a monastery dedicated to St. Mary but addresses the common people. Other sermons are addressed to university audiences: 15 contains several references to a university, and 19 speaks to scholars and refers to the recent victory in Normandy, apparently under Henry V, with a warning against taking false pride in battle. Similarly, 22 (addressing "Reuerendi magistri et domini"), 23 ("Venerandi domini et magistri"), and 24 ("Reuerendi mei, doctissimi domini et magistri," with an initial reference to the university, and ending, "Quod Frater Ricardus Cotell") address university audiences. Among the saints honored in this collection are St. Birinus, much worshiped in England but apparently not so elsewhere (28, also in O-19), and St. Alban (31).

The variety of occasions listed above, the diversity of audiences embracing both clergy and laypersons,[73] the strongly monastic or Benedictine character of the collection, the macaronic sermons shared with manuscript O, and the apparent similarity of one of its hands to the one that wrote O make it very probable that set 1 in O and this collection have common roots, perhaps even common authorship. To these common elements may be added the anti-Lollard stance taken throughout set 1

---

72. The chapter was evidently held on or around 14 September (as customary), because the sermon speaks not only of the chapter meeting but of the Nativity of BVM, the Exaltation of the Cross, and "the blessed martyrs": "In hac celebritate de quatuor hic solic' est predicari, vicelicet de huius sacri collegii eximia honestate, de beatissime Virginis sanctissima natiuitate, de sacrosancta crucis exaltacione, et de beatorum martirum coronacione" (f. 31).

73. In addition to the already mentioned sermons addressed to monastic audiences, sermon 17 speaks of "nos ecclesiastici et religiosi tam ad laudandum Deum nostrum quam ad edificandum nosmetipsos et proximum specialiter sumus electi" (f. 82v) and further of "nos pastores" (f. 84v), and it deals with the spiritual duties of monks and parish clergy. Sermon 33 begins with the address "Magistri reuerendi" (f. 165), but in its final exhortation, it speaks to both clerics and laypersons: "Si clericus es, lege et labora et quere Christum Iesum per scripturas...; et si laicus fueris, fac similiter: ingredere ecclesiam, audi ibi verba vite, interroga curatum tuum et eos qui legere nouerunt vbi Christum inuenire potueris, et inter sancta colloquia eorum stella gracie tibi apparebit" (ff. 170v–171).

of O, which in R is paralleled in three English sermons—20, 30 (which strongly repulses the Lollard attack on image worship and pilgrimages, f. 149v), and 32[74]—and in the Latin sermon 17.

The possible relationship between O and R can, on similar grounds, be extended to manuscript W (Worcester, Cathedral Library, MS F.10). This codex is composed of parchment and paper in an irregular fashion and written in a variety of hands, with the script changing over thirty times in the manuscript. The hands may be assigned to the second, going into the third, quarter of the fifteenth century.

Several codicological features provide some insight into the volume's genesis. It has a medieval foliation that runs from 1 with some slips to 320. In addition, it shows traces of three different sets of signatures. Two sets appear in the upper right and the lower right of the rectos respectively, and the third set is written in the lower left margin of the rectos, where many signatures are now hidden in the gutter. In at least one quire, the signatures appear on the versos. The three sets of signatures do not run parallel. Most interesting in this respect is the second set, in the lower right corners. It begins with quire 20 and then runs 21, 22, 23, 10, 11, 18, 19, 13, 14, 38, and so on. The booklets that make up the present manuscript—many of them of more than one quire, with their text often incomplete—were evidently arranged differently two or three times; the final sequence in which they now appear is marked by the last set of quire numbers (in the gutter) and by the medieval foliation. After this final arrangement, two more quires were added at the beginning, one of which contains material that completes two sermons that had been left incomplete in the earlier booklets and were now supplied with accurate *signes de renvoi*. The volume has no index or tabula. There are also some indications that this manuscript may have served as the exemplar for further copying, because at least three sermons (35, 82, and 85) are marked with the marginal note "scribatur"—"let it be written."

Some of the booklets have a certain degree of internal consistency. For instance, one of them contains sermons that are entirely in English (quire V, sermons 13–15); another contains sermons apparently attributed to a named preacher (quire VI, sermons 16–17); and yet another gathers sermons preached to an academic, clerical audience (quires XXI–XXIII,

---

74. All three have been edited by Horner (1975, 72–179).

sermons 122–37). But I am unable to detect any rationale for the overall sequence in which these booklets were combined, and this sequence changed in the early history of the collection. It appears that in the ordering of the copied material, haphazardness and the desire to collect what material was at hand played considerable parts, which would explain why sixteen sermons in the total of 167 items are repeated,[75] and why so many items are incomplete, normally at the end of a quire.

The collection forms a random mixture of sermons for selected Sundays and feast days of the church year and sermons for saints and for special occasions. Especially noteworthy among the latter are two sermons for a general chapter (sermons 28[76] and 71, the latter preached by John Fordham), three sermons for visitations (118, 130, and 135, the latter of a Benedictine monastery), one sermon for ordination to the priesthood (147), and three or four funeral sermons (83, 108, 158, and perhaps 144), of which one, for Lady Blackworth, distinguishes itself by the same etymological punning that occurs in sermon T-01 and elsewhere.[77] In addition to the Blessed Virgin, the saints honored include Alban (29), Benedict (113, 119, and 131), Cuthbert (64), King Edmund the martyr (123), and Patrick (62). Moreover, sermon 46 deals with Sts. Edmund [Rich] and Hugh of Lincoln and may have been given in a Carthusian house.

That this collection originated in a monastic milieu is confirmed beyond doubt by the presence of a large number of sermons addressed to a Benedictine audience or dealing with the ideals of the monastic life and its decadence (4, 5, 35, 102, 104, 105, 113, 116, 121, 124, 127, 128, 133, 153, 155, 156, and perhaps 138). One sermon is actually ascribed to a monk of St. Albans, Hugo Legat (2).[78] Two other preachers mentioned are Folsam (16 and 17) and Master John Fordham (71).[79] Sermon 29 may have been given at St. Albans, because it refers to "beatissimus

---

75. Complete collation of sermons 9 and 31 shows (a) that both derive from the same exemplar because they share curious and often manifestly erroneous readings, and (b) that 31 was copied from 9 because, while it corrects some of 9's dittographies, it introduces its own minor scribal errors and has about half a dozen longer eyeskips.

76. Edited by Pantin 1933.

77. See note 3 in this chapter.

78. Edited by Grisdale 1939, 1–21.

79. Folsam (or Folsham) apparently was a monk at Norwich. Master John Fordham was a monk at Worcester from 1396 to 1438; he held a D.Th. from Oxford (ca. 1407) and was president of the general chapter from 1420 to 1426 (Emden 1957–59, 2:705).

patronus noster Albanus" (f. 84ra). Similarly, sermon 127 speaks about "beato Petro apostolorum principe et huius sacri cenobii aduocato precipuo et patrono" (f. 240va) and may thus have been given at Gloucester.

An equally large number of sermons was preached to a university audience, including three that praise such aspects of medieval academic life as Peter Lombard's *Sentences* (22 and 26) and the pursuit of philosophy (119). If we may assume that the address "Magistri" indicates an academic audience, sermon 113 would be a university sermon given by a Benedictine on the feast of his order's founder. And sermon 134 is addressed to Benedictine monks elected to attend the university, in all likelihood Oxford.

Though many items in this collection are thus connected with monasticism, the collection at the same time shows a strong concern with the pastoral office (for instance, sermons 16, 23, 77, 89, 90, 102, 114, 122, 125, 137, and 143). Sermon 102 neatly combines the two features: its protheme addresses priests who have cure of souls, then later on the preacher refers to "nos religiosi, monachi, et fratres" (f. 195).[80] Other sermons bear no clear indications about their intended audiences or are explicitly directed, here and there, to the laity, as is 68, which, after speaking of the duty that both curates and parents have to teach and correct their subjects, ends with an exhortation to parents: "Et ideo, boni viri, vos qui habetis pueros ad custodiendum."[81]

These features would relate manuscript W closely to R and O.[82] Two more elements add strength to this relationship. First, several pieces take a clear anti-Lollard stand: sermon 20 criticizes the Lollards explicitly; 123 condemns their major attacks against heterodoxy; and the university sermon 102 enjoins on its clerical audience the duty to resist attempts

---

80. *Fratres* here may refer to friars. Sermon 145 includes some antifraternal material, criticizing their "three transgressions, namely, precious clothing, expensive inceptions, and fruitless sermons" ("tribus transgressionibus in fratrum mendicancium ordinibus, idest de vestium preciositate, de incepcionum su[m]ptuositate, et de predicacionum infructuositate," f. 274ra–b). The critique is attributed to "quidam modernus postillator." Two other possible references to mendicants occur in sermon 20, which speaks of a "frater predicator" who preached on the thema *Hic calix nouum testamentum est* on Palm Sunday, and in sermon 68, which refers to a "frater" who preached to the audience before the present occasion on confession and satisfaction.

81. That the remark aims at parents rather than schoolmasters is shown by an earlier reference to "viri et mulieres qui habent pueros suos ad regendum" (f. 126rb).

82. W shares one sermon with R; other W sermons appear also in A, H, S (four), Z, and Oxford Bodleian Library MS Barlow 24.

to dispossess the church (similar exhortations to ward off heretical teaching occur in 143 and 154). Second, to some extent W even shares the nationalistic tone of R, although the sermons collected in W cover a longer chronological range: sermon 1 laments the decay of England's former glory and 17 looks back to Crécy with nostalgia; 124 invites its audience to pray "pro rege nostro Richardo nunc nouiter creato [*read* coronato?]";[83] and 107, in illustrating the fall of the great, refers to the fates of the Duke of Dublin, the archbishop of York, and the count of Suffolk, an allusion to the events of 1387. These references place the composition of at least these particular sermons in the years between 1387 and 1399, although sermon 102 appears to have been composed in or shortly after 1410.[84] Apart from the present location of the manuscript, there is further evidence that the collection, or at least parts of it, comes from the Worcester Cathedral priory: three sermons (152, 154, and 155) bear the names of the local saints Oswald and Wulstan at their heads.

Of the 167 sermons collected in W, six are fully macaronic. The others range through the entire spectrum of types that were described in chapter 2, from purely Latin sermons, through types A, B, and minimal and marginal C, to sermons that are almost entirely in English.

Like the preceding volume, manuscript X (Worcester, Cathedral Library, MS F.126) is a large sermon collection evidently also made at Worcester Cathedral priory. It was written by several hands that date from the late fourteenth and early fifteenth centuries. The volume bears a medieval foliation. At the end, a hand contemporary with the texts has added an index of the sermons in the order in which they appear in the volume, giving their occasion, thema, and folio reference. A second "tabula de notabilibus que continentur in presenti volumine," being an alphabetical subject index that runs from Antethema to Ypocrita, was written or inserted on folios 264v–267; its entries are mostly based on marginalia that occur next to the sermons, both before and after this

---

83. Public prayer for the king and the royal family is a hallmark of monastic preaching.

84. In preaching against false heretics, without using the word *Lollards*, the preacher says: "Dicunt quod doctrina sua est comodifera regi et regno, sicut fecerunt in vltimo parliamento, vbi mouebant regem et proceres vt spoliassent ecclesiam possessionibus suis" (f. 193r–v). The reference would fit the presentation of the Lollard Disendowment Bill in (probably) 1410. An earlier petition for disendowment was presented to Parliament in 1371, but by two friars (see McKisack 1959, 289–91; Galbraith 1919, 579–82). See Hudson 1988, 337–42; 1978, 203–7.

table. In the top margin of folio 69 appears the inscription "Liber Beate Marie Wygornie."

The book is clearly the orderly product of collecting a large number of sermons for and by a monastic community. Its nearly 330 items are roughly divided into sermons *de tempore* (ff. 1–195) and *de sanctis* (ff. 200–307v). Toward the end of the latter section appear sermons for special occasions, such as the election of an abbot, visitation, dedication of a church, and profession. The latter sermons are neatly grouped together; for example, five sermons for an election (ff. 259–264) are followed by six sermons for visitation (ff. 271–278), and so on. Similar grouping occurs for sermons for feasts of the Blessed Virgin (ff. 283–307v), for Corpus Christi (ff. 247–257), and for other occasions throughout the volume. As already mentioned, the entire collection was finally provided with two indices.

This general impression of orderliness is disturbed, however, by the appearance of *de tempore* sermons among the sermons for saints' feasts and vice versa, and by the insertion of sermons on specific topics, such as the vanity of the world or the misery of the human condition, among *de sanctis* sermons. In addition, in neither section do the individual items follow the liturgical calendar with any strictness. The *de tempore* sermons, for instance, progress in general from Advent through the Christmas and Lenten seasons to Easter and the post-Easter season; but this pattern is constantly broken by such intrusions as a Palm Sunday sermon in the sequence of Advent sermons, or the recurrence of blocks of Advent or of Lenten sermons anywhere in the *de tempore* part. The reason for this lack of strict order is not difficult to see: the scribes must have copied different runs of sermons in a group. For example, on folios 165–183v appears a copy of the 55 *Collationes dominicales de evangeliis* by John Pecham, which are here numbered but not otherwise identified. They run in the order of the church year from the second Sunday of Advent to the twenty-fifth Sunday after Trinity, but they appear in this collection between a sermon for Ash Wednesday and one for the twenty-second Sunday after Trinity. Another run of sermons that can be attributed to a particular preacher—and is so in the manuscript—is by Master John Sene, monk at Glastonbury.[85] Several sermons are ascribed

---

85. He had received the D.Th. by 1360 and died before 1377, and there is some evidence that he was engaged in literary activity. See Emden 1957–59, 3:1662–63; Pantin 1931–37, 3:30, 201, 202; and Carley 1985, xxix–xxx.

to him in both the collection (f. 215v) and the table (for ff. 235, 246v), and he probably was the author of the entire block of sermons copied on folios 235–246.

The majority of sermons here collected is entirely in Latin, but some twenty-three items show a mixture of Latin and English of types A, B, and minimal and marginal C. One sermon contains just enough English elements to qualify for inclusion in the fully macaronic type C. One or two of the B sermons are remarkable for the richness and diversity of the English material they include.[86] Also noteworthy is the presence of at least four sermons in honor of the patron saint of Oxford, Frideswide, all in Latin.

For all their diversity, these thirteen manuscripts have a number of important features in common. They belong to three different kinds or types of late-medieval manuscripts: the notebook (T), the miscellany (D and L), and the sermon collection (the remaining ten books). Though written with differing degrees of care as shown in their script, apparatus, and corrections, none of them stand out by particularly artistic layouts or illuminations. These are not lavish products of bookmaking but relatively humble consumer goods made for study and consultation.

The ten collections of sermons or of material for preaching show a good deal of diversity, too, with respect to their provenance or affiliation. Four (Q, H, Z, and S) can, with a varying degree of certainty, be linked to the Franciscan order, and one (B) holds a sermon cycle ascribed to a famous Dominican preacher. What may come as a surprise is that four other manuscripts are unquestionably connected with the Benedictine order, as is established by evidence both external (in W and X) and internal (in R and O). The same diversity holds for the few names of individual preachers that appear in these manuscripts. Some named authors are Franciscans, one or two are Dominicans, and several are Benedictines. The surprise in this, again, is the relatively large share that Benedictine monks had in making and collecting sermons. No matter how groundbreaking the preaching of the friars had been in the thirteenth century or how much their example and practice may still have been guiding lights in England at the end of the fourteenth and through the

---

86. See Wenzel 1978, 82–86. Other English material from this collection has been quoted in Wenzel 1974a and 1974b, passim; 1986, see index, 259.

first half of the fifteenth century, the evidence before us speaks loudly of the monks' strong interest in preaching and of their painstaking cultivation of pulpit rhetoric.[87]

Diversity is also the first impression that arises from examining the audiences for which the collected sermons were intended. It is not always easy, if at all possible, to determine whether a given sermon was preached to, or intended for, a lay audience or the clergy. It may be right to assume that a battery of quotations from Aristotle or Avicenna indicates a learned audience, whereas bloodcurdling visions of the dead and conversion stories were meant to move the laity. Unfortunately, such a stylistic distinction was not always as neatly observed by late-medieval sermon writers as the modern scholar may wish; there are enough cases of sermons that mix these elements,[88] and others provide nonstylistic evidence of their audience that contradicts that simple dichotomy. Many sermons were written with no specific audience, or perhaps with *any* audience, in mind; hence they mixed stylistic elements rather freely. Yet if style is no reliable guide, the intended audience of these sermons can occasionally be inferred from external clues: a rubric here and there ("Sermo ad clerum"), formulas of address,[89] or explicit references in the texts to their listeners and their concerns.[90] These clues tell us that all the sermon collections under consideration contain sermons for the laity next to sermons for the clergy, in a very random mixture, as the preceding descriptions of the manuscripts have sufficiently shown.

One aspect of this matter should perhaps receive more emphasis: the preachers' concern with the pastoral office. Of the ten sermon collections analyzed, at least nine contain one or more sermons that deal specifically with the duties of the priesthood, either by outlining what a good priest should be like and do, or by castigating failures in these respects.[91] Even one of the miscellanies whose main interest seems to lie in devotional

---

87. See Wenzel 1993.

88. See, for example, the edited sermon O-07, which contains a good deal of medieval astronomy and also a tale about the servant of a Norman knight who used to swear by Christ's body and was cruelly punished for it. The audience of this sermon may have been mixed.

89. The formulas of address in medieval sermons need much further study. In Latin pieces, such addresses as "Reverendi" or "Venerandi" or "Reverendi patres" and the like would suggest a clerical audience, and this is very often borne out by internal references.

90. See the discussion earlier in this chapter.

91. The tenth manuscript, X, needs further study in this respect.

writings (D) gives some of its space to this topic. Furthermore, this concern is also found in those sermon collections that have a strong monastic affiliation—a somewhat perplexing relation because on principle monks did not have the cure of souls, at least not in parishes.[92]

Diversity and mixture characterize yet another aspect of these manuscripts: the occasions for which the individual sermons were created. The preceding analyses have revealed that, with one exception (and that a partial one, set 1 of B), the collections mix sermons from the two major cycles (*de tempore* and *de sanctis*) freely and present them in an absolutely random order. Our manuscripts are thus radically different from the great thirteenth-century collections of model sermons, from the contemporary Wycliffite sermons, and from other contemporary collections of Latin sermons made in England.[93] We have observed that in one manuscript (B) a random collection of sermons is preceded by a complete and orderly cycle, and that elsewhere (Q, X, and W) individual sermons for the same occasion or on the same topic are grouped together. But much more commonly, sermons were evidently copied higgledy-piggledy, with little concern for either occasion or audience. In their random order, however, these collections do show preferences for certain occasions of the church year. Thus, pieces for the Sundays in Lent, for Holy Week, and for Easter outnumber all other seasons, followed at some distance by sermons for Advent and Christmas. The same is true of sermons *de sanctis*, where the Blessed Virgin takes pride of place, followed by saints of particular interest to the English or to the Benedictine order.

It is therefore obvious that the manuscripts with which this study is concerned are not the products of making, or at least copying, cycles of sermons arranged in any kind of neat liturgical order, but instead collections of bits and pieces. This is plainly revealed by their physical makeup, their foliation and signatures, the presence of tables of contents, and even cross-references to other sermons in the same collection— features that often reveal the actual work and progression of whoever

---

92. But for evidence that monks engaged in preaching to the laity, see Wenzel 1993, 6–7, and especially Greatrex 1991, 219–22.

93. For example, the temporale and sanctorale cycles, both containing sermons on the epistles and gospels of the day, by Ralph Acton or Atton, writing in the fourteenth century (in Manchester, John Rylands Library, MS 367, and elsewhere; on Acton see Emden 1957– 59, 1:12). Another systematic collection is the very popular *Sermones dominicales* by John Felton, completed in 1431 (see Emden 1957–59, 2:676; Fletcher 1991).

brought these sermons and materials together. Hence, none of these manuscripts and their texts can claim the status of author's copies. One might think that the notebook of John Dygoun (T) contains some sermons in autograph, as could be suggested by the nature of the volume's makeup and its less careful handwriting. But this possibility is negated by the general character of the volume as a notebook, formed by a series of booklets into which preexisting material has been copied, often with identification of its sources, and, more to the point, by the fact that its one fully macaronic sermon, *Amore langueo*, already existed in a codex (S) dating from half a century before Dygoun's time. One would very much like to know what the exemplars from which the extant sermons were copied looked like: were they wax tablets or bits of parchment or paper, for instance; and did they contain fully worked-out sermon texts or merely notes taken during the sermon and subsequently elaborated by a scribe or reporter? Such questions are intriguing for the study of medieval sermons in general and become crucial in our investigation of linguistically mixed texts. But unfortunately the material evidence needed to answer them convincingly has disappeared. As regards macaronic sermons, I know of no extant wax tablet or *schedula* that contains a preacher's autograph or notes taken during his sermon.

None of these manuscripts contains any explicit statement that would tell us for whom and for what purposes the material was collected. There are no dedications to a religious or lay superior, no justifications for the time and efforts the scribe has spent on his work, no pious wishes that his labors may be useful and salutary for his readers—none of the various *rationes scribendi* employed in the prologues of so many medieval works.[94] And yet the nature of the material collected, its arrangement, and the codicological apparatus with which it was provided indicate that at least the manuscripts I have classified as sermon collections were compiled to provide preaching matter for study and further use by preachers.

---

94. Such prologues exist for some sermon collections made in fourteenth- and fifteenth-century England. For example, Ralph Acton (or Atton) provided his Latin sermon with a typical yet "personal" prologue ("Cum in ecclesia mea quietus residerem et loquendi ad populum per dies dominicos et festos mihi consuetudinem fecissem . . . ," Manchester, John Rylands Library, MS Latin 367, f. 1); John Waldeby, writing at the request of Abbot Thomas de la Mare of St. Albans, states that he is fashioning his exposition of the Creed, divided into twelve sermons, from notes made for his preaching at York (Oxford, MS Laud Misc. 296, f. 57ra–b); and the collection in Oxford, Trinity College MS 42, is dedicated to W. of C——kston, canon of Chichester.

Even manuscript Q, which has been called a "sermon diary," is not an account of sermons preached on successive dates but rather a collection of items ordered by principles other than chronology. The dominant characteristics of all thirteen manuscripts, therefore, are diversity and randomness, but a randomness that is not without purpose.

In this republic of sermon collections, the macaronic sermons are fully integrated citizens. They are always in a decided minority: eight out of a total of fifty-seven sermons in the best case, one out of 330 in the worst. The exception here is manuscript O, whose first part includes twenty-two macaronic sermons in a total of twenty-five. But this startling feature becomes less impressive when one considers that for the entire manuscript, which contains two sermon collections, the ratio is twenty-two out of forty-five. I know of no medieval manuscript that contains only macaronic sermons.

Further, sermons of type C always appear in the company of others that are entirely in Latin. Even in the exceptional first set of manuscript O, the twenty-two fully macaronic sermons rub elbows with two in Latin. Actually, the codices we have examined contain not just Latin and fully macaronic sermons but representatives of the other types of linguistically mixed pieces (types A, B, and minimal and marginal C) and even sermons that are predominantly English (types D or E).[95] The fully macaronic sermons we are investigating have in all cases been preserved with other types of linguistically mixed sermons and with sermons that are entirely in Latin. It would appear that for whoever collected these items, their language was of no great concern. As far as their preservation allows us to tell, type C sermons were neither privileged nor marginalized.

---

95. This is true of all thirteen manuscripts except the two miscellanies, D and L, which contain only one macaronic sermon each and otherwise Latin material. A good example of a type D sermon, which is all English but gives its division and some authorities in Latin, is Z-15.

CHAPTER 4

Macaronic Sermons

As we turn to fully macaronic sermons in particular and examine features already discussed in chapter 3—such as the makeup of individual manuscripts and the authorship, audience, and occasions of the sermons they preserve—the following pages may at first appear somewhat repetitive, but they will soon yield a more finely-tuned characterization of these sermons and lead us closer to such larger questions as how macaronic sermons came into being and whether they were actually preached in this form.

Regarding their authorship, type C sermons share the uncertainties we have observed previously. The collection in manuscript Q in general is linked to the Franciscan friar Nicholas Philip, but whether he was their author is not clear. None of the pieces in Q connected with the names of Melton and Holbeche is fully macaronic. Similarly, the macaronic sermons in R and in set 1 of manuscript O have been tentatively connected with the Benedictine Paunteley; but whether he was their author is far from certain. All the other pieces are nameless.

One reason for advancing Paunteley as the author of the O sermons was that three macaronic pieces in that manuscript also occur in R. There are two other cases in which a particular sermon has been preserved in multiple copies, both involving four different manuscripts each. Both are sermons on the passion of Christ, ostensibly made for Good Friday: *Amore langueo* (B-088, D-2, S-07, and T-07) and *Christus passus est pro nobis* (H-25, S-01, W-006, and Z-19). This sharing of evidently popular sermons is, again, in line with what we observed about sermon collections in general.

The occasions for which individual type C sermons were intended also follow the pattern established more generally by the manuscripts themselves. Of the forty-three separate sermons, all but four can be confidently assigned to a specific occasion on the grounds of either a rubric or strong internal evidence.[1] Most of them are for Sundays ranging through the entire church year, from Advent to the post-Pentecostal season; two sermons are for saints' feasts, the Assumption and the feast of St. Mark; two sermons are for funerals; and one piece is directed to the clergy. Within this broad range is a very strong concentration on the Lenten season: thirty sermons, which is nearly three-fourths of the total of macaronic pieces, are for occasions from the first Sunday in Lent to Easter; they include at least five sermons for Good Friday and two for Easter Sunday.[2] Both spread and concentration thus correspond exactly to the pattern we observed in the collections as a whole.

In discussing the occasions and other aspects of macaronic sermons, it must be remembered that the manuscripts under consideration are not systematic collections that contain one or more sermons in due order for each and every occasion throughout the church year, whether it is Sundays, saints' feasts, or special occasions. Rather, the manuscripts that have preserved macaronic sermons show a decided predilection for certain occasions and concerns, which may be summed up as calls for repentance, meditation on the passion of Christ, and, to a lesser extent, praise of the Blessed Virgin. Though these matters are difficult to quantify, I believe macaronic sermons show a slight difference in this respect: they seem to place an even greater emphasis on calls to repentance and meditation on the passion than do the entire group of sermons that are collected, in whatever linguistic form, in these manuscripts. This observation actually applies to any sermons that contain a significant amount of English material, including those of types B and minimal and marginal C. It is thus fair to say that the Sundays of Lent, Good Friday, and Easter were favorite occasions for the production of linguistically mixed and, especially, fully macaronic sermons. Such an emphasis accounts for the experience I have had again and again: in reading through manuscripts with basically Latin sermons written in England during the four-

---

1. Such as references to Christ's suffering "hodie" or calling to penitence "in hoc sacro tempore," though the latter could also refer to the Advent season.

2. The number of Good Friday sermons may actually be higher, because occasionally a sermon will be rubricked "in passione Domini," which can apply to both Passion Sunday or Good Friday.

teenth and early fifteenth centuries, one finds little if any English until one arrives at a sermon for Good Friday.[3]

To such favorite occasions for macaronic sermons I add favorite topics that similarly stimulated the production of linguistically mixed texts. The experience I have just described recurs here as well: a particular sermon will present pages on pages that are entirely in Latin until it turns to one of the "favorite topics"; then the language suddenly becomes macaronic. Such topics are, first of all, descriptions of Christ's passion, and next to them complaints at individual moral or social decadence, including tavern scenes and satiric pictures of youth. To illustrate this sudden appearance of macaronic sentences, I select cases from three sermons that contain some English material, but not enough of the kind to place them in type C. Such passages of heightened language mixture occur in fully macaronic sermons (type C) as well but naturally do not stand out as sharply there as they do in a more homogeneous Latin environment.[4]

W-066 provides a good example involving Christ's passion. The sermon is exclusively in Latin through its lengthy introduction and main division. The latter divides the thema into two parts: Christ's pain and passion, and his love and affection. Part 1 is then subdivided into three members: Christ's passion was most acute, universal, and ignominious. In the development of the second member ("universal"), English words, together with realistic details, begin to appear in the otherwise Latin text.

Vultis uidere quid passus est? Quando fuit eleuatus in cruce et corpus suum non habuit aliud **stayyng** nisi per manus et pedes que fuerunt clauate, dimiserunt pedem crucis cadere in profundo **morteys,** per

---

3. Among the manuscripts here surveyed, L is a good example, and the same is true of D and T. Another case in point is Oxford, Trinity College MS 42: its collected sermons show no English until one arrives at several for Good Friday, which belong to types B and marginal C. Bériou finds the same to be true of thirteenth-century sermons in France (1992, 276–77).

4. Any macaronic Good Friday sermon would furnish a good illustration of such clustering; see for instance *Amore langueo,* edited in appendix B, 1. For a macaronic cluster in the development of the transitoriness of youth, see the description of the gallant in W-102, printed in Wenzel 1986, 215. Two further good examples are a passage on the wheel of Fortune in O-08/49v–50 and another on pride in clothing in O-22/115r–v, quoted at the end of chapter 5.

quem casum pro quanto non dimiserunt istud cadere **softely** sed dimiserunt istud **altoschake**. Per quod **schakyng** quodlibet os transiuit extra iuncturam et perdidit locum suum naturalem.

(Do you want to see what he suffered? When he was lifted on the cross and his body had no other support than by his hands and feet that were pierced by nails, they let the foot of the cross fall into a deep hole, and they did not let it fall softly but with a great thump. Through this thump, every bone slipped out of its joint and lost its natural place.)[5]

This mixing of single English words into the Latin context continues for the remainder of the sermon. In the following paragraphs also appears another favorite topic for macaronic sentences, the transitoriness of life.

Est enim de gloria hominis hic in terra sicut de flore qui crescit in prato. In primo eius ortu est multum viuidum in se et pulcher et placens visui. Sed si pratum metatur et sol incaluerit, iste flos arescit et **fadiþ**, suus color euanescit. Et sic est de homine. Sit homo hodie quantumcumque **lusty and semely** ad visum; si cras accedat sibi modicus calor febris, robur et **lustys** deficiunt.

(For with man's glory here on earth it goes as it does with a flower that grows in the meadow. First, in its growth, it is very full of life, beautiful, and pleasing to behold. But when the meadow is cut and the sun grows hot, the flower dries and fades, and its color disappears. Thus it goes with man. Let him be as vital and pleasing to behold as possible today; if tomorrow a little heat of fever should come, his strength and vitality fall away.)[6]

A good example that develops a complaint at the degeneracy of the times macaronically can be found in B-111, on the thema *Convertimini ad Deum*. The sermon contains several English distinctions and message verses. One of them renders into English rhymes two Latin hexameters on the topos that virtues become vices.

---

5. W-066/120rb.
6. W-066/121rb.

Trewþe ys turnyd into trecherye,
Chast loue into lecherye,
Pleye and solas to velenye,
And holyday to glotonye.

These lines form the material and structure for further development. So far, the English elements in the sermon have been of types *a* and *b;* but now the language becomes, for a moment, genuinely macaronic.

Karissimi, sicud videtis mundus nunquam erat ita mirabilis [*read* miserabilis] sicut modo est, nec tanta caristia omnium rerum, et credo firmiter quod propter istas quatuor causas precedentes. Nam **wyt ys turnyd,**[7] etc. Consideremus modo omnes illos qui singulariter vocantur ingeniosi, siue in ecclesiastica curia siue in regia, et videamus propter que facta sunt ita singulariter nominati. Et videbimus propter cautelas, deceptiones quam propter pauperum tuitiones. Si sit aliquis quia sciat peruertere legem **vpsedoun** et sciat trahere eam ad libitum suum **after þat hys hond ys anoyntyd** vel magis vel minus non secundum intentionem legis, et ideo modo spoliet et defraudet proximos, non dicitur quod talis **ys a fals man** sed ingeniosus, **a wytty and a slye man**. Et non solum propter cautelas...

(Dearly beloved, as you see, the world was never so wretched as it is nowadays, nor was there ever such dearth of all things, and I firmly believe it is for these four causes. Because "wit is turned," etc. Let us consider all those who today are particularly called witty, whether in the church's court or the king's, and let us see for what deeds they have that strange name. We shall see that it is because of their tricks and deceptions rather than their legal protection of the poor. If there is one who knows how to turn the law upside down and to twist it after his will, according to whether his hand has been anointed more or less and not according to the intention of the law, and who thus will despoil and cheat his neighbors nowadays, such a person is called not false but witty and smart. And not only because of his tricks....)[8]

---

7. This phrase repeats the first line of the distinction but replaces *trewþe* with *wyt*.
8. B-111/187vb–188ra.

Similar macaronic sentences appear in the developments of the second and third topics, the latter including a little tavern scene.[9]

Another topic of social complaint frequently voiced in late-medieval sermons is false pride in clothing, and this, too, stimulated sermon writers to produce macaronic passages. In a sermon on the thema "Every realm that is divided against itself will be laid waste," the speaker first discusses earthly kingdoms and enjoins the need for unity, but then observes that nowadays justice has turned into trickery, and so forth. His text is entirely in Latin, except for two vernacular sayings—one by a tapster,[10] the other by a glutton feasting in the tavern[11]—and an English passage between them that is not introduced as a saying but instead switches the preacher's exhortation in a manner characteristic of genuinely macaronic elements.

Iam dierum nesciunt quid et quomodo vellent habere formam vestimentorum suorum in eo quod habent vestimenta sua contra naturam, **for-qwy it is a meruell to se a catt with two tallys, bot now a man or a woman wyll haue two talles, and yt ys more meruell, for a woman wyll haue a tayll a-fore off her scho and anoder byhynd off hyr gone. A man wyll haue two qwellbarowys off hys schowdyrs.** Set certe Deus non sic creavit hominem set ad ymaginem suam, et ipse non habet talia, scio.

(Nowadays they don't know what and how they want to have the shape of their clothes, because they have clothes against [the law of] nature. For it is a marvel to see a cat with two tails, but now a man or woman will have two tails, and it is an even greater marvel, for a woman will have a tail in front of her shoe and another behind her gown. A man will have two wheelbarrows off his shoulders. But surely God did not create man thus but rather in his own image, and he does not have such things as far as I know.)[12]

---

9. The sermon ends incomplete with this scene. The macaronic sentence is quoted in Wenzel 1986, 190.

10. "A cup of my ale and a kiss of my mouth is enough for a penny" (London, British Library, Harley 2388, f. 102v). For the Middle English text and the entire sermon, see Wenzel 1989, 281.

11. "Hauld, pely, hauld, for in fath þu has cost gude xvi d. to-nyght" (f. 103). I interpret this to mean: "Hold, belly, hold, for in faith you have cost me a good 16 pence tonight."

12. F. 103.

In discussing another sermon feature, their audience, the preceding chapter considered various kinds of relevant evidence—rubrics, forms of address, and internal remarks—and arrived at a complex picture according to which most of the sermon collections analyzed contained some sermons that were directed to a lay audience, others that aimed at the clergy, and some that evidently addressed both. The same picture holds for the fully macaronic sermons. Because many of them do not give a very firm indication of their intended audience, a convincing statistical account would be hard to reach. It is far more important and interesting to notice that a number of macaronic sermons are definitely directed to the clergy, and that others address a mixed audience of clergy and laity.

The main hint of a clerical audience comes from such address forms as "Reuerendi" or "Reuerendi domini." Such forms occur in several macaronic sermons found in different manuscripts.[13] A particularly clear case is W-102, where the clue to the sermon's audience given by its address form is supported by internal evidence. After its initial address of "Reuerendi domini" the sermon declares that Christ's special temple on earth is "the multitude and congregation of the faithful." Its stones are men and women, and its builders the "rectors, prelates, presbyters, and especially the preachers of God's word." After this initial image, the preacher addresses his audience again: "But, sirs, you and I whose task it is to build that temple must notice that some of these stones are soft . . . and others too hard." He then gives good advice on how to work with them so that a good building will emerge. Like Aristotle's mason,[14] pastors must use an adaptable rule: "Reverend sirs, you who have the cure of souls and have undertaken to build God a good temple, it is necessary that your rule of correction be flexible," and so on.[15] A ref-

---

13. A-33, B-136, O-22, W-072, W-102.

14. Aristotle's leaden rule used in making Lesbian moulding (*Nicomachean Ethics* 5.10. 1137v29–30) has become, in this sermon, a "magnus lathomus et edificator" named Lisbes, who "fecit sibi regulam plumbeam flexibilem" (f. 193).

15. "Reuerendi domini, speciale templum et habitacio quod Christus Filius Dei habet hic in terra est multitudo et congregacio fidelium. . . . Isti ecclesiastici cuiusmodi sunt rectores, prelati, et presbiteri, et specialiter predicatores verbi Dei qui habent custodiam et **warde** istius templi, oportet ipsos attendere quod sit deb[i]te preparatum. . . . Homines enim et mulieres erunt materia et lapides istius templi. . . . Sed domini mei, vos et me [?], quibus pertinet edificare istud templum, oportet vos attendere quod aliqui illorum lapidum sunt molles . . . et aliqui sunt adeo duri. . . . Reuerendi domini, vos qui habetis curam animarum

erence to the rule of St. Benedict and, later in the sermon, the phrase "we religious, monks, and brethren (or friars)" leave little doubt that the preacher was a (Benedictine) monk here speaking to fellow priests.[16]

Similar internal evidence in several other sermons points to a mixed audience of both clergy and laypersons. The examples already cited in chapter 3 are now joined by two more illustrations from type C sermons. O-13, evidently given on Holy Thursday, exhorts both groups at once.

And so you who are prefigured by Moses, give yourselves up to your cure of souls, engage in devout prayers and the understanding and contemplation of God. And you who belong to the laity, take your Our Father and your Creed and do not climb any higher.[17]

The *figura* alluded to is Moses, who ascended Mount Sinai while the Hebrews waited at the foot of the mountain (Exod. 19:17–20 and 20:18–21), one of the several images that the author of set 1 in O uses repeatedly to discuss the major divisions of society and the need for order and unity.[18] One might therefore think that addresses like the one quoted are merely rhetorical, spoken into a vacuum rather than to a specific congregation. But the long Good Friday sermon in L gives quite unequivocal evidence of addressing a mixed audience. After a lengthy introductory section, the preacher starts his sermon's main part with the words: "Now for the development of this sermon you will notice—first briefly in Latin for these clerics and afterward in English for all of you..." A short outline of the sermon in Latin follows. Then the preacher starts all over again: "The development that I have said for these clerics in Latin and that I intend to pursue is this..."[19]

---

et manucepistis Deo edificare bonum templum, oportet quod regula correccionis vestre sit flexibilis" (ff. 192v–193).

16. "Nos religiosi, monachi, et fratres" (f. 195).

17. "Ideo qui figuramini per Moisen, indulgete cure vestre, date vos deuotis precibus, cognicioni et contemplacioni diuine. Et vos qui estis de **laife, tak** þi Pater Noster **and** þi Credo, et non vlterius ascendas" (f. 80v).

18. Besides Moses on Mount Sinai, which is also used in sermon 24, the author uses images of the ship of state, in sermons 4, 16, and 25; the vineyard, in 7; and the temple, in 15 and 22.

19. "Nunc pro processu sermonis notabitis—primo breuiter in Latinis pro istis clericis et postea in Angl' pro vobis omnibus. Est igitur notandum quod... Processus huiusmodi quem dixi istis clericis in Latinis et quem intendo tenere est iste" (L-1/217v). Another case of this kind is B-115. After a protheme and division *intra* in Latin, the text continues:

I have quoted these passages to establish as firmly as possible that some fully macaronic sermons were written for audiences that included clerics or that were entirely clerical, even comprising a university audience (O-08). The particular significance of this fact lies in the light it sheds on the language used in preaching. It has been customary, for over a century and more, to determine the language in which a sermon was preached by the specific audience to which it was addressed: sermons for the clergy are said to have been given in Latin; those for laypersons, in the vernacular. That a significant percentage of macaronic sermons clearly address the clergy is an important factor in chapter 6, where I further discuss the phenomenon of these texts and the questions of their actual delivery.

Yet another and similarly important aspect of type C sermons is their form. In making their points and developing their matter, they employ all the well-known devices that are associated with late-medieval preaching[20]: scriptural, patristic, and other authorities; biblical *figurae;* exempla that derive from classical literature, medieval story collections, and hearsay or possibly the preacher's own experience; similes from every corner of life; images and *picturae* with parts and, frequently, inscriptions; verses, proverbs, and popular sayings; and the ubiquitous moral allegorization of whatever material comes to hand. Naturally, individual collections and, within them, individual sermons vary to some extent in their preference for what parts of this rich treasury of pulpit rhetoric they draw on. Thus, the sermons in Q use moralized images or sculptures less often than those in O; and among the Q sermons, some are considerably more elaborate and *curiosi* than others.[21] But these differences are minor and typical of any of these collections. On the whole, all macaronic sermons represent what previous students of medieval preaching have called the "popular sermon,"[22] whatever audience they address.

"Karissimi, sicut dixi istis literatis in verbis pro themate assumptis, pro processu sermonis nostri duo breuiter intelligere debetis: primo **an hol precious offeryng mannys soule to comfortyng**; item pro secundo **a fre and a profytabyl ȝeuyng mannes soule to strengþyng**. De istis duobus breuiter erit processus nostri sermonis" (199rb).

20. These are surveyed in some detail, as they appear in a preacher's handbook of the early fourteenth century, in Wenzel 1976, 41–49; 1978, 50–59.

21. Two sermons in Q (42 and 44) are labeled "curiosus" in the margin; see the extended comment in Fletcher 1986, 195–98. *Curiositas* here means not "outstanding whimsicality," as Fletcher seems to imply (198), but careful elaboration and elegance; see Wenzel 1986, 66, 75, with reference to Robert of Basevorn.

22. Notably Pfander 1937.

The term *popular,* however, is totally misleading if it suggests an audience of common laypersons whose attention had to be held by the sermonistic equivalent to Chaucer's "new tydings" and whose emotions had to be stirred by rather crude appeals to fear and wonder. That such devices were used in fourteenth- and fifteenth-century preaching, and that they occur in our fully macaronic sermons, cannot be denied. But their presence is no indication that these sermons were directed to weavers and mechanics. This fact has already emerged from my previous discussion of their audience. It emerges again when we consider their structure.

All known macaronic sermons, without a single exception, belong to the type called "scholastic sermon": they are based on a short biblical thema, which, after a protheme and introduction, is formally divided, with the divisions then being developed at some length. The introductory matter before the division may vary in form and length: some sermons have a carefully worked-out protheme that leads to the preacher's asking his congregation to pray; others begin directly with a prayer and general commendation or go at once into the division. However long or elaborate the introductory matter may be, the hallmark of the scholastic sermon, the *divisio thematis,* is always present. These features have been described often,[23] by both medieval *artes praedicandi* and modern students of preaching. That these components of a formal technique were applied consciously by the makers of macaronic sermons is shown by their use of the standard technical terms in both sermon texts and margins.[24]

Fully macaronic sermons not only observe the requirements of scholastic sermon structure in a general way; beyond that, they work out particular structural features with great care and technical skill. Two specific features demonstrate this characteristic with particular force: the final *unitio,* and what I can only call the sermon writers' academic concern with the division of their themata. The former is a device used at the end of the sermon to join together the main notions and key

---

23. See Wenzel 1986, chapter 3, esp. 66–69.

24. Type C sermons consistently use technical terms in their text. Beside the fairly ubiquitous *materia sermonis* (in the technical sense), *processus,* and *principalis,* one finds such terms as *antethema, divisio,* and the more specific ones discussed in text below. The sermons in set 1 of manuscript O are fairly regularly supplied with such terms in the margins, but the same is true of other manuscripts as well. Often divisions and subdivisions are marginally marked by some visual sign, and the beginnings of the principals are similarly indicated by at least a marginal number.

words developed in the preceding parts or principals of the sermon. In sermon O-07, edited in appendix C, the final paragraph adduces a biblical quotation not hitherto used in this sermon, whose phrases are explicitly linked to the key terms of the sermon's three principal parts. The quotation recalls the sermon's general structure and main topics, tying them up in a final knot, and at the same time leads to the concluding blessing. This device is used almost regularly in the macaronic O sermons and also appears in W-154, edited in appendix D. Many O sermons use a similar procedure to tie up the members of a subdivision within a principal.[25]

Such delight in formal structure and sermon rhetoric almost turned into an obsession for some macaronic sermon writers as they built their divisions. It is as if they felt a heavy obligation to furnish a formal *divisio thematis* in which the verbal material of the thema is analyzed, according to various possible procedures laid out by the *artes praedicandi,* into parts that are then confirmed, only to continue with another division that then provides the outline for the actual sermon. A relatively simple and succinct example occurs in Q-42. First, the preacher (a) repeats the thema, (b) divides its verbal material into three parts, (c) interprets these as a scriptural exegete would, and (d) confirms his interpretations with other scriptural authorities that contain the respective key terms of his interpretations.

(a) *Ve michi, mater mea,* vbi supra. Karissimi, (b) tria concipio in istis verbis, videlicet:

(c) a losse of hele and lykyng, in *ve;*
a body dressede to dying, ibi *ve michi;*
to a woman petously pleynyng, ibi *mater mea.*

(d) Pro primo dico quod concipio **a losse of hele and lykynge** in hoc verbo *ve,* vnde propheta in Psalmo: "Defecit in dolore vita mea." Pro secundo Job 33: "Consumpta est caro eius suppliciis." Pro tercio Jeremie 15: "Ve michi, mater; quare me genuisti?"

---

25. This connection of the sermon's main parts at the end is a feature taught by the major *artes praedicandi.* Basevorn calls it *unitio;* see Charland 1936, 306–7.

("Woe is me, my mother," as above. Dearly beloved, I find three things in these words, namely:

> a loss of health and joy, in "woe";
> a body prepared to die, in "woe is me":
> a pitiful complaint to a woman, in "my mother."

First I say that I find a loss of health and joy in the word "woe," whence the prophet says, in the Psalm: "My life is wasted with grief." For the second, Job 33: "His flesh is consumed with punishments." For the third, Jeremiah 15: "Woe is me, my mother; why have you borne me?")

Then, instead of developing these three parts, he continues, without any logical connection, to give a second division.

> Dolor iste siue passio potest assimulari bene **to**
>> **a man of ple and motyng,**
>> **a boke of scripture and wryting,**
>> **a harpe of melodye makyng**.

(This pain or passion can be well likened to a man of pleading and judgment; a book of scripture and writing; a harp of music making.)

This second division furnishes the topics that are subsequently developed in the remainder of the sermon, beginning with "Primo dico quod mors Christi potest assimulari **to a man of ple and motyng.**"[26]

Such a two-stage approach occurs in several other macaronic sermons, and (though this is not the case in the quoted example) sermon writers had clear verbal markers available to indicate this technique. The first part, the *divisio thematis* proper, usually begins with some reference to the words (*verba*) of the thema; the second, the actual division to be followed, uses the phrase *pro processu*. This is well shown in L-1, which marks the stages of its lengthy division with: "*In quibus verbis* aperte videre possumus.... Nunc *pro processu sermonis* notabitis..." That

---

26. Q-42/123; ed. Little 1943, 248.

sermon writers felt an obligation to proceed in this fashion is nicely shown in B-113. After a fairly substantial protheme that ends with an invitation to pray, the preacher announces: "Dearly beloved, I omit the introduction and division in order to be brief. For the development you should know . . ." He then launches into a division that is anything but simple, apparently making up for the admitted omission.[27]

We find here the successive application of the two traditional ways to divide the thema: *intra* (dividing the verbal matter of the thema) and *extra* (dividing a concept that is contained in or suggested by the theme).[28] The two techniques not only were recognized in a popular *ars praedicandi* attributed to St. Bonaventure but were linked there to different audiences, with the former being of greater appeal to trained exegetes (the clergy) and the latter more easily grasped by theologically untrained minds (the laity).[29] It is surprising that we should find both kinds used simultaneously in several macaronic sermons preserved in different manuscripts.

One further noteworthy aspect of dealing with the sermon thema is the technique of dividing it into more than one schema and then combining the resulting parts into a complex division. In the following example, the preacher first discusses the name of Jesus under its aspects of light, medicine, and food. Second, the preacher relates each aspect to a different class of rational beings. Third, he considers the modus operandi of each aspect and relates it back to a basic quality in God. Fourth, he ties the verbal and notional material that has thus been developed out of the single word *Iesus* into a division of three members, which then become the topics of the sermon proper.

Iesus, vbi prius. Sanctissimus doctor Bernardus *Super Cantica,* sermone XIIII, dicit quod istud venerabile nomen Iesus est (1) lux **briȝt schynyng,** medicina **releuynge,** et cibus **most norschynge.** (2) Ex quo est lux, **fendis of helle it a-ferid in derkenes.** Ex quo est medicina **hirlich men it helit of sekenes.** Ex quo est cibus, angelos celestes pascuit **in blissidnes.** (3) Sed ex quo hoc venerabile nomen Iesus est tante virtutis quod terret potentes, **þe frowarde fendes,** releuat [MS

27. "Karissimi, omissis introductione et diuisione vt breuius vos expediam, pro processu scire debetis" (B-113/193va).

28. In the quoted illustration, the divided verbal matter of the thema is *ve michi mater mea;* the divided concept is "pain," that is, *dolor* or *passio.*

29. See Wenzel 1986, 71, 89.

reuelat] misericorditer **seke creaturs,** et pascit graciose **heuonliche an-geles,** a forciori benedictus celi dominus qui vocatur Iesus habet istum triplicem modum operandi **on fend, man, and angel,** quia armatur in luce sicut princeps **almyȝty,** sanat **dedlich sekenes** sicut medicus **alwytty,** et pascit celicos spiritus sicut dominus **most goodly.** (4) Pro connexione istarum parcium dico primo:

—Quod omnipotens princeps Iesus sue armatura lucis vincit [MS dicit] nostrum inimicum tirannum **of derkenes;**

—quod omnisciens medicus Iesus sui surripo sanguinis sanauit **vrdlich men of hor dedle sekenes;**

—quod omnibonus dominus Iesus sue deitatis dulcedine pascit celicos angelos **in euerlastyng blissidnes.**

(*Jesus,* as quoted above. The most holy teacher Bernard, in his work *On Canticles,* sermon 14, says that the blessed name of Jesus is a bright-shining light, a medicine of relief, and most nourishing food. In so far as it is light, it frightens the fiends of hell in their darkness. In so far as it is medicine, it heals earthly men in their sickness. In so far as it is food, it feeds the heavenly angels in their bliss. But because this blessed name of Jesus has such power that it mightily frightens the froward fiends, mercifully relieves sick creatures, and graciously feeds the heavenly angels, a fortiori does the blessed lord of heaven who is called Jesus work in a threefold manner in fiend, man, and angel: he is armed in light like an almighty prince, he heals deadly sickness like a most skillful physician, and he feeds the heavenly spirits like a most benevolent lord. Tying these parts together, I say first that as an almighty prince, in the armor of his light, Jesus overcomes our enemy, the tyrant of darkness; that as an all-knowing physician, with the syrup of his blood, Jesus has healed earthly men of their deadly sickness; and that as an all-good lord, in the sweetness of his godhead, Jesus feeds the heavenly angels in everlasting bliss.)[30]

Dividing the thema thus into multiple triads and combining their corresponding elements into a complex division was, again, a trick of pulpit rhetoric taught by the major *artes praedicandi* of the time.[31] The resulting

---

30. O-05/28; I have added the numbers in parentheses for easier guidance.

31. Basevorn calls this technique *correspondentia* and considers various ways of achieving it: Charland 1936, 299–306. Other terms were also in use, such as *connexio partium* (as in quoted passage) or *connexio membrorum* (as in the edited sermon O-07, l. 144).

verbal artifact is a gem that scintillates with its logical processes and verbal ornaments, especially parallelism and rhythm. Such gems adorn a large number of macaronic sermons, not only in set 1 of O but in other collections. Now and then we can even hear echoes of criticism and a certain self-consciousness on the part of sermon writers with respect to such artistry. H-25, for example, begins with a long protheme that applies especially to preachers the point of the thema "Christ has suffered for us, giving you an example that you should follow." The protheme states that one of the examples Christ gave is that the words he spoke he did not speak as from himself (John 14:10). Therefore, preachers should likewise not speak as from themselves. But "a man speaks as from himself when he is intent on showing off his learning in dark figures, in subtle introductions and divisions, and in a profuse display of authorities."[32] This good advice is heeded in the following short introduction of the thema and its rather jejune division; but when the preacher comes to developing the principals, he cannot quite do so without dividing the first principal into three, and the third member of this subdivision further into another three parts.

However unappealing to modern taste such logical and verbal play may be, what matters for this study is that such work is not the product of spontaneous invention or the effluence of childlike minds open to God's spirit and speaking his truth as it comes to them. It is inconceivable that paragraphs like the one just quoted and some earlier ones could have been produced off-the-cuff. Instead, these macaronic sermons, in the form they have come to us, are first of all products of literary composition. In addition, the logical and rhetorical sophistication that informs their division—the heart of the scholastic sermon—argues that they resulted from careful, well-informed, and prolonged work that followed formal instructions that their writers had received at the university or at a house of studies. They may be "popular" in using the rhetoric of "popular" preaching, a term that would require readjustment in the light of what

---

32. "Primum verbum quod Christus dixit in exemplum predicatorum erat istud: 'Verba que ego loquor a meipso non loquor,' Iohannis 14. Et nota causam Iohannis 7 dicentis: 'Qui autem a seipso loquitur, querit gloriam suam. Qui autem querit gloriam eius qui misit illum, hic verax est.' Homo loquitur a seipso quando nimis ostendere nititur scienciam suam in tenebris figurarum, in subtilitatibus introduccionum et divisionum, et in multitudine auctoritatum literalium. Et vere multi tantum istis innituntur quod fructus sermonum multum subtrahitur" (f. 80). *Auctoritates literales* probably means "prooftexts with verbal concordance."

has just been said. They also may wear a rather bedraggled Latin garb that lets the native English underneath shine through in often embarrassing ways. But shapeless and inartistic products of the moment they are decidedly not.

CHAPTER 5

Macaronic Texture

The sermons studied here are compositions whose basic fabric is in Latin but in which parts appear in English. The latter should not be thought of as foreign elements woven into the basic fabric; the strands of the fabric themselves change here and there from one language to the other. I will now examine this macaronic texture more closely by looking at the frequency, length, and syntactic nature of the English elements. I will then address the question why the language switches as and where it does.

The forty-three sermons I have classified as fully macaronic vary considerably in length. Apart from incomplete pieces, their total number of words ranges from about 2,360 to over 17,000. An exact statistical account is nearly impossible to arrive at, for reasons that include the uncertainty about whether some elements in both Latin and English should be counted as one or two words and the defective state of manuscript Q, in which a good deal of material is illegible. Yet their average length can be estimated to lie somewhere between 5,000 and a little over 6,000 words. Only two sermons, H-25 and L-1, both for Good Friday, exceed this average considerably, extending to nearly 14,000 and over 17,000 words respectively. This wide variation in the total number of words applies equally to the number of English words contained in these sermons,[1] which ranges from about 130 to over 2,100. More significant than the actual number of English words is their proportion in the total number of words per sermon: it ranges from a low of 2.28 percent (in W-068) to an unusual high of 33.36 percent (in Q-20). In the three sermons I

---

1. I am here counting all English words, whether they belong to types *a, b,* or *c.*

have edited in appendices B–D, English words form 7.6 (S-07), 18.5 (O-07), and 2.8 (W-154) percent of the total number of words. The proportion of English material in these macaronic sermons is therefore always low and sometimes very low.[2]

We must therefore speak of Latin as the matrix or base language of these sermons on the basis of the proportion between the two languages alone. Occasionally this proportion approaches a point where the two languages are momentarily balanced, as in the following example from O-08:

> Quamdiu clerus **and þe laife** huius terre **werknet togedur** in vno **fagot and brendonn** super istum ignem, istud regnum **was ful warme and ful wel at hese.** Caritas **brande so hote,** þe **ley of loue was so huge,** quod **no Scottich miste ne no Frensche scouris** quierunt extinguere istam flammam. Sed nunc, prodolor, perfectus amor **is laid o watur,** caritas fere extinguitur, iste ignis **is almost out.** Quere vbi vis infra villam et extra, poteris **blowe** super vngues tuos **for any hete of loue.** Caritas est adeo frigida **as dumbeltomis. Fer truloue is hard to finde, miche similacion** þer **is, faire cher faileth not,** picta verba sunt sufficiencia, set fidencia modica est. Vix aliquis confidit alteri . . .[3]

But such balance lasts only for a few sentences, after which Latin again becomes the dominant language; and such passages in which English elements constitute half of the vocabulary are very rare in the corpus.

More importantly, Latin forms the syntactic matrix into which the English elements are always fully integrated, a matrix that follows the patterns of classical Latin morphology and syntax without question. There are occasional slips in gender and in verbal endings, and the classical tense rules are by no means strictly observed, as they were not in medieval Latin generally. And the vocabulary and style of these sermons are so heavily influenced by native English idioms as to make a classicist cringe—*facit tremare pilastros*, as a later macaronic poet has

---

2. See appendix E for a table indicating the total number of Latin words, of English words, and of switches from Latin to English in the forty-three macaronic sermons.

3. O-08/50v. A similar passage from the same sermon is the description of Fortune's wheel, quoted in chapter 3 as an example of favorite macaronic passages. This sermon was preached at Oxford to the clergy.

it.[4] But the basic features of Latin grammar—the distinctions of number and gender in nouns and adjectives, and of person, number, tense, mood, and voice in verbs—are faithfully adhered to. Latin grammar therefore was fairly solidly ingrained in the minds of whoever composed these sermons. This is shown with particular clarity at places where the language switches in the middle of a smaller syntactic structure.[5] For example, in the phrase "liberacionem **of wa** et tribulacione" (L-1/220), the ablative case of *tribulacione* is evidently due to the implied preposition *de*, here replaced by English **of**. Similarly, in "verba mee **prechinge**" (O-11/69), the feminine gender of *mee*, which could not possibly be determined by the English noun **prechinge**, must have been determined by an assumed Latin noun, such as *predicatio*.[6] Similar cases are "**ful** fixis stellis" and "de vestro **malady**," in the edited sermon O-07 (ll. 159 and 468).

The English elements in these sermons belong to all the classes and categories recognized by Modern English descriptive grammar.[7] They may be single words, phrases, clauses, or entire sentences. In the category of single words, all eight traditional word classes are represented. Nouns ("vita nostra propter eius **vnstedfastnesse** comparatur," B-127/220rb) and proper nouns ("ista dies vocaretur **Blake Moneday**," B-113/193va)—including foreign names ("**Egesip** nec **Quintilian**," etc., O-08/49v)—adjectives ("viri ecclesiastici qui sunt valde **ware**," L-1/219v), verbs ("hec **browgth** illum gloriosum solem," B-136/245rb), and adverbs ("ista virgo fuit **indirliche** pulcra," Q-20/63) are naturally predominant. But the smaller classes also furnish some good examples. An isolated pronoun appears in "fecerunt eum portare **himself** suam propriam dampnacionem" (L-1/223); the definite article in "þe draco auaricie" (O-07, l. 293); a preposition in "sciuit me iuuare **of** xii annis" ("he could help me for twelve years," L-1/222v); a conjunction in "fame **and** siti" (O-04/20); and even an exclamation in "**Alas**, victum non habeo" (O-07, ll. 576–77). Though the English vocabulary utilized in C sermons is

---

4. Quoted by Paoli 1959, 6.

5. Cases of English words with Latin endings are extremely rare. I have encountered only *sufferabat* (Q-19/58) and *doungeriosa* (W-072/131rb).

6. These examples would constitute firm evidence that their writers thought not in the vernacular, as some students of medieval preaching maintain, but in Latin; see further chapter 6.

7. In the following discussion, I have utilized the system and terminology of structural grammar as developed by Charles C. Fries, W. Nelson Francis, and others.

heavily Germanic in origin, words of Latin or Romance background occur with regularity.

English phrases, too, are represented with examples of all the various possibilities: noun phrases ("quilibet libenter audit **hys owen leden,**" B-113/193va), verb phrases ("postea **eer castin** in puteum inferni," L-1/220), prepositional phrases ("si deberet stare **at þe barre** coram iusticiario," B-113/194ra), and structures of coordination ("tunc fuit auditus **wele fer and wyde,**" L-1/216v). We likewise find examples of all the major kinds of English clauses: main clauses ("Statim sicut videt ciuitatem, **he brast on for to gretin,** sic quod vix potuit loqui," L-1/216), coordinate clauses ("Simplex homo vellet habere bona mercatoris, et mercator bona simplicis, **and lordis wold haue al y-fere,**" B-136/246vb), and various kinds of subordinate clauses.

Potestis videre vlterius **how wonderful he ys to mannys sy3th** (B-136/247ra: noun clause).

Et anatematizauit sibi ipsi si nouit eum vel sciuit **qwat he ment** (L-1/221: noun clause).

Communiter circa auroram oritur vna leuis aura **þat bryngeth down þe dewe** (B-136/246rb: relative clause).

Hoc videntes presbiteri et clerici qui custodierunt oblationes, irruerunt in eum et cum lignis et fustibus verberauerunt eum **þat wo was hym þat euer he was yborn,** ita quod vix euasit cum vita (B-113/195vb: clause of result).

Quantum teneor diligere Deum qui me fecit **3er i was novt** (L-1/217: clause of place or time).

Quen my strength was most, paciebar graues penas, proprium cor aperui ad tibi dandum graciam et misericordiam (O-01/6: clause of time).

Sohtfast and verray God as he was, humiliauit se sic nobis quod exinaniuit seipsum (L-1/218: concessive clause).

Transfer a me **ys cuppe 3at Y ne drink it no3t,** idest istam passionem, **3at Y suffir it no3t** (L-1/219v: clause of result).

Ipsi ita rude traxerunt eum **3at 3e rouis of 3e wondis hengin to 3e clo3is and made al 3e woundis to bledin al new** (L-1/224v: clause of degree).

To complete the picture, I add one example of a complex English sentence—"**Mede may spede þer no riȝth ys**" (R-12/68v)—and another of a sequence of English sentences:

> þen he seyþ y shal openly shewe my wreþ on ȝou and y shal deme ȝou ryȝt aftur ȝoure dedus. And þus y shal put to ȝou all ȝoure wykked leuyng þat ȝe han offended me wit fro þe tyme þat ȝe were bore to ȝoure last endyng. þer y nul not spare ȝou ne haue mercy on ȝou but as ȝe haue dysseruud so ȝe shul haue. And þenne ȝe þat take lytul hede of me shul wel know þat y am ȝoure lord. (W-152/287vb)

These examples tell only part of the whole story, because the boundaries between English and Latin by no means always coincide with the boundaries of syntactic units, be they phrases, clauses, or entire sentences. On the contrary, the switch often occurs in the middle of a syntactic structure, and conversely syntactic structures in English are occasionally juxtaposed without a break. In the following examples, all from the edited sermon O-07, the English continues beyond a first syntactic unit or the end of a clause or sentence, into the beginning of another clause or sentence.

> Depricemur Deum pro misericordia **and help, doutles** vult misereri nobis **and send vs comfort** de celo (ll. 128–29).
> Effudit sanguinem cordis sui pro nostro **sake, and of his endles mercy** fecit istud pactum nobiscum (527–28).
> Fige tuam spem et cor super illos sanctos **and beseche hom of help. And dowtles** si ita feceris **and be** in voluntate dimittendi peccatum tuum . . . (566–68).
> **And a vicius man with all. þis** vitam duxit ȝeris and dayes (571–72).
> Suum corpus et anima reuiuebantur **and rose fro deth to lyue. In schewyng** sui terribilis vultus . . . (213–14).

In contrast to English elements that extend beyond the boundaries of syntactic units, we also find many cases in which the language changes within the boundary of a smaller syntactic structure. Such switches occur perhaps most dramatically within compound verb forms or verb phrases, such as: "fuit capella **bild** in honore omnium sanctorum" (573–74) or "**he most** conuertere faciem suam" (454–55). Equally striking are switches in structures of modification, whether the head element is in Latin— "omnes ramos **vnthrifti**" (16)—or in English—"**of men** Ecclesie" (334).

A similarly striking example from this sermon involves the English syntactic pattern "he offered up," here rendered with a switch that puts the prepositional adverb in English: "et obtulit **up** sanguinem" (212). Another structure that thus mixes languages in its components is the prepositional phrase. Usually both the preposition and its object are in English, as in "articulum **of his ioyful ascencion**" (229) and many other cases; but not infrequently the preposition is in Latin and its object in English, as for instance in "pro **scharpe schowris**" (110–11). There are even a few cases where only the preposition is in English and its object reverts to the preceding Latin, such as "vna **of** manna" (B-113/195vb), though no such cases occur in O-07.

Among the syntactic structures that mix the two languages in this fashion, the most remarkable is the structure of coordination. Sermon O-07 begins at once with such a case: "Gracia **and comfort**" (2). This pattern occurs very frequently in O-07 as well as throughout the corpus of macaronic sermons. It applies not only to nouns, as in the given example, but to adjectives, "Si vites sint fertiles **and likinge**" (11–12); verbs, "Iste ramus non potest flecti **ne be crocud**" (38); and other units including phrases and clauses, of which many can be found in sermon O-07. Its reverse, beginning with English and changing to Latin, recurs as well, though perhaps not as frequently: "non solum **gouernors** sed omnes homines" (29–30) or "quidam sunt **as stiburne** et duri cordis quod . . ." (82). As the two parts thus coordinated are often synonymous or nearly so, one might think of such structures as macaronic doublets, that is, structures of coordination in which a single thought is expressed twice by elements taken from different etymological backgrounds or, as here, from different languages. The use of etymological doublets was very dear to late fourteenth- and fifteenth-century writers and translators in England, who often coordinated words of Germanic and Romance or Latin provenance in this way.[8] Given the large number of similar macaronic doublets in the sermons under discussion, it would seem undeniable that these texts shared a peculiar stylistic penchant of contemporary vernacular writers.

Can one go further and claim that the desire for macaronic doublets

---

8. For a recent discussion, see Mueller 1984, 147–61, and literature cited there. But notice that fondness for doublets was not restricted to English writers. Lazzerini (1971, 287) calls attention to the "coppia sinonimica" in the macaronic sermons of Michel Menot.

actually caused macaronic texts of this kind to come into being? Was this well-attested stylistic penchant the creative force behind macaronic writing? I do not believe the evidence allows for such a view. Genuine macaronic doublets form only a minority of macaronic structures of coordination. In sermon O-07 I find forty–one of the latter,[9] of which, by a generous count,[10] only twelve could possibly be considered doublets. In addition, our macaronic texts contain a good many doublets that are not macaronic but all English. Some examples from O-07 are **"ar prouyn-yd and nurchid furd," "neuer so fair ne so lusti," "stakis and stodis,"** and **"grangynge and grennynge"** (ll. 12–13, 93–94, 78, and 97–98). Though doublets undeniably form a favorite stylistic device in the sermons studied, they do not explain why their writers created macaronic texts.

The discussion of macaronic structures of coordination has led to the question whether their writers' fondness for any particular linguistic or stylistic features might explain why the language shifts, and shifts so frequently. Another feature of this kind is the recurrence of favorite words or phrases in English. Given the structural importance of *concordantia vocalis* in scholastic sermons (to which category all our macaronic sermons belong),[11] and given the repeated use of the same material, often in large blocks, by the same sermon writer or collector (of which the sermons in O are a fine example), it will not surprise us to find that within a single sermon or several pieces in the same collection, certain English words or phrases recur repeatedly. Thus, O-24, on *Intravit castellum* ("He entered a castle," Luke 10:38), advises the proud, avaricious, and envious to enter the spiritual castle and save themselves in the towers of humility, almsgiving, and charity. In developing the tower of humility, the preacher speaks of various turrets on this tower that have different functions, and in describing them, he uses the English noun **turrett** and its plural seven times in as many sentences. Similarly, much of the English vocabulary used in developing the image of the ship of state in O-10 appears again when the same image is reused in O-16, 23, and 25 (such words as **hindcastel, ouerseile, wawe, stormis,** and others).

---

9. I have only counted structures of coordination whose coordinated elements are Latin and English, not those in which one coordinated element is itself macaronic, as in "vites domini **and railis** communitatis" or "þai **are raisid vp** et vnita **to stif stacus.**"

10. I have included, for instance, "humiles **and buxum**" and "**as stiburne** et duri cordis," where the synonymity of its two coordinated members could be questioned.

11. On *concordantia vocalis,* see Wenzel 1986, 74–79.

Apart from such repetition tied to the key terms of a single sermon or to the reuse of material in several sermons, it is possible to identify some English expressions that must have been favorites of individual preachers. For example, in several sermons, the author of set 1 in O uses the single words þus and **truliche**, the phrase **welthe and prosperite**, and the construction **be x never so y** (also used with other verbs). Other macaronic collections or writers have different preferences. Thus, the macaronic sermons in manuscript Q employ the construction **it farith . . . as it doith** frequently (Q-19, 20, 21 several times, and 23). A peculiar collocation that recurs not only in O sermons but throughout the corpus is the phrase **lustis and likingis** ("desires and pleasures");[12] outside O the phrase appears in B-127, L-1, Q-20, 21, 23, and 24, and W-068.

The last-quoted phrase is further distinguished by its alliteration, and the collocation enjoyed such popularity in English prose and verse texts outside the macaronic sermons, including works by Langland, Chaucer, and Malory, that it held the rank of an alliterative formula.[13] It also occurs with some frequency in the contemporary Lollard sermons edited by Cigman.[14] This raises the questions of how much alliteration occurs in the English elements of our macaronic sermons and whether the tendency to produce alliterating phrases might explain the changes from Latin to English.

In the texts I have examined, alliteration occurs with great frequency, particularly in O, but likewise in the other manuscripts that contain macaronic sermons. Some examples from the latter are:

operantur **al by line and leuel** (A-33/100)
sit **redy to reseyuyng** (B-113/193rb)
iste murus **wulle fle and falle** (O-02/8)
nunquam fui **crafty clarioun** (O-02/11v)
lati rami, articuli, **fadoun fast** (O-03/14v)
scuti fuerunt **longe and large** (O-04/25v)
On þe fynd be fers super te (O-06/39)
made of marbilstonys (Q-20/64v)

---

12. In O-04, 16, 18, and 23.
13. See MED, s.v. "liking" and "lust."
14. See Cigman 1989, 4/146; 19/261; 60/249; 97/150; 213/228–29; 214/240; 234/962, 969.

sunt **fayr fals spekers** (R-12/67)

þus **the sely parayl ys ponisched** istis cornubus quod þey **smerte ful sore** (R-12/69)

habeas mundi **wele at wylle** (W-154, l. 73)

Occasionally, alliteration binds the elements throughout an entire sentence and beyond.

Non est confidencia nec stabilitas **in þis wordli wele.** Vides ad oculum: heri **a lord now a lost man,** heri episcopum **now a begger,** heri **a kinge now a caytif.** (O-08/49v)

Here and there such alliteration even extends beyond the English element:

naues onustas [MS anustas] **wit fode** fidei (O-02/9)

tarit tamdiu ad tabernam (O-02/12)

sua humilitas **of herte** (Q-20/64)

per plurima tempora grauiter **gronyng** (W-102/193v)

Docuitne nos leccionem arsmetrice **to kountyn and to kalkylyn** et cognoscendum numeros (W-102/194v)

On some rarer occasions, alliteration is even joined to punning:

non vultu ficto **and ficle** verbis sed pleno corde (O-14/91)

diu laborauit grauiter **in grauynge** istorum signorum (O-07, ll. 225–26)

Whether such alliterative collocations are the product of a conscious stylistic intention is hard to say. Though widespread and more frequent than any other stylistic device, they are not a dominant feature; in the totality of English material, they form only a small segment. Nor do they give the reader the same impression of the *recherché,* the sought-after effect, that strikes one so forcefully in reading fourteenth-century alliterative poetry. Contrary to the latter, in our macaronic sermons, alliterative phrases tend to "come naturally" as part and parcel of the native idiom, as in such common phrases as, **fairest of flouris** (O-11/71v), **day of dome** (Q-21/67v), or **drope of dew** (B-127/220vb). Moreover, by shifting from one language to the other, the possible alliteration of an English phrase that may have been in the mind or ear of the sermon writer is frequently lost. For instance, in some passages, the collocation **lustis and likinge,** which occurs more often than any other in and outside these macaronic sermons, is not realized and instead yields to the mixed phrase **luste** *et delectacio* (Q-25/81v).[15] The same failure to realize alliteration appears in the longer sentence that was quoted a few lines above ("Non est confidencia . . . "), where the expected **bishop,** to alliterate with **begger,** appears as Latin *episcopus.* I therefore do not believe it possible to argue convincingly that the urge or desire to create or preserve alliterative phrases explains the appearance of English elements in macaronic sermons.[16]

Another stylistic feature that raises the same question is structural parallelism. The edited sermon O-07, for example, contains the sentence

Pro isto caput meum **was al toprickid,** corpus meum **al tobetonn and rent,** et cor **clef o too** (364–65),

in which the pattern of switching from Latin subject to English predicate is followed through three coordinated clauses. Such macaronic parallelism appears more than once, in O and in other sermons. In a different example, the English elements form the initial words of successive phrases, thereby producing a kind of macaronic anaphora.

þus ignis caritatis extinguitur, þus humor deuocionis arescit, þus tota spiritualis vita subtrahit se per istos **cursed errours.** (O-10/64)

Again, one is compelled to ask whether the bilingualism of these sentences might not be the result of conscious stylistic artistry. Yet, again, I hesitate to extend local cases into a general principle that would explain the entire phenomenon of macaronic texture, because on the whole the evidence for such a generalization is unconvincing.

Cases of such macaronic parallelism are relatively infrequent, and our texts contain too many instances where the author plainly missed a good opportunity to create it. Two examples of the latter, again from O-07,

---

15. Similarly, "plenus carnalibus voluptatibus et corporalibus **lykynggis**" (Q-24/79v).

16. This and other phenomena of macaronic texture deserve further analysis by a trained linguist. In the two last-quoted examples, for instance, one could conceivably see an underlying force of alliteration at work: *l*ust—de*l*ight/de*l*ectacio; *e*piscopus—*b*eggar.

will suffice. Both express conventional triads of medieval thought (power/ wisdom/goodness in the persons of the Holy Trinity; vegetative life/ sensation/intelligence in the human soul), but in neither case is the Englishing of the key terms carried through all three members, as it would have to be, and could have easily been, if full macaronic parallelism had been intended.

> Pater celi misit **donn** suam virtuosam potenciam in memoriam, Filius **parfith wisdom** in intellectum, et Spiritus Sanctus graciosam bonitatem in liberam voluntatem (407–10).
> **Mankinde**... habet **lyuing** cum arboribus, **feling** cum bestiis, et intelligere cum angelis (486–88).

A final element that claims our attention in the search for possible stylistic causes of macaronic texts are English proverbs and proverbial expressions. In a number of cases, an English proverb is quoted in its entirety.

> **Schal neuer cloc henne be wel crowing cok**. (O-16/98v)

So are English proverbial expressions:

> Reuera, isti caupones circa quadriuium adeo bene possunt sagittare ad capucia illorum aut **pype in an hywy leff**. (W-102/194)[17]

Both items are inserted into the context as if they were quotations, even if they appear without an introductory phrase, such as "sicut vulgariter dicitur" or the like; hence they form *a* elements according to the classification I gave in chapter 2. The two quoted expressions are entirely in English, but in many more cases, English proverbs mix English and Latin:

> Vt vulgariter dicitur: "He þat **wil** in curia nunc manere, **he most couuray wel fouell**." (O-09/57v)[18]

---

17. Whiting and Whiting 1968, 172.
18. "He who wants to stay at court must curry well Favell" (Whiting and Whiting 1968, F85, from the English *Proverbs of Wisdom*).

Anima huius peccatoris est in via saluacionis, quia reperit misericordiam inter **stirop and** terram. (O-22/118)[19]
Quere vbi vis infra villam et extra, poteris **blowe** super vngues tuos
for any hete of loue. (O-08/50v)[20]

The O sermons are particularly rich in such proverbial expressions in
macaronic form, and several of them occur more than once. For example,
the expression "something is laid a-water" (or "on water"), meaning
that it is disregarded or treated lightly,[21] occurs as "perfectus amor **is
laid o watur**" (O-08/50v; cf. O-05/30v) and "honor **is leyd a watur**"
(O-13/80v). Likewise, the proverb "He who hews above his head will
have chips fall in his eye"[22] is used several times as a warning to the
laity not to probe into theological matters that lie beyond their ken.

Tandiu ciderunt supra caput quod **chippis** ceciderunt in oculos eorum
pro incredulitate et instabilitate fidei. (O-13/80v)
Adeo diu secauerunt supra suum capunt [!] quod þe **chippis** corruerunt
in oculos nostros. (O-16/98v)

And parsons are similarly warned not to preach above their congrega-
tions' heads.

Si docebis aperte plebem tuam, **hewe not** supra caput tuum, ne capias
altas materias que transcendunt ingenium tuum, ne forte þou **trippe
beside þe truthe.** (O-10/63)[23]

Another example involves the phrase "stepping over a straw,"[24] an act
apparently considered dangerous in folklore—especially if two straws lay
crosswise—and hence condemned by preachers as superstitious.

---

19. "He finds mercy between the stirrup and the ground," that is, while he is falling,
before it is too late. Not in Whiting and Whiting 1968.
20. "Blow on your nails," as one of the last remedies in extremely cold weather; Whiting
and Whiting 1968, N2.
21. Whiting and Whiting 1968, W77.
22. Whiting and Whiting 1968, C235.
23. Whiting and Whiting 1968, H221.
24. Whiting and Whiting 1968, S814.

Tales falsi iudaiste sunt nimis multi, vt dicitur, qui habent conscienciam **of stepping ouer a straw**. (O-05/30v)

The proverbial phrase, which is here entirely in English, appears elsewhere macaronically.

Si habes conscienciam **to trede on a crossid** stramen. (O-22/113v)

Yet another example concerns the expression "to set a rush of" something or someone, in the sense of not giving a hoot.[25] In their polemic against the Lollards, the C sermons use the phrase several times.

[The Lollards] iecerunt conscienciam ad gallum, þai **set not** unum cirpum per papam et totam eius potestatem. (O-06/35)

And they use it with the adjective *one* included in the English.

Non ponderabant excomunicaciones nec censuras Ecclesie, iecerunt conscienciam ad gallum, þai **set not a** cirpum per papam et totam eius potestatem. (O-24/125)

The two quotations just given present a proverb in macaronic form (with the word *rush* appearing as Latin *cirpum,* hardly a common word); in addition, they contain a second proverbial expression, which is here given in unmixed Latin: *iecerunt conscienciam ad gallum* ("they cast their conscience to the cock").[26] Such vernacular proverbs or proverbial expressions rendered in pure Latin occur quite often. In a tale in which several devils discuss whether a dying sinner will be theirs, the fourth warns his colleagues, as it were, not to count their chickens before they are hatched, using the following medieval equivalent:

Piscamini ante rethe. Nisi melius ludatis, decepti estis. Si petat misericordiam semel ex corde, potest decipere vos omnes.

(You are fishing before the net. Unless you play better, you will be

---

25. Whiting and Whiting 1968, R249.
26. Meaning "to neglect"; Whiting and Whiting 1968, C353.

cheated. If he [the sinner] asks once for mercy, from his heart, he can deceive all of you.)[27]

"Fishing before the net" is attested as a proverbial expression in fifteenth- and sixteenth-century English texts, yet here it appears purely in Latin.[28] The same phenomenon occurs again in another O sermon.

Si sit fur uel mechus, dicit quod erat fatum suum, erat aptum sibi ante camisiam, erat Dei ordinacio, natus erat sub tali planeta, non potuit vitare.

(If he is a thief or womanizer, he says it was his destiny, it was thus made for him before the shirt, it was God's foreordination, he was born under such-and-such a star, he could not avoid it.)[29]

The phrase "something is made (or shaped) before a person's shirt (or gown)," which may be modernized as "a person's genes predispose him or her to sin," is well attested as an English proverbial expression from Chaucer on,[30] yet here it is rendered in Latin. To the two cases from O sermons, I add another from manuscript Q, to show that the phenomenon is not limited to the former. The preacher of Q-21 declares that the devil's bondage is so great that it deprives man of his free will: *Inuitis dentibus tuis facit te peccare* ("He makes you sin against your will," f. 67v). *Inuitis dentibus* renders the Middle English phrases **maugre your teeth** or **unthonc your teth,** both common proverbial expressions.[31]

The same process of rendering an English expression in either Latin or a macaronic form affects not only proverbs but more general idiomatic phrases. Our sermons contain many instances of English idiomatic expressions preserved in their native form. Some examples from O-07 are:

---

27. O-12/78.
28. Whiting and Whiting 1968, N91.
29. O-13/82.
30. Whiting and Whiting 1968, D106. Latin versions of the expression occur in a text written very early in the fourteenth century, *Fasciculus morum* V.xii.149 and VII.vii.85 (Wenzel 1989, 476, 670).
31. Whiting and Whiting 1968, T406 and 418.

þis is gret ruthe (l. 70)
set to hond (73)
wytout grangynge and grennynge (97–98)
bere not to purpose (104)
make we oure mone (116)
pipin al amys (344)
rend lith from lith (379)
it frete away þe hold rust (425)
it wold not away (417)

Yet exactly as in the case of proverbial expressions (which often are hard to differentiate from idiomatic ones), the author of this sermon evidently experienced a strong pressure to formulate even these idiomatic phrases in Latin. The last one mentioned, for example, occurs macaronically a few lines later, as "noluit **away**." Similar combinations of a Latin verb with an English prepositional adverb occur more than once: "misit **doun**," "offerebant **up**," "defert **abowte**," and so forth. A different but equally striking case of macaronizing an English idiomatic expression is "si ceperimus **hede**" ("if we took heed") in Q-23/74v.

This process even extends to the point where it yields English idioms in entirely Latin shapes. Thus, the long passage quoted in chapter 1 contains the clause *cepit tres discipulos secum,* whose *cepit . . . secum,* instead of the biblical verb *assumpsit* (Matt. 17:1), is clearly a calque of the English clause "he took . . . with him." Some other examples are:

loquebatur . . . extranee, "he spoke strangely" (L-1/223v, H-25/94v)
sine pluri, "without more" (L-1/220v)
quid pro, "what for" (L-1/217v; compare Chaucer, KnT 1453; ReT 3967; SqT 54, 397; PF 15)
mutare continenciam suam, "change her countenance [or disposition]" (L-1/219)
accepit quasi suam licenciam ab eis, "he took, as it were, his leave from them" (L-1/219)
capias michi pulcrum hominem, "take me a beautiful person," in the sense of "give me, suppose there is" (L-1/220v)
habet vt apparet mundum ad votum, "he has, as it seems, the world at his will" (W-154, 41–42)

habuit mercatores sufficientes, "he has merchants enough" (W-154, 318)[32]

voluerunt cepisse fugam, "they wanted to take flight" (O-25/129v)

Not surprisingly, such calques occur also as single words or noun phrases, such as *media* ("means"), *capitaneus* ("chief"), *dies bone Veneris* ("Good Friday"), *magisterium* ("mastery, the upper hand"; ME **maistrie**), *superconfidencia* ("presumption"; ME **overhope,**) *schira* ("shire"), *par precum* ("a pair of beads"), and many others.

The unfinished state of Latham's *Dictionary of Medieval Latin from British Sources* does not yet allow us to determine whether all these calques existed outside our sermons, but the material already published, for letters A–H, suggests strongly that these phrases were common in Anglo-Latin during and after the thirteenth century. How far the formation of such calques may have gone is sometimes hard to gauge, because of the high incidence of abbreviation in the scripts that have preserved them and clear indications that the scribes did not always know what to make of them (especially in O). Hence one wonders whether the manuscript reading *noluit dare sursum* at O-06/37 might indeed stand for "he did not want to give up." If it does, our fifteenth-century sermon writers would have felt quite at home with American junior Latinists and their *da mihi fracturam* ("give me a break").

The process of macaronization extends to other elements besides English idioms and proverbs. As is well known, late medieval preachers liked to formulate certain functional parts of their sermons in vernacular rhymes, whether the original was Latin prose or verse.[33] One of these parts was the sermon thema. In our macaronic texts, its rhymed English rendition is, on occasion, subjected to macaronization. The following couplet, for example, translates the thema *Intrauit castellum* of Luke 10:38:

Modur and maiden þat neuer did mysse
Intrauit castellum **of ioy and blisse.** (O-24/124)

In this case, the mixture may have a functional purpose, because the

---

32. Similarly, apparently, in O-09/58: "magna iuramenta sufficiencia" ("great oaths enough").

33. See Wenzel 1978.

Latin words preserve the thema in its original form.[34] But the same is not true in the following translation of the thema *Fructus iusti lignum vite* (Prov. 11:30; O-17/100v):[35]

þe holi crosse, þe liuelich tre,
Est þi frute if þou riȝtful be.

Macaronization likewise affects other verses that we know existed completely in English and acquired a mixed shape in the hands of these sermon writers. In sermon O-09, for instance, the preacher introduces a description of an image of the god of mercy that contains several inscriptions.

In signum huius, deus pietatis olim pingebatur in similitudine hominis habentis in manu scissum cor in duas partes. In vna parte scribebatur: "**Qwan mercy** vocatur, venit statim." In altera parte: "**Merci is rediest** vbi **synne is most**." Et in circuitu: "**Merci abidid and locud al dai qwan man fro synne** vult diuertere." Ista ymago, iste deus pietatis, est Iesus.[36]

The quotations in this text imply three couplets that elsewhere have been preserved entirely in English:

Ȝif sinne nere, merci nere non.
Wan Merci is cald, he comet anon.

þer Merci is rediest wer sinne is mest.
þer Merci is lattest were sinne is lest.

---

34. Similarly in O-14/85: "*Ecce rex venit,* Mattei XXI. Anglice: **Synful man, behold and se,** / **A blisful** rex **comus to** þe."

35. A similar mixture occurs in sermon O-22 on the thema *Statuit eum supra pinnaculum templi* (Matt. 4:5), which is translated into the English verse: "**On** þe **hy pinnacle of** þe **tempul** / **Oure Lord was sette to** þe **exemple**" (f. 113). After the division follows this macaronic verse:
þus þat þin hert schul hine nolet,
but holich per amorem to God be knyt,
opon þis pinnacle oure Lord was set (f. 114v).

36. O-09/59v. On the use of such *picturae,* see Smalley 1960, chapter 7, especially 179. On inscriptions in them, which I have classified as "message verses," see Wenzel 1978, 81; 1986, esp. 121.

Merci abidet and loket al dai
Wan mon fro sinne wil torne away.[37]

The preacher of O-09 is quoting these lines accurately, though in macaronic form. That he had no objection to quoting them elsewhere entirely in English is evident from his reusing the topic in O-12.

Lego quod deus pietatis olim pingebatur in similitudine iuuenis cum aperto corde. In vna parte erat scriptum: **"Ner syn wer, merci wer non."** In alia: **"Merci is rediest qwer synne is most."** Ista ymago signat verum deum pietatis et misericordie, Christum Iesum.[38]

The preceding discussion of several grammatical and stylistic features in the macaronic texture of the sermons we are studying (doublets, alliteration, syntactic parallelism, and proverbs and proverbial expressions) has repeatedly compelled us to ask whether any of them might have been the motivating force behind the shifting from Latin to English. I think the answer must be no. Such features do not occur as frequently and consistently as they must if they are to be credited with such a causative role, and the macaronization of the conventional English elements just considered directly contradicts such a hypothetical function for these stylistic elements. What else might have possibly caused the switching? Why would a sermon writer, penning his discourse in Latin, every so often change to English, for a word, a phrase, or a sentence or more, and then return to Latin?

If we exclude from consideration elements that are clearly glosses, translated or quoted authorities, and parts of the division, subdivision, or distinctions—English elements of types *a* and *b*, according to my earlier classification—an answer that may suggest itself with all the power of the obvious is that sermon writers changed from Latin to their native English when they sought for a word or phrase for which they lacked a Latin term or when the English came to their mind more readily than the foreign equivalent. The primary test case for this hypothesis would be passages that involve some technical vocabulary. Here, one would expect technical terms to be given in the language in which they occur

---

37. From BL MS Harley 7322; edited in Wenzel 1986, 121.
38. O-12/77v.

more naturally: Latin words for learned matters, English ones for every-day affairs. Sermon O-07 serves as a good case in point.

The sermon utilizes four special images that draw on a technical lexicon: the care of the vineyard (ll. 8–47), drawing a circle with a compass (189–98), the moon in eclipse (271–79), and making polyphonic music (339–48). Of these four, the last two are definitely learned, even academic, images, and it is therefore not surprising that their key terms all occur in Latin (though with English glosses for *[circulus] equans* and *deferens*). Caring for the vineyard, however, brings us closer to the peas-antry, and here the writer turns to a vernacular vocabulary for such technical features as stakes, rails, pruning, and propagating. Lastly, the image of drawing a circle with the compass belongs to both the world of commoners and that of learned men, because compasses were used by stone masons as well as artists. And here this sermon consistently uses the English word **cumpas**. One is tempted to conclude that the writer of this sermon switched to the English term because its Latin equivalent, *circinus*, was not known to him or at least was not part of his active Latin vocabulary. Though at first glance plausible, such an explanation is hard to prove. And against it stands some evidence that *circinus* was not a stranger to English sermon writers in the early fifteenth century. The word is used in other sermons, even if not by the author of set 1 in O.[39]

That the sermon writer's supposed lack of a technical term in Latin and his substituting a vernacular equivalent for it is insufficient for explaining shifts from Latin to the vernacular can also be proven neg-atively with the following example. In W-154, edited in appendix D, the preacher, who is quite liberal with the use of single English words, likens slanderers to a horseleech and briefly describes this animal's natural properties. He does not call the animal by its standard Latin name, *sanguissuga*. Nor does he use the vernacular term one might expect,

---

39. "Si vis habere graciam in bonis tuis temporalibus et placere Deo þer **wyth, it must fare be þe as it doth** per latomum et suum circinum. Videtis bene ad oculum quod quando latomus vult facere vnum circulum, ipse situat vnam tibiam circini in vno puncto et circumducit aliam tibiam per circuitum, et quamdiu punctus medius **is kept,** circulus est verus et perfectus satis" (Q-29/77). Compare "Sicut enim geometer capiens regulam et circinum metitur cum eis longitudinem et latitudinem, rotunditatem et angulos rerum proponit, sic confessor postea integraliter audierit confessionem, cum circino discrecionis et regula sue racionis mensuraret circumstancias peccatorum et condiciones peccantium" (W-072/132v), which is also a type C sermon.

"horseleech." Instead, he refers to it as *medicus equinus*, an obvious Latinization of the Middle English noun that is not without a certain comic effect.[40]

Therefore, the occasional use of the vernacular for technical terms does not generally explain the phenomenon of switching between the two languages. In addition to the cited instances that cast doubt on such an explanation, one finds that in many cases the same concept, though part of a technical lexicon, is expressed in both languages. A good example is the notion of "pruning" or "cutting away": the section on caring for the vineyard in sermon O-07 uses both the English phrase **cutte away** and its Latin equivalent *abscindere*. The suggestion that the language switches where technical terms are more easily available in the vernacular does not even work in the limited context of a technical discussion. It does so even less when applied to macaronic texts generally.

The same holds true of English idiomatic expressions, that is, phrases peculiar to the vernacular for which an exact or even approximate counterpart in Latin would have been hard to find. Again, one would expect that in a medium that tolerated language mixture, such expressions would have been written down in their native English. But though such phrases often do occur in English, they appear just as frequently in the form of Latin or macaronic calques. Macaronic switching thus penetrates to the very heart of the English lexicon, and it occurs even more frequently in areas where the vocabulary is less idiomatic or technical. Hence it becomes all the more difficult to find a good linguistic or psychological reason for the switches. I fail to detect any linguistic or psychological reason why, in the same narrative context, the writer of O-07 should say "niger vt **pich**" at one point (l. 362) and "nigrum ut pix" a few lines later (378, both meaning "black as pitch"),[41] or why, in a sequence of the devil's actions, he should state, "eruit sibi ambos oculos, pene-

---

40. W-154, l. 367. See *MED,* s.v. "hors-leche."

41. Similar cases are **suttelte**/*subtilitas* in W-154, 234 and 235 (in adjacent sentences) and *magisterium*/**maistrie** in Q-42/123v–124 (over some distance). It can be argued that in these two cases the phonetic similarity of the two terms caused the writers to slip from one language into the other; another case of this kind would be the proverbial phrase "stepping over a **straw**/*stramen*" quoted earlier in this chapter. On the basis of such cases, one may reasonably ask whether perhaps the phonetic identity or similarity in the two languages, including phrases that begin with such words as *in*/**in** or *est*/**is,** may account for the switching. But even a cursory reading of a macaronic paragraph quickly shows that such rare cases hardly explain the general phenomenon of code switching.

trauit eius cor cum furca," and then switch to "**and reuyd him** de ista vita" when the corresponding Latin phrase *et rapuit eum* would have done just as well and surely was as readily accessible to him (371). Sentences like "**Our lord . . . schal kepe hom** a voragine auaricie, a vento superbie **and** a **waweys** luxurie" (O-04/27) or "flumina crescebant, þe **wawis wex** adeo **hwge** quod . . ." (O-16/97) defy attempts to explain such quick and frequent shifting back and forth.

One must conclude that the macaronic texture of these sermons was caused neither by the unavailability of technical words or idiomatic expressions in Latin nor by their writers' desire to create alliteration, macaronic doublets, parallelism, and other stylistic effects. Rather, their switching is a random phenomenon for which all-encompassing causes, whether linguistic, stylistic, or psychological, are hard to find. This randomness is beautifully illustrated by the phrase "of your [or his] sickness," which in sermon O-07 appears in all three possible forms: English ("**of þi maledy**," ll. 444–45), Latin ("a sua infirmitate," 454), and macaronic ("de vestro **malady**," 468).

Despite their random mixture of languages, these sermons are by no means lacking in rhetorical force, which pervades and expresses itself through both languages. English elements are not used here for the same purpose and with the same "wit" as Latin phrases are used by Dante, Langland, or Chaucer's Chauntecleer. But despite, and perhaps even through, the linguistic mixture, a rhetorical effectiveness comes about that aims at moving and stirring the audience's emotions. To balance the somewhat dry analysis of the preceding pages, I conclude this chapter with a macaronic paragraph that should be read out and allowed to have its effect without concern about what may account for its switches. As the preacher appeals to his audience to reject pride, here in the form of feminine dress, by calling for self-knowledge and the memory of human mortality, he hammers his message in with a sequence of short clauses in paratactic juxtaposition and uses verbal, clausal, and sentence repetition, climax, rhetorical questions, direct address (here to a singular audience), authoritative quotations, various forms of *cursus,* and such topoi as the Nine Worthies and the *ubi sunt* formula, all leading to a climax that contrasts beauty with virtue in the brevity of a proverb decked in alliteration.

Isto modo,
quamuis habeas singulares virtutes,

licet creuisti super generosam stipitem,
   venisti de sublimi progenie,
set not þin hert to hie ne superbias,
   instatue speculum—teipsum—coram visu tuo,
   cogita quid es.
Quid es, credis?
Secundus philosophus dicit quod homo est manicipium mortis,
   a manciple,
   a seruant,
   an homage to deth.
Be þou neuer so quik,
      so qwyuer
      aut **liuelich,**
habes cutem **þat deth is in,**
   geris mortem circa te,
be þou neuer so fair ne so fresche of hu.
Licet erigas cornua in sublime,
      hangist super ea **perre and preciouse stonis,**
      facis frontem tuam **as gay** vt frons templi
         —sicut propheta dicit: "Circumornate vt similitudo
         templi"—,
      lauas et vngis,
      facis **a gay meror** de teipsa **men to gasyn oponn,**
quis es, credis?
Sanctus Bernardus dat **an homli descripcioun:**
   es nisi terra et cinis,
      et pudet dicere solum quod est suus textus:
         saccus plenus **of filth,**
         saccus plenus fimo,
         saccus plenus stercoris,
   es nisi **a filth,** quantumcumque sis pulcra.
Cogita tunc quam turpis es,
salta de pinnaculo superbie,
iacta cornua ad diabolum,
descende et agnosce teipsum.
Non es melior quam patres tui,
   cape exemplum de eis,
   sint tibi speculum.

Qui est nunc Nabugodonosor et rex Antiochus
   qui statuebantur olim supra altum pinnaculum superbie?
Vbi est presignis Iosue et Iulius imperator, rex Arthurus et magnus
    Alexander,
   qui statuebantur olim supra suppremum honoris pinnaculum?
Omnes isti erant **homageris** morti,
   fecerunt homagium et transierunt,
   saltauerunt de vita ad mortem.
Abierunt hi, **and þou schalt aftur,** nescis vbi nec quando.
Statue hoc speculum, tuum mortale corpus, ante visum tuum,
memento quod morieris, quia memoria mortis faciet te
    noscere teipsum.
Fac isto modo speculum miticie de teipso proprio visui,
   let no couetise acumbre þe,
   let no bewte blinde þe,
quia quantumcumque sis pulcher aut **fresche of hu,**
non es speculum sine macula,
   es turpiter maculatus,
quia sepe þe **more bewte, þe lasse bownte;**
    þe fairer face, þe fowler soule,
      sicut cotidie auditur.

(In this way, though you may have individual virtues, even if you
have grown from a noble stem and come from an exalted line, do
not set your heart too high so that you may not become proud.
Put a mirror, yourself, before your eyes; consider what you are.
What are you, do you think? The philosopher Secundus says that
"man is a slave to death, a manciple, a servant, a vassal to death."
However much alive, agile, or lively you may be, you have a skin
with death inside, you carry death around you no matter how fair
or fresh in complexion you may be. Though you may raise your
horns on high, hang jewels and precious stones on them, make
your face as bright as the front of the temple—as the prophet says,
"They are adorned round about like a temple" [Ps. 143:12]—wash
and anoint yourself, make a bright mirror of yourself for men to
gaze upon—who are you, do you think? St. Bernard gives a homely
description: you are but dust and ashes, and—I am ashamed to
quote his text—"sack full of filth, sack full of dung, sack full of

excrement, you are but filth, however beautiful you are." Consider how vile you are. Jump off the tower of pride, throw your horns to the devil, come down and recognize yourself. You are no better than your forefathers; take an example from them. Let them be a mirror for yourself. Where is now Nebuchadnezzar and king Antiochus, who were once placed on the high pinnacle of pride? Where is the famous Joshua and Caesar, king Arthur and Alexander the Great, who were once placed on the highest pinnacle of honor? They all were vassals to death. They did their homage and went away; they jumped from life to death. They have gone, and you will go after them, you do not know where or when. Place that mirror, your mortal body, before your eyes, remember that you will die, for the memory of death will make you know yourself. In this way make a mirror of humility of yourself for your own eyes, let no false desires encumber you, let no beauty blind you, for however beautiful or fresh of complexion you may be, you are not a mirror without blemish, you are terribly stained, for always "the more beauty, the less goodness; the fairer the face, the fouler the soul," as we hear it every day.)[42]

Can one deny that in the hands of this preacher, macaronic texture has become an effective instrument of pulpit oratory?

---

42. O-22/115r–v.

CHAPTER 6

Bilingualism in Action

Though the rhetorical art of the passage quoted at the end of the preceding chapter does not appear consistently on every page of every
macaronic sermon, it is sufficiently widespread to suggest, together with
the preachers' use of sophisticated structural devices typical of the scholastic sermon, that these sermons are products of deliberate rhetorical
artistry. This would at once imply that they are literary and the result
of written composition. Just as it is unlikely that the structural devices
analyzed in chapter 5 are inventions of the moment, so it is unlikely
that the means of persuasive rhetoric in the quoted passage would, at
the moment of delivery, have come naturally to even the most talented
or inspired preacher. These sermons, therefore, owe their shape to careful
composition applied either before or after their delivery. Since I have
found no evidence that they were made from *reportationes* or notes taken
during the delivery of a sermon and later elaborated at leisure,[1] it is

---

1. Such evidence would be: (a) in the case of variant versions of the same sermon,
different elaborations made by different note-takers or writers, including differing lengths
of the sermon development or the presence or absence of the protheme and of the opening
and closing formulae (see Lecoy de la Marche 1886, 330–31); and (b) in the sermons
themselves, direct remarks to the effect that "here he [i.e., the preacher] said . . ." or the
like. The manuscripts here studied contain several pieces of evidence that approach the
latter kind, for instance: R-16 ("Introduccio istius thematis isto modo fiebat"; but notice
that the syntax then shifts from reporting to command: "Et adducantur auctoritates ad
materiam pertinentes . . . probetur per auctoritates et sufficientes et pertinentes," f. 82); a
note in S, f. 65r–v ("Et persuasit predicator . . ."); and W-020 ("Frater predicator habuit
istud thema in die ramis palmarum, hoc scilicet: Hic calix nouum testamentum est," f.
68v). All these instances are notes, not developed sermons. Perhaps the weightiest case of
such a direct remark occurs in R-03, the funeral sermon for Abbot Walter Froucetur, where
the omission of part 2 is stated retrospectively: "Secundum principale non dicebatur ob
temporis breuitudinem" (f. 20). But notice that the passive form *dicebatur* allows us to

105

likely that they are copies of sermons (see chap. 3) that were originally written out before their delivery. Though very little is known about the working habits of medieval sermon writers, whether monks, friars, or parish priests, we do at least know from monastic records that the task of preaching the important chapter sermon was assigned years in advance to talented monks, usually more than one,[2] and that the labors of those who preached to monastic audiences were deemed sufficiently great to receive some remuneration.[3]

These sermons bear very clear traces that they were written for readers. Many include commands presumably directed to a preacher that tell him how to proceed in his sermon at a given point, whether to "note the story about..." ("nota narracionem," W-154, l. 498) or to "make the recapitulation" ("tunc fiat recapitulacio," Q-42/126v), with the announced story or recapitulation omitted from the written text. Occasionally they also contain cross-references either to passages within the same sermon ("require superius," L-1/218v) or to other sermons in the same collection, whether these are still extant or not.[4] This can only mean that these macaronic sermons were composed, or at least copied and collected, for perusal and perhaps study by fellow preachers. These features are not limited to sermons of type C but occur with equal frequency in other types, including fully Latin pieces.

Yet they *are* sermons, compositions that address and appeal to an audience of listeners, that follow exactly the rules or recommendations laid out by contemporary *artes praedicandi,* and that at least occasionally refer to specific times and places; one entire collection even records the years and towns at which, presumably, they were delivered.[5] What, then,

---

think that the remark comes from the preacher's own pen, not a *reportator*'s, who would have written *dicebat* or *dixit*. With respect to full C sermons, I have found no evidence of type (b); and the four sermons that survive in more than one copy contain no evidence of type (a) either. Such evidence exists for sermon collections from France and Italy; see below, note 26. With respect to England, Owst (1926, 234) states that there is no evidence of *reportatio*, though he then, in his rather typical fashion, goes on to speculate. For more recent studies of *reportatio* in England, see Roberts 1968, 56–62 (Stephen Langton); O'Carroll 1984, 117 (Richard Fishacre); Archer 1984, 20–21 (Philip Repingdon, bishop of Lincoln, 1405–19); Forde 1989 (Nicholas Hereford, 1382).

  2. See for example Pantin 1931–37, 2:23, 26, 97, 156, 179, 216–17.

  3. See Pantin 1931–37, 2:217, 3:185, 256; Pearce 1916, 113, 144.

  4. For cross-references to other pieces in the same collection, see chapter 3 on manuscripts B, O, and Z.

  5. In manuscript Q; see the discussion in chapter 3. Similarly, the sermons in B have

is the relation between the written form in which they have been preserved and their oral delivery, especially in regard to their linguistic form? Modern students of medieval preaching have fairly unanimously asserted that sermons given to the common people were delivered in the vernacular, whereas sermons to the clergy were preached in Latin, but both were written out or down in Latin, the official language of the clergy.[6] This simple picture may be accurate for earlier times,[7] but it obviously does not fit the subject of this study,[8] because here, as we have seen in chapters 3 and 4, the same written medium is used for sermons addressed to either of the two audiences, and this written medium is not pure Latin but a mixed language. Whatever we may be able to deduce about the language these sermon writers had in mind for the actual delivery, when writing them down, they utilized a linguistic mixture.

In an attempt to explain the phenomenon of these macaronic sermons in the England of about 1400, I propose the following model of their genesis. The sermons evidently rest on the basis of an English text. By "basis"—perhaps "Gestalt" might be a better word—I mean the stage that lies behind their written form. This could have been a purely mental conception, an actual sermon delivered from the pulpit, or a written text. Which of these possibilities obtains is hard to prove, though I give precedence to the option of a purely mental conception because I have found no clear evidence for the other two, evidence that would derive from external remarks about preachers and their craft, from surviving sheets containing drafts of complete sermons or at least notes or outlines,[9] or from indications of *reportatio*.

---

a number of marginal references to small country towns, which I interpret as places where they were preached.

6. See the further discussion in text below, with citation of Lecoy de la Marche at note 24.

7. Yet one wonders what language Master Nicholas of Ewelme, chancellor of Oxford University, would have used when he preached in public "clero et populo" in the cemetery of St. Frideswyde in 1268; see Anstey 1868, 1:36.

8. An official text that, in my view, plainly contradicts Lecoy de la Marche's clear-cut alignment of language and audience is the license that the famous canon lawyer William Lyndwode received in 1417, allowing him "verbum Dei clero et populo in lingua Latina seu vulgari licite proponere et praedicare." This seems to state that he may preach to whatever audience, both clergy and people, in either Latin or the vernacular (Wilkins 1737, 389). Such licenses were required by the constitutions of Bishop Arundel in 1408 (ibid., 315).

9. Owst (1926, 59) calls attention to Cambridge, Gonville and Caius College MS 356,

It is much easier to show that, with some exceptions to be specified presently, this basis was an *English* text—"text" here understood as either a verbal or a purely mental construct embracing all the possibilities just mentioned. The evidence for its being in the vernacular is rich and of various kinds. Some sermons contain explicit remarks that the preacher is addressing his audience, or part of it, in English. In chapter 4 I quoted sermon L-1 with its two outlines, the first explicitly spoken in Latin to the clergy, the second in English to the rest of the congregation. Further, after stating the initial thema in Latin, many sermons continue at once to translate it into English, thus following a practice that was international and prescribed from the thirteenth century on.[10] A good example occurs in X-3.

> *Extrema gaudii luctus occupat,* Prouerbiorum 14. Karissimi, ista verba
> que nunc dixi in latinis possunt sic dici in Anglico:

> **Worliche blysse and joye al-so**
> **Endite3 in sorwe and wo.** (X-03/29rb)

That in more than one case such a translation is announced but not given will require further attention later.

Another unequivocal piece of evidence for the sermon's English basis occurs in Q-42. In its second principal, Christ's passion is compared to a book written with all the letters of the alphabet. Developing this image, the preacher goes through the alphabet and finds an aspect of Christ's suffering for each letter, in English: **angussyng, bledyng, cursyng,** and so forth. What clinches the case for the primacy of English is the letter *g,* for which the preacher finds Christ's **greting.** Because this Middle

---

a "sermon note-book" perhaps made by an Austin friar. The rarity of such a document for England is emphasized by James (1907, 405). Rough sermon notes can be found elsewhere, as for instance in Oxford, New College MS 88, with many marginalia. The subject calls for much further examination of sermon manuscripts. Sermon outlines are often written out in a form that is as finished as that of model sermons; see for example those appended to many copies of *Fasciculus morum* (Wenzel 1978, 47–49).

10. Honorius of Autun, *Speculum ecclesiae:* "Ad omnes sermones debes primum versum Latina lingua pronunciare, dein patria lingua explanare" (*PL* 172:829–30). An *ars praedicandi* preserved in a fifteenth-century manuscript at Esztergom and entitled *Modus sermonizandi in capitulo* begins: "Primo dic thema in latino, deinde thema dic in theutunico"; see Newhauser 1987, 110.

English noun was ambiguous, meaning both "greeting" and "weeping," the sermon writer at once provides it with a clarifying gloss in Latin.

Septima littera est G et signat his **greting**, latine salutacio.[11]

Another aspect of macaronic sermons that points to their English basis is that a good deal of their Latin lexicon is flagrantly patterned on or translated from Middle English, as we saw in the discussion of English idioms in chapter 5.

Yet another kind of evidence that the basis of these sermons was an English text can be found in their treatment of biblical and patristic quotations. We know from sermons that have been preserved entirely in English (i.e., type E) that preachers liked to first quote authorities in Latin and then translate them into English.[12] These Latin authorities are the exceptions in the otherwise English basis that I mentioned earlier. An unedited English sermon in manuscript B, for example, has the following quotation of Luke 11:28:

þer-for þus seyth Luke yn hys gospel, Luce XI: Beati qui audiunt verbum Dei et custodiunt illud. **þey ben y-blessyd, seyth he, þat heryn þe word of God almyȝthy and kepyth hyt <in dede>.** (B-116/201ra)

Similar examples recur in the Middle English sermons edited by Ross and elsewhere.[13] The same procedure also appears in some macaronic sermons of type C, as in the following instance from L-1:

Ideo dicit per Ieremiam prophetam: "In caritate perpetua dilexi te," Ieremie 31; "**in love,** inquit, **þat hevirmore schal lastin haf y louid te.**" (L-1/217v)

---

11. Q-42/125, edited in Little 1943, 252; "weeping," **wepynge,** is used for the (Latin) letter *v*. Latin glosses for English words, as in the quoted sentence, occur with some frequency in other macaronic sermons—for example, "**godys of hows,** domus, **and** ..." (Q-25/82v); or "sicut est þe **day rew** vel aurora" (B-136/245va).

12. This practice was likewise followed on the Continent; see Lecoy de la Marche 1886, 250–51; Bériou 1987, 1:103.

13. For example, Ross 1940, 3/6–7, 3/29–31, 12/29–31, and passim; Cigman 1989, 2/35–38, 14/66–68, and passim; Grisdale 1939, 2/26–27, 2/32–33, 22/24–30, and passim.

More remarkable about this general practice in late-medieval vernacular preaching is that in our macaronic sermons the process of translating
a Latin authority breaks down and yields to macaronization, which often
results in a near-repetition of the authority in bilingual form or even
entirely in Latin, a result that completely counteracts the original intention of Englishing the Latin authority. To demonstrate, I choose again
some examples from L-1. The first is a macaronic rendering of a biblical
quotation.

> Sicut dixit Apostolus Ad Hebreos 5, "cum clamore valido et multis
> lacrimis offerens exauditus est pro sua reuerencia." "**Wyt a greyt cry,**"
> inquit Apostolus, "et multis lacrimis ipse fecit suam oblacionem,"
> idest sui preciosi sanguinis, "et fuit exauditus in sua **bindinge for ys
> reuerens.**" (L-1/216v)

The same process affects patristic authorities.

> Vt dixit Jeronimus super illud Psalmi *Speciosus forma*: "Nisi ha-
> buisset, inquit, in uultu quoddam occulis sidereum, nunquam eum
> statim secuti fuissent apostoli, nec qui ad comprehendendum eum
> venerant corruissent." "**Ne had he had** in sua facie **a manere of sterre
> lyt** (ad trahendum hominem et homines ad amorem quando voluisset
> et ad terrendum homines quando voluisset), **schundirde neuer ȝe apos-
> tils at fowl him at his first calling,** nec illi qui venerant ad capiendum
> eum **a falle swa doun o bakke at his first loking.**" (L-1/220)

In both cases, the rendition of the original authority is more than simple
translation, whether English or macaronic, and it might therefore more
properly be called a paraphrase that includes verbal substitution (*in sua
facie* for *in uultu*) and commentary, a process reminiscent of Langland's
use of Latin tags in *Piers Plowman*.[14]

What matters here is that the text of the quoted authority itself is
rendered not entirely in English but in a linguistic mixture. In the fol-

---

14. This phenomenon of "rendering" biblical and other authorities in the vernacular
in a process close to paraphrasing needs further study. One wonders, for instance, whether
the threat of Lollardism might have caused preachers to substitute paraphrase for straight-
forward translation.

lowing example, again from L-1, the rendition appears without any English at all:

Sicut testatur ipsemet in ewangelio: "Maiorem dileccionem nemo habet quam vt animam suam ponat quis pro amicis suis." Maiorem, inquit, dileccionem non potest homo habere quam quod det suam vitam pro amico suo. (L-1/218)

It looks as if in these cases the English translation of a Latin authority, or part of it, was retranslated into Latin. This phenomenon is not restricted to L-1; it occurs similarly throughout, and is very characteristic of, the macaronic sermons in Q.

The main and fundamental authority for a scholastic sermon was its biblical thema. This was normally announced in Latin and then translated into English verse or prose, often with a connecting marker, such as "anglice." In this situation, too, the English occasionally became retranslated into Latin or disappeared altogether. An example of the former occurs in R-12. After the initial prayer, the preacher repeats the thema, *"Exiuit de templo,* ubi prius," and continues, "Anglice," but what follows is not in English but in Latin: "Christus *exiuit de templo.*" After that an alternate rendering is introduced with "vel sic," and then we get an English translation in verse (R-12/63). The English rendition disappears completely, for example, in the edited sermon W-154 (ll. 2–3) and in the following case: "Ista sunt verba euangelii sancti Marci et sunt dicta in lingua materna. Experiencia docet..." ("These words are from the gospel of St. Mark and are in our mother tongue. Experience teaches us...," H-18/52v).[15] The omission of the English rendering could be due to the scribe, but whether or not this is the case, there was a stage before the written form at which the "text" was in English.

---

15. It is possible to interpret the words *sunt dicta in lingua materna* as "they were said in the mother tongue," which would then make this sermon a record kept by either the preacher or a *reportator,* much like the sermons by Fitzralph. What argues against this possibility is that for such notes Fitzralph regularly uses the medieval instead of the classical perfect (*ostensum fuit,* etc.), as do the writers of macaronic sermons I have read. Another example of omitting the announced translation occurs in B-093, a sermon entirely in Latin. After a short introduction leading to prayer and the repetition of the thema *Stephanus plenus gratia,* the text continues: "Ista verba pro themate sumpta scribuntur in epistula hodierna et sic secundum nostram linguam sunt interpretanda. Querunt quidam doctores et clerici numquid..." (f. 159ra). The same phenomenon occurs in bilingual sermons produced in France; see Bériou 1987, 2:10, 11, 36, and passim.

To give this hypothetical basis or Gestalt a written form, the sermon writers then used Latin. This choice is not at all astonishing, because Latin remained, as it had been for over a millennium, the official language of the church and the clergy until at least the end of the fifteenth century, enjoying prestige, universality, and perhaps the advantage of a medium that was closed to peasants and heretics.[16] One may, at this point, object that my suggested model unnecessarily introduces a rather vague concept, that of an English basis. Why not simply say that English sermons were translated into Latin? The reason for the suggested model touches the heart of this discussion: I wish to avoid the term *translation* for the process I am describing precisely because it implies or at least suggests a concrete exemplar, whether oral (the sermon as delivered from the pulpit) or written (notes taken during the sermon or prepared by the preacher before the delivery), and a choice between two languages. It forecloses the alternate possibility that a purely mental conception of the sermon was expressed bilingually, not by default but deliberately. It is astonishing that in the case of the sermons here studied, the result of writing out the English basis was not pure Latin but a mixture of Latin and English. The preceding chapters furnish evidence of various sorts that this mixture did not result from the sermon writers' carelessness or incompetence. The texture of these macaronic compositions, the nature of the language mix they employ, denies the theory that they came about as a compromise between the traditional requirement of writing sermons in Latin and the writers' lack of the mastery of the Latin vocabulary they would have needed for doing so successfully. Whether the macaronic form was deliberately intended is, for the moment, a moot question; but that form was certainly tolerated, and it was tolerated by writers who otherwise show a high level of intelligence and clerical training.

We must, therefore, think of these sermon writers as functionally and fluently bilingual. This view and the analysis on which it is based find unexpected and strong support in modern studies of bilingualism.[17]

---

16. See Owst 1926, 223-29; Clanchy 1979, 157. Owst and other students have suggested that writing the sermons in Latin, especially those that criticized the clergy, would have "kept them away safely from the inquisitive eyes of the laity," and that especially in the early fifteenth century, Latin might have been preferred out of "a fear of the taint of heresy"; Owst 1926, 224, 229. These points are repeated, for example, in Dolan 1989, 30-31.

17. This paragraph is indebted to the summaries and critical reviews of contemporary work on bilingualism in Beardsmore 1986, Hamers and Blanc 1989, and Romaine 1989.

Though the latter deal primarily, even exclusively, with observable oral discourse, their major insights fully apply to the written texts of this study. Of central relevance here is the concept of "code-switching," defined as "the seemingly random alternation of two languages both between and within sentences."[18] Recording and analyzing the discourse of contemporary bilingual speakers in the United States, Great Britain, and elsewhere has shown that such code-switching affects all parts of speech and syntactic units. In analyzing the discourse of speakers who mix languages within the sentence (i.e., who practice intrasentential code-switching), a distinction may be made between a pragmatic approach, which seeks for motivations for the switching, and a grammatical one, which is primarily concerned with the linguistic constraints on code-switching. In pursuing the latter, linguists have found that code-switching is not "random" but constrained by the rules of the two grammars involved. These bilingual speakers know and master the grammars of both languages; they are totally competent and fluent speakers in both.[19]

Code-switching is, thus, essentially different from linguistic borrowing.

In general, it would not be correct to say that speakers code-mix or switch to fill lexical gaps. . . . Although it is popularly believed by bilingual speakers themselves that they mix or borrow because they don't know the term in one language or another, it is often the case that switching occurs most often for items which people know and use in both languages.[20]

As far as motivations for the switching are concerned, the same linguists argue that it

---

18. Poplack 1980, 581. It should be noted that Poplack's use of *random* in this definition means "without grammatical rules or constraints" (a point that Poplack's investigation comes to deny) and thus differs from my earlier use of the term as "without observable grammatical or psychological motivation" with respect to the shifting from one language to the other.

19. One major exception to this statement is that such competence need not cover the lexicon of both languages equally; a bilingual speaker may not master the special vocabulary of certain fields in both languages with equal competence. This observation applies to cases in macaronic sermons where the technical vocabulary was more readily available in English than in Latin, as shown in chapter 5.

20. Romaine 1989, 132.

is basically stylistic and that code-switching is to be treated as a discourse phenomenon which cannot be handled satisfactorily in terms of the internal structure of sentences.[21]

Modern bilingual speech that mixes languages within sentences is basically a "discourse strategy" that parallels style-switching in monolingual speakers (such as the use of the historical present in conversation): "Mixing and switching for fluent bilinguals is thus, in principle, no different from style-switching for the monolingual. Bilinguals just have a wider choice."[22] Therefore, "code-switching, rather than representing debasement of linguistic skill, is actually a sensitive indicator of bilingual ability."[23]

These findings made by linguists, combined with the results of my investigation of macaronic sermon texture, force me to reject several general explanations of macaronic texts that have been advanced in the past. The latter rest primarily on the pioneering and seminal study of thirteenth-century preaching in France, based on close inspection of a large number of manuscripts, by Albert Lecoy de la Marche. In this most influential investigation of preaching in the high Middle Ages, which has cast much light as well as a long shadow on subsequent studies of preaching in countries other than France, Lecoy de la Marche devoted an entire chapter to the question of what language was used in actual preaching. He announced the following two principles, based on external and internal evidence:

All sermons addressed to the faithful [i.e., the laity], even those

---

21. Romaine 1989, 111.

22. Romaine 1989, 132. Romaine also points out "that one of the most common discourse functions of code-switching is to repeat the same thing in both languages" (ibid.)—an aspect paralleled by the frequent macaronic structures of coordination and doublets discussed in chapter 5. A basic study of code-switching as a "discourse strategy" is Gumperz 1982, chapter 4, which concludes that "code-switching signals contextual information equivalent to what in monolingual settings is conveyed through prosody or other syntactic or lexical processes" (98). I must add, however, that the acceptability of switching in the material studied by Gumperz is considerably more restricted than what I find in C sermons: "Switching is blocked where it violates the speaker's feeling for what on syntactic or semantic grounds must be regarded as a single unit" (ibid., 90). In contrast, the C sermons are full of cases where the switching occurs in the middle of such units.

23. Poplack 1980, 581.

written in Latin, were preached entirely in French. Only the sermons addressed to the clergy were ordinarily preached in Latin.[24]

In both cases, however, the sermons were normally written out in Latin, the international language of the clergy.

Turning to sermon texts that mix Latin and French, Lecoy de la Marche distinguished between two different situations: where a Latin authoritative text is followed by a French "commentaire," and where French phrases or single words are interwoven into the Latin text (1886, 253). Regarding the second situation—which is the one of direct interest for us—he distinguished further between the following cases (255–57):

1. A simple sketch or draft, or else the *reportatio* of a cleric who, in writing down the sermon, used Latin here and there when he did not recall the preacher's actual French words.
2. French phrases in Latin texts that are quotations of verses or proverbs that the redactor wanted to leave in their original form or else did not know how to translate into Latin.
3. Texts in which parts of Latin phrases or words are followed by their French equivalents, which the writers added to help their confreres in their task of delivering to the faithful, in French, the entire, basically Latin passage. These, in other words, are translation helps for technical terms and such. Such glosses may also occur in the margins.
4. French words or short phrases without their Latin equivalent. These occur "either in order to avoid needless repetition or because the writer did not know the learned idiom perfectly" (257).

---

24. *"Tous les sermons adressés aux fidèles, même ceux qui sont écrits en latin, étaient prêchés entièrement en français. Seuls, les sermons adressés à des clercs étaient ordinairement prêchés en latin,"* Lecoy de la Marche 1886, 235 (emphasis in original). H. Martin (1988, 560 n. 21) reminds us that the principle was already announced by Mabillon. Subsequent writers have added that sermons preached to nuns were usually in the vernacular, too; see, for example, Owst 1926, 223. Boeren (1956, 170) points out that there were exceptions even in the early thirteenth-century university sermon, when some preachers used the vernacular before clerics. A similar exception to Lecoy de la Marche's principle was Abbot Samson of Bury St. Edmunds, who assured a hesitant fellow monk chosen to become prior that he needed not worry too much about his insufficiency in Latin because, among other things, "in multis ecclesiis fit sermo in conventu Gallice vel potius Anglice"; see Richter 1979, 93 n. 46.

If we examine these categories (which, unfortunately, fuse two different matters—the nature of the linguistic mixture, and motives that would explain it) in the light of my preceding chapters, we find that the first does not address the nature of the mixture with any specificity; that the second and third concern what I have called *a* elements; and that only the fourth deals with *c* elements, which alone constitute genuinely macaronic sermons. My analysis of the texture of type C sermons has shown that, contrary to Lecoy de la Marche's claim (in his fourth group), vernacular words that are not glosses very often repeat what has already been said in Latin (especially the macaronic doublets), and that in the overwhelming majority of cases, it is plain that the writer was perfectly capable of expressing his thought in the learned idiom. To Lecoy de la Marche's conclusion that "we have not found any hybrid phrases that cannot be related to one of these raisons-d'être, and if one were to discover any, this would only be an exception,"[25] I am forced to say that in the C sermons I have studied, this "exception" covers the majority of hybrid or macaronic elements.

Lecoy de la Marche's study has profoundly influenced later pronouncements about macaronic sermons made by students of such texts from France and England. Especially the role of *reportatio* in creating macaronic texts has been, and is being, further studied.[26] Where surviving manuscripts allow us to see the linguistic state of both the recording made during the sermon and its subsequent elaboration, as for instance in the case of Peter of Limoges examined by Bériou, it appears that *reportatores* took notes of a vernacular sermon in Latin (because that language offered a richer system of abbreviations, which would have made the recording faster) but slipped into the vernacular whenever they had no Latin equivalent at hand or when a passage in the sermon contained a vernacular expression or saying they wanted to preserve in its original form.[27] But this explanation of macaronic texts does not hold for the sermons studied here. As I pointed out earlier, apart from there being no evidence of *reportatio,* our macaronic sermons bear all the stylistic features of fully

---

25. "Nous n'avons point remarqué de phrases hybrides qu'on ne puisse rapporter à l'une de ces raison d'être; et si l'on en découvrait, ce ne serait qu'à l'état d'exception" (Lecoy de la Marche 1886, 257).

26. See Hamesse 1986; Bériou 1978; Bériou 1987, 1:59–64; Bériou 1992; Bataillon 1989; Delcorno 1986; Rusconi 1989; Völker 1963. For England, see above, note 1.

27. Bériou 1978. See also Parkes 1991.

developed and elaborated compositions, whether they were written before or after delivery; and the two specific reasons advanced by Bériou—linguistic incompetence and the desire to preserve vernacular sayings—are roundly contradicted by the analysis I have undertaken in this chapter and in chapter 5.

The same objections also apply to the limited attention that has been given to macaronic sermons from England. For example, A. G. Little, who edited the macaronic sermon Q-42, comments on its linguistic form as follows:

> The sermon is written in Latin with an admixture of English. English words and phrases are sometimes introduced promiscuously but generally on a systematic plan. The summaries or headings of divisions and subdivisions (which in Latin sermons are given in rhymed Latin) are here given in rhymed English. The sermon was delivered in English. Those parts in which the exact wording was essential to the proper construction of the sermon are in English. For the rest, where only the meaning and not the exact form was important, a practised preacher could easily discourse in English on the basis of a Latin text, and it would certainly be easier and quicker to write out the sermon in Latin, with its fixed spelling and universally recognized system of abbreviation, than in English which had neither of these advantages.[28]

The essential parts that Little speaks of, if in English, represent *a* or *b* elements according to my earlier classification and therefore do not constitute a sermon of type C. But sermon Q-42 is full of *c* elements, that is, of English material that by definition does not have such structural functions; I count over sixty of them.[29] And these are certainly not introduced "on a systematic plan." As was the case with Lecoy de la Marche, Little's explanation does not fit the linguistic facts of Q-42 or of the other type C sermons.

In a more recent study of preaching in northern France between 1350 and 1520, Hervé Martin reconsiders the questions of what language

---

28. Little 1943, 247.
29. These include a number of phrases that are part of speeches by historical characters or abstractions. One might challenge their being considered *c* elements; but they are certainly not glosses, translations of Latin quotations, vernacular quotations, divisions, and so on.

sermons were preached in and what might explain the macaronic texts. For him, things are "perfectly clear" and "no longer a matter for debate":[30] sermons to the laity were delivered in French, those to the clergy, in Latin; written texts are in Latin, occasionally with some elements left in French for various reasons; and in the actual delivery, a preacher would render such a bilingual written text monolingually, according to his audience.[31] The elements left in French, in the written text, are rhymed divisions, precise translations of authorities, glosses, idiomatic expressions that were almost untranslatable, and words for which the Latin equivalent did not occur to the writer.[32] Yet when Martin discusses cases where the Latin equivalent supposedly did not occur to the writer's mind, he is faced—as I am, in analyzing macaronic sermons from England—with situations where a vernacular word remained untranslated (as he views it) though its Latin equivalent was present to the writer's mind. Martin concludes that this indicates

that Pierre-aux-Bœufs thinks primarily in the vulgar tongue. . . . In these circumstances, the orator [meaning translator or writer] is carried along by the *élan* that pushes him towards his mother tongue. But he must brake very quickly, in the name of theology, of science, and of seriousness.[33]

Martin's suggestion that those who wrote out macaronic sermons thought in the native tongue agrees with my proposal that the English basis existed as a purely mental conception. But I do not think that the preacher's being carried away and then recovering his theological or scientific dignity explains the switching I have analyzed in chapter 5. Such a putative emotional élan might account for a higher incidence of English elements in sections that deal with Christ's passion, but it does

---

30. Schneyer, too, in his history of Catholic preaching, states that discussions about the language of preaching "sind . . . längst abgeschlossen" (1969, 128). However, Schneyer was less intimately familiar with sermons from the fourteenth and fifteenth than he was with those from earlier centuries.

31. This also seems to be Horner's view on the macaronic sermons in O and R: "The sermons have been preserved in this bilingual fashion so that a preacher wishing to use a sermon could adapt it readily to either a clerical or lay audience" (1989, 321 n. 34).

32. H. Martin 1988, 560–63.

33. H. Martin 1988, 563, my translation. Pierre-aux-Bœufs, who flourished at the beginning of the fifteenth century, is the preacher especially studied by H. Martin.

not explain the constant and evenly distributed switching in genuine type C sermons. I consider Martin's and similar discussions to be misguided because they are determined by the traditional view of a strict separation of Latin versus vernacular preaching according to audience and preclude an unbiased linguistic analysis of the macaronic texts.[34] One would like to ask Lecoy de la Marche and his followers in what language preachers delivered sermons that bear clear indications of being addressed to an audience of both clerics and layfolk.[35]

Does this mean that our type C sermons were actually preached in their macaronic form? This suggestion goes straight against the greatest virtues of Anglo-Saxon culture, common sense and pragmatism; and one can well understand the reluctance of modern scholars to entertain the possibility of preaching the word of God in a form that supposedly would not have been understood by the masses. Yet what else explains their particular linguistic shape?

A number of remarks made by late-medieval Englishmen speak of the use of both Latin and English in contemporary preaching. For instance, a fifteenth-century legend says of a friar:

And firste he prechide gud latyne,
And sythyne Inglysche gud and fyne.[36]

And Chaucer's Pardoner declares:

And in Latyn I speke a wordes fewe,
To saffron with my predicacioun,
And for to stire hem to devocioun.[37]

---

34. I notice that Richard Hunt, too, was uncomfortable with the Mabillon/Lecoy de la Marche principle in his discussion of the sermons by Alexander Nequam; see Hunt 1984, 92–94.

35. Apart from what macaronic sermons themselves have revealed about mixed audiences (see chapters 3 and 4), there is external evidence that such audiences existed. As shown above, ch. 2, note 2, the constitutions for the provincial chapter of the Benedictine order decreed that on the first day of the chapter a sermon was to be preached in Latin to the assembled clergy, and on the third day another "sermo ad populum in lingua vulgari" (Pantin 1931–37, 2:58, 60–61; see also 1:88, 266, and 2:7). In 1423 the sermon on the third day was preached by Dr. Iohannes Derham "clero et populo" (ibid., 2:155, my emphasis). For an instance of a mixed audience in the thirteenth century, see above, note 7.

36. De miraculo Beate Marie, ll. 52–53, in Horstmann 1881, 503.

37. Chaucer, The Pardoner's Tale, ll. 344–46.

More specific remarks made here and there tell us that such bilingualism occurred in various forms and at different occasions in late-medieval preaching. Apart from outstanding preachers who are on record as having been able to preach in two or three different languages,[38] preachers of the later middle ages continued the practice, attested from earlier centuries,[39] of preaching in the vernacular and then writing out their own sermons in Latin, usually in a more polished form. Richard Fitzralph tells us in his sermon diary that he preached many of his sermons *in vulgari,* yet his notes and complete sermons are entirely in Latin.[40] In the 1420s, two friars testified that they had preached in the vernacular and had subsequently written their sermons out in Latin.[41]

Sometimes a preacher, conversely, delivered his sermon in Latin and then, still in the pulpit, translated it into the vernacular, a situation evidently envisioned in the first couplet quoted above. A funeral sermon preached by Bishop Grandisson of Exeter in 1341 was "first given in Latin and then in French."[42] At a later time and in a different country, Giles of Viterbo "also had a penchant for repeating in the vernacular what he had just declaimed in Latin. . . . It was not dissimilar to the way the popes themselves preached in the Middle Ages."[43] And I suspect that Wyclif's remark "In duplici ergo lingua est fides Christi populo reserenda" ("The faith of Christ must be laid open to the people in two languages") is to be understood similarly as referring to preaching in either Latin or the vernacular.[44]

A different type of mixture occurred when, within the same sermon,

---

38. For example, Adam Orleton, successively bishop of Hereford, Worcester, and Winchester (1317–45), preached in the vernacular (English?), French, and Latin; see Haines 1978, 56, 70, 165. Similarly, Abbot Thomas de la Mare of St. Albans (1349–96), before becoming abbot, spent three years learning how to preach "tam in lingua Anglica quam Latina" (Riley 1867, 2:380). Thomas Walsingham also reports that he could preach in all three languages (ibid., 3:409–10). Even as early as the end of the twelfth century, Odo of Canterbury preached in French, Latin, or Middle English (Searle 1980, 306–8).

39. A good example is sermon 65 by Peter of Blois, which he says he had given "laicis satis crude et insipide (sicut eorum capacitatis erat)" and then written out "in Latinum sermonem" in a more elaborate form, at the bidding of a friend (*PL* 207:750).

40. Gwynn 1937; Walsh 1981, 182–238.

41. Owst 1926, 225.

42. Owst 1926, 265.

43. O'Malley 1979, 27.

44. The remark occurs in a context that argues that the gospel must be preached in the language people are most familiar with; *Speculum secularium dominorum* i (in Wyclif 1913, 75).

the preacher used Latin to address the clergy and English to address the laity, both simultaneously present in his audience. Direct evidence for such a procedure comes from sermon L-1 and has been quoted earlier.[45] A specific application of this principle occurs in the sermons of Ranulphe de la Houblonnière (ca. 1225?–88). These form an exact French counterpart to our macaronic sermons from England, showing the same mixture of Latin with *c* elements (as well as *a* and *b* ones) in French. In one of them, evidently preached to a mixed audience, the use of both languages allowed the preacher to reserve for the clergy in his audience certain remarks that might have scandalized the common people.

Caueant ergo ne hodie istam oblationem faciant, donec se purgauerunt, et precipue caueant sibi sacerdotes qui hanc eamdem oblationem faciunt in sacramento altaris pro se et pro populo. Hoc dicas eis latinis uerbis, non laicalibus, propter scandalum.

(Let them take care not to make such an offering today until they have cleansed themselves, and let especially the priests take care, who make this offering in the sacrament of the altar for themselves and for the people. *Tell them so in Latin, not in the vernacular language, in order to avoid giving scandal*).[46]

Finally, preachers changed from one language to the other not only out of consideration for their audience and the potentially inflammatory effect of their remarks, but out of respect for authoritative texts. Thus they commonly quoted authoritative passages in Latin and then translated and developed them in the vernacular. Occasionally such linguistic dignity is bestowed not only on biblical and patristic but on scientific authorities. A fine example appears in sermon B-136, on Canticles 6:9, "Who is she who comes forth as the morning rising, fair as the moon, bright as the sun?" In discussing "the morning rising," the preacher cites a number of authorities on the beginning of dawn and the altitude of clouds that is involved in it: Albumasar, Ptolomaeus, Pliny, and Roger Bacon. After he has done so, he continues with "Dixi in latinis quod sunt diuersa dicta de altitudine nubium" ("I have said

45. See above, chapter 4, note 19.
46. Bériou 1987, 2:52–53, ll. 344–48 (my emphasis), and her remarks at 1:103 n. 27.

in Latin that there are different authorities concerning the altitude of clouds")—a clear indication that after this barrage of Latin authorities, the sermon continued in English, though its written form at this point is Latin.[47]

Similar privileging might even extend as far as the major sermon division. Among our macaronic sermons, L-1 presents first a division in Latin, then one that was presumably spoken in English.[48] The text preserved in the manuscript tells us quite clearly what the preacher did in the pulpit: "Nunc pro processu sermonis notabitis primo breuiter in Latinis pro istis clericis et postea in Angl' pro vobis omnibus" ("Now, for the further development you shall note, first briefly in Latin for these clerics and then in English for all of you," L-1/217v). The written record of the sermon has indeed preserved the first version of the same division in Latin, the second in macaronic form. Another case of this kind but without class differentiation (i.e., clerics versus lay audience) is X-3, where the division is first written out in Latin only ("Pro processu istius sermonis...") and then followed with the words "Dicatur processus Anglice sic," which leads at once to the same division in rhymed English lines (X-3/29rb). Obviously, in the actual delivery, the division was first spoken in Latin and then followed by a vernacular or macaronic rendition.[49] In his handbook on preaching, Robert Basevorn even reports

---

47. B-136/245ra. The sermon as a whole is type C.

48. The same situation may possibly occur in S-07 also, if its first word, here edited as *prolatiue,* is to be read as *primo latine;* see the edition in appendix B.

49. I add some further cases in which the preserved text tells us that the preacher switched to English after he had given introductory material (beyond the thema) in Latin: In B-115, after giving a division with confirmation, all in Latin, the text continues: "Karissimi, sicut dixi istis literatis in verbis pro themate assumptis pro processu sermonis nostri, duo breuiter intelligere debetis: primo **an hol precious offeryng**... De istis duobus breuiter erit processus nostri sermonis" (f. 199rb). Similarly, in B-135, after repeating the thema, the preacher continues: "Karissimi, ista verba que dixi in latino scribuntur in epistula Pauli et tantum signant in anglico. Karissimi..." But here the written text contains no English (f. 242rb). Much earlier, in 1345, Fitzralph noted in his sermon 6 on Corpus Christi that, after the initial prayer, he first gave a preview of the sermon in Latin, which he then repeated in English: "vt sub breuibus verbis ac leuibus et latino describam sermonis nostri materiam, et postmodum loquar ad populum expressius atque rusticius in uulgari, videtur michi..." (f. 4). Later he records the switch again: "quod sequitur de isto sermone dictum fuit ad populum in vulgari, et repetita fuerunt primo in vulgari ista vltimo hic premissa, et consequenter prosecucio sic fiebat. Dico primo..." (ibid.). Pace Gwynn and Walsh, MS Bodley 144, from which I quote (f. 7r–v), does list the sermon's occasion, although uncharacteristically at its end. A similar preview of the sermon seems to occur at the beginning of the edited sermon *Amore langueo* (S-07, etc.).

that English preachers sometimes give the division in Latin to keep lay people from preaching—the *subtilitas* of the Latin division should scare them off or at least teach them proper respect![50]

Such remarks and examples show that fourteenth- and fifteenth-century preachers used both languages in delivering the same sermon. Yet the various situations they reflect do not include genuine macaronic texts of the kind this book is concerned with, that is, texts in which the language changes within the sentence; and so our question whether these macaronic sermons were actually preached in this form is still unanswered. One longs, at this point, for a clear, unequivocal testimony—whether made with praise or blame—that such preaching did occur. Such testimony is not entirely lacking. Fra Tommaso Antonio of Siena (A.D. 1395) is reported as having "given a devout sermon in Latin before the people and, according to custom, somewhat in the vernacular."[51] It is not absolutely clear whether *aliqualiter in vulgari* implies intrasentential code-switching. But another witness, and one of much greater relevance to England, leaves less doubt. According to the statutes of the Carthusian order, "Let it be up to whoever gives the sermon to speak Latin or vulgar *or in a mixture*" (my emphasis).[52]

The possibility that macaronic sermons were preached has been entertained by a few previous scholars. Pfander, in studying popular sermons by English friars, recorded his suspicion that "at times sermons were delivered in a mixture of Latin and English," but he did not pursue the matter more closely.[53] Even Martin is willing to allow for some exceptions to his rigorous view.[54] A much stronger case was made by Lucia Lazzerini

---

50. "Multi illiterati usurparent sibi actum praedicandi, nisi quia vident tantam subtilitatem, ad quam attingere nequeunt. Et propter eandem causam, quando laicis praedicant, praemittunt thema suum cum divisione sua in latino, quia hoc facere est difficile idiotis" (Basevorn, *Forma praedicandi* 7, in Charland 1936, 244–45).

51. "Sermonem devotum feci in latino coram populo et iuxta morem aliqualiter in vulgari" (quoted in Lazzerini 1971, 241).

52. "In dispositione facientis sermonem sit loqui latine vel vulgariter vel mixtim" (*Statuta antiqua,* I, cap. xxxii, par. 5; in *Statuta ordinis cartusiensis a domino Guigone priore cartusie edita,* Basel 1510). I owe this reference to Gillespie 1989, 167. To what extent this admittedly very isolated disposition could have influenced non-Carthusian preaching, or conversely might reflect preaching in other orders, remains an open question.

53. Pfander 1937, 7.

54. "On ne peut exclure que la langue vulgaire ait été truffée de latin, surtout quand il s'agissait de développer une argumentation théologique, les enchaînements conceptuels se faisant plus facilement dans la langue savante" (H. Martin 1988, 560). But again, this

in a virtual monograph on the *Latinus grossus* (gross or rustic, i.e.,
macaronic, Latin) of some late-medieval preachers in Italy. Against Lecoy
de la Marche, she maintained that the Latin-Italian mixture in these
texts cannot be explained as the result of translation. She adduced the
testimony of Fra Tommaso Antonio quoted above and of later fifteenth-
and sixteenth-century writers. Lazzerini's study has the virtue of paying
close attention to the actual texture of the sermons under consideration.
Her findings parallel many points that my analysis of macaronic sermons
from England have brought out, from the prevalence of doublets (Lazzerini 1971, 287) to macaronic density in the treatment of certain favorite
topics (237), the presence of a rhetorical style (274–82), and the insufficiency of causes that would explain the mixture otherwise.[55]

The objection to the view that macaronic sermons were actually
preached rests on the assumption that their audiences were monolingual,
in our case English-speaking only. But what if they were bilingual, such
as would have been the case with university or monastic audiences? My
analysis of the various collections and manuscripts in which type C
sermons occur brought to light that in many cases not only were these
collections made by and for a monastic readership, but individual sermons in them were preached to a clerical audience or to one that contained both clergy and laypersons, often at Oxford or some monastic
community.[56] In these cases, the condition for macaronic preaching would

---

rhetorical situation does not explain the macaronic sermons from England, and Martin's
remark proceeds from the assumption that the sermons here envisioned were preached in
the vernacular.

55. "La non-causalità della mescidanza, che si è manifesta con tanta evidenza nel corso
della nostra analise, costituisce senza dubbio un grave colpo per le teorie volte ad apporre
a tutti i casi d'ibridismo, senza eccezione, l'etichetta di 'semplice accidente' dovuto alla
trascuratezza o all'ignoranza d'ipotetici traduttori" (Lazzerini 1971, 290).

56. According to various pieces of monastic legislation issued in England throughout
the fourteenth and fifteenth centuries, Benedictine monks were trained, either in their
monastery or at Oxford, to preach in either Latin or English. The constitutions of Benedict
XII in 1336 call for the establishment of a common house of studies and for sending a
determined number of monks to the university. Two years later, the acts of the first
provincial chapter of the united province of the Benedictines in England decree that "every
prelate (i.e., abbot or prior) should appoint and ordain those in his convent whom he
knows to be able and fit for the office of preaching, to preach the word of God both in
private and publicly, with knowledge and discretion" (Pantin 1931–37, 2:11–12). Some
years thereafter, the constitutions of the provincial chapter edited by abbot Thomas de la
Mare (after 1349, perhaps in 1363) declare that "we order that those who are sent to the
university, for no other reason than that they may learn how to preach the word of God

have been fulfilled. The macaronic sermons in manuscripts O, R, W, and X could certainly have been delivered in that form. The circumstantial evidence for other cases is perhaps not quite as strong, but even such an unlikely candidate for macaronic preaching as manuscript Q possesses several features that make macaronic delivery possible. Q contains sermons made and/or collected and probably also preached by a member of the Franciscan order, that putative powerhouse of popular preaching and sympathy with the common folk, not likely to have indulged in appealing to popular emotions in a mixture of Latin and English. Yet the collection includes several pieces addressed to the clergy, and the macaronic sermons in it are full of material more suitable for a learned audience than for the laity. The same holds for the C sermons in the second part of manuscript B. One can, therefore, make a fairly good case that these macaronic sermons were written for audiences that would have been capable of understanding their linguistic mixture in oral delivery. And the quotation from the Carthusian statutes about mixed sermons fairly clinches the case for macaronic preaching at least by monastic preachers or to monastic audiences.[57]

A final argument for macaronic delivery derives from the near-oral style of these sermons, in which the shifts from Latin to English occur as smoothly and "naturally" as they do in the code-switching of bilingual speakers. To illustrate this style, I choose a short passage from Q-19, an Advent sermon on "Your savior will come." Its second principal, on God's coming to people daily with his grace, begins as follows:

Dixi eciam quod venit in hominem et **doith** omni die **by grace of þe godhede.** Karissimi, debetis intelligere quod **it farith** per graciam Dei **as it doith** per solem. Videtis bene ad oculum quod quando sol splendet **bry3te,** splendet ita prompte in loco qui est inmundus sicut in loco qui est mundus, in domo qui est clausus sicut in domo qui est apertus, in casu illi qui fuerint in domo clauso voluerint aperire hostia et

---

properly, should, according to the disposition of the prior or the more mature students, preach frequently both in Latin and in the vernacular, in our study house at Oxford or wherever the prior and the mature students may decide, so that they can do so the more freely and promptly when it is time to recall them to their monastery" (Riley 1867, 2:460). These provisions are repeated and expanded in the statutes of 1444 (Pantin 1931–37, 2:214–15). See also Wenzel 1993.

57. For preaching at the provincial chapters of the Benedictines, about which we have fairly good information, see chapter 2, notes 2–3.

fenestras et **letyn it in.** Veraciter recte sic **it fary3th** per graciam Dei:
it is ita prompta malo sicut bono, peccatori sicut iusto, ita quod non
est defectus in Deo qui tribuit graciam; set si aliquis defectus sit, **it
is of mennys wicked hertis** qui possent recipere graciam Dei et nolunt.
Et ideo dicit Parisiensis *De fide et legibus,* capitulo 2: "**It is skilful
and** racionabile," dicit iste clericus, "quod lumen gracie diuine non
ingrediatur **þat manis herte** qui ponit obicem mortalis peccati
þera3enis."

(I have further said that he comes to people and does so every day
through the grace of his godhead. Beloved, you must understand that
it goes with the grace of God as it does with the sun. You see well
with your eyes that when the sun shines brightly, it shines as readily
on a place that is unclean as on one that is clean, in a house that is
closed as in one that is open, if those who are in the closed house
will open the doors and windows and let it in. Truly, in just this way
it goes with God's grace: it is as ready for an evil person as for a
good one, for a sinner as for a righteous person, so that there is no
fault in God, who distributes his grace. But if there is any fault, it
rests in people's wicked hearts, who could receive God's grace and
do not wish to. And therefore the Parisian master, in chapter 2 of
his book *On Faith and Laws,* says: "It is sensible and reasonable,"
says this cleric, "that the light of divine grace should not enter that
person's heart who puts the obstacle of deadly sin thereagainst.")[58]

Here, a spiritual truth is explained by comparison with an everyday
observation, and the moral drawn from it is supported with an authoritative quotation. The Latin is punctuated with English words and
phrases, all but one[59] of Germanic origin, but these do not call attention
to themselves. The passage lacks the direct emotional appeal that characterized the paragraph quoted at the end of the preceding chapter and
its concomitant rhetorical devices, such as repetition, parallelism, rhetorical questions, and so on. It is plain and progresses at a steady, if

---

58. Q-19/59. The reference is to William of Auvergne, *De fide,* chapter 2, in *Opera
omnia,* vol. 1, p. 8, col. b: "Meritoque gratiae lumen divine cor illius ad illustrandum
non ingreditur, qui obicem illius opponit peccati."

59. The noun **grace;** but this is part of the repeated division, i.e., a *b* element.

unexciting, pace, as it ought to at this point of the sermon. It is effective in its economy, clarity, and forward movement, which culminates in the moral point that one should not place obstacles in the way of God's coming. These are the major virtues of expository prose, and I think the macaronic texture of this passage achieves them very well.

Could the sermons that mix their basic Latin with a substantial number of English c elements represent an attempt to create a mixed language made for special bilingual audiences, a language that with its combined virtues of lucid expository prose and heightened rhetorical appeal was well suited for delivery from the pulpit? If such a view is acceptable, these sermons are products of a linguistic aggiornamento and a stylistic trial that runs parallel to, though in the reverse direction of, the aureate diction used by some contemporary poets, that is, the practice of decorating English verse with fanciful Latinate words.[60] Like the latter, macaronic Latin was short-lived and probably a stylistic step in the wrong direction, though the play element present in both these stylistic trials has continued to appeal to the taste or fancy of speakers fluent in both languages. This suggestion may appear to contradict my attempt in chapter 1 to set macaronic sermons apart from both the witty parody by humanist poets and the privileging of Latin sentences in macaronic hymns and the poetry of Dante and Langland. The seeming contradiction is resolved when we consider that these macaronic sermon texts came about not as an intentional stylistic device but as the natural result of written discourse by fluent bilingual speakers. In any case, far from being an awkward compromise that reveals linguistic incompetence, the mixed Latin of these sermons can, and I believe should, be taken as an indication that at the time, and perhaps in a specific milieu, Latin was very much a living idiom.

I also believe that there is very little firm ground for the argument that the Latin of these macaronic sermons and of sermons that are entirely in Latin must be the result of translation from a preexistent concrete English text because it is full of vernacular idioms awkwardly rendered into Latin (i.e., calques). Most of such latinized English idioms can be found in other contemporary documents. This evidently was the

60. The basic study is still Mendenhall 1919. For more recent analyses of aureate diction in Lydgate, see Ebin 1979, 336 n. 36, to which should be added Norton-Smith 1966, 192–95.

way late–medieval English citizens wrote and talked when they wrote
and talked in Latin (as did, mutatis mutandis, contemporary Frenchmen
and Italians). Not that around the year 1400, a more classical Latin, or
at least what was perceived as such, lay beyond the capacities of literary
Englishmen. John of Whethamstede, abbot of St. Albans, is well known
for his cultivation of *florida verborum venustas,*[61] and the same classicizing style appears in a number of sermons that stand next to type C
sermons in the manuscripts I have described. For instance, a sermon on
"Gather in the house of discipline" (Ecclus. 51:31), preached by Master
John Fordham at the general chapter of, presumably, the English Benedictines, begins thus:

> Amantissimi patres et domini. Oriens splendor solis iusticie candorque
> lucis eterne et speculum sine macula deifice maiestatis, ipsa videlicet
> sedium diuinarum assistrix sapiencia, vt radios sue discipline mor-
> talibus graciosius communicaret, informatricis super se assumpsit
> officium; religionem monasticam, vt causa salutaris scola foret con-
> ueniens, quasi ex tot preciosis construxit lapidibus quot in eadem
> fulgencia incitamenta splendent virtutum, et ne ipsa more Achademie
> crebra temptacionum violencia velut quodam terremotu concussa sub-
> itaneam pateretur ruinam, ipsam quasi columpna septemplici fulcien-
> do septiformi munere Spiritus Sancti nobiliter insigniuit, vt iam de
> ipsa verificatur quamuis sub methafore quodam inuolucro: Sapiencia
> edificauit sibi domum.

> (Most loving fathers and lords, the rising splendor of the sun of justice,
> the brightness of eternal light, and the spotless mirror of the divine
> majesty, namely, Wisdom, who sits next to the divine seats, to com-
> municate the rays of her teaching more graciously to mortals, took
> on herself the office of teacher. That it might be a convenient school
> for the sake of salvation, she built the monastic way of life, as it
> were, out of as many precious stones as brilliant promptings to the
> virtues to shine forth in it; and that this way of life may not, like
> the Academy, be shaken by frequent violent temptations, as if by an
> earthquake, and suffer ruin, she fortified it with seven columns and
> gloriously marked it with the sevenfold gift of the Holy Spirit, so that

61. See Jacob 1933.

it is true of her, albeit under the veil of a metaphor, that "Wisdom has built a house for herself.")[62]

This is not quite Ciceronian prose, but in its vocabulary, learned references, and complicated word order the quoted passage smells of the lamp—Master John Fordham worked hard to impress his learned colleagues with what he must have thought was a discourse worthy of the occasion.[63] His is a very far cry from the style we observed in the previous quotation. The Latin in our type C sermons is humbler and folksier in grammar and style; yet it formed a tool that would have been totally serviceable and effective in teaching and moving its audience.

---

62. W-071/130rb.

63. One is reminded of the style cultivated by Peter of Blois: "copious, ornate, learned, glowing with burning words . . . its involved and intricate course through a maze of Scriptural and classical allusions and metaphors" (Southern 1970, 125). Peter of Blois is quoted in several sermons of R and W. For a brief characterization of the "elevated prose" style of medieval sermons and its difference from (genuine) classicizing tendencies in the twelfth century, see J. Martin 1982.

Appendices

Inventories of Manuscripts and Sermons

The following descriptions furnish bibliographical details concerning the thirteen manuscripts discussed in chapter 3 and list all the late-medieval sermons they contain. Measurements are given in millimeters; the detailed collations are entirely my own. For each sermon, I give:

1. the occasion as noted in the rubric at the beginning of the sermon
2. the thema, with biblical locus and occasion if present
3. reference to the modern Vulgate, in square brackets
4. the opening words of the sermon
5. folio reference
6. occasion of the sermon, without brackets if stated in the initial rubric, and in brackets if inferred from other marginalia or references in the sermon and
7. the type of the sermon according to the classification presented in chapter 1.

Asterisked sermons are type C.

A

Cambridge, University Library, MS Ii.3.8

Paper, with parchment flyleaves in front and back. ii + 177 + iii + pastedown. Dimensions: 295 × 220, written space of sermons 245 × 175. Collation: I–IV^{12} (medieval foliation: i–xxiii, 1–48), V^{10} (49–58), VI^{10} (59–68), VII^{10} (69–76, 78–79; medieval 77 excised), VIII^{10} (80–89), IX^{12} (90–100, unnumbered [100A]), X^{12} (101–110, 1102 [old 111], 1103 [old 112]), XI^{12}

(1104 twice [old 113–114], 1105, 106–109, 110, cxi–cxiiii), XII[12] (cxv, cxvi, cxvii twice, cxviii–cxxi, leaves 9–12 excised), XIII[12] (cxxvi–cxxxvii), XIV[12] (138–149), XV[12] (150–161; 152–153 wanting), XVI[12] (162–170, leaves 10–12 excised), 174–176. Medieval foliation as indicated (and used in the following analysis). Ff. 1–33 are written in two columns, the remainder in long lines, in several hands ranging from early to very late in the fifteenth century. Secundo folio: *iste et persequentes.*

Owner's note, f. 176: John Morton [Merton? Melton?], bought from William Denham [?], belonging to Thomas . . .

Literature: Owst 1926 and 1933 (passim); Erb 1971; Stemmler 1975.

As noted in the catalog (Cambridge University 1858, 3:411–12), the manuscript contains three treatises on the Decalogue (Bloomfield 5618, 2086, and 0450, on ff. 1–18, 18v–31, and 31v–36v, respectively), an *ars praedicandi* (Caplan *Suppl.* b, ff. 37–40v), and then a series of fifty-eight sermons *de tempore* in irregular order and some sermon material, such as exempla, commonplaces with English translation, expanded distinctions, and skeleton sermons (ff. 41–169). Many sermons are incomplete, ending with the marginal note "vacat" (f. 53) or "non plus in copia" (76, 78, 89v), and the scribes have frequently left blank spaces. As it is not always easy to distinguish between a full sermon and an extended distinction, I follow the medieval table of contents (ff. i–ii), which refers to a total of fifty-eight sermons, giving fifty-six themata, for two of which it lists two different sermons each.

A-01. Apprehende arma et scutum et exurge in adiutorium, Psalmo 32 [Ps. 34:2]. Si debilis quisquam bellum inire debeat cum aduersario forti et astuto—Ff. 41–43v. Type A.

A-02. Hortamur vos ne in vacuum graciam Dei recipiatis, 2° Ad Corinthios [2 Cor. 6:1], et in epistula hodierna. Karissimi, Ista dicitur dominica in quadragesima. Est quadragesima dies quadraginta dierum incipiens—Ff. 43v–45v, incomplete. 1 Lent. Type 0.

A-03. *Sermo in die Parasseues.* Christus passus est pro nobis, 1 Petri 2° [1 Pet. 2:21]. Racio potest assignari quare hodie sancta ecclesia a Spiritu docta—Ff. 46–47, incomplete. Good Friday. Type 0.

A-04. Lapis solutus calore in es vertitur, Iob 28 [Job 28:2]. Ista verba, dilectissimi, si ad literam intelligantur, veritatem habent, set spiritualiter—Ff. 47v–48. [St. Thomas the Apostle.] Type 0.

A-05. Veni, Domine Iesu, Apocalipsis vltimo [Rev. 22:20]. Scitis quod vnumquodque naturaliter sanitatem corporis diligit—Ff. 49–50. [Advent season.] Type 0.

A-06. Penitenciam agite, Matthei 3° [Matt. 3:2]. Dilectissimi, Sapiens rex Salomon qui scienciam docet—Ff. 50–51. Type 0.

A-07. Parce, Domine, parce populo tuo, Joel 38 primo capitulo [Joel 2:17]. Karissimi, Quando aliquis populus verberibus opprimitur grauioribus, tanto idem populus ad Deum calmat [!] feruencius—Ff. 52–53, incomplete, with marginal note "vacat." Type 0.

A-08. Vltra non serviamus peccato, Ad Romanos vi° [Rom. 6:6]. Wlgariter dicitur, "Stultus est qui potest eligere et capit partem peiorem"—Ff. 53–54. Type 0.

A-09. Orate vt non intretis in temptacionem, Matthei 26 [Matt. 26:41]. In quibus Salvator duo facit: primo ad ipsum interueniendum nos inuitat, secundo causam interueniendi manifestat—Ff. 54–55. Type 0.

A-10. Hortamur vos ne in vacuum graciam Dei recipiatis [2 Cor. 6:1]. Hec gracia est remissio peccatorum—Ff. 55–56. Probably not a sermon, but referred to in tabula. Type 0.

A-11. Tene quod habes, Apocalipsis 3° [Rev. 3:11]. Karissimi, Magne virtutis est amicum adquerere [!], set maioris est amicum adquesitum retinere. Set tu, quicumque Christiane, hodie in ecclesia—Ff. 56–57v. [Easter.] Type 0.

A-12. *Prima dominica quadragesime.* Ecce nunc dies salutis, Corinthiorum 6° [2 Cor. 6:2]. Karissimi, Infirmis multiplicibus egritudinibus laborantibus maxima materia consolacioni quando veniens ad eum medicus—Ff. 58–59, incomplete. 1 Lent. Type 0.

A-13. Christus passus est pro nobis vobis relinquens exemplum vt sequamini vestigia eius, Petri 2 [1 Pet. 2:21]. Christus de mundo transiens multas angustias et tandem mortem sustinuit—Ff. 59–60, incomplete, with marginal note "hic adde." Type 0, but translation of *O vos omnes* in bottom margin of f. 59v.

A-14. *Dominica secunda quadragesime.* Hec est voluntas Dei, sanctificacio uestra, Thessalonicensium 4 [1 Thess. 4:3]. Scribitur, karissimi, Luce 12: "Seruus sciens voluntatem Domini"—F. 62r–v. 2 Lent. Type 0.

A-15. Panem de celo prestitisti eis omne delectamentum in se habentem. Sapiencie xvi [Wisd. 16:20]. Boni et mali homini [in MS Merton 248: Boni homines et mulieres] sine gracia Dei et eius adiutorio—Ff. 66–71. [Corpus Christi.] A variant in Oxford, Merton College 248, ff. 131rb–132va, where it is ascribed to Friar Lawrence Bretown. Type C marginal.

A-16. Memorare testamenti altissimi, Ecclesiastici 28 [Ecclus. 28:9]. Valerius libro suo primo capitulo narrat quod maiores natu Romanorum opera predecessorum suorum egregio carmine—Ff. 71–74v. Type B2.

A-17. Benedictus qui venit in nomine Domini, Matthei 20 [Matt. 21:9]. Karissimi, Secundum philosophos et eciam astrologes [!] inter omnes planetas sol—Ff. 74v–76, incomplete with marginal note "non plus in copia." [Palm Sunday.] Type A.

A-18. Ecce rex tuus venit tibi mansuetus [Matt. 21:5]. Introduccio fuit de breui honore hodie Christo collato . . . Rex iste mansuetus Christus est—Ff. 76v–78, incomplete with marginal note "non plus in copia." [Palm Sunday.] Type 0.

A-19. *De passione Christi.* Per proprium sanguinem introiuit semel in sancta, Ad Hebreos 9° [Heb. 9:12]. Karissimi, In principio debetis scire sicud docet beatus Anselmus—Ff. 78v–80. Good Friday. Type B2.

A-20. *Pro quadragesima et aliis temporibus anni.* Dominus hiis opus habet, Matthei 21° [Matt. 21:3]. Karissimi, Sum nuncius ad vos arduis negociis et missus ex parte regis et tocius consilii ad notificandum vos de magna taxacione—Ff. 80v–82, incomplete? Lent and other seasons. Type C marginal.

A-21. Panem nostrum cotidianum da nobis hodie, Matthei vi° [Matt. 6:11], in ewangelio et in oracione communi. þe bred þat fedeʒ vs eueri day þou graunte vs lord þis esterday. Karissimi, Qualiter hec verba sunt ad propositum aduertamus—Ff. 82v–83v, incomplete? Easter. Type B2.

A-22. Luna mutatur, Ecclesiastici xxvii [Ecclus. 27:12]. Reuerendi mei, Vt directe descendam ad materiam sermonis, scire debemus secundum Ysodorum Ethim. quod luna mutatur variis temporibus—Ff. 83v–85v. Easter. Type C minimal, rich in B2 elements. The text ends: "Vnde tota die predicaui de inconstancia, iam intendo vobis predicare de constancia et quare tenebimus nobiscum illum reuerendum Dominum quem accepimus. 'Tene,' inquit, 'quod habes,' Iohannes in Apocalipsi."

A-23. Tene quod habes, ne alius accipiat a te coronam [Rev. 3:11]. Non est enim magnum bonum amicum adquirere, set pocius magnum est amicum adquesitum tenere. Pro quo scire debemus si tenere voluerimus hunc regem regum—Ff. 85v–86. Easter. Type C minimal. Continuation of A-22?

A-24. Heu, heu, heu, Ezechielis 6 [Ezek. 6:11, 9:8, 11:13]. Heu, casus accidit dolorosus: punctus qui erat in circuli medio non contentus tali loco tam abcessit rupto circulo—Ff. 86–89v, incomplete, with marginal note "non plus in copia." Type B2, rich.

*A-25. *De corpore Christi.* Sic honorabitur quem rex voluerit honorare, Hester [Esther 6:9]. Pro processu sermonis debetis scire quod quatuor personas in mundo isto video honorari, scilicet sapientes, diuites, strenuos, et prelatos—Ff. 90–91v. Corpus Christi. Type C.

A-26. *Dominica prima quadragesime.* Ecce nu[n]c dies salutis, 2ª Corinthiorum 6° [2 Cor. 6:2]. Prima dies exploracio sue culpe, secunda culpe deploracio, tercia eiusdem explicacio—Ff. 91v–92, incomplete. 1 Lent. Also O-39, q.v. Type B1.

A-27. Caritas operit multitudinem peccatorum, prima Petri 4° [1 Pet. 4:8]. Karissimi, Quatuor sunt experimenta per que literas priuatas potest homo legere—Ff. 92v–93. Type 0.

A-28. Lacrimis cepit rigare pedes eius, Luce 7° [Luke 7:38]. Vbi describitur vt desolata vt humiliata narra de muliere meretrice quam desponsauit imperator quidam—Ff. 93-94, incomplete. Type C marginal.

A-29. Iesu fili Dauid, miserere mei, Matthei iii [Matt. 15:22; cf. Mark 10:47; Luke 18:38]. Karissimi fratres, Hester 3° scribitur quod cum filii Israel grauiter—Ff. 94v–96v, incomplete. Type B2.

A-30. *Dominica quarta quadragesime.* Clama que non parturis, Ad Galatas 5° et Ysaye 54° [Gal. 4:27 and Isa. 45:10]. Karissimi, Solent clamatores publici et precones ad promulgandum leges seu edicta regum et principum—F. 97r-v, incomplete? 4 Lent. Type B1.

A-31. *Sermo in aduentu Domini.* Veniens veniet et non tardabit, Abacuc 1° [Hab. 2:3]. Notandum, karissimi, quod secundum veritatem et ecclesie consuetudinem triplicem recitamus Christi aduentum—Ff. 97v–98v, incomplete? The text ends, "et dicatur exposicio huius euangelii etc." Advent. Type 0.

A-32. Gloria in altissimo Deo et in terra pax hominibus bone voluntatis, Luce 12 [Luke 2:14]. Hodie recolit sancta ecclesia, fratres karissimi, prerogatiua gaudia que humiliter angeli de natiuitate—Ff. 98v–100. Christmas. Type 0.

***A-33.** *Dominica 2ª quadragesime.* Hec est voluntas Dei, sanctificacio vestra, Ad Thessalonicenses 4° [1 Thess. 4:3]. Reuerendi mei, Sicud dicit beatus Gregorius in Registro—Ff. 100-100A, v. 2 Lent. Type C.

A-34. Penitenciam agite, Matthei 3 et pro themate hodierno [Matt. 3:2]. Karissimi, Quia per totum hoc sacrum tempus quadragesimale est dedicatum hominibus ad agendam penitenciam—Ff. 101-105v. Lent. Type 0.

A-35. Quare rubrum est indumentum tuum, Ysay et capitulo [Isa. 63:2]. Secundum sentenciam doctorum hec fuit questio angelorum in die ascensionis Domini—Ff. 106-1104bis, verso (i.e., canceled 114v);

incomplete. Also S-19; Z-20; and Cambridge, University Library MS Ee.6.27, ff. 73–84v. Type B2. See further under Z-20.

A-36. Miserere mei, Domine, Matthei 15 et in ewangelio presentis dominice [Matt. 15:22]. Karissimi, Sicud testatur sacra scriptura 2° Regum 12, cum rex Dauid suggestionem [!] diaboli fedasset—Ff. 1105 (i.e., canceled 115)–108. 2 Lent. Also H-2. Type A.

A-37. Cum ieiunasset quadraginta diebus et quadraginta noctibus, postea esuriit, Matthei 4° [Matt. 4:2]. Pulcrior modus et nobilior docendi est quod magister prius faciat documentum—Ff. 108–109. Type 0.

A-38. Cum ieiunas, vnge capud tuum et faciem tuam laua [Matt. 6:17]. Dignitas ieiunii multipliciter commendatur: a loco—Ff. 110–CXIv. Type 0.

A-39. Ipse vulneratus est propter iniquitates nostras et eius liuore sanati sumus, Ysaie 53 [Isa. 53:5]. Crist ys wounded for oure wikkednesse and we buþ ful heled of oure siknesse. Tractaturi de passione Domini secundum quod modo solempnizat Ecclesia—Ff. CXIv–CXVII bis. [Passion.] Type A.

A-40. Probet seipsum homo et sic de pane illo edat, prima ad Corinthios xi° [1 Cor. 11:28]. Applicando materiam collacionis ad circumstancias huius festi, notandum, karissimi, quod quisquis reficere debet amicum—Ff. CXVII bis–CXXI. [Corpus Christi?] Type B1.

A-41. *Dominica prima quadragesime.* Quid hic statis, Matthei 20 capitulo [Matt. 20:6]. In principio huius collacionis recomendatis omnibus . . . Reuerendi, secundum mortem [!] laudabilem Ecclesie diucius approbatam solet filius post decessum patris—Ff. CXXVI–CXXVIIv. [Septuagesima?] Type 0.

A-42. Videte, vigilate et orate, Marci 13 [Mark 13:33]. Summus sacerdos noster Iesus Christus, qui de celis descendit vt seipsum hostiam viuam Deo Patri—Ff. CXXVIIv–CXXXIv. [To parish priests.] Type 0.

A-43. *Dominica in passione Domini.* Qaure [!] non creditis, Iohannis 8 et in euangelio hodierno [John 8:46]. Reuerendi mei, Inuenio scriptum Exodi 4 quod cum Pharao rex Egipciorum fuisset rebellis voluntati diuine—Ff. CXXXIv–CXXXIIIv. Passion Sunday. Type B1.

A-44. Declina a malo et fac bonum, Psalmo 36 [Ps. 36:27]. Gracia omnipotentis . . . Reuerendi domini, Sicut nos dococet [!] experiencia, siquis habens dominum—Ff. CXXXIV–CXXXVI. Type B1.

A-45. *Sermo in natiuitate Domini.* A, a, a, Ieremie primo [Jer. 1:6]. Pro introduccione notandum quod propter tres proprietates que inveniuntur in Christo et eciam in hac littera a conuenienter potest a assumi pro themate—Ff. CXXXVI–CXXXVII. Christmas. Type B2.

A-46. *Sermo de ascensione Domini.* Sedet a dextris Dei, Marci vltimo [Mark 16:19]. Dicitur communiter quod boni rumores letificant corda, etc. Set optimos—Ff. CXXXVII–138. Ascension. Type B2.

A-47. *Dominica prima quadragesime.* Ecce nunc dies salutis, 2 Corinthiorum 6 et epistula hodierna [2 Cor. 6:2]. Istud verbum vobis veraciter prolatum supponit quod perdidistis optimum diligibile, scilicet salutem, et inuenistis maximum odibile, scilicet infirmitatem—Ff. 138–140. 1 Lent. Also W-163. Type B1.

A-48. Redde racionem villicacionis tue, Luce 16 et in ewangelio hodierno [Luke 16:2]. Noueritis, karissimi mei, quod Christus autor veritatis et doctor in libro suo de euangelio Matthei 20 assimulans regnum celorum patrifamilias—Ff. 140–144, incomplete. 9 after Trinity. By Thomas Wimbledon. For other copies in Latin and English, see Owen 1966, 176 n. 3; and Knight 1967, 3–20. Also H-5 and Oxford Trinity College MS 42, ff. 47–56. Type 0.

A-49. *Dominica 23 post festum sancte Trinitatis.* Viam Dei in veritate doces, Matthei 22 et in euangelio presentis dominice [Matt. 22:16]. In principio . . . Reuerendi domini, Refert euangelium hodiernum quod Pharisei consilium inierunt—Ff. 144v–147v. 23 after Trinity. Type C marginal.

A-50. Quomodo stabit regnum, Luce 11 et in euangelio presentis dominice [Luke 11:18]. In principio . . . Karissimi, Sicut dicit Sapiens Ecclesiastici 10, regna perduntur—Ff. 147v–150v. 3 Lent. Type B1. Sympathetic to Lollards. Perhaps preached at the time of Pope Boniface IX (1389–1404).

A-51. [Loquimini veritatem] [Eph. 4:25; *thema not given at the beginning*]. Sciendum est quod cum Moyses duceret populum—F. 154r–v, incomplete. Type 0.

A-52. Clama ne cesses, exalta vocem tuam quase tuba [Isa. 58:1]. Hic precipit Dominus clamare et non cessare—F. 154v. Only 8 lines, marked "antethema," but referred to in tabula. Type 0.

A-53. Beati qui audiunt verbum Dei [Luke 11:28]. Tria sunt qui a multis maxime desiderantur—F. 155. Marked "antethema," but referred to in tabula. Type 0.

A-54. Ductus est Iesus in desertum a spiritu vt temptaretur a diabolo, Matthei 4 et in euangelio dominice instantis [Matt. 4:1]. Gracia . . .

Reuerendi mei, In exordio nostre collacionis . . . Reuerendi, Verba . . . Karissimi, Testante beato Gregorio omnis Christi accio—Ff. 157v–159. 1 Lent. Type A.

A-55. *Sermo in natali Domini.* Vnus est et secundum non habet, Ecclesiastes 4 [Eccles. 4:8]. þer is on and swsch anothur was neuer non. Reuerendi mei, Fuit vnum genus hominum qui voluit libenter audire— Ff. 159v–161. Christmas. Type C marginal.

A-56. Venite, benedicti Patris mei, Matthei 25 et introitu misse hodierne [Matt. 25:34, introit for Easter Wednesday]. Reuerendi domini, Nouerunt iuris periti, homo qui habet magnam causam—Ff. 161–164. Easter Wednesday. Type B2.

A-57. Letare, Galatarum 4 et in epistula hodierne [corrected from hodierna; Gal. 4:27]. Quantus est dolor et tristicia cum quis a suo solo exulat naturali—Ff. 164–166v. 4 Lent and the feast of St Gregory (i.e., 1374, 1385, 1396, or 1458). Also Brinton sermon 36. Type A.

A-58. Comedite, Matthei 26 [Matt. 26:26]. Auicenna primo canone docet quod iter agens debet precipue esse sollicitus de nutrimento, et statim ostendens quale debet esse nutrimentum dicit—Ff. 167–169. Type 0.

B

Cambridge, University Library, MS Kk.4.24

Parchment. 304 leaves, the last pastedown. Dimensions: ca. 275 × 196, written space 218/225 × 138/142. Collation: 38 quires of 8. Three medieval foliations: (a) upper right of rectos, 1–115 (modern 1–114, the skip occurs between modern 41 and 44), erased; (b) upper right of rectos, 116–296 (modern 121–301), in the hand of the rubricator and perhaps main scribe—this foliation is used in the indices; (c) upper left of versos, 1–303 (modern 1–301, skipping two numbers at modern 43), seemingly by a later hand. See discussion in chapter 3. Medieval quire signatures partially visible: Arabic 1 through 7, occasionally Roman i through iiii (?). Written in two columns of 46 lines (except modern ff. 303–304), in one Anglicana hand of s. xv¹. Colored initials: alternating blue and red in part 1, blue in part 2 through B-143. Secundo folio: *et expectauit vt ferret.*

The volume contains two sets of sermons.

Set 1: *Exortationes fratris Johannis de Bromiard de ordine fratrum predicatorum* (1ra, with flourished initial; similar explicit, 114va), ff. 1–114va. Seventy-six numbered sermons *de tempore* and *de sanctis,* in the order of the church year. Followed by three indices: (1) ff. 114va–115ra, "Tabula thematum Exhortationum sequentium [!]," a list of the feasts and themata of the preceding *Exhortationes;* (2) ff. 115ra–120va, "Tabula realis sermonum precedentium," a table of subjects in alphabetical order, from *Ab infantia* to *Christianus*; (3) f. 120v, in three cols., "Tabula vocabulorum," from *Armatura* to *Christus,* in the order of first letter and second vowel.

Set 2: ninety-two sermons *de tempore, de sanctis,* and for some special occasions, in irregular order, ff. 121r–301v. Followed (ff. 302rb–303v) by a late fifteenth-century "Tabula sermonum operis precedentis," an index of sermon themes for both sets, in the order of the church year (1 Advent to All Souls), referring to the third medieval foliation. Many sermons of set 2 are incomplete, with the scribe leaving blank spaces but no *signes de renvoi.*

About twenty place names from Bedfordshire and Buckinghamshire appear in at least twenty-three places in the top margins, throughout the manuscript; see discussion in chapter 3.

On f. 303v is an indulgence granted by bishop John [Carpenter] of Worcester, given at his manor of Northwyke and dated 6 June 1464.

In the following list, the sermons of both sets are numbered consecutively, and the occasions indicated before the thema are as they appear marginally at the beginning of the sermons (i.e., not as written in the upper right of the rectos).

B-001. *Dominica prima aduentus Domini.* Induimini Dominum Iesum Christum, Romanorum 13, et legitur in epistula [Rom. 13:14]. Induimini inquit Dominum Iesum Christum, hoc est habitu gracie—Ff. 1ra–2va. 1 Advent. Type A.

B-002. *Dominica 2ª.* Honorificetis Deum, Romanorum 15.a, et in epistula [Rom. 15:6]. Tribus modis quilibet seruiens tenetur honorare dominum suum—Ff. 2va–4rb. 2 Advent. Type 0.

B-003. *Dominica 3.* Illuminabit abscondita tenebrarum et manifestabit abscondita, 1 Corinthiorum 4 [1 Cor. 4:5]. Primo peccator ad hoc quod Deum in natalicio digne recipiat—Ff. 4ra–5vb. 3 Advent. Type 0.

B-004. *Dominica 4.* Dominus prope est, Philippensium 4.b, et in epistula [Phil. 4:5]. Dominus inquit prope est, ergo peccantes penitenciam fortiter agant—Ff. 5vb–7ra. 4 Advent. Type 0.

B-005. *In nativitate Christi.* Dat omnibus affluenter, Iacobi 1 [James

1:5]. Quia isto die filius datus est nobis, Ysaie 9. Primo ista die dat omnibus affluenter—Ff. 7ra–8vb. Christmas. Type A.

B-006. *Item in natiuitate Christi.* Venit Deus, \Exodi 20/ 1 Regum 4 [Exod. 20:20 and 1 Sam. 4:7]. Cum larga distributione graciarum, cum magna curacione animarum—Ff. 8vb–10ra. Christmas. Type 0.

B-007. *Item in natiuitate Christi.* Venit lumen tuum, Ysaie 40 [Isa. 60:1]. Spiritualium tenebrarum expulsiuum, animarum infirmarum sanatiuum—Ff. 10ra–11va. Christmas. Type 0.

B-008. *In die sancti Stephani.* Leuaui oculos meos, in Psalmo [Ps. 120:1]. Stephanus in tormentis Iudeorum sic eleuat oculos—Ff. 11va–12va. St. Stephen. Type 0.

B-009. *In die sancti Iohannis.* Hic est discipulus ille, Iohannis vltimo [John 21:24]. Primo hic est discipulus ille quem Christus ceteris altius illuminabat—Ff. 12va–13va. St. John Evangelist. Type 0.

B-010. *In die sanctorum Innocentium.* Ipsorum est regnum, Matthei 5 [Matt. 5:3]. Et hoc quadruplici racione, per rationem videlicet mundicie et castitatis—Ff. 13va–14rb. Holy Innocents. Type 0.

B-011. *Sancti Thome.* Hic homo iustus erat, Luce 24 [Luke 23:47]. Quia reddebat que sunt Cesaris Cesari, que sunt Dei Deo—Ff. 14rb–15va. St. Thomas of Canterbury. Type 0.

B-012. *Sancti Siluestri.* Iusticias dilexit, in Psalmo [Ps. 10:8]. Et hoc ostendit tripliciter: primo mandatis Dei humiliter obediendo [MS: homini amicabiliter subveniendo]—Ff. 15va–17ra. St. Sylvester. Type 0.

B-013. *Dominica infra octauam natalis.* Si filius et heres, Galatarum 4, et in epistula [Gal. 4:7]. Triplicem legimus hereditatem: bonorum appetendam—Ff. 17ra–18rb. Sunday in the Octave of Christmas. Type 0.

B-014. *In circumcisione Domini.* Plenitudo legis est, Romanorum 13 [Rom. 13:10]. Querenti quid sit finis circumcisionis vel purificationis—Ff. 18rb–20ra. Circumcision. Type A.

B-015. *Dominica infra octauam circumcisionis.* Venit in terram, Matthei 2 [Matt. 2:21]. Christus venit in terram vt nos inuitaret et vt nos desponsaret—Ff. 20ra–21rb. Sunday in the Octave of Circumcision. Type 0.

B-016. *In epiphania.* Adorabunt eum omnes reges, in Psalmo [Ps. 71:11]. Non solum isti qui hodie optulerunt ei aurum, thus et mirram—Ff. 21rb–22rb. Epiphany. Type 0.

B-017. *Dominica infra octauam epiphanie.* Querebamus te, Luce 2, et in euangelio [Luke 2:48]. Beati qui in morte poterent Christo dicere veraciter, Domine Iesu—Ff. 22rb–23vb. Sunday in the Octave of Epiphany. Type 0.

B-018. *Dominica prima post octauam epiphanie.* Spe gaudentes, Romanorum 12, et in epistula [Rom. 12:12]. Vult enim Apostolus quod simus illa spe gaudentes que habet quatuor conditiones—Ff. 23vb–24vb. 1 after Octave of Epiphany. Type 0.

B-019. Mundare, Matthei 8, et in euangelio [Matt. 8:3]. Quod tunc dixit Christus leproso ab eo sanato, dicit nunc cuilibet Christiano—Ff. 25ra–26ra. [2 after Octave of Epiphany.] Type 0.

B-020. *Dominica 3ª post octauam epiphanie.* Domine, salua nos, Matthei 8, et in euangelio [Matt. 8:25]. Tu Domine salua nos qui saluas largiter bene operantes—Ff. 26ra–27rb. 3 after Octave of Epiphany. Type 0.

B-021. *Dominica 4ª post octauam epiphanie.* Induite vos sicut electi Dei, Colossensium 3, et in epistula [Col. 3:12]. Induite inquit vos indumento purgatiuo, ornatiuo, defensiuo, et pugnatiuo—Ff. 27rb–28rb. 4 after Octave of Epiphany. Type 0.

B-022. *Dominica 5 post octauam epiphanie* [f. 28rb]. Pax Christi exultet in cordibus vestris, Colossensium 3, et in epistula [Col. 3:15]. Sic inquam sit in cordibus vestris quod habeatis pacem cum Christo—Ff. 28va–29ra. 5 after Octave of Epiphany. Type 0.

B-023. *Dominica in septuagesima.* Quid hic statis, Matthei 20.b, et in euangelio [Matt. 20:6]. Questioni huic respondebo quod hic statis vel saltem de iure stare deberetis—Ff. 29ra–31rb. Septuagesima. Type 0.

B-024. *Dominica in sexagesima.* Hec dicens clamabat, Luce 8.b, et in euangelio [Luke 8:8]. Clamatur triplici de causa. Nam clamat diligens ad errantem ut redeat—Ff. 31rb–32va. Sexagesima. Type 0.

B-025. *Dominica in quinquagesima.* Vidit et sequebatur, Luce 18 in fine, et in euangelio [Luke 18:43]. Istud verbum in Deo ostendit miraculi operationem propter quod ille—Ff. 32va–34rb. Quinquagesima. Type 0.

B-026. *In die cinerum.* Penitentiam agite, Matthei 4.a [Matt. 4:17]. Tria ostendam: quare est penitendum, quando est penitendum, et quomodo est penitendum—Ff. 34rb–35rb. Ash Wednesday. Type 0.

B-027. *Dominica 1ª quadragesime.* Non in solo pane viuit homo, Matthei 4.b, et in euangelio [Matt. 4:4]. Idest non in vno genere set in triplici genere panis—Ff. 35rb–37rb. 1 Lent. Type 0.

B-028. *Dominica 2ª quadragesime.* Sanata est, Matthei 15.f, et in euangelio [Matt. 15:28]. Istud euangelium de muliere Cananea congrue legitur isto tempore—Ff. 37rb–38vb. 2 Lent. Type 0.

B-029. *Dominica 3ª quadragesime.* Cum eiecisset demonium, locutus est, Luce 11.c, et in euangelio [Luke 11:14]. Legimus de triplici eiectione et de triplici locutione—Ff. 38vb–40rb. 3 Lent. Type 0.

B-030. *Dominica 4ª quadragesime.* Seruit cum filiis suis, Galatarum 4.f, et in epistula [Gal. 4:25]. Quilibet Christianus seruit Deo vel de iure seruire deberet—Ff. 40rb–41vb. 4 Lent. Type 0.

B-031. *Dominica in passione.* Abscondita est fortitudo eius, Abacuc 3.b [Hab. 3:4]. In aliis dominicis diebus precedentibus legimus de alico miraculo Dei—Ff. 41vb–43rb. Type 0.

B-032. *Dominica in ramis palmarum.* Benedictus qui venit, Iohannis 22.b, et legitur isto die [John 12:13]. Deus benedicit hominem et homo benedicit Deum—Ff. 43rb–44vb. Palm Sunday. Type 0.

B-033. *In die cene.* Gaudium est in celo super vno peccatore penitentiam < agente >, Luce 15.c [Luke 15:7]. Qui in expulsione penitentium de ecclesia in die cinerum dictum fuit eis—Ff. 44vb–45vb. Maundy Thursday. Type 0.

B-034. *In die parasceues.* Exiit Iesus portans spineam coronam, Iohannis 19.a [John 19:5]. Legimus de exitu Dei et de exitu hominis—Ff. 45va–47va. Good Friday. Type 0.

B-035. *In die pache in missa.* Conuocat amicos, Luce 5 [Luke 15:6]. Sicut homines mundiales facientes festa sua mundialia—Ff. 47vb–49ra. Easter. Type 0.

B-036. *In die pasce post prandium, etc.* Quomodo Christus surrexit a mortuis et infra ita nos, Romanorum 6 [Rom. 6:4]. Aduertite quadruplicem resurectionem—Ff. 49ra–51va. Easter. Type 0.

B-037. *In crastino pasche.* Cognouerunt eum, Luce 24.c, et legitur in euangelio [Luke 24:31]. Triplex cognitio est cuilibet Christiano necessaria, Dei, sui, et proximi—Ff. 51va–52vb. Easter Monday. Type 0.

B-038. *Dominica prima in octaua pasche.* Hoc est testimonium, Iohannis 5, et legitur in epistula [1 John 5:11]. Legimus de triplici testimonio. Primum habuit Christus in preterito—Ff. 52vb–54ra. Octave of Easter. Type A.

B-039. *Dominica 1 post octauam pasche.* Christus passus est pro nobis, 1 Petri 2.f, et legitur in epistula [1 Pet. 2:21]. Christus ergo passus est pro nobis propter quatuor raciones—Ff. 54ra–55va. 1 after Octave of Easter. Type A.

B-040. *Dominica 2ª.* Sic est voluntas Dei, 1 Petri 2.d, et epistula [1 Pet. 2:15]. Vt pacem cum Deo constanter custodiatis, illa namque pax bona est—Ff. 55va–56rb. 2 after Octave of Easter. Type 0.

B-041. *Dominica 3ª.* Ille arguet mundum, Iohannis 16, et in euangelio [John 16:8]. Christus dicit in euangelio quod Spiritus Sanctus arguet mundum de triplici culpa—Ff. 56rb-57vb. 3 after Octave of Easter. Type 0.

B-042. *Dominica quarta.* Estote factores verbi, Iacobi 1, et in epistula [James 1:22]. Primo estote factores verbi Dei omnipotentis—Ff. 57vb-59ra. 4 after Octave of Easter. Type 0.

B-043. *In rogationibus.* Qui petit accipit, Luce 2, et in euangelio [Luke 11:10]. Qui petit, inquit, accipit si habeat tria per que meretur petitio sua exaudiri—Ff. 59ra-60rb. Monday of Rogation Days. Type 0.

B-044. *In ascensione.* Abiit in domum suam, Matthei 9 [Matt. 9:7]. Super quo est aduertendum quod Deus facit quadruplicem domum—Ff. 60rb-61vb. Ascension. Type A.

B-045. *Dominica infra octauam ascensionis.* Estote prudentes, 1 Petri 4.c, et in epistula [1 Pet. 4:7]. Sicut in hoc mundo dicitur esse prudens mundanus homo qui scit multa bona adquirere—Ff. 61vb-62vb. Sunday in Octave of Ascension. Type 0.

B-046. *In pentecoste.* Accipiebant Spiritum Sanctum, Actuum 8 [Acts 8:17]. Illi sancti apostoli accipiebant, et vos per Dei graciam accepistis—Ff. 62vb-64va. Pentecost. Type 0.

B-047. *De Trinitate.* Omnia operatur Deus tribus, Iob 33 [Job 33:29]. Hec est Patris potentia, Filii sapientia, et Spiritus Sancti misericordia et clementia—Ff. 64va-66rb. Trinity. Type A.

B-048. *In festo Corporis Christi.* Extendit manum suam, in Psalmo [Ps. 54:21]. Quotiens audistis missam vel itis ad communicandum in bona vita vel digne—Ff. 66rb-68va. Corpus Christi. Type 0.

B-049. *Dominica 1ª post Trinitatem.* Fili, recordare, Luce 16, et legitur in euangelio [Luke 16:25]. Fili, inquam, recordare trium: primo tue nature miserrime ne superbias—Ff. 68va-70va. 1 after Trinity. Type 0.

B-050. *Dominica 2ª.* Vocati sunt, Luce 14, et in euangelio [Luke 14:24]. Ex quo omnes vocati sunt a Deo ad gloriam celestem—Ff. 70va-72va. 2 after Trinity. Type 0.

B-051. *Dominica 3ª.* Peccatores recipit, Luce 15, et in euangelio [Luke 15:2]. Nota circa peccatorem tria recipiuntur consideratione digna—Ff. 72va-74va. 3 after Trinity. Type 0.

B-052. *Dominica 4ª.* Reuelationem filiorum Dei expectat, Romanorum 8.d, et in epistula [Rom. 8:19]. Oportet quod quilibet Christianus expectet Deum ad corporis et anime refectionem—Ff. 74vb-76va. 4 after Trinity. Type 0.

B-053. *Dominica 5*[a]. Vocati estis, 1 Petri 3.d, et in epistula [1 Pet. 3:9]. Vocati estis ad tria: primo ut peccatum deseratis—Ff. 76va–78rb. 5 after Trinity. Type 0.

B-054. *Dominica 6*[a]. Mortuus est peccato, Romanorum 6, et in epistula [Rom. 6:7]. Est mortuus peccato quilibet bonus Christianus, quia sicut mortuus mundo—Ff. 78va–80rb. 6 after Trinity. Type 0.

B-055. *Dominica 7*[a]. Misereor super turbam, Marci 8, et in euangelio [Mark 8:2]. Legimus de triplici misericordia, Dei ad hominem et hominis ad seipsum—Ff. 80rb–81va. 7 after Trinity. Type A.

B-056. *Dominica 8*[a]. Si filii et heredes, Romanorum 8, et in epistula [Rom. 8:17]. Ex quo sic est quod filii Dei sunt heredes celi, multum deberet quilibet—Ff. 81va–83rb. 8 after Trinity. Type 0.

B-057. *Dominica 9*[a]. Diffamatus est quasi dissipasset bona illius, Luce 16, et in euangelio [Luke 16:1]. Deus qui Sapientie 7 omnium bonorum mater est fecit quatuor bona—Ff. 83rb–85va. 9 after Trinity. Type 0.

B-058. *Dominica 10*[a]. Erat quotidie docens, Luce 19, et in euangelio [Luke 19:47]. Christus docuit et docet omnem Christianum tria pertinentia ad Deum—Ff. 85va–86vb. 10 after Trinity. Type 0.

B-059. *Dominica XI*[a]. Descendit hic iustificatus, Luce 18, et in euangelio [Luke 18:14]. Legimus de triplici descensu: Dei, hominis, et demonis—Ff. 86vb–88va. 11 after Trinity. Type A.

B-060. *Dominica 12*[a]. Fiduciam talem habemus ad Deum, Corinthiorum 3, et in epistula [2 Cor. 3:4]. Talem fiduciam et talem intentionem habemus quod qui ponit totam fiduciam—Ff. 88va–90ra. 12 after Trinity. Type 0.

B-061. *Dominica 13*. Beati oculi qui vident, Luce 10, et in euangelio [Luke 10:23]. Beati oculi qui vident tria, scilicet agenda, timenda, et speranda—Ff. 90ra–91va. 13 after Trinity. Type 0.

B-062. *Dominica 14*[a]. Iesu preceptor, miserere nostri, Luce 17.c, et in euangelio [Luke 17:13]. Circa istum gloriosum preceptorem poteritis tria videre—Ff. 91va–93va. 14 after Trinity. Type 0.

B-063. *Dominica 15*. Primum querite regnum Dei, Matthei 6, et in euangelio [Matt. 6:33]. In istis verbis Christus docet totum processum vite nostre—Ff. 93va–95ra. 15 after Trinity. Type 0.

B-064. *Dominica 16*. Defunctus efferebatur filius, Luce 17, et in euangelio [Luke 17:12]. In tribus vocabulis tria se offerunt intuenti: peccantis conditio—Ff. 95ra–96va. 16 after Trinity. Type 0.

B-065. *Dominica 17*[a]. Recumbe in nouissimo, Luce 14, et in euangelio

[Luke 14:10]. Tria sunt que habent diuersum nouissimum finem: culpa, natura, et gratia—Ff. 96va-98ra. 17 after Trinity. Type 0.

B-066. *Dominica 18.* Diliges, Matthei 22, et in euangelio [Matt. 22:37]. Diliges Deum integraliter, diliges eciam teipsum rationabiliter, diliges proximum generaliter—Ff. 98ra-99rb. 18 after Trinity. Type 0.

B-067. *Dominica 19*[a]. Remittuntur tibi peccata, Matthei 9, et in euangelio [Matt. 9:2]. Ad hoc quod peccata peccatori remittantur ad suam saluationem tria requiruntur—Ff. 99rb-100vb. 19 after Trinity. Type 0.

B-068. *Dominica 20*[a]. Congregauerunt omnes, Matthei 22.b, et in euangelio [Matt. 22:10]. Deus congregat omnes obedientes, homo omnes iuuantes, diabolus omnes peccantes—Ff. 100vb-102rb. 20 after Trinity. Type 0.

B-069. *Dominica 21.* Accipite armaturam, Ephesiorum vltimo e, et in epistula [Eph. 6:13]. Quidam accipiunt armaturam contra iustum malitiose—Ff. 102va-103vb. 21 after Trinity. Type 0.

B-070. *Dominica 22.* Patientiam habe, Matthei 18.f, et in euangelio [Matt. 18:26]. Deus patitur et humiliter et frequenter dura pati permittit tria genera hominum—Ff. 103vb-105va. 22 after Trinity. Type 0.

B-071. *Dominica 23*[a]. Reddite, Matthei 22, et in euangelio [Matt. 22:21]. Reddite, inquam, tria: de promissis solutionem, de acceptis rationem, de offensis satisfactionem—Ff. 105va-107rb. 23 after Trinity. Type 0.

B-072. *Dominica 24*[a]. Deo per omnia placentes, Colossensium 1, et in epistula [Col. 1:10]. Ad hoc quod Deo per omnia placeamus oportet quod habeamus tria—Ff. 107rb-108vb. 24 after Trinity. Type 0.

B-073. *Dominica 25.* Sapiens erit, Ieremie 23, et in epistula [Jer. 23:5]. Hoc namque de Christo dicitur, qui sapientiam suam ostendit in tribus—Ff. 108vb-109vb. 25 after Trinity. Type 0.

B-074. *In dedicatio[ne] ecclesie.* Factum est conuiuium magnum in domo, Thobie 2 [Tob. 2:1; cf. Tob. 7:9, etc.]. In domo ecclesie factum est illo die conuiuium magnum indulgentie—Ff. 109vb-111ra. Dedication of church. Type 0.

B-075. *In omni festo beate Marie.* Fecit mihi magna, Luce 1 [Luke 1:49]. Istud verbum est verbum Virginis gloriose regratiantis Deo de magnis beneficiis—Ff. 111ra-112vb. Blessed Virgin. Type 0.

B-076. *De omni sancto vel sancta.* Elegit eum, Ecclesiastici 4 [Ecclus. 45:4]; Elegit eam, in Psalmo [Ps. ?]. Plurimorum sanctorum: Elegit viros sanctissimos, Paralipomenon 19 [1 Chron. 19:10]; vel: Eos elegit

Deus, Paralipomenon 29 [2 Chron. 29:11]. De vtroque simul: in Psalmo: Viam veritatis elegi [Ps. 118:30]. Triplex est electio, diuina, humana, et prophana—Ff. 112vb–114va. Any saint. Type 0.

B-077. Mulier sapiens edificat sibi domum, mulier insipiens destruit constructam [Prov. 14:1]. Multe benedictiones fiunt in dedicatione ecclesie—F. 121ra–va. [Dedication of church.] Type 0.

B-078. *Item de dedicatione ecclesie.* Sanctificaui domum hanc, 2 Regum 9 [1 Kings 9:3]. Karissimi, Decens est et conueniens regie magestati vt non solum habeat aulam—Ff. 121va–123rb. Dedication of church. Type 0.

B-079. *De eodem.* Sanctifica te, Actuum 21 [Acts 21:24]; vel sic: Hec est voluntas Dei, sanctificatio vestra, Ad Thessalonicenses 4 [1 Thess. 4:3]; vel sic: Sanctificaui domum hanc, 3 Regum 9 [1 Kings 9:3]. Karissimi, Quatuor genera domorum inuenio in sacra scriptura que dedicantur—Ff. 123rb–125vb, incomplete? Dedication of church. Type C marginal.

B-080. *Ad clerum.* Custodite sacerdocium vestrum, Numeri 18 [Num. 18:7]. Domini reuerendi mei, Res in se nobilis ac preciosa aliis vtilis et fructuosa—Ff. 125vb–127rb. To the clergy. Type 0.

B-081. *In visitatione.* Glorificent Deum in die visitationis, 1 Petri 2 [1 Pet. 2:12]. Reuerendi patres et domini, In principio nostre breuissime collationis . . . Hec verba tam ad visitantes quam ad visitatos—Ff. 127rv–128va. Visitation. Type 0.

B-082. *Dominica in passione Domini.* Qui ex Deo est, verba Dei audit, Iohannis 8, et in euangelio hodierno [John 8:47]. Reuerendi domini et amici, Tria videntur michi esse necessaria cuilibet—Ff. 128va–129vb. Passion Sunday. Type 0.

B-083. *Dominica in passione vel in ramis palmarum.* Apertus est liber, Apocalipsis 5 [Rev. 20:12]. Est liber vnus de quo fit mensio in sacra scriptura quem vidit Iohannes—Ff. 129vb–134vb. Passion Sunday or Palm Sunday. Type A.

B-084. *De eodem.* Ortum est bellum satis durum, 2 Regum 3 [2 Sam. 2:17]. Karissimi, Inuenio in sacra scriptura Exodi 17 semel populum Israeliticum—Ff. 134vb–138rb, incomplete. Passion Sunday or Palm Sunday. Type B2.

B-085. *Item dominica in passione.* Veritatem dico, Iohannis 8 [John 8:45]. In sacra scriptura plura inueniuntur exempla quomodo sancte et iuste viuentes—Ff. 138va–139ra. Passion Sunday. Type 0.

B-086. *De eodem vel in die parasceues.* Secundum legem debet mori,

Iohannis 19 [John 19:7]. Karissimi, Scribitur Ad Galatas propter transgressores lex posita est—Ff. 139ra–142vb. Passion Sunday or Good Friday. Type 0.

B-087. *De eodem.* A, a, a dicite quia prope est dies Domini, Joelis 1.e [Joel 1:15]. Si quis mirabilia audiret vel videret qualia nunquam audierat—Ff. 142vb–143vb. Passion Sunday or Good Friday. Type 0.

*B-088. *In passione vel in parasceue.* Amore langueo, Canticorum 2 [Song of Sol. 2:5]. Prolatiue potest dici sic: Karissimi, Sicut manifeste videtis—Ff. 143vb–150ra. Passion Sunday or Good Friday. Also S-07, T-07, D-2. Type C. Edited in appendix B.

B-089. *Ad clerum.* Uidete, Luce 21 [Luke 21:8?]. Ista congeries literarum "videte" potest esse vna dictio—Ff. 150ra–153va. To the clergy. Type 0.

B-090. Elegit eam in habitationem sibi, Psalmo 131 [Ps. 131:13]. In his mundanis principum et dominorum dominiis video quod secundum cursus—Ff. 153va–155rb. Type A.

B-091. Hoc est corpus meum, Corinthiorum 2 [1 Cor. 11:24]. Teste Seneca in suis prouerbiis quietissime viuerent homines—Ff. 155rb–157va. [Corpus Christi.] Type 0.

B-092. *In die natalis Domini.* Natus est vobis hodie Saluator, Luce 2 [Luke 2:11]. Karissimi, Domini terreni in die natali sui solent esse gratiosi—Ff. 157va–159ra. Christmas. Type 0.

B-093. *In die sancti Stephani.* Stephanus plenus gratia, Actuum 6 [Acts 6:8]. Auxilium et gratia Dei omnipotentis per gloriosam intercessionem . . . Ista verba pro themate sumpta—Ff. 159ra–160ra. St. Stephen. Type 0.

B-094. *In die sancti Iohannis.* Diligebat Iesus sequentem, Iohannis ultimo [John 21:20]. Reuerendi patres et domini, Saluator noster nos instruere desiderans—Ff. 160ra–161rb. St. John Evangelist. Type 0.

B-095. *De sancto Thoma Cant'.* Hic perfectus est vir, Iacobi 3 [James 3:2]. Reuerendi domini et amici, Si loquamur de isto nomine Thomas, videtur totaliter—Ff. 161rb–162rb. St. Thomas of Canterbury. Type 0.

B-096. *In die circumcisionis Domini.* Nomen eius Iesus, Luce 2 [Luke 2:21]. Karissimi, Secundum Ysodorum Ethimologiarum 1, quod recte nominatum est sortitur nomen—Ff. 162rb–163vb. Circumcision. Type 0.

B-097. *In die epiphanie.* Venimus adorare eum, Matthei 3 [Matt. 2:2]. Karissimi mei, Hec fuerunt verba regum qui adorauerunt Filium Dei—Ff. 163vb–165rb. Epiphany. Type 0.

B-098. *Dominica 1ª aduentus Domini.* Exulta, filia Syon, iubila, filia

Hierusalem; ecce rex tuus venit iustus et saluator et pauper et ascendens super asinam et pullum asine, Zacharie 9.b [Zech. 9:9]. Voluntas terreni regis in diuersis ciuitatibus scitur per suas literas—Ff. 165va–166va. 1 Advent. Type 0.

B-099. *Dominica 2ᵃ aduentus Domini.* Christus suscepit uos in honorem, Ad Romanos 15.b [Rom. 15:7]. Vbi tria notantur: redemptoris benignitas in confortando, Christus—Ff. 166va–168rb. 2 Advent. Type A.

B-100. *Dominica 3 aduentus Domini.* Tu quis es? [Matt. 11:3?]. Puer tener et iuuenis sub matris custodia delicate nutritus—Ff. 168rb–171rb. 3 Advent. Type 0.

B-101. *In festo sancte Trinitatis.* In tribus complacitum est spiritui meo, Ecclesiastici 25 [Ecclus. 25:1]. Sapientissimus Salomon Prouerbiorum 30 capitulo ait: "Tria michi deficilia"—Ff. 171rb–172vb. Trinity. Type B1.

B-102. *In festo corporis Christi.* Hic est panis, Iob [!] 6 [John 6:50]. Karissimi, Legitur in libro Regum quod Ioab qui princeps exercitus Dauid fuit—Ff. 172vb–175ra. Corpus Christi. Type B2.

B-103. *Dominica pro estate.* Quid faciendo vitam eternam possidebo? Luce x [Luke 10:25]. In quanto quis appetit aliquam rem quam non habet, diligentius inquirit—Ff. 175ra–176ra. Type 0.

B-104. *In natiuitate beate Marie.* In me spes vite, Ecclesiastici 24 [Ecclus. 24:25]. Ieronimus de Beata Virgine dicit sic: "Si omnia membra essent lingue"—F. 176ra–vb. Nativity of BVM. Type 0.

B-105. *In assuntione beate Marie.* In plenitudine sanctorum detentio mea, Ecclesiastici 24, et in epistula hodierna [Ecclus. 24:16]. Reuera, summa felicitas est cuilibet illam rem possidere quam summe diligit—Ff. 176vb–177vb. Assumption of BVM. Type 0.

B-106. *In tempore belli.* Adiuua nos, Deus, Paralipomenon 14 [2 Chron. 14:11]. Necessitas et miseria homines compellit vt auxilium inuocent a potente—Ff. 177vb–179ra. In time of war. Type 0.

B-107. *De sancto Iacobo.* Iste est amicus meus, Canticorum 3 [Song of Sol. 5:16]. Karissimi mei, Signum magnum amicicie est quod vnus libenter audiat bona—Ff. 179ra–180va. St. James. Type B2.

B-108. Ecce nunc tempus acceptabile, 2 Corinthiorum 6 [2 Cor. 6:2]. Istud tempus, karissimi, vocatur a clericis ver, hoc est tempus vernale—Ff. 180va–184vb, incomplete. [Lent.] Type C marginal.

B-109. *De ascensione Domini.* Relinquo mundum et vado ad Patrem, Iohannis 16 [John 16:28]. Anglice: Al þys wordyl Y forsake, and to my fader þe wey Y take. Videmus enim in natura—Ff. 185ra–186ra. Ascension. Type A.

B-110. *In ascensione Domini.* Ascendit Deus in iubilo, Psalmo 36 [Ps. 46:6]. Anglice: God ys went into heuene with ioye and blysse and myry steuene. Reuerendi, Pro processu nostri sermonis—F. 186ra–vb. Ascension. Type B2.

B-111. Conuertimini ad Dominum [Hos. 14:3?]. Pro processu debetis scire quod quatuor inconuenientia sive incomoda—Ff. 186vb–189ra, incomplete. Type C marginal.

B-112. *Dominica 15ᵃ.* Dum tempus habemus, operemur bonum, Ad Galatas 6 [Gal. 6:10]. Karissimi, Sicut dicit beatus Augustinus super illud Psalmi: "Incensa et suffossa"—Ff. 189rb–193ra, incomplete. 15 after Trinity. Type C marginal.

*****B-113.** *Feria 2ᵃ pentecostes.* Lux venit in mundum, et dilexerunt homines magis tenebras, Iohannis 3 [John 3:19]. Into þys wordel ys ycome ly3th, but men loueþ more þe derke ny3th. Karissimi, In predicatione verbi Dei si ex verbis predicatoris—Ff. 193ra–196ra. Monday after Pentecost. Type C.

B-114. *In die pasche.* Alleluya, Apocalipsis [Rev. 19:1]. Narrat, karissimi, Giraldus historiagraphus de quodam rege qui Persis regnabat—Ff. 196ra–198vb. Easter. Type B1.

B-115. *In die pasche.* Verus panis dat vitam, Iohannis 6 [John 6:33]. Karissimi, Debetis intelligere quod preter panem materialem duplex inuenitur panis—Ff. 198vb–201ra. Easter. Type B2.

B-116. *In die pasche.* Custos domini sui gloriabitur, Prouerbiorum 27 [Prov. 27:18]. Karissimi, Vt dicit Augustinus *De ciuitate Dei* 13: "Omnes homines cupiunt et desiderant"—Ff. 201ra–203rb. Easter. Type D.

B-117. *Bonus modus et processus introducendi sententiam excommunicationis 4 temporibus anni.* Securis ad radicem posita est, Matthei 3 [Matt. 3:10]. Anglice: þe axe ys set at the rote. Leue syrys, 3e wete3 wel 3at a man—Ff. 203rb–205ra. Ember Days. Type D.

B-118. *Item alius bonus modus introducendi casus generalis sentensie.* Cepit colere terram et plantauit vineam, Genesis ix [Gen. 9:20]. Good men, þese wordys byth þus moche to sey yn englysch . . . 3e wetyþ wel þat a good hosbund—Ff. 205ra–209ra. Ember Days. Type E.

B-119. *In die pasche.* Probet seipsum homo et sic de pane illo edat, 1 Corinthiorum xi [1 Cor. 11:28]. Karissimi, Videmus ad oculum quod si corporalis medicina sumatur—F. 209ra–va. Easter. Type 0.

B-120. *In die pasche.* Custodite sicut scitis, Matthei 27.f [Matt. 27:65].

Quanto res est melior in se et quanto maius damnum prouenit ex eius perditione—Ff. 209va–211rb. Easter. Type 0.

B-121. *In die pasche.* Comedite panem, Prouerbiorum ix [Prov. 9:5]. Homo ex duplici natura componitur, scilicet ex corpore et anima—Ff. 211rb–213rb. Easter. Type 0.

B-122. *In die pasche.* Venias hodie ad conuiuium quod paraui, Hester 5 [Esther 5:4]. Videtis quod quando filius regis magni desponsatur, post desponsationem—F. 213rb–vb. Easter. Type 0.

B-123. *Feria 2 ebdomade pasche.* Mane nobiscum, Domine, quoniam aduesperascit, Luce 24 [Luke 24:29]. Anglice: Wone wyth vs, lord, ful of myȝth . . . Genesis 19 habetur quod Abrahe sedenti—Ff. 213vb–215ra, incomplete. Easter Monday. Type A.

B-124. *In die pasche.* Custodi partem tuam, 2 Machabeorum 1 capitulo f [2 Macc. 1:26]. Scitis, karissimi, quod homo est creatura composita ex duabus partibus—Ff. 215ra–217rb. Easter. Type B1.

B-125. *Dominica 2ª post pascham.* Peccatis mortui iustitie viuamus, 1 Petri 2.d [1 Pet. 2:24]. Si lex condita sit super duobus articulis, oportet obligatos illi legi—Ff. 217rb–218rb. Easter Monday. Type 0.

B-126. *In die epiphanie.* Obtulerunt ei munera, aurum, thus, et mirram, Matthei 2 [Matt. 2:11]. Karissimi, In verbis propositis tanguntur duo, videlicet magorum oblatio—Ff. 218rb–219ra, incomplete. Epiphany. Type 0.

B-127. *Dominica 15ª.* Dum tempus habemus, operemur bonum, Ad Galatas 6 [Gal. 6:10]. Worke we þe goode faste . . . Karissimi, Debetis scire quod tempus diuiditur—Ff. 219vb–223va, incomplete. 15 after Trinity. Type C marginal. Among various portents of the coming judgment, including civil strife, wars, hunger, and pestilence, the preacher mentions a recent earthquake, perhaps referring to 1382: "Non sunt multi anni elapsi a tempore quo erat generalis terre motus per vniuersam Angliam" (f. 221vb).

B-128. *In die cinerum.* Reuertimini et viuite [Ezek. 18:32]. Karissimi, Secundum communem famam nunquam fuerunt homines ita maliciosi—Ff. 223va–226va, incomplete. Ash Wednesday. Type C minimal.

B-129. *Amicus vocatur quadrupliciter.* Vocati estis, 1 Petri 3 [1 Pet. 3:9]. Scitis, karissimi, quod quatuor modis solet quis vocare amicum suum—Ff. 226vb–229va, incomplete. [5 after Trinity?] Type C minimal.

B-130. *Pro mortuis.* Memento finis, Ecclesiastici 17 capitulo [Ecclus. 36:10]. Karissimi, Sicut videtis nunquam fuerunt homines ita dediti mundo, luxurie—Ff. 229vb–232va, incomplete. The dead. Type C marginal.

B-131. *Dominica 1ª quadragesime.* Illi soli seruies, Matthei 4 [Matt. 4:10]. To god and to no mo . . . [written before the thema]. Reuerendi domini, Secundum beatum Gregorium . . . in omni quod cogitamus—Ff. 232vb–234va, incomplete. 1 Lent. Type C marginal.

B-132. *De aduentu Domini.* Ecce venio cito, Apocalipsis 10 [Rev. 3:11 etc.]. Reuerendi mei, Debetis scire quod de quadruplici aduentu Christi—Ff. 234vb–238ra. Advent. Type C marginal.

B-133. *In die pasche.* Tene quod habes, Apocalipsis 3 [Rev. 3:11]. Reuerendi mei, Sicut scribit Discoriades libro 2, capitulo 57, in India inferiori est arbor—Ff. 238ra–240rb. Easter. Also S-04. C marginal.

B-134. *In festo Trinitatis.* In nomine Patris et Filii et Spiritus Sancti, Matthei [Matt. 28:19]. Sancta Trinitas, cuius memoria generaliter per totam ecclesiam hodierna die recolitur—Ff. 240rb–242ra. Trinity. Type A.

B-135. Surge qui dormis, Ad Ephesios 5 [Eph. 5:14]. Karissimi, In tribus periculis solent homines in lecto dormientes euigilare—Ff. 242rb–243vb. Also H-22 and Cambridge Gonville and Caius College MS 334, ff. 181ra–182va. Type 0.

*B-136. Que est ista que progreditur sicut aurora consurgens, pulcra vt luna, electa vt sol? Canticorum 6 [Song of Sol. 6:9]. Reuerendi mei, Quia prerogatiua Virginis benedicte non potest sufficienter—Ff. 243vb–247rb. Type C.

B-137. Qui manducat viuet, Iohannis 6 [John 6:58]. Karissimi, Beatus Bernardus dicit et eciam Philosophus quod ignis—Ff. 247rb–248rb, incomplete. [Corpus Christi.] Type 0.

B-138. Exiit qui seminat seminare semen suum [Luke 8:5]. Seminat Christus, seminat diabolus, seminat homo—Ff. 248va–249rb. [Sexagesima.] Type 0.

B-139. *Dominica in septuagesima.* Voca operarios et redde illis mercedem [Matt. 20:8]. Multi sunt vocati in vineam set quidam venire noluerunt—Ff. 249rb–250rb. Septuagesima. Type 0.

B-140. Qui est ex Deo, verba Dei audit [John 8:47]. Ergo ad destructionem consequentis, qui non audit verbum Dei non est ex—Ff. 250rb–251rb. [Passion Sunday.] Type 0.

B-141. Cum venerit spiritus veritatis, docebit omnem veritatem, Iohannis 16 [John 16:13]. Sciens Iesus discipulos de absentia eius dolentes, consolabatur eos—Ff. 251rb–253ra. [4 after Easter?] Type 0.

B-142. *Dominicia 1ª quadragesime.* Viuit homo [Matt. 4:4?]. Ex sacra scriptura patet quod sepius per deuote orationis instantiam—Ff. 253ra–256ra. 1 Lent. Type 0.

B-143. Vexatur qui non respondit, Matthei 15 [Matt. 15:22–23]. Vt comuniter ratione vtentibus exprimitur quod quanto quis dure—Ff. 256ra–258ra. [2 Lent?] Type 0.

B-144. Orate pro inuicem vt saluemini, Iacobi 5.f [James 5:16]. Impotentes virtute orationis a periculis se defendunt quod viribus naturalibus—Ff. 258ra–261rb, incomplete. [Rogation Days?] Type 0.

B-145. Vbi est Deus? [?]. Inter omnes questiones in sacra scriptura motas assumpta pro themate—Ff. 261va–263rb. [The academic tone and absence of penitential exhortation make it unlikely that this sermon is intended for Ash Wednesday, as might be suggested by the thema from, possibly, Joel 2:17.] Type 0.

B-146. Tres sunt qui testimonium dant, Iohannis 5.e [1 John 5:7]. Sacra scriptura approbante inueni quod quatuor pro processu sermonis sunt notanda—Ff. 263rb–265ra. Type 0.

B-147. *Dominica 3ª quadragesime.* Reuertar [Luke 11:24]. Inter clementiam et vindictam naturalis ordo statuit vt prius attemptetur clementia—Ff. 265ra–268rb. 3 Lent. Also O-32; q.v. Type 0.

B-148. *Epiphania.* Ortus est sol, congregati sunt [Ps. 103:22]. De nocte quamdiu solis absentia durat tria incomoda sequuntur—Ff. 268rb–269rb. Epiphany. Type A.

B-149. Voca operarios et redde illis mercedem [Matt. 20:8]. Vita hominis sicut ferrum est. Nam sicut ferreum instrumentum non vsitatum—Ff. 269va–273vb. [Septuagesima?] Type A.

B-150. *In die cinerum.* Conuertimini ad me in toto corde vestro, Ioelis 2, et in epistula hodierna [Joel 2:12]. Karissimi, Loquitur 3 Regum 20 quod cum rex Ezechias egrotaret—Ff. 273vb–274va. Ash Wednesday. Type 0.

B-151. *Dominica in quinquagesima.* Fides, spes, caritas, tria hec, 1 Corinthiorum 13, et in epistula hodierna [1 Cor. 13:13]. Quam necessarium est cuilibet ad eternam salutem festinanti scire—Ff. 274va–276rb. Quinquagesima. Type 0.

B-152. *Dominica 1ª quadragesime.* Dominum Deum tuum adorabis, Matthei 4, et in euangelio hodierno [Matt. 4:10]. Ratio edocet naturalis quod quilibet deberet illud libenter facere—Ff. 276rb–279va. 1 Lent. Type 0.

B-153. *Dominica 4 quadragesime.* Filii promissionis sumus, Ad Galatas 4.c, et in epistula hodierna [Gal. 4:28]. Cum Saul rex Israel preuaricatus esset legem Dei, statim malignus spiritus—Ff. 279va–281ra. 4 Lent. Type 0.

B-154. *Dominica 1ª quadragesime.* Exhibeamus nos Dei ministros in pacientia, 2 Corinthiorum 6 [2 Cor. 6:4]. Minister escas apponere potest, sed edentibus saporem dare non potest—Ff. 281ra–282vb. 1 Lent. Type 0.

B-155. *Dominica 1ª quadragesime.* Nunc dies salutis, 2 Corinthiorum 6 [2 Cor. 6:2]. Karissimi, Secundum Augustinum *De verbis Apostoli,* omelia 88, ex quo Adam lapsus est—Ff. 283ra–284vb. 1 Lent. Type 0.

B-156. *Dominica 1ª quadragesime.* Dominum Deum tuum adorabis, Matthei 4 [Matt. 4:10]. Iob: "Quam mutationem dabit homo pro anima sua?" Abraham ait pueris suis—Ff. 284vb–285rb. 1 Lent. Type 0.

B-157. *Dominica 1ª quadragesime.* Si filius Dei es, dic, Matthei 4, et in euangelio hodierno [Matt. 4:3]. Crisostomus in *Imperfecto,* omelia 13: "Filii carnales si similes sint"—Ff. 285rb–286rb. 1 Lent. Type 0.

B-158. *Dominica 1ª quadragesime.* Dic vt lapides isti panes fiant, Matthei 4 [Matt. 4:3]. Iuxta illud quod Apostolus dicit Ad Thimotheum 2 capitulo, Obsecro ergo primum omnium—Ff. 286rb–289ra. 1 Lent. Type 0. A version of Richard Fitzralph's antifraternal sermon 67, given at St. Paul's Cross, London, on 1 Lent. The invitation to pray for the royal family has been changed to "pro statu domini nostri regis," and references to other sermons by Fitzralph and the lengthy discussion of the history of the friars' privileges to hear confession, etc., have been omitted. But the antifraternal thrust of Fitzralph's sermon is fully preserved.

B-159. *Dominica 2ª quadragesime.* Miserere mei, fili David, Matthei 15, et in euangelio [Matt. 15:21]. Reuerendi et amici karissimi, Duabus de causis potest Filius Dei filius Dauid appellari—Ff. 289ra–290vb. 2 Lent. Type 0.

B-160. *Dominica 2ª quadragesime.* Domine, adiuua me, Matthei 15 [Matt. 15:25]. Debilis et impotens, pauper et indigens, pauidus et timens habent materiam—Ff. 290vb–291vb. 2 Lent. Type 0.

B-161. *Dominica 2ª quadragesime.* Filia mea a demonio male vexatur, Matthei 15 [Matt. 15:22]. Cum rex Saul preuaricatus esset legem Dei ac mandata, spiritus malus—Ff. 291vb–292vb. 2 Lent. Type 0. Same opening as B-153, but only for a few sentences.

B-162. *Dominica 3ª quadragesime.* Erat Iesus eiiciens demonium et illud erat mutum, Luce xi, et [in] euangelio hodierno [Luke 11:14]. Karissime [!], Hoc nomen Iesus vocabulum est eximie pietatis ac dulcedinis—Ff. 292vb–294rb. 3 Lent. Type 0.

B-163. *Dominica 3ª quadragesime.* Christus dilexit nos, Ephesiorum

5 [Eph. 5:2]. Ratio edocet quod homo paruipendit ea que vilia sunt, sed ea que preciosa—Ff. 294rb–295rb. 3 Lent. Type 0.

B-164. *Dominica 3ª quadragesime.* Estote imitatores Dei, Ad Ephesios 5 [Eph. 5:1]. Secundum artem medicine contraria contrariis curantur. Aqua et ignis—Ff. 295rb–296rb. 3 Lent. Type 0.

B-165. *Dominica 4ª quadragesime.* Signa faciebat super his qui infirmabantur, Iohannis 6.a [John 6:2]. Triplex est infirmitas corporalis: quedam extra corpus vt in manibus—Ff. 296rb–297va. 4 Lent. Type 0.

B-166. *Dominica 4ª quadragesime.* Quid dicit Scriptura, Ad Galatas 4, et in epistula hodierna [Gal. 4:30]. Karissimi, Apostolus 2 Corinthiorum 3 dicit quod non sumus sufficientes cogitare—Ff. 297va–298vb. 4 Lent. Type 0.

B-167. Ecce ascendimus, etc. [Luke 18:31]. Iste ascensus Domini in materialem Hierusalem signat nostrum ascensum spiritualem—Ff. 298vb–300ra. [Quinquagesima?] Type 0.

B-168. Gratia super gratiam mulier sancta et pudorata; et in eodem: Narratio fatui quasi sarcina in via, in labiis sensati inuenitur gratia [Ecclus. 26:19; 21:19]. Sensatus est cui res sapiunt prout sunt. Item notandum quod Beata Virgo comparatur cristallo—Ff. 300ra–301ra. [BVM?] Type 0.

B-169. *Dominica in passione.* Emundabit conscientiam nostram ab operibus mortuis ad seruiendum Deo viuenti, Hebreorum 9, et in epistula hodierna [Heb. 9:14]. Karissimi, Si reducamus ad memoriam humani generis principium et consequenter—F. 301ra–vb. Passion Sunday. Type 0.

D

Dublin, Trinity College, MS 277

Paper. 564 pages. Mid–xv.

The manuscript has been fully described and analyzed in Colker 1991, 1:509–32. Besides the sermons listed here, it also contains sermons ascribed to Augustine, Bernard, and Maurice de Sully (Colker items 53, 67, and 105–6).

D-1. *Sermo de assumpcione.* Que est ista que progreditur quasi aurora consurgens, etc. [Song of Sol. 6:3]. Sicut dicit Anselmus *De conceptu virginali,* capitulo 2, triplex est rerum cursus—Pp. 93–96. Assumption of BVM. Type 0. Colker no. 7.

*D-2. *Sermo de passione Christi in die parasceues facienda.* Amore langueo, Canticorum 2° capitulo [Song of Sol. 2:5]. Prolatiue potest dici sic: Karissimi, Sicut manifeste videtis—Pp. 185–198. Good Friday. Also B-088, S-07, and T-07. Type C. Colker no. 50. Edited here in appendix B.

H

London, British Library, MS Harley 331

Paper. 99 leaves. Dimensions: ca. 225 × 147, written space ca. 172 × 118. Collation: I–IV¹⁶ (ff. 1–64), V¹⁰ (65–66, 68–75; f. 67 is an added leaf, smaller in size and unrelated in content), VI²⁴ (76–99). Medieval foliation: 89–154 (modern 1–66), 155–167 (modern 68–80), continued 168–186 in modern pencil (modern ff. 81–99). Medieval quire signatures on verso: 8–12 and *vltimus*. Written in long lines in several hands of xv². Secundo folio: lost.

An old shelf mark 38.A.11 is on f. 1 top. At bottom of f. 14v is written "Thomas Chamburleyne" in the hand that wrote the quire signatures, which is different from the text hands and in lighter brown ink.

After the final eleven lines of an incomplete sermon, the volume contains twenty-five complete sermons, theological notes, and part of a theological treatise (with "Capitulum 12. Notandum quod quadruplex est Dei derelicio," f. 67).

H-01. Iesus, Mathei 4° capitulo [Matt. 4:1, etc.]. Tria mouent me istud thema accipere: dede, nede, and spede—Ff. 1–5. Also Z-03. Type B1.

H-02. *Dominica 2ª quadragesime.* Miserere mei, Domine, Mathei xv, et in euangelio presentis dominice [Matt. 15:22]. Karissimi, Sicut testatur sacra scriptura ii Regum 12 capitulo, cum rex David suggestione diaboli fedasset—Ff. 5–9v. 2 Lent. Also A-36. Type B1.

H-03. Quo abiit Symon, i Machabeorum 5 [1 Macc. 5:21]. Reuerendi mei, Christus Dei Filius loquens suis discipulis in parabolis Luce 19 sic inquit: "Homo quidam nobilis abiit"—Ff. 9v–13. Also W-083 and W-092. Type 0.

H-04. Maria, Luce primo, et in euangelio hodierno [Luke 1:27]. O gloriosa domina excelsa supra sydera, inebriare nos digneris tanquam infantulos—Ff. 13–15. Type 0.

H-05. Redde racionem villicacionis tue, Luce 16 capitulo [Luke 16:2]. Noueritis, karissimi mei, quod Christus auctor veritatis et doctor in libro

suo de euangelio Mathei 28 assimulans regnum celorum patrifamilias—
Ff. 15-18. By Thomas Wimbledon; also A-48. Type 0.

H-06. *Sermo generalis.* Si secundum carnem vixeritis, moriemini, Romanorum 8 [Rom. 8:13]. Istud taliter declaratur: Notandum est cuicumque quod quilibet existens in mundo tres habet capitales inimicum [!]—
Ff. 18-21. General sermon. Type C marginal.

H-07. *Sermo in die pasche.* Surge et comede, 3 Regum 19 [1 Kings
19:5]. Dicit Gregorius in *Morum* quod qui Deo loqui desiderat de nulla
re confidere debet nisi de gracia Dei—Ff. 21-23. Easter. Also Z-14.
Type B1.

H-08. Surrexit Dominus vere, Luce 24 [Luke 24:34]. Karissimi, Sicut
medicina corporalis si fuerit conueniens complexioni recipientis multociens cum bona gubernacione est causa salutis—Ff. 23v-26v. Also Z-
26. Type 0.

H-09. Dirigite viam Domini, Iohannis primo [John 1:23]. Karissimi, In hoc euangelio ostenditur quomodo Iudei audientes mirabilem
nativitatem—Ff. 26v-27v. Type 0.

H-10. *Sermo de festo omnium sanctorum.* Merces vestra copiosa est
in celis, Mathei 5 [Matt. 5:12]. Karissimi, Sicut legitur in euangelio
Mathei 4, Christus ante passionem suam circuibat Galileam—Ff. 27v-
31v. All Saints. Also Z-24. Type A.

H-11. *In die omnium sanctorum.* Beati misericordes quoniam ipsi
misericordiam consequuntur, Mathei 5 [Matt. 5:7]. Pro processu sermonis debetis notare quod misericordia est amor sive voluntas relevandi
miserum—Ff. 32-35. All Saints. Type 0.

H-12. *In die sancti Thome.* Euge, serue bone, Luce xix^mo [Luke 19:17].
Karissimi, In euangelio hodierno Christus redemptor noster ostendit
nobis per parabolam principaliter tria—Ff. 35-38. St. Thomas of Canterbury. Type 0.

H-13. *In die epheme* [read *epiphanie*]. Apertis thesauris suis optulerunt ei munera: aurum, thus, et mirram, Mathei 3° [Matt. 2:11]. Karissimi, In hoc euangelio ostenditur quomodo nato Saluatore nostro in
Bethelem [!] Iude—Ff. 38-41. Epiphany. Type 0.

H-14. *In die circumcisionis Domini.* Circumcidimini Domino, Ieremie
4 capitulo [Jer. 4:4]. Karissimi, Hodie celebrat Ecclesia festum de circumcisione Domini, qui circumcisus fuit in octava die a sua nativitate—
Ff. 41-43. Circumcision. Type 0.

H-15. *De assumpcione.* Intrauit Iesus in quoddam castellum, et mulier
quedam, etc., Luce 10 [Luke 10:38]. Karissimi, Erat quondam rex nobilis

habens duos filios et quatuor filias—Ff. 43–47. Assumption of BVM. Type B2.

H-16. *De sancto Iohanne Baptista.* Preibis enim ante faciem Domini parare vias eius, Luce 1, et ad propositum huius solempnitatis [Luke 1:76]. Verba ista fuerunt data prophetice de sancto Baptista—Ff. 47–49. St. John the Baptist. Type 0.

H-17. *Sermo de natiuitate sancti Iohannis Baptiste.* Tu puer propheta altissimi vocaberis, Luce 1, et ad propositum huius festi [Luke 1:76]. Sanctus Iohannes Baptista fuit sanctificatus in vtero matris sue—Ff. 49v–52. Nativity of St. John the Baptist. Type 0.

H-18. *Sermo generalis.* Videte, vigilate, et orate, Marci 13 [Mark 13:33]. Reuerendi mei, Testante scriptura sacra solebant sancti se dare oracioni—Ff. 52–54v. General sermon. Type 0.

H-19. *Dominica 1 in quinquagesima.* Iesu, fili David, miserere mei, Luce 18 [Luke 18:38]. Karissimi, Antequam Christus passus fuit suam passionem dolorosam, quasi prophetice ostendebat suis discipulis—Ff. 54v–62v. Quinquagesima. Type 0.

H-20. *Sermo natiuitatis sancte Marie Virginis.* Ego quasi vitis fructificavi suavitatem odoris, Ecclesiastici 24 [Ecclus. 24:23]. Karissimi, Christus in euangelio Iohannis 14 vocat seipsum vitem—Ff. 62v–65. Nativity of BVM. Type B1, with the English division added in the bottom margin (f. 63).

H-21. *In exaltacione sancte crucis.* Qui ambulat in tenebris nessit quo vadit, Iohannis xii° capitulo, et in euangelio hodierno [John 12:35]. Karissimi, Euangelium hodiernum ostendit quomodo Christus ante passionem suam manifestauit Iudeis—Ff. 65–66, incomplete. Exaltation of the cross. Type 0.

H-22. *Sermo generalis pro tota quadragesima.* Surge qui dormis, Ad Ephesios vi° capitulo [Eph. 5:14]. Karissimi, In tribus periculis solent homines evigilare in lecto dormientes: in periculo ignis—Ff. 68–69v. Lent. Also B-135 and Cambridge, Gonville and Caius College MS 334, ff. 181ra–182va. Type 0.

H-23. Manhu, Exodi 16 capitulo [Exod. 16:15]. Karissimi, Sacra scriptura nos docet, sicut legitur in veteri testamento, quod filii Israel exeuntes—Ff. 70–71v, incomplete? Type B1.

H-24. Ego sum vitis, vos palmites, Iohannis 15, et in euangelio hodierno [John 15:5]. Karissimi, Ut experimentum docet multociens quando aliquis dominus uel paterfamilias conducit operarios—Ff. 72–75. Type 0.

*H-25. Cristus passus est pro nobis, vobis relinquens exemplum vt sequamini, 1ᵃ Petri 2° [1 Pet. 2:21]. Anglice: Crist in hys passion reliquit exemplum . . . Quamuis hec verba dicantur generaliter omnibus Christianis—Ff. 80–99. [Good Friday.] Also W-006, S-01, and Z-19. Type C.

L

London, Lambeth Palace, MS 352

Parchment. ii + 226 leaves. xiv/xv.

The manuscript has been described and analyzed by James and Jenkins 1930–32, 466–70. Besides John Waldeby's exposition of the Pater Noster, here called *Itinerarium salutis* (which is composed as a series of sermons, ff. 25–54v), and over seventy paragraph-length summaries of sermons on Sunday themata (ff. 57–83), the volume contains one full-length, independent sermon:

*L-1. Dilexit nos et lauit nos a peccatis nostris in sanguine suo, Apocalipsis 1 [Rev. 1:5]. Reuerendi mei, Sponsa grata pro cuius amore sponsus eius in bello fuit occisus—Ff. 216–224v. [Good Friday.] Type C.

O

Oxford, Bodleian Library, MS Bodley 649

Parchment. i + 216 + ii leaves. Dimensions: 230 × 145/150, written space 140/146 × 100. Collation: I¹² (medieval ff. 1–12), II¹² (13–24), III¹² (25–37, no 33), IV¹² (38–49), V¹² (50–61), VI¹² (62–73), VII¹² (74–85), VIII¹² (86–97), IX¹² (98–110, no 99), X¹² (111–122), XI¹² (123–134), XII¹² (145[!]–156), XIII¹² (157–168, 164 twice, no 165), XIV¹² (169–180), XV¹² (181–192), XVI¹² (193–204), XVII¹² (205–216), XVIII¹² (217–228). Medieval foliation (as indicated) and quire signatures a–t (intermittently preserved), quire m wanting (ff. 135–144). Written in one column by one hand of the early fifteenth century, most likely at Oxford. The scribe may have been John Swetstock. Secundo folio: *perfeccio mentis.*

The volume includes two sets of sermons: (1) 1–25, ff. 1–133 (134 is blank); (2) 26–45, ff. 145–227. The sermons have been analyzed by Horner 1989, whose numbering includes nonsermon items (notes and narrationes, mostly in the second part). They have attracted the attention of several scholars: Owst 1933 (pp. 6, 29, 52, 70–75, 84, 158, 161, 190, 225, 239, 272, 311, 328, 332, 352, 398, 510, 535); Haines 1972, 1975, 1976, and 1989; Horner 1989; and Hudson 1988 (436–37). I follow the medieval foliation.

*O-01. Nvnc dies salutis, 2ª Ad Corinthios vi [2 Cor. 6:2]. Anglice: Alle seke . . . hele. Lego in scriptura sacra Exodi xvii° quod quando crudelis tirannus Amalec—Ff. 1–8. [1 Lent.] Type C.

*O-02. Assumpsit eum in ciuitatem, Mathei iiij^to, etc. [Matt. 4:5]. Deus qui fudit suum sanguinem pro humano peccato et sustulit mortem . . . Assumpsit . . . Anglice: He toke . . . Tutissima ciuitas—Ff. 8–13v. [1 Lent.] Type C.

*O-03. Magna est fides, Mathei xv° [Matt. 15:28]. Lego in sacra scriptura Danielis 4to quod magnus ille rex Nabogodonosor vidit in visione grandem arborem—Ff. 14–19v. [2 Lent.] Type C.

*O-04. Domine, adiuua me, Mathei 15, et in dominice instantis euangelio [Matt. 15:25]. þe help and þe comfort . . . Vt lego in sacra scriptura Apocalipsis 5 þe evangelista Iohannes—Ff. 19v–27. [2 Lent.] Type C.

*O-05. Iesus, Mathei xv, et in euangelio hodierno [Matt. 15:21]. þe gracius comfort omnipotentis . . . Reuerendi domini, Sicut lego in sacra scriptura Apocalipsis X°—Ff. 27–34. [2 Lent.] Also R-14. Type C.

*O-06. Fortis armatus custodit atrium, Luce xi° [Luke 11:21]. Anglice: A my3ti werrour . . . Lego 2° Machabeorum XI quod quando maledictus rex Anthiocus—Ff. 34–40v. [3 Lent.] Type C.

*O-07. De celo querebant, Luce xi, et in euangelio hodierno [Luke 11:16]. Gracia and comfort benedicte Trinitatis intercessione . . . Venerandi domini, Verba que sumpsi . . . þai so3t fro heuon. Domini, Specialis vinea—Ff. 40v–48. [3 Lent.] Type C. At end, "quod Io. S." Edited here in appendix C.

*O-08. Videbant signa, Iohannis 5, et in euangelio hodierno [John 6:2]. Lego in scriptura sacra Apocalipsis xii quod sanctus euangelista Iohannes vidit magnum et mirabile signum—Ff. 48–54. [4 Lent.] Type C. Partially identical with O-11.

*O-09. Abiit Iesus, Iohannis vi [John 6:1]. Reuerendi domini, Autores qui tractant de naturis dicunt quod est naturale odium, inimicicia inter regem auium aquilam et venenosum serpentem—Ff. 54–60v. [4 Lent.] Type C.

*O-10. Abiit trans mare, Iohannis 6 [John 6:1]. Reuerendi domini, Acerbum mare quod Christus transiit et quod nos o[mnes] oportet superuelificare—Ff. 60v–68. [4 Lent.] Type C.

*O-11. Videbant signa, Iohannis 5, et in euangelio hodierno [John 6:2]. Lego in sacra scriptura Apocalipsis xii quod sanctus euangelista s. Iohannes vidit magnum mirabile signum—Ff. 68v–74. [4 Lent.] Type C. Protheme identical with O-08, but without the reference to Oxford.

*O-12. Pontifex introiuit in sancta, Ad Ebreos ix [Heb. 9:11–12?]. Anglice: þe bischop hath entred . . . Lego 2° Paralipomenon quod gloriosus rex Salamon fecit sibi statlich trone—Ff. 74–79v. [Passion Sunday.] Also R-02. Type C.

*O-13. Christus introiuit in sancta, Ad Ebreos ix [Heb. 9:12]. Lego in sacra scriptura Exodi xx° quod postquam omnipotens Deus—Ff. 79v–85. [Passion Sunday.] Type C.

*O-14. Ecce rex venit, Mathei xxi [Matt. 21:5]. Anglice: Synful man . . . Vt auctores nature dicunt, Bartholomei xii *De Naturis,* est quoddam genus virtuosorum lapidum, magnetes scilicet—Ff. 85–91. [Lent.] Type C.

*O-15. Exiuit de templo, Iohannis viii [John 8:59]. Summus celi pontifex qui isto sacro tempore paciebatur passionem et mortem . . . In huius sermonis exordio exorabimus . . . Speciale templum—Ff. 91–96v. [Passion Sunday.] Also R-12. Type C.

*O-16. Domine, salua nos, perimus, Mathei 8ᵘᵒ [Matt. 8:25]. Non miremini quod sumpsi ista verba pro themate, quia isto die quidam habent missam principalem de ieiunio, quidam de sancto M[arco] . . . Ista fuerunt verba apostolorum—Ff. 97–100, incomplete. [St. Mark, mentioned on f. 98v.] Type C.

*O-17. Fructus iusti lignum vite, Prouerbiorum xi [Prov. 11:30]. þe holi crosse . . . Secundum doctores iusticia est virtus reddens vnicuique quod suum est—Ff. 100v–102, incomplete. Type C.

*O-18. Sanauit eum, Luce xiiii, et in dominice presentis euangelio [Luke 14:4]. Lego in sacra scriptura Iosue VII° capitulo tempore quo magna ciuitas Iericho destrueretur—Ff. 102v–105v. [17 after Trinity.] Type C.

O-19. Vestiuit pontificem, Leuitici viii° [Lev 8:7]. Scriptura sacra Exodi xxviii° et Leuitici viii et Magister Historiarum super illis locis dicunt quod summus pontifex veteris legis erat vestitus tribus solemnibus ornamentis—Ff. 106–107v, incomplete. [St. Birinus.] Also R-28. Type C minimal.

O-20. Sacerdos est angelus, Malachie 2° [Mal. 2:7?]. Reuerendi patres et domini, In gloriosissimo templo celestis Ierusalem ab arca fecundissima paternalis memorie manna profluit—Ff. 108–109v. Type 0.

O-21. Quasi flos rosarum in diebus veris, l° capitulo [Ecclus. 50:8]. Increate splendor sapiencie ab eterni solis cardine progrediens sui ortus fulgore temporanee nostre mortalitati serenus illuxit—Ff. 110–111. Type 0.

*O-22. Statuit eum supra pinnaculum templi, Mathei 4to [Matt. 4:5]. Deus qui statuebatur supra pinnaculum crucis pro hominis peccato . . . Reuerendi domini, In huius sermonis exordio eamus . . . Anglice: On þe hy pinnacle . . . Speciale templum et habitacio—Ff. 112v–119. [1 Lent.] Type C.

*O-23. Dies mei transierunt quasi nauis, Iob ix° [Job 9:26]. Deus qui fecit diem et noctem . . . Dies hii cito complentur, tempus nostre mortalis vite cito euanescit—Ff. 119v–124. Funeral sermon for Knight John D. Type C.

*O-24. Intrauit castellum, Luce x° [Luke 10:38]. þe souerayne lord celi et terre . . . Anglice: Moder and maiden that neuer did mysse . . . Fortissimum et pulcherrimum castell—Ff. 124–128v. [Assumption of BVM.] Type C.

*O-25. Qui nauigat mare enarrat pericula, Ecclesiastici xliii° [Ecclus. 43:26]. Suppremus princeps celi et terre Deus . . . Anglice: Qwo sailet . . . vel sic: Vr maryner . . . Magnum mare quod Dominus noster transiuit—Ff. 128v–133. Type C. Preached by a Benedictine in the time of Henry V, after Agincourt. Edited in Haines 1976.

O-26. Ascendens Iesus in nauiculam transfretauit, Mathei xi [Matt. 9:1]. Beati homines in hac peregrinacione langore cruciantur, timore consternantur, fauore demendantur—Ff. 145–148, incomplete. The text ends, "et perfice vltra questiones secundum alphabetum." [19 after Trinity?] Type 0.

O-27. Induite vos armaturam Dei [Eph. 6:11]. Intelligatis quod armatura fidelium debet esse oracio. Vnde dicit Bernardus—Ff. 148–150, incomplete. [21 after Trinity.] Type 0.

O-28. Videte quomodo caute ambuletis [Eph. 5:15]. In hiis verbis docet nos Apostolus subtilem theoricam et vtilem practicam. Nam docet nos speculari subtiliter—F. 150, incomplete. [20 after Trinity.] Type 0.

O-29. Dedit dona hominibus, Ad Ephesios 6 [Eph. 4:8]. Karissimi, Si consideremus vniuersorum dominum, eum tam auidum humani amoris inueniemus—Ff. 150v–157v. [Pentecost.] Type A.

O-30. Caritas operit multitudinem peccatorum, 1 Petri 4 [1 Pet. 4:8]. Quatuor sunt experimenta per que literas priuatas potest homo legere—Ff. 157v–159, incomplete? [6 after Easter.] Type 0.

O-31. Amore langueo, Canticorum 2 [Song of Sol. 2:5]. Karissimi,

Septem signa amoris et langoris considero que isto die humano generi acciderunt. Nam isto primus homo fuit creatus—Ff. 159–164, incomplete. [Good Friday.] Type C minimal. The opening section is very reminiscent of B-088, etc.

O-32. Reuertar, Luce xi [Luke 11:24]. Inter clemenciam et vindictam ordo struitur vt preacceptetur clemencia, postea sequatur vindicta—Ff. 164–168v, incomplete. [3 Lent.] Also B-147. Type B2: one English distinction appearing in the bottom margin, and one English gloss; on two occasions the scribe announces an English translation without giving it.

O-33. Veni et vide, Iohannis 1 [John 1:45]. Ante incarnacionem genus humanum fuit lanceatum tribus lanceis, 2° Regum 18: dolore propter amissionem status innocencie—Ff. 168v–169v, incomplete. Type 0.

O-34. *De beato Martino.* Non potest ciuitas abscondi supra montem posita, Mathei 6 [Matt. 5:14]. Solent homines commendare ciuitates propter quatuor condiciones, videlicet propter murorum altitudinem— Ff. 169v–174v, incomplete. St. Martin. Type 0.

O-35. *De sancto Edmundo.* Ecce rex vester, Iohannis 9 [John 19:14]. Karissimi, Regna solent distingui per arma et per regem, per loquelam et per legem—Ff. 174v–177v, incomplete. St. Edmund. Type 0.

O-36. *De sanctis apostolis Philippi et Iacobi.* Statuit duas columpnas in porticu [MS: porticii] templi, 3 Regum 7 [1 Kings 7:21]. Dicit Augustinus de verbis Apostoli quod templum Dei istis duobus columpnis— Ff. 177v–178v, incomplete. Sts. Philip and James. Type 0.

O-37. *Sermo de beato Thoma apostolo.* Deus meus et dominus meus, Iohannis 20 [John 20:28]. Secundum commentarium Boecii *De consolacione* tres fuerunt vite famose—Ff. 178v–183, incomplete? St. Thomas the Apostle. Type 0.

O-38. *Collacio.* Vade, Iohannis 4 [John 4:16 or 4:50]. Narrat di'i Agellius in quodam libello *De bellis Armenie* de quodam rege generoso— Ff. 188v–189, incomplete. [21 after Trinity?] Type 0.

O-39. Ecce nunc dies salutis, 2ᵃ Ad Corinthios 6 [2 Cor. 6:2]. Prima dies exploracio sue culpe, secunda culpe deploracio, tercia eiusdem explicacio, quarta Dei imploracio—Ff. 192–194, incomplete? [1 Lent?] Also A-26, which stops two sentences before the end in O-39 and only alludes to the fable of the fox and the dove, which is here told in full. Type C marginal.

O-40. *Katerina.* Quasi si sit rota in medio rote, suple: apparuit beata Katerina, Ezechielis primo [Ezek. 1:16]. Refert historia 3 Regum primo quod rex Dauid senuerat habebatque etatis plurimos annos—Ff. 194–201v. St. Catherine. Type 0.

O-41. *Sermo de omnibus sanctis.* Beati qui per portas intrant ciuitatem, Apocalipsis vltimo [Rev. 22:14]. Karissimi, Ista verba scribuntur in ultimo loco sacre scripture et possunt esse verba ecclesie—Ff. 201v–206. All Saints. Type 0.

O-42. *Sermo de mortuis.* Libera nos a malo, Amen, Mathei [*blank*] [Matt. 6:13]. Karissimi, Anime defunctorum penis purgatorii deputate duplici malo inuoluuntur—Ff. 207–213. The dead. Type 0. Partially (ff. 207–209) edited by Palmer 1983.

O-43. Ipsum elegit ab omni viuente, Ecclesiastici 45 [Ecclus. 45:20]. Karissimi, Scitis quod primus parens in mundi primordio se cum suis subiugauit multiplici obproprio—Ff. 213–217. [St. John the Baptist.] Type 0.

O-44. *De sancto Barnaba.* En morior, Genesis 25 [Gen. 25:32]. Karissimi, Barnabas interpretatur filius concludens. Sed quid isto die verius sibi concludere poterat—Ff. 217–220v, incomplete. St. Barnabas. Type 0.

O-45. *Sermo de beato Andrea.* Crucifixus sum, prima Ad Corinthios primo [1 Cor. 1:13?]. Secundum Varronem hec fuit tragedia peccati mortalis quod reclinabatur in lectulo ad similitudinem hominis—Ff. 220v–227. St. Andrew. Type 0.

Q

Oxford, Bodleian Library, MS Lat.th.d.1 (SC 29746)

Parchment and paper. i + 182 leaves. Due to the volume's damaged and brittle state, a careful collation is extremely difficult to make and hazardous. See Madan 1905, 685; Fletcher 1986. Apparently made up of several booklets; see Fletcher 1986, n. 2. Written in long lines, in one hand of xv[1]. Medieval foliation, partially visible, in upper right of rectos: 1–170 (twice) for modern 5–175. Secundo folio: lost.

On f. 178r–v, a late fifteenth-century hand has added a table of sermons, listing themata, folios, and occasions. These medieval folio references agree with the medieval foliation. The table has allowed Fletcher and me to reconstruct the themata of the earlier sermons. After the table had been made, 4 bifolia were added (modern ff. 1–4 and 179–181), on which an alphabetical index was begun from *Aaron* to *Amicus,* in the order of ff. 179, 1–4, 180–181.

For authorship, see discussion in chapter 2. An owner's note on f. 180 reads: "Liber iste post decessum patris ac fratris thome goddard bachalarii spectat ad conventum Fratrum Minorum babwellie, exaratum Norwici anno Domini 1538."

Literature: Owst 1926, 59 (cf. 27, 83, 150, 231, 249); Owst 1933, 6, 268, 278; Little 1943; Fletcher 1986.

The volume contains about fifty–seven sermons and a number of notes, tales, lists of sermon themes, and sermon outlines (f. 5r–v). I follow Fletcher's numbering but omit items that are not independent sermons.

Q-01. Four themata with processus for Advent (see Tabula). The second and fourth are recognizably on Ecce rex tuus venit [Matt. 12:5]— F. 5r–v. Type B1, at least.

Q-02. Expectabant redempcionem Israel [Luke 2:38?]—Ff. 6–8. General sermon. Type B1, at least.

Q-03. Preparate corda vestra [1 Sam. 7:4]—Ff. 9–11. General sermon. Type B1, at least.

Q-04. Quecumque scripta sunt [Rom. 15:4]. Alle thynges . . . —Ff. 14–15. 1, 2, and 3 Advent. Type B1, at least.

Q-05. Vnanimes uno ore honorificetis Deum [Rom. 15:6]—Ff. 17v–18v. 2 Advent. Type B1, at least.

Q-06. Graciam Dei recipiatis, 2 Ad Corinthios 6° [2 Cor. 6:1]. Karissimi, Secundum Boecium [?] in suis distinccionibus recepcio gracie diuine in nobis tria facit—Ff. 30v–33. 1 Lent. Repeated as Q-16. Type B1?

Q-08. Est nomen Iesus [Luke 2:21]—Ff. 34–36v. Circumcision. Type B1, at least.

Q-09. Hoc vobis signum, Luce 2°, et in principio istius solempnitatis euangelii [?] [Luke 2:12]—Ff. 36v–38v. Christmas. Type 0?

Q-10. Mementote mirabilium eius que fecit [Psalmo xiv] [Ps. 104:5]. Reuerendi, Thomas *De veritatibus theologie* [libro iiii . . .] in incarnacione tripliciter: tamquam . . . , secundo vt magister ad discipulos—Ff. 39–41. Christmas season. Type B2.

Q-15. Sequebatur eum multitudo magna, Iohannis 6°, et in euangelio hodierno [John 6:2]. Reuerendi mei, Dicit enim Boicius in suis distinccionibus quod ad sequendam aliquam predam absentem tria sunt que iuuant hominem—Ff. 45–48. [4 Lent.] Type B1.

Q-16. Graciam Dei recipiatis, 2ᵃ Ad Corinthios 6°, et in instantis dominice epistula [2 Cor. 6:1]. Reuerendi mei, Secundum Boicium in suis distinccionibus recepcio gracie diuine in nos tria facit—Ff. 48-51. [1 Lent.] Repeats Q-06. Type B1.

Q-17. Dominus est, prima Ad Corinthios 2° [1 Cor. 4:4]. Reuerendi, Secundum Holket in postilla sua super Sapienciam tria requiruntur ad hoc quod aliquis sit verus dominus—Ff. 51v-54. Type B1.

Q-18. Pater meus glorificat me, Iohannis 8° [John 8:54]. Karissimi, Quamuis ista verba dicantur de Patre in diuinis [?] et Christo eius filio— Ff. 54v-57. Type B1.

***Q-19.** *Sermo pro toto aduentu Domini.* Saluator tuus veniet, Ysaie 62 [Isa. 62:11]. Karissimi, Videtis bene ad oculum et verum est quod quando est ita quod rex vel aliquis dominus veniet ad vnam ciuitatem— Ff. 57v-61. Advent season. Type C.

***Q-20.** *In natiuitate Domini.* Natus est nobis hodie Saluator, Luce 2° capitulo [Luke 2:11]. Karissimi, Videtis bene ad oculum quod homines huius mundi habent lykyng and will ad audiendum thre maner of thydinggis—Ff. 61-65v. Christmas. Type C.

***Q-21.** *Pro quadragesima.* Penitenciam agite, appropinquabit enim regnum celorum, Mathei 3° et 4° [Matt. 3:2 and 4:17]. Auxilium et gracia, etc. Karissimi, Bene videtis ad oculum et verum est quod si aliqua comunitas, ciuitas, vel villa scholde fallen in a daunger erga regem—Ff. 66-69. Lent. Type C.

***Q-22.** *In die pasche.* Dii estis, Psalmo 80 [Ps. 81:6]. Ecce constitui te deum, Exodi 7ᵐᵒ capitulo [Exod. 7:1]. Quocumque die comederitis ex eo eritis sicut dii, Genesis 3° capitulo [Gen. 3:5]. Karissimi, Dicit Glosa super illo textu "Siquidem sunt dii multi, nobis tamen vnus est Deus," primo Corinthiorum 8° [5-6], quod iste terminus "deus" intelligitur tribus modis in sacra scriptura—Ff. 69v-74. Easter. Another version Q-25. Type C. The text before "Quocumque die" appears in the top margin.

***Q-23.** *Processus de gracia pro quocumque themate.* [Gracia]. Reuerendi [?], Pro processu debetis intelligere quod sicut diuersi doctores dicunt qui tractant de ista materia, gracia accipitur duobus modis—Ff. 74v-78v. Type C.

***Q-24.** *Antethema et introduccio de gracia.* Auxilium et gracia, etc. Karissimi, Debetis intelligere sicut dicit vnus magnus clericus, et est venerabilis Beda *De ymagine mundi*, iste clericus dicit quod est vna certa insula—Ff. 79-80. Type C. At the bottom of fol. 78v, the following themata appear: Graciam Dei recipiatis, 2ᵃ Ad Corinthios 6° capitulo [2 Cor. 6:1]. Vnicuique vestrum data est gracia, Ad Ephesios 4° capitulo

[Eph. 4:7]. Dabit Dominus graciam populo suo, Exodi xi° capitulo [Exod. 11:3].

*Q-25. *In paschate.* Dii estis omnes, Sapiencie 80 [Ps. 81:6]. Glosa dicit er' [*read* super] 8ᵐ capitulum prime epistule Ad Corinthios sic: "Iste terminus 'deus', inquid, tripliciter accipitur in scriptura"—Ff. 80–84. Easter. A version of Q-22. Type C.

Q-26. Custodite sicud scitis, Mathei 27 [Matt. 27:65]. Karissimi, Secundum beatum Augustinum super Psalmum 7 duo sunt effectus medicine—Ff. 84–86v. Easter. Type B1.

Q-27. *Sermo in synodo.* Sacerdotes sanctificentur, Exodi 19, et pro themate hodierno [Exod. 19:22]. Reuerendi domini patresque amantissimi, Cum secundum commentatorem super Dionisium *De diuinis nominibus* sanctificacio sit ab omni immundicia pura et immaculata vita—Ff. 87–89. Synod. Type 0.

Q-29. *Sermo comunis pro dominicis prima, 2ᵃ, 3ᵃ, et 4ᵃ quadragesime.* Ecce nunc tempus, 2ᵃ Ad Corinthios vi° [2 Cor. 6:2]. Karissimi, Inter omnia que perdimus [?] iactura temporis est maxima in hac vita—Ff. 91–93v. 1–4 Lent. Type B2. The few legible traces of the rubric indicating the sermon's occasion are confirmed by the tabula. The sermon is provided with separate introductions for the four Sundays of Lent, which are clearly marked in the margin:

1. Ecce nunc tempus, as above.
2. Domine, adiuua me, Mathei 15 [Matt. 15:25]. Karissimi, Dicit Saluator noster Iohannis 15, Sine me nichil potestis.
3. Locutus est mutus, Luce 11° [Luke 11:14]. Karissimi, Licet ista verba dicantur.
4. Erumpe et clama, Ad Galatas 4° [Gal. 4:27]. Karissimi, Debetis scire pro processu sermonis quod triplex est clamor.

Q-30. *Quadragesima.* Ecce nunc tempus, 2ᵃ Ad Corinthios 6° [2 Cor. 6:2]. Dicit Ianuensis [?] . . . quod tria visum corporalem proprie impedire possunt—Ff. 94–96. Lent. Type B2.

Q-31. *Tempore quadragesime. In ramis.* Ecce [. . .], et in euangelio hodierno [Matt. 26:36, etc.?]. Karissimi, Rogatus breuem sermonem facere ideo breue verbum as[sumpsi?], quod est nisi due sillabe, scilicet "ecce"—Ff. 96v–99. Lent or Palm Sunday. Type C marginal.

Q-32. *Sermo prima dominica quadragesime.* Graciam Dei recipiatis, 2ᵃ Ad Corinthios 6° [2 Cor. 6:1]. Karissimi, Apostolus in epistula hodierna hortatur uos ne in vacuum graciam Dei recipiatis—Ff. 99v–100v. 1 Lent. Type 0.

Q-33. *Dominica 2ª quadragesime.* Miserere mei, fili Dauid, Mathei 15º [Matt. 15:22]. Karissimi, Dicit Philosophus 2º *De celo et mundo* quod omne graue naturaliter appetit descendere—Ff. 100v–102. 2 Lent. Type B1.

Q-34. *Sermo pro visitacione fratrum.* Tres sunt qui testimonium dant, prima canonica Iohannis capitulo 5º [1 John 5:7]. Karissimi patres, Sicut scitis vnumquodque principiatum de quanto similius, propinquius, ac conformius existit primo principio—Ff. 102v–103v. Visitation sermon. Type 0.

Q-35. *Dominica 4ª post pasca.* Spiritus veritatis docebit vos omnem veritatem, Iohannis 16º [John 16:13]. Tribus modis, karissimi, secundum Magistrum Sentenciarum et doctores peccatum committitur—Ff. 103v–104v. 4 after Easter. Type 0.

Q-36. *Dominica 7 post Pentecostes. Sermo in visitacione fratrum.* Ex fructibus eorum cognoscetis eos, Mathei 7º [Matt. 7:16]. Karissimi, Rector et redemptor generis humani assimilando hominem arbori iuxta illud dictum philosophi Secundi—Ff. 104v–107. 7 after Easter; visitation sermon. Type 0.

Q-37. *Pro visitatione.* Relictis omnibus secuti sunt eum, Luce 5º [Luke 5:11]. Hec verba ad litteram dicuntur de beatis apostolis qui propter Deum reliquerunt recia—F. 107r–v. Visitation sermon. Type 0. Before the thema: "Reuerendi patres fratresque predilecti, Quia ante quamlibet visitacionem ordinariam saltem in publico laudabili consuetudine solent visitatores per modum collacionis aliquid visitandis proponere, igitur vt conformem me aliqualiter eisdem, sit hoc thema preuium."

Q-38. *Sermo de sanguine et passione Domini.* Que vtilitas in sanguine meo, Psalmo 69º [Ps. 29:10]. Karissimi, Hec verba sic dici possunt: Qwhat profyȝte is heere in myn blode. Doctor Crisostomus—Ff. 108–113. Passion, Good Friday. Type A.

Q-39. *De pascione Domini.* Redempti estis sanguine Iesu, 1ª Petri 4º [1 Pet. 1:18–19]. Karissimi mei, Secundum Crisostomum in *Imperfecto,* omelia prima, Christus habuit tres dignitates—Ff. 113v–115, 102. Passion, Good Friday. Type C marginal. The sermon ends on f. 115, with a renvoi to an alternate ending on 102.

Q-40. *De passione.* Exiuit sanguis et aqua, Iohannis 10 [John 19:34]. Karissimi, Viri ecclesiastici laicis [tenen]tur doctrinam salutarem prebere principaliter propter duas causas—Ff. 115v–118v. Good Friday. Type B1.

Q-41. *De Domini passione.* Extra portam passus est, Ad Hebreos 13 [Heb. 13:12]. Karissimi, Ieremie 7 habetur et dicitur predicatori: "Sta in porta domus Dei, predica verbum istud, et dic." Karissimi, Ad presens in nostro proposito per portam domus Domini—Ff. 119v–123, 119r (headed "Finis sequentis sermonis, scilicet Extra . . ."). Good Friday. Type 0.

*Q-42. *Sermo in die parasceues.* Ve michi, mater mea, Ieremie 15° capitulo, etc. [Jer. 15:10]. Quare rubrum est indumentum. Gentes videntes nouam rem et inconsuetam multum mirantur—Ff. 123v–126v. Good Friday. Type C. Edited in Little 1943.

Q-43. *De Domini passione.* Vidi librum scriptum intus et foris, Apocalipsis 5° [Rev. 5:1]. Karissimi, Videtur michi quod est de nobis et de Saluatore nostro sicut de magistro et eius discipulis—Ff. 127–129v. Good Friday. Type B2.

Q-44. *In ramis palmarum.* Risus dolore miscebitur, Prouerbiorum 14° [Prov. 14:13]. Karissimi, In predicto themate continetur plenarie quid legit Ecclesia et canit in presenti sollempnitate—Ff. 129v–132v. Palm Sunday [and Good Friday]. Type C minimal.

Q-45. Nunc clamemus in celum et miserebitur nostri Deus, Machabeorum 1° [1 Macc. 4:10]. Karissimi [?], Ista fuerunt verba Iude Machabei pugnatoris strenui—Ff. 133–135v. Rogation Days. Type C marginal. Fletcher's (1986) item 46 is a "historia de tribus inimicis" and intended to conclude the preceding sermon ("Nota hanc historiam quia concludit predicta"). On f. 133v, "Nota bene Phelyp. wulcy [?]," not noticed in Fletcher, appears in the text, perhaps derived from a marginal note?

Q-47. *Feria tercia.* Nunc clamemus, vbi supra [1 Macc. 4:10]. Karissimi, Habetur in euangelio hodierno quod quando Christus predicauit hic in terris dixit inter alia sic: "Si quis vestrum habebit amicum"—Ff. 136–137v. Tuesday of Rogation Days. Type C marginal.

Q-48. *Feria quarta.* Nunc clamemus, etc. [1 Macc. 4:10]. Karissimi, Dominus Iesus Christus cum discipulis suis post resurreccionem aliquantulum commoratus instante iam tempore quo corporaliter ab eis erat recessurus—Ff. 137v–139. Wednesday of Rogation Days. Type C marginal.

Q-50. Petite et dabitur vobis, Luce xi capitulo [Luke 11:9]. Karissimi, In principio huius sermonis due possunt hic queri questiones. Prima est, Quis est ille—Ff. 139v–142. Rogation Days. Type B1.

Q-51. *In rogacionibus.* Orate pro invicem vt saluemini, Iacobi vltimo, et in epistula Rogacionum [James 5:16]. Reuerendi, Sicut docet Hugo de Sancto Victore in libello suo *De virtute oracionis,* duo sunt que precipue nos ad orandum videntur excitare—Ff. 142v–143v. Rogation Days. Type B1. Written in the top margin of f. 143 is "Helbech."

Q-52. *Sermo processionalis.* Vnanimes estote in oracione, 1ª Petri 3° [1 Pet. 3:8]. Dicit Ysidorus *De summo bono* quod seruus Dei quocienscumque aliquo vicio tangitur—F. 144r-v, incomplete (noted in the table). Sermon for procession. Type B.

Q-53. *De sanguine, pro dominicis pascionis et ramis palmarum et feria sexta parasceues.* Sanguis Christi emundabit conscienciam nostram, Ad Hebreos 9° capitulo, et pro themate hodierno [Heb. 9:14]. Reuerendi, Quia vt dicit Augustinus, et ponitur in canone 28, questione 1, *Ex hiis,* quilibet iudicabitur—Ff. 145–149. Passion Sunday, Palm Sunday, Good Friday. Type C minimal.

Q-54. *Dominica in ramis.* Sanguis meus effundetur in remissionem peccatorum, Matthei 26°, et in processione hodierna [Matt. 26:28]. Reuerendi mei, Sicut testatur Apostolus Ad Hebreos 9, in antiqua lege sine sanguinis effusione non fiebat—F. 149v. Palm Sunday. Type 0. Only an introduction: "Pro processu sermonis dic si placet sicut in precedenti sermone, scilicet *Sanguis Christi emundabit,* etc."

Q-55. *Eciam in parasceue sermo.* Que vtilitas in sanguine meo, Psalmo 29° [Ps. 29:10]. Karissimi, Sicut sciunt scolastici qui fuerunt in vniuersitatibus, vtputa Oxon' vel Cantebrig'—F. 150. Type 0. Only an introduction, to be followed by *Sanguis Christi emundabit conscienciam.*

Q-56. Quanto magis sanguis Christi, Ad Hebreos 9° [Heb. 9:14]. Nota quod in veteri testamento reperiuntur sex genera animalium quorum sanguis effundebatur in illis sacrificiis legalibus—F. 150r-v. Type 0. Only notes for a sermon, ending "Nota bene et tracta sicut vis."

Q-58. *De Sancto Spiritu vel dominica infra octauam ascencionis.* Mittam vobis spiritum veritatis, Iohannis 16° capitulo, et in instantis dominice euangelio [John 15:26]. Karissimi mei, In huius sermonis exordio secundum laudabilem consuetudinem necessarium est—Ff. 151v–154v. Sunday after Ascension. Type B2.

Q-59. *In professione nouicii.* Ecce agnus Dei, Iohannis primo [John 1:29]. Quamuis, karissimi, ista verba historialiter et ad litteram dicantur de nostro Saluatore—Ff. 155–156. Profession of a novice. Type 0.

Q-61. In duobus mandatis tota lex pendet, Mathei 22° [Matt. 22:40]. Karissimi, Racio d[ictat?] et experiencia probat quod omnis—Ff. 157–159. Type B1. Written before the thema is "Sermo Melton de x preceptis."

Q-62. *Sermo communis de Beata Virgine.* Ora pro nobis, quoniam mulier sancta es, Iudith 8° [Jth. 8:29]. Anglice: As þou art . . . Karissimi, Racio dictat et exemplo confirmatur quod quando malefaceres [*read* malefactores] timent castigari propter demerita sua—Ff. 159-161v. Common sermon for BVM. Type C minimal. F. 159 top margin: "Melton."

Q-63. Exspectat Dominus vt miseriatur nostri, Ysaie 30 [Isa 30:18]. Anglice: Oure Lord . . . Karissime [*or corrected to* karissimi?], Audi, peccator, Dei benignitatem: qui iuste poterit punire exspectat tibi conferre graciam et misericordiam—Ff. 162-164v. Type C minimal. Before the thema: "Sermo de misericordia Melton."

Q-64. *Sermo generalis de conuersione peccatoris.* Conuertimini ad me in toto corde vestro, Ioelis 2° [Joel 2:12]. Anglice: With all ȝour herte . . . Karissimi, Videmus ad oculum quod quando pater videt filium suum male morigeratum—Ff. 165-166. General sermon. Type B2. F. 165 top margin: "Melton." The sermon is followed, on 166, by a separate paragraph of twenty-one lines marked "Introduccio bona," not noted by Fletcher. It begins, "Aristoteles habet et racio docet quod omne naturale existens extra locum suum," and evidently could introduce a sermon on "Conuertimini ad me et conuertar ad vos" [Zech. 1:3].

Q-65. *In parasceue.* Agnus qui in medio troni est reget eos, etc., Apocalipsis [Rev. 7:17]. Karissimi, Quando Deus fecit hominem, constituit eum dominum mundi—Ff. 166v-170v. Good Friday. Type B2.

Q-66. *In parasceue.* Sustinuit crucem confusione contempta, Hebreorum 12° [Heb. 12:2]. Karissimi, Inter omnia annualia Romanorum habetur quod Rome inventa fuit vna mensa aurea—Ff. 171-173. Good Friday. Type B2.

Q-67. *In paschate.* Qui custos est domini sui gloriabitur, Prouerbiorum 27° [Prov. 27:18]. Karissimi, Si enim ita esset quod rex Anglie vel Francie traderet custodiam ciuitatis vnius cuidam in terra sua—Ff. 173-175. Easter. Type C marginal. See Q-70.

Q-68. *In corpore Christi.* Iste est panis quem dedit vobis dominus ad vescendum, Exodi xvi° [Exod. 16:15]. Karissimi, Debetis intelligere quod triplex est panis—Ff. 175v-176v. Corpus Christi. Type B. In top margin of 175v: "Holbeche."

Q-70. Custodi virum istum, 3 Regum 20° [1 Kings 20:39]. Karissimi, Sic in Anglico: Kepe þu well . . . Karissimi, Ista est dies in qua omnes debemus venire ad mensam Domini—F. 177v. [Easter.] Type B1. Introduction only, with reference to Q-67; the present item is also noted there, f. 173, bottom margin: "Nota aliud thema s. Custodi virum istum in fine libri pro eodem processu." Q-70 is followed by another thema, "Custodite sicut scitis" [Matt. 27:65], without further text; cf. Q-26.

R

Oxford, Bodleian Library, MS Laud misc. 706

Parchment. ii + 188 + i leaves.

The manuscript has been described and analyzed in Horner 1975 and 1989, 316–20.

Dimensions: 225/230 × ca. 155, written space 154 × 108. Collation: The volume is made up of several booklets and was bound at St. Peter's Abbey, Gloucester, in the late fifteenth or early sixteenth century. In the binding, one folio was lost and two bifolia were bound out of order. There are several divergent modern foliations after f. 170. For easier reference, I have throughout preserved the earliest modern foliation, which is in ink from 1 to 175 and then in pencil (176a–181). I^{12} (ff. 1–12), II^{12} (13–24), III^{12} (25–36), IV^{12} (37–48), V^{12} (49–60), VI^{12} (61–71a, 71b), VII^{12} (72–83), VIII^{12} (84–95), IX^{12} (96–107), X^{12} (108a, 108b–118), XI^{12} (119–130), XII^{10} (131–140; the correct order is 133, 134, 131, 132, 135, 136, 139, 140, 137, 138), XIII^{12} (141–152), XIV^{12} (153–161a, 161b–163), XV^{12} (164–175), XVI^{10} (176a–176e, 177–181). At least three sets of medieval quire signatures: (1) center of lower margin: h–m for II–VI, d–g for VII–X, n–o for XI–XII, b–c for XIII–XIV; (2) center of lower margin: ii–xv for II–XV; (3) extreme lower right, mostly cropped: small letter and Roman numeral, never on first leaf of quire: a–b in II–III, e in IV, g–h in V–VI, a–d in VII–X. Written in long lines by several hands of xv^1. Secundo folio: *reuoluat quilibet*.

The volume belonged to John Paunteley (f. 181v), a Benedictine monk from St. Peter's Abbey and "sacre pagine professor" at Oxford around 1410. On f. i verso is a list of 27 + 1 "conciones," with thema, biblical source, and folio; omitted are sermons 16, 17, XX, 28, 29, 33.

Literature: Coxe 1973; Horner 1975, 1977, 1978, 1989; Haines 1989, 203–4.

Besides the sermons listed here, the volume contains the *Tractatus de accione elementorum* by John Chilmark (ff. 176a–179v).

R-01. Qvomodo stabit regnum, Luce 11 capitulo [Luke 11:18]. Sicut

testatur Sapiens, Sapiencie 6 capitulo, sapiencia et observancia precep-
torum Dei—Ff. 1–5v. [3 Lent.] Type 0.

*R-02. Pontifex introiuit in sancta, Ad Hebreos ix [Heb. 9:11–12?].
Anglice: þe bischope . . . Libro 2° Paralipomenon est scriptum quod gloriosus rex Salamon fecit sibi a statelich trone—Ff. 005v–012v, 063. [Pas-
sion Sunday.] Also O-12. Type C.

R-03. *Sermo Iohannis Paunteley in exequiis Walteri Froucetur, abbatis
Glouc', anno Domini millesimo CCCC° xii°, iii° die mensis Maii.* Fluuius
egrediebatur de loco, Genesis 2 capitulo [Gen. 2:10]. Anglice sic: Water
is went out of the reuer. Totus iste mundus potest dici magnus fluuius—
Ff. 13–20. Burial of Walter Froucetur ("sermo funeralis est" in table).
Type C minimal. Preached by John Paunteley. Edited in Horner 1975,
180–215, and in Horner 1977.

R-04. *Sermo de sancto Bernardo. Dominica in palmis coram quodam
episcopo.* Pater, dimitte illis, Luce 23 [Luke 23:34]. Karissimi, Celestis
magister ea quibus indigemus quomodo assequi debeamus edocens, "Petite," inquit—Ff. 20–27. Labeled "sermo de domino Bernardo" in the
table; the sermon contains one reference to Palm Sunday. Type 0.

R-05. Ascendit aurora, ascendit aurora, Genesis xxxii° capitulo [Gen.
32:26]. Reuerendi in Christo patres atque domini, Celestis imperii \celice
regionis/ piissime imperator eterne claritatis lumine naturaliter circum-
fulsus—Ff. 27–30. [Assumption of BVM.] Also W-004. Type 0.

R-06 *Sermo capitulo generali.* Quattuor facies vni erant, Ezechielis
1mo [Ezek. 1:6]. Karissimi, Beatus Gregorius 8 *Morum* de predicatoribus
loquens dicit quod vis et summa [*read* sentencia?] loquencium quadr[i]-
faria qualitate distinguitur—Ff. 30–39. General chapter sermon [of Cis-
tercians]. Type 0.

R-07. Ego propono animam meam, Iohannis 10 [John 10:15]. Beatus
Augustinus sermone *De fide* conuenientem modum nostre redempcionis
insinuans—Ff. 39–44. Type 0. At end (f. 44) an introductory prayer:
"In principio sermonis recommendo vobis dominum papam, omnes
prelatos . . . "

R-08. Clamauit miserere mei, Mathei 15 [Matt. 15:22]. Sicut narrat
Macrobius in *Saturnalis* libro 2, consuetudo Romanorum fuit quando
obsidebant ciuitatem hostium—Ff. 44–49v. Type C marginal.

R-09. Maria, Luce primo capitulo, et in euangelio hodierno [Luke
1:27]. In principio nostre collacionis breuissime, ut impetremus graciam
curramus ad nostram Mariam. Bernardus dicit: "Si queris"—Ff. 49v–
52v. [Annunciation.] Type 0.

R-10. Accipite Spiritum Sanctum, Iohannis 10 [John 20:22]. Consuetudo erat apud milites circa obsidionem Troie commorantes omni die quo ad bellum procederent—Ff. 52v-57v. [Pentecost.] Type B1.

R-11. Benedicta tu, Luce 2 [Luke 1:28, 42]. Reuerendi et domini, Sicut 3° Regum 10° legitur, illustris rex Salamon habuit in mari classem magnam—Ff. 57v-62v, incomplete? Type C minimal.

***R-12.** Exiuit de templo, Iohannis viii° [John 8:59]. Summus celi pontifex qui isto sacro tempore paciebatur passionem et mortem . . . In huius sermonis exordium exorabimus . . . Speciale templum—Ff. 63-70v. [Passion Sunday?] Also O-15. Type C.

***R-13.** Iesus, Mathei xv°, et in ewangelio hodierno [Matt. 15:21]. þe gracowsus comfort omnipotentis . . . Reuerendi domini, Sicut lego in sacra scriptura Apocalipsis x°—F. 71a r-v, incomplete. [2 Lent.] Also O-05. Type C.

***R-14.** *Sermo obiti.* Pvlcritudo agri mecum est, Psalmo xlix°, et pro themate hodierno [Ps. 49:11]. Karissimi \mei/, Secundum Gwidonem et alios dictatores idem est dictu pulcritudo agri et pulcher ager—Ff. 72-80. Burial, of Thomas Beauchamp ("sermo funeralis" in table). Type C. Edited in Horner 1975, 216-49, and in Horner 1978.

R-15. *De corpore Christi.* Probet seipsum homo [1 Cor. 11:28]. Non inueniuntur in aliqua ciuitate seu villa regni tot acute argumentaciones seu arguentes—Ff. 80-82. Corpus Christi. Type C marginal.

R-16. *In crastino pasche.* Redde quod debes, Mathei 18 [Matt. 18:28]. Benedicat nos Deus, etc. [really part of the sermon?] Introduccio istius thematis isto modo fiebat, scilicet quod duo sunt que maxime quemlicet [!] hominem obligant ad reddendum—F. 82. Easter Monday. Type 0.

R-17. *Dominica 3ª quadragesime.* Locutus est mutus, Luce 11, et in euangelio hodierno [Luke 11:14]. Reuerendi, etc., Inmensa Dei bonitas cuncta que ab inicio creauit et fecit—Ff. 82-86v. 3 Lent. Type 0.

R-XX. Seruitus non habet hereditatem [Eph. 5:5]. Anglice: Seruage and bondage haue not heuen herytage, other ellus the seruage of synne haue not heuen wymne, etc.—F. 86v. Type A. The quoted text is all that is given of this sermon.

R-18. *Ad visitacionem.* Venio querens fructum, Luce xiii° [Luke 13:6]. Reuerendi patres et domini, Qualiter ad reuelacionem [!] nostre indigencie in principio cuiuslibet nostri operis—Ff. 86v-89v. Visitation [of a Benedictine community]. Type 0.

R-19. *Dominica secunda quadragesime.* Vocauit nos Deus, prima Ad Tessalonisenses capitulo 4 [1 Thess. 4:7]. Venerandi domini, Secundum doctores causa quare Apostolus scripsit hanc epistulam erat ista: gentiles in primitiua ecclesia—Ff. 89v–98. 2 Lent. Type 0.

R-20. *Dominica tercia quadragesime.* Venit ira Dei, Ad Ephesios 5, in epistula que hodierne diei [Eph. 5:6]. Gentil Iesu, in whom ys comprehendit myȝth, wit, comfort, and vertu, be medyacioun . . . Cristis pepul, þe most opun knowynge experience scheuyth—Ff. 98–109. 3 Lent. Type E. Edited in Horner 1975, 72–110.

R-21. *Dominica palmarum.* Hec [!] sentite in vobis, quod et in Christo Iesu, Ad Philippenses 2° [Phil. 2:5]. Karissimi, Hoc nomen Iesus nomen est dignitatis regie; ideo debet adorari—Ff. 109–118, incomplete. Palm Sunday. Type B2.

R-22. Dominus tecum, Luce 1°, et in euangelio hodierno [Luke 1:28]. Reuerendi magistri et domini, Sicut legitur in quodam sermone quem beatus Bernardus fecit de isto sancto festo, omnipotens Deus quando creauit hominem—Ff. 119–123v. [Annunciation.] Type A.

R-23. Magna est fides tua, Mathei 15 [Matt. 15:28]. Teste scriptura sacra Genesis 2° capitulo Deus fecit paradisum voluptatis in quo plantauit omne lignum—Ff. 123v–129. [2 Lent?]. Type 0.

R-24. Veritatem dico, Iohannis 4° [John 8:45, 46]. Iesus via, veritas, et vita: via ad patria ducens . . . Venerandi mei, Perpendens ego talis—Ff. 129–130v, 133–134. Type B1. At end: "Quod Frater Ricardus Cotell."

R-25. Quomodo stabit regnum, Luce xi, et in ewangelio presentis dominice [Luke 11:18]. Quamuis a seculis in regibus magna fuerit gloria, machina multiplex, et regna varia—Ff. 132, 135–136. [3 Lent.] Type 0.

R-26. *Dominica 4ª aduentus.* Tv quis es, Iohannis primo, et in ewangelio presentis dominice [John 1:18]. Peregrinus ingrediens terram extraneam multas solet de statu ab indigenis questiones recipere—Ff. 134v, 131–131v. 4 Advent. Type 0.

R-27. In principio erat uerbum, Iohannis primo capitulo [John 1:1]. Reuerendi patres et domini, In principio huius sermonis breuissimi recommendatis omnibus . . . Eternitatem omnipotentis uerbi eternaliter apud Deum—Ff. 139–140, incomplete. Type 0.

R-28. Vestiuit pontificem, Leuitici viii° [Lev. 8:7]. Scriptura sacra Exodi xxviii° et Leuitici viii° et iiii [*read* Magister] Historiarum super illis locis dicit quod summus pontifex veteris legis erat vestitus tribus solempnibus qua—Ff. 140v, 137–138v, incomplete. [St. Birinus.] Also O-19. Type C minimal.

R-29. Sol egressus est super terram, sol egressus est super terram, Genesis xix capitulo [Gen. 19:23]. In Christo merito recolendi patres atque domini, Ante radios matutinos fulgentis aurore duo prenotanda signorum indicia solis ortum visibilis solent precedere—Ff. 141–143v. [Vigil of Christmas.] Type 0.

R-30. Estote sicut filii, Ad Ephesios 5 [Eph. 5:1]. Sextus Iulius *De bello Cesaris* refert quod fuit venerabilis princeps . . . Beth ʒe as gode childur . . . Be thys worthy prince I vndurstond at this tyme Crist—Ff. 144–152v, incomplete. 3 Lent ("sermo in tempore tribulacionis" in the table). Type E. Edited in Horner 1975, 111–46.

R-31. Coronauit eum in die leticie, Canticorum 3° [Song of Sol. 3:11]. Venerandi patres et magistri, Triumphantis milicie princeps coronatus residens in excelsis ineffabilem sue diuinitatis magnificenciam—Ff. 153–156, incomplete. [St. Alban.] Type 0.

R-32. Fructus lucis est in bonitate, Ad Ephesios 5to, et in epistula dominice iam instantis [Eph. 5:9]. Venerandi patres et amici, As þe famwes clerk Lincolniensis rehersit in his tretis that he made, *De spera celesti,* sex signes þer be—Ff. 156–163v, incomplete. [3 Lent.] Type E. Edited in Horner 1975, 147–79.

R-33. [Inuenisti graciam apud Deum (Luke 1:30).] Beginning missing; text begins, "Gabriel racionabilis est"—Ff. 164–171, acephalous. Type B1.

S

Oxford, Balliol College, MS 149

Parchment, in two parts. i + 221 leaves. End of xiv and xiv².

The manuscript has been described and analyzed by Mynors 1963, 130–35. In the (medieval) binding, two bifolia were exchanged between quires d and e, affecting modern ff. 39/44 and 51/56; the error was noticed and corrected by means of medieval *signes de renvoi.*

Sermons 1–23 in part 1, written in long lines in two hands (1–17 and 20–23; 18–19) of the late xiv. Sermon 24 in part 2. The manuscript contains a note, written in the main hand of part 1, which must be a copy of notes taken by a named but unidentified parish priest, who says he was born on 25 April 1361; see Mynors 1963, 132–33.

*S-01. Christus passus est vobis relinquens exemplum vt sequamini, 1 Petri 2 [1 Pet. 2:21]. Anglice sic: Crist in hys passion reliquit vobis quomodo schil doun, etc. Quamuis hec verba dicantur generaliter

Christianis omnibus—Ff. 1–15v. [Good Friday.] Also H-25, Z-19, and W-006. Type C.

S-02. *Sermo sabato quatuor temporum in aduentu Domini.* Factum est verbum Domini super Iohannem, Luce 3°, et in euangelio hodierno secundum vsum sancte Romane ecclesie et nostrum [Luke 3:2]. Iohannes Euangelista Filium Deum Christum comparat verbo dicens in principio— Ff. 15v–19v. Saturday of Ember Days in Advent. Type B2.

S-03. *De corpore Christi sermo.* Memoriam fecit mirabilium suorum misericors Deus, escam [Ps. 110:4–5]. Secundum sanctos Gregorium, Augustinum, et alios doctores, verbum comparatur cibo—Ff. 19v–23. Corpus Christi. Also W-007. Type B1.

S-04. *Sermo in die pasce.* Tene quod habes, Apocalipsis 3 [Rev. 3:11]. Reuerendi mei, Sicut scribit Dyascorides libro 2, capitulo 97, in India inferiori est arbor—Ff. 23–25v. Also B-133. Easter. Type C marginal.

S-05. *Sermo in die pasce.* Gaudere oportet quia frater tuus reuixit, 15 [Luke 15:32]. þe by-ouys to be glad . . . Sicut dicit scriptura sacra, Christus est frater noster—Ff. 25v–28. Easter. Type C marginal.

S-06. Ministri Christi sunt, 1 Corinthiorum xi [2 Cor. 11:23]. Secundum beatum Bernardum quatuor sunt quibus seruitur in hoc mundo: Mundus, caro, demon, et Deus—Ff. 28–31. Also W-010 and W-032. Type 0.

***S-07.** Amore langueo, Canticorum 2 capitulo [Song of Sol. 2:5]. Prolatiue [*corr. to* primo latine] potest dici sic: Karissimi, Sicut manifeste videntes [!]—Ff. 31–38v. [Good Friday.] Also B-088, D-2, and T-07. Type C. Edited in appendix B.

S-08. *Sermo in dominica in ramis palmarum.* Ite, soluite, et adducite, Mathei 21, et euangelio hodierno [Matt. 21:2]. In hiis verbis exprimit triplex misterium [!] apostolorum prelatorum—Ff. 38v, 51r–v, 40–41. Palm Sunday. Type 0.

S-09. *Pasche.* Panis cor hominis confirmet, Psalmo c^{mo} iii° [Ps. 103:15]. Inter ceteras peticiones quas posuit Dominus in oracione dominica—Ff. 41–43v, 56r–v. Easter. Type C minimal.

S-10. *Dominica prima quadragesime* [f. 56v]. Illi soli seruies, Deuteronomii ii°, et in euangelio hodierno [Deut. 6:13; cf. Matt. 4:10]. Carissimi mei, Esset voluntas mea hac vice aliquem sermonem vobis dicere ad presens ad honorem Dei . . . Quilibet homo in toto mundo deberet—Ff. 45–46. 1 Lent. Type 0.

S-11. *De aduentu Domini.* Parate viam Domini, Marci 1 [Mark 1:3].

Sicut in primo parente per diabolum via nobis patuit ad mortem, ita in Iesu Christo—Ff. 46–50v. Advent. Type 0.

S-12. *Sermo in die cinerum.* Conuertemini ad me in toto corde vestro, Ioelis ii capitulo, et epistula hodierna [Joel 2:12]. Quia totaliter auerti a Deo est dampnabile, et solum parcialiter reuerti ad Deum est culpabile—Ff. 50v, 39r–v, 52r–v. Ash Wednesday. Type 0.

S-13. Homo in cinerem reuertetur, Iob 34° capitulo [Job 34:15]. Reuerendi patres, Ex natura corumptiua racione regulata, vt "homo"—Ff. 52v–55. Type 0.

S-14. Cum fortis armatus custodit atrium suum, in pace sunt omnia que possidet, Luce xi° [Luke 11:21]. Anglice: Wyle the stronge y-armed... Primo that ys araied abell for to fiȝite... Ad hoc quod firma sit custodia—Ff. 55r–v, 44r–v, 57–59. Type B2.

S-15. Suscitare super pastorem meum, Zacharie 13 capitulo [Zech. 13:7]. Patris [!] mei, reuerendi domini et magistri, Iuxta sentenciam Saluatoris michi deccorantis imperantis n[u]nc predicator habeo existere veritatis—Ff. 59–63. Type 0. At the thema, marginal: "Sermo Iohannis de scrata f. Minorum."

S-16. *Dominica 3 quadragesime.* Ambulate in dileccione sicut Christus dilexit, Ad Ephesios 5 [Eph. 5:2]. Karissimi, Inuenio quod tria modernis temporibus diliguntur a multis—Ff. 65v–72. 3 Lent. Also in W-009 and W-031. Type B2.

S-17. *Sermo generalis de dileccione.* Ambulate in dileccione [Eph. 5:2]. Sicut Augustinus in Epistula ad Mecedones, bonos vel malos mores non faciunt nisi boni et mali amores—Ff. 72–75. General sermon. Type B2.

S-18. Exiit qui seminat seminare semen, etc., Luce viii, Mathei xiii [Luke 8:5 and Matt. 13:3]. Verba ista sunt bene exposita a Christo Saluatore nostro—Ff. 75v–77. Type 0.

S-19. Quare rubrum est indumentum tuum, Ysaie 63° capitulo [Isa. 63:2]. Secundum sentenciam doctorum hec fuit questio angelorum in die assencionis Domini et erit questio iudicandorum—Ff. 77v–83v, 77, incomplete. (The two lines at the top of f. 84 do not belong to this sermon.) [Good Friday.] Also A-35, Z-20, and Cambridge University Library MS Ee.6.27, ff. 73–84v; see also S-20. Type B1. See further under Z-20.

S-20. *Sermo Chambron in die parascheues.* Qvare rubrum est indumentum tuum, Ysaie 63° capitulo [Isa. 63:2]. Secundum sentenciam doctorum hec fuit questio angelorum in ascensione \aut in die ascencionis/ Domini, et erit questio iudicandorum—Ff. 84–86v. Good Friday. A shorter version of S-19. Type B1. The preacher is Chambron.

S-21. *Dominica 5* [?] *post epiphaniam, Mathei 13; dominica septuagesime, Mathei 20; dominica 21, Mathei 18; et sermo generalis.* Simile est regnum celorum homini [Matt. 13:45, 20:1, and 18:23]. Inuenio quod regnum celorum aliquando vocatur sancta ecclesia, aliquando anima humana, aliquando mansio angelorum et animarum sanctarum—Ff. 86v–87, incomplete. 5 [?] after Epiphany, Septuagesima, 21 after Trinity, and general sermon. Type 0. Only thirty lines, after which: "Residuum istius sermonis quere quere [!] in papiro post sermonem Miserere mei, etc., ad hoc signum," but the paper leaf or quire referred to is wanting.

S-22. [Miserere mei.] [The opening of the sermon is missing; the extant text begins just before the main division:] supra caput scripsit: Hic est deus pietatis et misericordie—Ff. 87–90, acephalous. Type 0. At the beginning of the text, "Hic deficit; require in papiro ad hoc signum," but the paper leaf or quire referred to is wanting.

S-23. *Sermo Chambron dominica 3 quadragesime.* Reuertar in domum meam vnde exiui, Luce xi° [Luke 11:24]. Karissimi, Presenti dominica de muto a demonio vexato tractatur, ad designandum duplicem effectum predicandi—Ff. 90–92v. 3 Lent. Type C minimal. Preacher: Chambron.

S-24. Querite et inuenietis, Mathei 7 et Luce ii [Matt. 7:7 and Luke 11:9]. Hodie sancta mater ecclesia recolit magos ab oriente uenisse et Christum natum diligenter inquisisse—Ff. 219–220v. Type 0.

T

Oxford, Magdalen College, MS 93

Paper, ii + 309 + ii leaves.

The manuscript was analyzed in Coxe 1973, 2:49–51. It has since then been refoliated.

Dimensions: ca. 290 × 220, written space 228 × 175; sermon T-07: leaf 294 × 220, written space 214 × 150. Collation: I⁸ (ff. 1–8), II⁸ (9–16), III⁸ (17–24), IV⁸ (25–32), V⁸ (33–40), VI⁴ (41–44), VII⁸ (45–52), VIII⁸ (53–60), IX⁸ (61–68), X⁸ (69–76), XI⁸ (77–84), XII⁸ (85–92), XIII⁸ (93–101, leaf 8 excised), XIV¹² (102–113), XV⁸ (114–121), XVI⁸ (122–129), XVII¹⁰

(130-139), XVIII[8] (140-147), XIX[20] (148-167), XX[4] (168-171), XXI[8] (172-178, leaf 8 lost), XXII[8] (179-184, leaves 1 and 8 lost), XXIII[12] (185-196), XXIV[8] (197-202, leaves 2 and 7 wanting), XXV[10] (203-212), XXVI[14] (213-226), XXVII[10] (227-236), XXVIII[8] (237-244), XXIX[8] (245-252), XXX[8] (253-260), XXXI[8] (261-268), XXXII[8] (269-276), XXXIII[8] (277-284), XXXIV[8] (285-292), XXXV[6] (293-297, leaf 6 excised), XXXVI[8] (298-305), XXXVII[8] (306-309, leaves 5-8 ripped out). Medieval quire signatures in several repeated sets (e.g., I-VI = medieval A-F, VII-XII = medieval A-F, etc.), indicating that the present volume was made up from several booklets. Written by several hands of the late fifteenth century, including that of John Dygoun. A notebook; see the discussion in chapter 13. Secundo folio: *Quecumque scripta sunt.*

Written on f. 311v, upside down, is "Liber M. Johannis Dygoun reclusi Bethlehem de Schene."

For contents see Coxe 1973. The new foliation is as follows: (1) ff. 1-42; (2) ff. 45-91; (3) ff. 93-97v; (4) ff. 102-111; (5) ff. 114-120; (6) f. 122; (7) ff. 122-123; (8) ff. 123-124; (9) f. 127r-v; (11) ff. 133-136; (17) ff. 157-160; (18) ff. 160v-167v; (20) f. 171v; (22) ff. 175v-176; (23) ff. 190, 179-183v; (24) ff. 185-192v; (25) ff. 198-201; (26) ff. 203-206; (27) ff. 213-224; (28) f. 224r-v; (29) f. 226r-v, possibly the conclusion of (31); (30) ff. 227-233; (31) ff. 233-236v, 226r-v; (32) ff. 237-244v; (33) ff. 245-266v, 268r-v; (34) ff. 268v, 267 (Bloomfield Incipits 8951); (35) ff. 269-275v, 277-280, 282-295v; (36) ff. 298-301v; (37) ff. 301v-304v; (38) ff. 306-309v.

T-01. Mortuus viuet, Iohannis 11 [John 11:25]. Lincolniensis *Dicto* 25 dicit et ponit tres mortes: corporis, anime, et gehenne—Ff. 130-132. Type B2. The sermon clearly ends on f. 132: "Dic hic narracionem de Egesippi et ibi fac finem." Evidently a funeral or memorial sermon for Isabel Fullthorp.

T-02. Mortuus viuet, Iohannis 11, et pro themate hodierno [John 11:25]. Gracia Domini nostri Iesu Christi, etc. Apostolus Paulus scribens 1 Ad Thimotheum 2.a petit ante omnia—F. 136v, incomplete. [Funeral or commemoration of a dead woman.] Type 0. It is not clear whether the distinctions on death, Latin and English, on f. 136 are intended for this sermon; if they are, the sermon is Type B1.

T-03. *In festo annunciacionis beate Marie.* Salutate Mariam, Ad Romanos vltimo [Rom. 16:6]. Karissimi, In isto festo sacratissimo Deus tria mirabilia fecit—Ff. 140-143v. Annunciation of BVM. Type B1.

T-04. *Annunciacionis.* Concipies et paries filium, Luce 1 [Luke 1:31]. Karissimi, In omni actu tria requiruntur, scilicet tempus, modus, et causa—Ff. 144-147. Annunciation of BVM. Type 0.

T-05. Ambulate, Ad Ephesios v^{to} [Eph. 5:2 etc.]. Karissimi, Homo existens de paupertate magna sequuntur eum multe miserie—Ff. 148-149. Type B2.

T-06. Ecce morior cum nichil horum fecerim, Danielis xiiii [Dan. 13:43]. Karissimi, In hiis verbis Christus pro nobis in cruce pendens ostendit se suis amicis conqueri flebiliter—Ff. 149-151. Type 0.

*T-07. Amore langueo, Canticorum 2° [Song of Sol. 2:5]. Probatiue potest dici: Karissimi, Sicut manifeste videtis—Ff. 152-157. [Good Friday.] Also B-088, D-2, and S-07. Type C. Edited here in appendix B.

T-08. Credite, Marci xi [Mark 11:24]. Gracia Domini nostri Iesu Christi, etc. Karissimi, Si aliquis imperator vel rex mandaret populo cui preest—Ff. 168-169, incomplete. Type A.

T-09. *Dominica 19.* Ascendens Iesus in nauiculam transfretauit ... potestatem talem hominibus, Mathei 9 capitulo, a; Marci 2; Luce v [Matt. 9:1-8]. In isto euangelio declaratur nobis miraculum per quod Dominus noster Iesus Christus ostendit potenciam sue deitatis—Ff. 172-174, incomplete? 19 after Trinity. Type 0.

T-10. *Dominica prima aduentus Domini.* Rex tuus venit, Mathei 21.a [Matt. 21:5]. Primo est considerandum quid est quod Iesus appropinquans Ierosolimis—Ff. 174-175v, incomplete. 1 Advent. Type 0.

W

Worcester, Cathedral Library, MS F.10

A composite volume of parchment and paper. ii + 336 leaves. Dimensions: 300 × 220, written space variously ca. 204/232 × 145/175.

Collation: I² (parchment; modern f. 1; leaf 1 excised), II¹² (2-8, 8x, 9-12), III¹⁰ (13-17, leaves 6-10 excised), IV¹² (18-29; medieval quire 1/1/?), V¹² (30-41, medieval quire 2/2/ii), VI¹² (42-53, medieval quire 4/19/iii), VII¹² (54-65, medieval quire 5/20/?), VIII¹² (66-75, leaves 11-12 excised; medieval quire 6/21/v), IX¹² (76-87, medieval quire 7/22/?), X¹⁰ (88-97, medieval quire 8/23/vii), XI¹² (98-109, medieval quire 9/10!/viii), XII¹² (110-121, medieval quire 10/11/ix), XIII¹² (122-132, leaf 10 ripped out; medieval quire 11/18!/x), XIV¹² (133-144, medieval quire 12/19/xi), XV¹² (145-156, medieval quire 13/13!/xii), XVI¹² (157-

168, medieval quire 14/14/xiii), XVII^{12} (169–179, leaf 12 ripped out; medieval quire 15/38!/xiiii), XVIII^{12} (180–189, leaves 1–2 excised; medieval quire ?/?/?), XIX^{12} (190–201, medieval quire 17/30!/xvi), XX^{12} (202–203, 203x, 204–212, medieval quire ?/18?/xvii), XXI^{12} (213–224, medieval quire 19/29/xviii), XXII^{12} (225–236, medieval quire 2./24!/xix), XXIII^{12} (237–248, medieval quire ?/25/xx), XXIV^{12} (249–259, leaf 12 excised; medieval quire 2./26/xxi), XXV^{2} (a paper bifolium, 260–261), XXVI^{8} (262–269, medieval quire ?/?/?), XXVII^{12} (270–283, with an added paper bifolium, 280–281; medieval quire 23/16/xxiii), XXVIII^{12} (284–294, 294x, medieval quire ?/?/?), XXIX^{10} (295–304, medieval quire ?/31/.xv), XXX^{8} (305–312, medieval quire ?/32/xxvi), XXXI^{8} (313–320, medieval quire ?/33/xxvii), XXXII^{12} (321–332, medieval quire ?/3.?/xxviii), XXXIII^{4} (333–336, medieval quire ?/?/?). Medieval foliation 1–320 with several errors. Traces of three different systems of medieval quire signatures appear on the opening folios: (a) Upper right of recto; (b) lower right of recto, both in Arabic numerals; (c) lower left of recto, in the gutter, in Roman numerals. In the collation above, I give what signatures are visible as a/b/c.

Parchment leaves: i, ii, 1, 225, 236, 237, 248, 249, 279, 283, 284, 285, 294, 294x, 333, 334, 335, 336. The codex comprises a number of booklets distinguishable by varying size, layout (either long lines or two columns), hands (a variety of fifteenth–century Anglicana hands with more or less dominant secretary features), and watermarks. Secundo folio: *tum vbertatem*.

Written on f. 335v are pentrials including "Willelmus, Wedmore, Johannes," and "Iste liber constat W Frampton." Written on f. 336 is "Meldenham Wygornye." Above it is "an inscription in which consonants are substituted for vowels: normalized it reads 'Iste liber constat dompno tome meldenham.' Meldenham was prior from 1499 to 1507" (Young 1944, 65).

Literature: Owst 1933, 15, 21, 38, 58, 86, 107–9, 120, 156, 179, 187, 225, 271–72, 332, 373–74, 407, 414, 427, 441, 452, 455, 509, 527–28, 530, 533, 542.

The manuscript contains 167 sermons, with occasional notes and narrationes between them.

W-001. Magna est fides tua, Mathei xv° [Matt. 15:28]. O altitudo incomprehensibilis bonitatis et pietatis Domini Dei nostri—Ff. 5v–8. [2 Lent.] Repeated as W-034. Type 0.

W-002. *Sermo Hugonis Legat in passione Domini.* Accipiant repromissionem vocati, accipiant repromissionem vocati [Heb. 9:15]. The helpe and the grace of Crist Iesu be with vs now and euere, Amen. I rede in Genesi . . . þat God thorw þe heȝe loue—Ff. 8–13v. Passion Sunday. Type E. Edited in Grisdale 1939, 1–21.

W-003. Dominus in celo parauit sedem suam, Psalmo cii° [Ps. 102:19]. Sicut testatur Ysydorus *Ethimologiarum* libro 18, inter omnia que debent preparari—Ff. 13v–14v, incomplete. [Ascension.] Type B2.

W-004. Ascendit aurora, Genesis xxxii° capitulo [Gen. 32:26]. Reuerendi in Christo patres atque domini, Celestis imperii piissimus imperator humanam nuper cernens naturam—F. 16r–v. [Assumption of BVM?] Also R-05. Type 0.

W-005. *In vigilia natalis Domini.* Protulit terra herbam virentem, Genesis 1° capitulo [Gen. 1:12]. Reuerendi patres et domini, Postquam genus humanum nostri primi parentis Adam exigente demerito—F. 17r–v. Vigil of Christmas. Type 0.

*****W-006.** *Optimus sermo de passione Christi.* Christus passus est vobis relinquens exemplum vt sequamini, Petri 2 [1 Pet. 2:21]. Anglice sic: Cryst in hijs passyone reliquit exemplum . . . Quamuis hec verba dicantur generaliter omnibus Christianis—Ff. 18–26v. Good Friday. Also H-25, S-01, and Z-19. Type C.

W-007. Memoriam fecit mirabilium suorum misericors Dominus, escam [Ps. 110:4–5]. Secundum sanctos Gregorium, Augustinum, et alios doctores, verbum comparatur cibo—Ff. 27–29v. [Corpus Christi.] Also S-03. Type B1.

W-008. Panis dat vitam, Iohannis 6 [John 6:33]. Karissimi, Verbum Dei frequenter dicitur verbum vite quia sicut panis corporalis—Ff. 29v–31. [Corpus Christi?] Repeated as W-030. Type B2.

W-009. Ambulate in dilectione sicut Christus dilexit, Ad Ephesios 5 [Eph. 5:2]. Karissimi, Inuenio quod tria modernis temporibus diliguntur a multis—Ff. 31–36. [3 Lent?] Repeated as W-031; also S-16. Type B2.

W-010. Ministri Christi sunt, 1 Corinthiorum xi [2 Cor. 11:23]. Secundum beatum Bernardum quatuor sunt quibus seruitur in hoc mundo: mundus, caro, demon, et Deus—Ff. 36–38v. Repeated as W-032; also S-06. Type 0.

W-011. Flos de radice ascendet et requiescet, Ysaie xi [Isa. 11:1–2]. Experimur naturaliter, karissimi, quod arbores et herbe naturaliter producunt folia ante florem—Ff. 38v–41v. Repeated as W-033. Type 0.

W-012. Accipite Spiritum Sanctum, Iohannis 20 [John 20:22]. Karissimi, Scitis quod est vulgare et commune dictum quod omne promissum est debitum—F. 41v, incomplete. [Pentecost.] Type 0.

W-013. Liberauit nos, Ad Galatas 4°, et in epistula presentis dominice [Gal. 4:31]. The helpe and þe grace . . . Crysten peple, thier wordis þat I af take—Ff. 42ra–47va. [4 Lent.] Type E. Edited in Grisdale 1939, 22–50.

W-014. Christus semetipsum optulit Deo, Christus etc., Ad Ebreos 9no [Heb. 9:14]. The help and te grace . . . Cristen peple, þes wordes þat ich ha take to prech of—Ff. 47va–52vb. [Passion Sunday.] Type E. Edited in Grisdale 1939, 50–80.

W-015. Acceperunt ramos palmarum, Iohannis xii [John 12:13]. Seneca libro secundo *De beneficiis* capitulo 20, þis clerk tellyt that ther was—Ff. 52vb–53vb, incomplete. [Palm Sunday.] Type E.

W-016. Lignum vite in medio paradisi, Genesis xi° [Gen. 2:9]. Reuerendi patres, In gloriosissimo paradiso orbis architipi, quem inmensa magestate solus inhabitat rex regum et dominus dominancium—Ff. 54–57v. [Sermon to clergy.] The opening twenty-eight lines are repeated on f. 73va–b and canceled. Type 0. Written in the top margin of f. 54 is "Folsam," evidently the name of the preacher.

W-017. Accipite armaturam Dei, Ad Ephesios 6 [Eph. 6:13]. In quibus verbis includuntur tria necessaria in omni sermone. Quiscumque predicaret oportet eum habere—Ff. 57v–62v. Type C marginal. Written before thema is "Folsam."

W-018. Beati qui audiunt verbum Dei, Luce xi^{mo} [Luke 11:28]. In quibus verbis quia virtuosa operacio consulitur vobis in audiendo verbum Dei—Ff. 62v–66v. [Lent.] Type C marginal.

W-019. Requiescet pax, Luce 14 [Luke 10:6]. Karissimi, Mathei 12 legitur quod postquam Christus iecisset demonium ab vno ceco et muto—Ff. 66v–68v. Repeated as W-096. Type B1.

W-020. Iesus exiuit de templo [John 8:59]. Primo in antetema qualiter sol habuit quoddam templum, cuius templi descripcio habetur in Ouidio *De transformatis*—F. 68v. Type B1. Only a note on the parts of a temple and their moral meaning. Followed by another note recording a similar moralization of the chalice, from a sermon of some "frater predicator" on the thema "Hic calix nouum testamentum est" preached on Palm Sunday; see chapter 6, n. 1.

W-021. Veni ad me, Regum xvii° [1 Sam. 17:44]. Sicut iudicio naturali cognoscimus quod quando aliquis artifex presumptuosus suscipit aliquod opus—Ff. 69–73va. [Assumption of BVM.] The first seventeen lines are copied again (with slight changes) on f. 179v and canceled; the original following folio has been ripped out. Type 0.

W-022. *Introitus Sentenciarum.* Lignum vite in medio paradisi, Genesis 2° capitulo [Gen. 2:9]. Reuerendi magistri, patres, et domini, Fons sapiencie, verbum Dei, in orto anime racionalis scaturiendo emanaciones—Ff. 74ra–75va. Academic sermon, introduction to Peter Lombard's *Sentences.* Type 0. This sermon seems to replace another on the same thema, W-016, which was copied or begun to be copied before it and then was canceled.

W-023. Multi sunt vocati, Mathei 20 [Matt. 20:16]. Reuerendi patres et magistri, Vt vinea Domini Sabaoth ecclesia militans sponsa Christi in triplici actu—F. 75vb, incomplete. [To clergy?] Type 0.

W-024. Habundant passiones Christi, 2° Ad Corinthios primo [2 Cor. 1:5]. Summus rerum pontifex solo sue bonitatis intuitu cuncta esse producens—Ff. 76ra–77rb. [Passion.] Type 0.

W-025. Erumpe et clama, Ad Galathas 4ᵗᵒ [Gal. 4:27]. Reuerendi domini, Prò materia huius sermonis diligenter est notandum quod tria precipue faciunt hominem clamare—Ff. 77va–78vb. Type 0.

W-026. Ego Iohannes vidi ciuitatem, Apocalipsis 23° capitulo [Rev. 22:8]. Reuerendissimi magistri, patres et domini, Princeps philosophorum Aristoteles—Ff. 78vb–80ra. [Academic sermon on the *Sentences.*] Type 0.

W-027. *Introitus Sentensiarum.* Semper laus in eius ore, Psalmo 33° [Ps. 33:2]. Reuerendi domini, patres, et magistri, Secundum beati Augustini doctrinam maior est sacre scripture subtilitas—Ff. 80ra–81rb. Academic sermon on the *Sentences.* Type 0.

W-028. *Sermo in conuocacione vel in capitulo generali.* Principes populorum congregati sunt, Psalmo 46 [Ps. 46:10]. Qui autem nunc prelati vocantur, olim populi dicebantur. Ideo dicit Iohannes Crisostomus—Ff. 81rb–83rb. Convocation or general chapter. Type 0. Edited in Pantin 1933.

W-029. *Sermo ad clerum vel ad prelatos bonus.* Speciosus est in splendore, Ecclesiastici 43° [Ecclus. 43:12]. Oriens sol iusticie et splendor lucis eterne ab interius penetralibus celestis archani mundum foras voluit euocare—Ff. 83rb–84va. Sermon to clergy; in honor of St. Alban; on basis of prayer for Pope Boniface XI and "King H." dateable to 1399–1404. Repeated as W-099. Type 0.

W-030. *Optimus sermo de sacramento altaris.* Panis dat vitam, Iohannis 6 [John 6:33]. Karissime [!], Verbum Dei frequenter dicitur verbum vite, quia sicut panis corporalis—Ff. 84vb–86ra. [Corpus Christi?] Repeats W-008. Type B2.

W-031. Ambulate in dilectione sicut Christus dilexit, Ad Ephesios 5 [Eph. 5:2]. Karissimi, Inuenio quod tria modernis temporibus diliguntur de multis—Ff. 86ra–90rb. [3 Lent?] Repeats W-009; also S-16. Type B2.

W-032. Ministri Christi sunt, 1 Corinthiorum xi [2 Cor. 11:23]. Secundum beatum Bernardum quatuor sunt quibus seruitur in hoc mundo: mundus, caro, demon, et Deus—Ff. 90rb–92va. Repeats W-010; also S-06. Type 0.

W-033. Flos de radice ascendet et requiescet, Ysaie xi [Isa. 11:1–2]. Experimur naturaliter, karissimi, quod arbores et herbe naturaliter producunt folia ante florem—Ff. 92va–95rb. Repeats W-011. Type 0.

W-034. Magna est fides tua, Mathei xv° [Matt. 15:28]. O altitudo incomprehensibilis bonitatis et pietatis domini Dei nostri—Ff. 95va–97vb. [2 Lent?] Repeats W-001. Type 0.

W-035. In gloria requiescet, Prouerbiorum xiiii° [Ecclus. 14:26]. Reuerendi patres et domini, Triplici radio virtuali exigitur quilibet operator spiritualis verbum Dei seminaturus—Ff. 97vb, 285rb–v, 3–5v. [Assumption of BVM.] Type 0.

W-036. Petite [et accipi, *canceled*], Luce xi [Luke 11:9]. Karissimi, Legitur in Vitis Patrum quod petenti a quodam sancto verbum Dei— Ff. 98ra–99vb. Type 0.

W-037. Est vita eterna vt cognoscant te, Iohannis xvii, et in ewangelio vigilie ascensionis [John 17:3]. Fratres, Sicut homo constans ex duplici natura, corporali videlicet et spirituali—Ff. 100ra–101vb. [Vigil of Ascension.] Type A.

W-038. Vt testimonium perhiberet de lumine, Iohannis i [John 1:7]. Solent testes veridici ad testimonium ducti de scitis deponere—Ff. 101vb–102ra. Type 0.

W-039. Venit, Iohannis 1 [John 1:7 or 11]. Solent duces et reges incliri [!] principes potentes et strenui—F. 102ra–b. Type 0.

W-040. Non, Iohannis 1 [?]. Duo loc[cuc]ionum sunt genera, et due sunt species diuinitus accepte sermonum—F. 102rb–vb. Type 0.

W-041. *De sancto Edmundo.* Erat lux vera que illuminat, etc. [John 1:9]. Karissimi, Pro quo omnium mortalium laborat fama—Ff. 102vb–103va. St. Edmund, but the sermon speaks about St Catharine. Type 0.

W-042. Dedit, Iohannis 1 [John 1:12]. Inter liberales et prodigos sic solet plurimum variari condicio—Ff. 103va–104ra. Type 0.

W-043. Dedit, vbi prius [John 1:12]. Secundum sentenciam Philosophi 4 Ethicorum generalium personarum condicio sic in accepcione—F. 104ra–va. Type 0.

W-044. Potestatem, Iohannis 1 [John 1:12]. Motus continui mundi, carnis, et diaboli sic corda hominum ventilant—Ff. 104va–105ra. Type 0.

W-045. Fuit homo, Iohannis 1 [John 1:6]. Primus parens cum dati sibi premii dignitate reiecta—F. 105ra–vb. Type 0.

W-046. Omnis [*for* omnes?], Iohannis primo capitulo [John 1:7?]. Karissimi, Beatus Bernardus *De gracia et libero arbitrio* capitulo 8 probare videtur—Ff. 105vb–106rb. Type 0.

W-047. Venientem, Iohannis 1° [John 1:9]. In aduentu regis et principis, domini eximii et potentis ad ciuitatem aliquam—Ff. 106va–107ra. Type 0.

W-048. Hominem, Iohannis i [John 1:9]. Karissimi, Licet prophecie ac sacre pagine detractatores videantur asserere—F. 107ra–va. [St. Andrew?] Type 0.

W-049. In mundo erat, Iohannis primo [John 1:10]. Karissimi, Tam fide quam scripturis testantibus—F. 107va–b. Type 0.

W-050. Mundus, Iohannis 1 capitulo [John 1:10]. Karissimi, Sicut dicit Crisostomus omelia 18 *Operis imperfecto*[!], Non est in mundo—107vb–108rb. Type 0.

W-051. *De sancto Nicholayo.* Eum, Iohannis 1° [John 1:10]. Karissimi, Sicut dicit beatus Augustinus *De perfeccione iusticie,* "Dominus," inquit Augustinus, "iusticiam comprehendit"—F. 108rb–va. St. Nicholas. Type 0.

W-052. *In concepcione beate marie.* Non cognouit, Iohannes 1° [John 1:10]. Princeps seculi, princeps mundi, princeps tenebrarum et miserie—Ff. 108va–109rb. Conception of BVM. Type 0.

W-053. Cognouit eum, Iohannis 1° [John 1:10]. Coram sapiente et iudice qui negocia sua sunt facturi—109rb–110rb. [On BVM.] Type 0.

W-054. Sedit in solio regni sui, Hester i° capitulo [Esther 1:2]. Solebant magno por'e [*for* magne potencie?] dignitate prefecti vt reges illustres et domini, magne sciencie veritate prouecti vt doctores nobiles et magistri—Ff. 110rb–111va. [Academic sermon, praise of theology.] Type 0.

W-055. Non affectamus laudes, Ieronimus in prologo libri Hester [Jerome's prologue to the Book of Esther]. Karissimi, Vt dicit Gregorius 2 *Morum,* laus humana oculis oblata mortalibus mentem operantis inmutat—F. 111va–b. Type 0.

W-056. Cunta faciebat consilio, Hester i [Esther 1:13]. Mundi sapiens architectus cunta disponens numero, pondere, et mensura, Sapiencie 9— Ff. 111vb–112va. Type 0.

W-057. Inuenit graciam in conspectu illius, Hester 2° [Esther 2:9]. Multos et in multis legimus Christum Dominum quesiuisse quem multos in multis legimus inuenisse. Magdalena Christum inuenit—Ff. 112va–113rb. Type 0.

W-058. Flectebant genua et adorabant, Hester [Esther 3:2]. Multos constat coram Deo indies genuflectere—F. 113rb–vb. ["Isto tempore sacro."] Type 0.

W-059. *De sancto Gregorio.* Hoc honore condignus est, Hester 5to [Esther 6:11]. Karissimi, Sanctos [?] multos quos ad honoris fastigium non ambicio popularis—Ff. 113vb–114va. St. Gregory. Type 0.

W-060. Stabat in ministerio regis, Hester 7mo [Esther 7:9]. Secundum quod dicit Augustinus 11 *De ciuitate Dei,* capitulo 12, omnes de suo perseuerancie premio certi—Ff. 114va–115ra. Type 0.

W-061. Quid vis fieri, Hester 9 [Esther 9:12; cf. 7:2]. Sicut dicit Hugo de Sancto Victore, capitulo de oracione, Dei beneficia ad memoriam reuocemus—F. 115ra–va. Type 0.

W-062. *De sancto Patricio Hybernie episcopo.* Fecit signa multa, Hester 11 [Esther 10:9]. Solent magni et magnifici regum precipue fulti subsiduis non exigua facere—Ff. 115va–116rb. St. Patrick. Type 0.

W-063. Humiles exaltati sunt, Hester 12 [Esther 11:11]. Sicut Augustinus quarto *Contra Iulianum,* capitulo 22, et capit a Tulio *De re publica*, sicut dicit ibidem Tullius inquit Augustinus hominem—Ff. 116rb–117ra. [Lent.] Type 0.

W-064. *De sancto Cuthberto.* Eius imperio subiecti sumus, Hester 13 [Esther 13:1]. Augustinus *83 questionum,* questione 63, duabus personis, videlicet sacerdotali et regina [!], ad quas sacrosancta unicio pertinebat— F. 117ra–vb. St. Cuthbert. Type 0.

W-065. Nunc inuoca Dominum, Hester 14 [Esther 15:3]. Sicut dicit Augustinus in libello suo *De miseria hominis:* "Qicquid videt, quicquid splendit, quicquid pulcherrimum est"—Ff. 117vb–118va. Type 0.

W-066. [Amore langueo (Song of Sol. 2:5), *marg.*]. Induite, Ad Ephesios 4to [Eph 4:24]. Rex sanctorum conforta me principatum tenens et da sermonem rectum et bene sonantem—Ff. 118va–121vb, incomplete. [Good Friday.] Type C minimal. The thema is "Amore langueo"; at the head of the sermon is written "Antethema."

W-067. *Nota istum sermonem pro cena Domini.* Rex tuus venit tibi,

Mathei 21° [Matt. 21:5]. In quibus verbis ostenditur iocundissimum matrimonium vmquam factum inter potenciam et misericordiam Dei—Ff. 122ra–124va. Maundy Thursday. Type C marginal.

*W-068. *Die parasceue.* Secundum gloriam eius multiplicata est ignominia eius [1 Macc. 1:42]. In quibus verbis potestis videre duo tangencia Christi personam—Ff. 124va–126va. Good Friday. Type C.

W-069. Existis in desertum, Mathei xi° [Matt. 11:7]. Reuerendi magistri, patres, et domini, Nostri thematis verba tam historice quam allegorice diligenter indaganti occurret triplex esse desertum—F. 126va–b, incomplete. [3 Advent?] Type 0.

W-070. Sanguis Christi emundabit conscienciam uestram, Ad Hebreos 9 capitulo [Heb. 9:14]. Tria inuenio in sacra scriptura que mundant humanam conscienciam. Primum est sermo diuinus—Ff. 127ra–130ra. [Lent.] Type C minimal.

W-071. *Sermo magistri Iohannis Fordham in capitulo generali.* Congregate vos in domum discipline, Prouerbiorum xi° capitulo, et pro themate hodierno [Ecclus. 51:31]. Amantissimi patres et domini, Oriens splendor solis iusticie candorque lucis eterne et speculum sine macula deifice maiestatis—Ff. 130rb–131rb, incomplete. General chapter. Type 0. On Fordham see chapter 3, note 79.

*W-072. *Pro patria* [read *penitencia?*]. Conuertimini, Ioelis 2° capitulo [Joel 2:12]. Reuerendi domini, Duos dominos I rede of in sacra scriptura qui continue sunt contrarie et aduersantes—Ff. 131rb–132v. [Lent, perhaps Ash Wednesday: "Isto sacro tempore quadragesime futuro" and "iam instantibus penitencie sacratis diebus."] Type C.

W-073. Ductus est Iesus in desertum a spiritu vt temptaretur a diabolo, Mathei 4 [Matt. 4:1]. Ad literam iam post lapsum [read baptismum] suum recessit in desertum et ibi temptatus est a diabolo— F. 133ra–b, incomplete. [1 Lent?] Type 0.

W-074. *Dominica 2ª quadragesime.* Domine, adiuua me, Mathei 3° [Matt. 15:25]. Tria sunt circa que versatur intencio predicatoris: primum vt informet peccatores—Ff. 133rb–134va. 2 Lent. Type 0.

W-075. Erat Iesus eiciens demonium, et illud erat mutum, et cum eiecisset demonium locutus est mutus, Luce xi [Luke 11:14]. Hoc euangelium octo continet. Primo Saluator miraculum operatur—Ff. 134vb–135va. [3 Lent?] Type 0.

W-076. Nolite conformari huic seculo, Romanorum 12, et in epistula hodierna [Rom. 12:2]. Reuerendi magistri, patres, et domini, In principio huius colacionis nolite confirmari [!] huic seculo. Reuerendi domini, Quia testante beato Iohanne—Ff. 135va–136va. [2 after Epiphany.] Type 0.

W-077. Quamuis eminens sciencia desideranda sit in pastore, tamen competens tolleratur, secundum Apostolum Ad Corinthios octavo: "Sciencia inflat"—Ff. 136vb–138rb. Type 0. This item has no thema or standard sermon structure, though it ends with the normal closing formula: "oportet vos intrare in regnum celorum, ad quod nos perducat qui sine fine viuit et regnat. Amen." It expounds the articles of faith, commandments, petitions, virtues, vices, and some other matter and may be a simple priest's manual.

W-078. Adueniente iam et iminente tempore miseracionem et miseriarum Domini Iesu—F. 138va, incomplete. Four points for meditation on Holy Thursday. Possibly not a part of a sermon but a guide to meditation. Type 0.

W-079. In nomine Patris et Filii et Spiritus Sancti [Matt. 28:19]. Quanta sit dignitas humane condicionis—Ff. 138vb–139ra, incomplete. Contains references to a "sermo precedens," whose first of the four parts announced in the division was given before none. Type 0.

W-080. Seminauit bonum semen in agro, Mathei xiii° [Matt. 13:24]. Patres et domini reuerendi, Ager veteris sinagoge quem a publica via gencium ceremoniarum pluralitas clausura notabili circumserit—Ff. 139rb–140va. [Academic sermon; praise of theology and Peter Lombard.] Type 0.

W-081. *Sermo de morte.* Sic est omnis qui natus est, Iohannes 3° [John 3:8]. Ad ea que sunt de iure nature omnis creatura particeps obligatur, sed mori est connaturale homini—Ff. 140va–141vb. On death. Type 0.

W-082. *De rogacionibus.* Orate pro inuicem vt saluemini, Iacobi 5 [James 5:16]. Scitis quod quando aliquis aduocatus est iturus ad curiam— Ff. 141vb–142va. Rogation Days. Type 0.

W-083. *Sequitur sermo de vno mortuo.* Qvo abiit Symon, 1 Machabeorum 5 [1 Macc. 5:21]. Reuerendi mei, Christus Filius Dei loquens discipulis suis dicens in parabolis Luce 19 sic inquit: "Homo quidam nobilis abiit"—Ff. 142va–144rb. Funeral sermon. Repeated as W-092; also H-03. Type 0.

W-084. *Sermo in rogacionibus.* Clamemus in celum et miseretur nostri Deus noster, Machabiorum primo capitulo 4 [1 Macc. 4:10]. Karissimi mei, Cristus Iesus Matthei 5 dat nobis vnum sanum consilium—F. 144rb–vb, incomplete. Rogation Days. Type B2.

W-085. Sitis ipsi sapientes, 2 Ad Corinthios xi [2 Cor. 11:19]. In has [!] verbis notantur diuersa intra homini [!]. Primo vita secundum racionem—Ff. 145ra–150rb. Type C marginal.

W-086. Quid hic statis tota die ociosi, Mathei 20, etc. [Matt. 20:6]. In quibus verbis comprehendi possunt duo conueniencia predicatoribus verbi Dei—Ff. 150rb–153vb. Type 0.

W-087. Probet seipsum homo et sic de pane edat, 1 Corinthiorum 11 [1 Cor. 11:28]. In quibus verbis duo sunt consideranda. Primum est discussio seu consideracio cuiuslibet hominis in seipso—Ff. 154va–158va. Type A.

W-088. In finem dilexit. Iohannis xiii, et in euangelio hodierno [John 13:1]. Karissimi, Sicut dicit beatus Iohannes euangelista, Dominus noster Iesus Christus appropinquante die passionis—Ff. 158va–162rb. Type C minimal.

W-089. Sic currite vt comprehendatis, 1 Ad Corinthios 9, et in epistula presentis dominice [1 Cor. 9:24]. Karissimi, Ad disponendum et preparandum nos ad currendum—Ff. 162rb–166rb. [Septuagesima.] Type B1.

W-090. *Duodena passionis Christi.* Audiat terra verba oris mei [Deut. 32:1]. Ecce iam videmus quomodo celum et terra et omnia elementa accusantur de morte—F. 169r–v. Type 0.

W-091. Reuertar, Luce 11ᵐᵒ [Luke 11:24]. Naturalis ordo fatetur vt prius attemptetur clemencia et postmodum sequatur vindicta—Ff. 170–173v, incomplete. [3 Lent?] Type 0. Cf. sermons B-147 and O-32.

W-092. *Sermo in obitu notabilis persone.* Quo abiit Symon, 1 Machabeorum 5 [1 Macc. 5:21]. Reuerendi mei, Christus Filius Dei loquens discipulis suis dicit in parabolis Luce 19 sic: Inquit, "homo quidam nobilis abiit"—Ff. 173v–176. Funeral of an important person. Repeats W-083; also H-03. Type 0.

W-093. *Sermo in rogacionibus. / Sermo bonus dominica 4ᵃ quadragesime [marg.].* Veritatem dico vobis, quare non creditis. Iohannis 8, et in euangelio hodierno [John 8:46?]. Domini et amici, Hec verba fuerunt Christi ad Iudeos et possunt esse predicatorum—Ff. 176–179v. 4 Lent. Repeated as W-112. Type B2.

W-094. *In assencione Domini.* Ascendit in montem, Mathei 5° capitulo [Matt. 5:1]. Karissimi, Sicut sacra commemorat scriptura, dum Christus fuit in hoc mundo tribus vicibus ascendit in montem—Ff. 179v–181v. Ascension. Type 0. This sermon evidently replaces W-021, whose beginning "Reuerendi domini, Racione naturali cognoscimus quod cum aliquis artifex presumptuosus suscipit aliquod opus" appears on f. 179v and is canceled.

W-095. Omnis lingua confiteatur, Ad Philippenses 2° [Phil. 2:11]. Karissimi, Secundum Ysidorum *Ethimologiarum* libro 9, capitulo primo, sicut sunt tres lingue principales—Ff. 181v–183v. Type B1. Perhaps only a protheme, leading to the division.

W-096. Requiescet pax, Luce 10 [Luke 10:6]. Karissimi, Matthei 12 legitur quod postquam Iesus iecisset demonium ab vno ceco et muto— Ff. 183v–185. Repeats W-019. "In hoc sermone multum tractat de pace" is written on f. 184, top margin. Type B1.

W-097. *In parasceue.* Quid faciam de Iesu, Mathei 21 [Matt. 27:22]. Hec verba dici possunt a beata Virgine Maria vel sancta Ecclesia et a peccatrice anima—Ff. 185–187v. Good Friday. Type 0.

W-098. *In parasceue bonus* [*sermo*]. Occiditur Christus, Danielis 9 [Dan. 9:26]. Hec verba prophecie per multa curicula annorum ante Christi adventum et mortem spiritu prophetico erant prenunciata—Ff. 187v–188v, incomplete. Good Friday. Type 0. Followed (f. 189r–v) by a copy of the end of W-113, which has been canceled.

W-099. Speciosus est in splendore, Ecclesiastici 43° [Ecclus. 43:12]. Oriens sol iusticie et splendor lucis eterne ab interius penetralibus celestis archani mundum foras voluit euocare cuncta—F. 189v, incomplete. [Sermon to clergy.] Repeats W-029. Type 0.

W-100. Oculi mei semper ad Dominum [Ps. 24:15]. Nota quod diabolus laqueum parat vt animas quasi aues capere queat—F. 190r–v. Type 0.

W-101. Descende priusquam moriatur filius meus, Iohannis 4, et in euangelio dominice iam instantis [John 4:49]. Reuerendi magistri, patres, et domini, Primi hominis miseria et pii redemptoris misericordia in serie presentis euangelii pariter includuntur—Ff. 190v–192v. [21 after Trinity.] Type 0.

*W-102. Venit, Mathei 21, etc. [Matt. 21:5]. Reuerendi domini, Speciale templum et habitacio quod Christus Filius Dei habet hic in terra est multitudo et congregacio fidelium—Ff. 192v–195, incomplete? [Sermon to clergy.] Type C.

W-103. Fructum afferunt, Luce 8, et instantis dominice euangelio [Luke 8:15]. Reuerendi magistri, patres, et domini, In agro dominico fructificantes in triplicem solent statum distingui—Ff. 195–196v. [Sexagesima.] Type 0.

W-104. *In natiuitate Beate Virginis.* Lux orta est, Ysaie ix capitulo [Isa. 9:2]. Reuerendi patres et domini, Fons et origo sapiencie, virtutum largitor, et remunerator meritorum—Ff. 196v–198v. Nativity of BVM. Repeated as W-159. Type 0.

W-105. Abite liberi ad patrem, Genesis 44 [Gen. 44:17]. Reuerendi patres et domini, Postquam primus parens de patria libertatis in locum miserabilis servitutis—Ff. 198v–200v. [Deposition of St. Benedict.] Repeated as W-160. Type 0.

W-106. *In natiuitate sancte Marie.* Ego quasi vitis fructificaui, Ecclesiastici 14 [Ecclus. 24:23]. Reuerendi domini, Que, qualis, et quanta sit benedicta Virgo cuius concepcionem hodie celebramus—Ff. 200v–201v. Nativity or Conception of BVM. Repeated as W-161. Type 0.

W-107. Ite in castellum, Mathei xxi° [Matt. 21:2]. Reuerendi patres, In primeva creacione generis humani graciosa bonitas omnipotentis Dei dedit prothoparenti nostro Ade pro se et omnibus suis castellum—Ff. 201v–206, incomplete. [Palm Sunday.] Repeated as W-151. Refers to the falls of the duke of Dublin, the archbishop of York, the count of Suffolk, and other magnates, which occurred in the late 1380s. Type C marginal.

W-108. Nigra sum et formosa, Canticorum primo [Song of Sol. 1:4]. Solet esse assercio popularis colorem nigram indelectabilem esse—Ff. 206–209, incomplete. [Funeral of Lady Blackworth.] Type C marginal.

W-109. Cooperatores simus veritatis; hec verba sunt in tercia canonica euangeliste Iohannis [3 John 8]. Honorabiles magistri, patres, atque domini, Teste beato Augustino *De vita beata,* capitulo xxvii°, illa est plena satietas animorum—Ff. 209–210v. Type 0.

W-110. Dicit Dominus, lauda, filia Syon [Zeph. 3:14]. Hiis verbis Dominus filiam Syon ad laudem inuitat. O Beata Virgo potest dici filia Syon—Ff. 210v–212. Type 0.

W-111. Ecce nubecula parva quasi vestigium hominis assendebat de mari, iii Regum 18 [1 Kings 18:45]. Legitur Genesis 31 de Iacocob [!] qui luctabatur cum angelo, cui dixit angelus—F. 212r–v, incomplete. Sermon in praise of BVM. Type 0.

W-112. Veritatem dico, quare non creditis michi, Iohannis 8, et in euangelio hodierno [John 8:46?]. Domini, Hec verba fuerunt Christi ad Iudeos et possunt esse predicatorum populo—Ff. 213–215. [Passion Sunday?] Repeats W-093. Type B2.

W-113. *De sancto Benedicto.* Surgam et ibo ad patrem, Luce 15 [Luke 15:18]. Reuerendi magistri, patres, atque domini, Grauis offensa peccatoris et grandis clemencia redemptoris in hodierna Christi parabola innuuntur—Ff. 215–217v. St. Benedict. Type 0. See W-098.

W-114. Conuersi estis nunc ad pastorem, prima Petri 2 [1 Pet. 2:25]. Quamdiu oues non sunt sub manu pastores [!], tamdiu sunt in periculo—Ff. 217v–218v. [To clergy?] Type 0.

W-115. *Sermo in natali.* Natus est hodie Saluator, Luce 2° capitulo

[Luke 2:11]. Reuerendi patres mei, Hodie vt solempnizat Ecclesia dum vox angelica sonuit—Ff. 218v–219. Christmas. Type 0.

W-116. *Sermo in passione.* Grauiter vulneratus sum, 3 Regum 23 capitulo [1 Kings 22:34]. Karissimi, Predicator verbi Dei predicato debet sic vilescere ut vulneret superbos exemplo—Ff. 219–220v. Passion. Repeated as W-148. Type 0.

W-117. Pax vobis, Luce vltimo et Iohannis 20 [Luke 24:36 and John 20:20]. Reuerendi patres et domini, Cum iuxta laudabilem ordinis nostri consuetudinem visitacionem precedere sermo debeat salutaris—Ff. 220v–221v. [Visitation of monastery.] Type 0.

W-118. Videte vocacionem vestram, Ad Corinthios primo [1 Cor. 1:26]. Reuerendi patres et domini, Triplicem inuenio in sacra scriptura vocacionem—Ff. 222–223. [Visitation sermon?] Type 0.

W-119. Benedictus es in templo, Danielis 4to [Dan. 3:53]. Benedictus Deus in donis suis et sanctus in omnibus operibus suis—Ff. 223–224. [St. Benedict.] Type 0.

W-120. Purum diligenter monstrat. Textus est Philosophi 2° *De sompno et vigilia,* capitulo 2° [Aristotle *De insomniis* 2 (460a.14–15)]. Reuerendi mei, Quia nouerit vestra discrecio quod inter consuetudines quas mater nostra venerabilis antiquitus exercuit—F. 224r–v, incomplete? [Academic sermon in praise of philosophy.] Type 0.

W-121. *De castitate.* Timentibus Deum orietur sol iusticie, Machabeorum 3° capitulo [Mal. 4:2]. Reuerendi mei, Quia secundum Philosophum anima in sua prima creacione est tabula nuda—Ff. 225ra–227va. Type 0.

W-122. *De bono exemplo aliis proponendo.* Expectamus Dominum, Ad Philippenses 3° [Phil. 3:20]. Iustissimi iudicis sentencia diffinitiua exigentibus parentis nostri demeritis in hanc insulam deportati ut per gloriam resurreccionis reformemur—Ff. 227va–229rb. [To clergy?] Type 0.

W-123. *De sancto Edmundo.* Regnabit rex, Ieremie 23, et in epistola dominicali hodierna [Jer. 23:5]. Reuerendi magistri, patres, et domini, Ierarcha suppremus rex omnipotens Deus noster mundi minoris regimen—Ff. 229rb–231ra. St. Edmund the king. Type 0.

W-124. Hodie incipiam te exaltare, Iosue iii capitulo [Josh. 3:7]. Reuerendi patres et domini, Sine gracia [*read* gracie] specialis influencia ipsius fontis misericordie celestium atque terrestrium conditoris—Ff. 231ra–235ra. [Assumption of BVM.] Prayer "pro rege nostro Richardo nunc nouiter creato" [*for* coronato in 1377?]. Type 0.

W-125. *Alius sermo.* Vt filii lucis ambulate, Ad Ephesios 5° [Eph.

5:8]. Reuerendi domini et magistri, Tria conspicio necessaria cuilibet viatori que fideles animos ad spiritualem progressum dirigunt indefessos—Ff. 235ra–237ra. [To clergy.] Type 0. Like the preceding sermon, this also deals with chastity.

W-126. *Sermo de assumpcione beate Marie Virginis, etc.* Data est ei corona, Apocalipsis vi [Rev. 6:2]. Reuerendi patres et domini, Secundum quod dicit Eustachius 8 *Ethicorum,* capitulo 23°, dare est quoddam honorificum et diuinum—Ff. 237ra–239ra. Assumption of BVM. Type 0.

W-127. *Alius sermo.* Edificauit domum suam super petram, Mathei 7° [Matt. 7:24]. Reuerendi patres et domini, Ad hec precipue debet quilibet pronuncians verbum Dei se habere, vt audientes retrahat a peccati consuetudine et eius accionibus—Ff. 239ra–240va. Type 0. Preached to a monastic audience of a house dedicated to St. Peter (at Gloucester?): "Potestis secure cum Beato Petro apostolorum principe et huius sacri cenobii aduocato precipuo et patrono illam querere questionem a Domino que scribitur Mathei 19: 'Ecce nos reliquimus. . . .'"

W-128. *Alius sermo.* Qui humiliatus fuerit, erit in gloria, Iob 22° capitulo [Job 22:29]. Reuerendi patres et domini, Tria considerantur in sacra scriptura de quibus viatori cuilibet conuenit gloriari—Ff. 240va–242rb. Type 0.

W-129. *Alius sermo.* Intelligite hec qui obliuiscemini Deum [Ps. 49:22]. Est autem notandum secundum beatum Augustinum *De doctrina Christiana* quod officium doctoris ecclesiastici seu predicatoris est docere populum—Ff. 242rb–246vb. [Good Friday.] Type B2.

W-130. *Alius sermo.* Videamus si floruerit vinea, Canticorum 7° capitulo [Song of Sol. 7:12]. Reuerendi patres ac domini, In predicatore verbi Dei tria specialiter requiruntur—Ff. 246vb–248va. [Visitation of a monastic community.] Type 0.

W-131. Labora vt bonus miles Christi, 2ª Ad Thimotheum 2° [2 Tim. 2:3]. Reuerendi magistri, patres, et domini, Sicud miles mundialis militare habet in defensione regni—Ff. 248va–250vb. [St. Benedict.] Type 0.

W-132. Vocauit multos, Luce xiiii, et in euangelio presentis dominice [Luke 14:16]. Infelix morsus fructus prohibiti quem divina primis parentibus interdixit autoritas—Ff. 250vb–253ra. [2 after Trinity.] Possibly preached on 29 June 1427 or 1432. Type 0.

W-133. Amore langueo, Canticorum 2° [Song of Sol. 2:5]. Reuerendi patres et domini, In hiis verbis duo possumus intueri que preces orancium cicius faciunt exaudiri—Ff. 253ra–255rb. [Good Friday.] Type 0.

W-134. Elegit vos Deus, iiª Ad Thimotheum 2° [1 Cor. 1:27?, Eph.

1:4?]. Discretor cogitacionum et cordium, Deus noster, cuius inuestigabiles vie—Ff. 255rb–256va. [Advent?] Type 0.

W-135. Flores apparuerunt in terra, Canticorum 2° capitulo [Song of Sol. 2:12]. Reuerendi patres et domini, Secundum beatum Ambrosium in *De paradiso,* fons ineffabilis bonitatis, rerum omnium conditor—Ff. 256va–257vb. [Visitation of monastery.] Type 0.

W-136. Ecce nunc dies salutis, 2° Ad Corinthios 6° [2 Cor. 6:2]. Beda super Apocalipsim in principio inter diuersas condiciones de audiendo verbum Dei duas recitat—Ff. 257vb–259vb, incomplete. [Lent.] Type 0.

W-137. [Acephalous.] A sermon on spiritualis fraternitas and the duties of a good pastor. The surviving text begins "in pacis, vnitatis, et dileccionis firma obseruacione," near the end of the first member of the first principal, which discusses spiritual brotherhood in mouth, heart, and deed—F. 260ra–va. [Visitation sermon.] Type 0.

W-138. Data est ei corona, Apocalipsis vi° capitulo [Rev. 6:2]. Reuerendi patres et domini confratresque karissimi, Vt refocilletur fames interior anime—Ff. 260v–261v, incomplete. [Vigil of the Assumption of BVM? "Die quasi crastina."] Type 0.

W-139. Requiem quesiui, Ecclesiastici xxiiii° capitulo [Ecclus. 24:11]. Reuerendi patres et domini, Indigens alieno presid[i]o ad ipsius concurrit clemenciam—Ff. 262–264. [Assumption of BVM?] Type 0.

W-140. Nunc bene, primo Machabeorum 12° capitulo [1 Macc. 12:18]. Karissimi, Ex dictis sancti Augustini 12 *De ciuitate,* capitulo primo, patet quod bene esse et male cuiuscumque racionalis creature—F. 264r-v. [Christmas?] Type 0.

W-141. [Regnum surget (Luke 21:10).] Beginning missing. The text begins, "per medicinarum sumpcionem"—Ff. 265–266v, acephalous and incomplete. Type B1.

W-142. Preparate corda vestra Domino, primo Regum 7° capitulo [1 Sam. 7:3]. Karissimi mei, Triplici instante causa solemnitatis huius diei nobis merito congruit corda Domino preparare—Ff. 267v–269, incomplete. [Ash Wednesday.] Type 0.

W-143. Florete flores, Ecclesiastici 39ⁿᵒ [Ecclus. 39:19]. Venerandi patres et domini, Rosa refulgens ciuitatis superne, pater ille suppremus et rector Olimpi—Ff. 269r–b; 1–2. [To monastic community.] Type 0.

W-144. Lauit nos in sanguine suo, Apocalipsis 1 capitulo [Rev. 1:5]. Reuerendi domini, Secundum Hugonem 4 *Super Angelicam Ierarchiam,* capitulo 4, mundum esse oportet qui alios mundare debet—Ff. 270ra–272va. [Good Friday.] Type 0.

W-145. Iudea abiit in Galeliam [!], Iohannis 4°, et in euangelio hodierno

[John 4:3, 4:47?]. Amantissimi domini, Sicut scribit Remigius in suis interpretacionibus, hec diccio Iudea secundum ebraicam accepcionem—Ff. 272vb–274rb. [21 after Trinity?] Type 0.

W-146. Gentes ignorant Deum, Ad Tessalonicenses 4° [1 Thess. 4:5]. Attestante sentencia patrum et doctorum tria sunt que ignoranciam causant Dei—Ff. 274va–276va. Type 0.

W-147. *In celebracione ordinum.* Illi soli seruies, Mathei 4° [Matt. 4:10]. Karissimi, Dicit Philosophus 3 *Ethicorum* quod aliter iudicat studiosus et aliter pravus—Ff. 276va–278va, incomplete. Celebration of Holy Orders. Type 0.

W-148. Grauiter vulneratus sum, Regum 22 [1 Kings 22:34]. Karissimi, Predicator verbi Dei debet sibi vilescere vt vulneret superbos exemplo sue humilitatis—Ff. 278va–280ra, incomplete. [Passion.] Repeats W-116. Type 0.

W-149. Vade et noli amplius peccare, Iohannis 8° [John 8:11]. Ista verba dixit Iesus cuidam mulieri deprehense in adulterio—Ff. 280ra–281va. Type A.

W-150. [Acephalous.] End of a sermon, perhaps on *sanguis*; the text begins "sumus cum Christo per baptismum in mortem"—F. 282ra–b. Type 0.

W-151. Ite in castellum, Mathei etc. [Matt. 21:2]. Non erunt nisi quasi flores sine fructu, quia sicut Apostolus dicit 1° Ad Corinthios 13, "Si linguis"—Ff. 282rb–285ra, incomplete. [Palm Sunday.] Type C marginal. This repeats W-107 but lacks its beginning (approximately two pages).

*W-152. A Domino corripimur vt non cum hoc mundo dampnemur, prima Ad Corinthios xi^mo, et in epistula instantis solempnitatis [1 Cor. 11:32]. Domini, Lego in scriptura sacra iii Regum 18 capitulo quod sanctus propheta Helias cum offerret sacrificium—Ff. 286ra–288ra. [Maundy Thursday.] Type C. In top margin: "Iesus, Maria, Oswaldus, Wlstanus, Benedictus et Thomas succurrant michi, Amen."

W-153. Ecce quomodo amabat, Iohannis xi° capitulo [John 11:36]. Reuerendi patres et domini, In huius exilis collacionis exordio Patris potenciam, Filii sapienciam, ac Spiritus Sancti benignissimam clemenciam—Ff. 288ra–289rb. [To monastic audience.] Type 0.

*W-154. Quem teipsum facis, Iohannis viii capitulo, et in ewangelio hodierno [John 8:53]. Ista verba primitus recitata sunt scripta . . . et sunt tantum dicere in anglicis . . . Domini, Si consideracionem habere vellemus ad statum, gradum, et dignitatem—Ff. 289rb–291va. [Passion.] Type C.

Edited in appendix D. In top margin of f. 289rb: "Iesus, Maria, Oswaldus, Wlstanus, Benedictus et Thomas succurrant michi."

W-155. Wlnerasti cor meum, sponsa. Canticorum 4° capitulo [Song of Sol. 4:9]. Reuerendi patres et domini, In huius exilis collacionis exordio inuocato Sancti Spiritus auxilio in omni bono opere necessario requisito—Ff. 291vb–292vb. [Good Friday.] Type 0. In top margin of f. 291vb: "Iesus, Maria, Iohannes, Oswaldus, Wlstanus, Benedictus . . . "

W-156. In ciuitate sanctificata requieui [Ecclus. 24:15]. Reuerendi domini, Sicut ciuium societati firma sit proteccio in ciuitate de qua sceleris et peccati plena fit eieccio per sanctificacionem—Ff. 293–294x,v, incomplete? [Assumption of BVM?] Type 0.

W-157. Transiet de morte ad vitam, Iohannis 9 [John 5:24]. Secundum Philosophum a fine denominandum est vnumquodque—Ff. 306va–307rb. Type 0. Follows a longer treatise and material on death; possibly not a sermon.

W-158. *Nota hanc* [!] *sermonem pro exsequiis alicuius mortui.* Cuius est ymago hec, Luce 19 [Matt. 22:20 or Mark 12:16; cf. Luke 20:24]. Videmus quod quando quis debeat alteri obligari pro aliqua certa re— Ff. 307rb–308vb. Funeral sermon. Type 0.

W-159. *Sermo de natiuitate Beate Virginis.* Lux orta est, Ysaie ix capitulo [Isa. 9:2]. Reuerendi patres et domini, Fons et origo sapiencie, virtutum largitor, et remunerator meritorum—Ff. 308vb–312rb. Nativity of BVM. Repeats W-104. Type 0.

W-160. Abite liberi ad patrem, Genesis 44 [Gen. 44:17]. Reuerendi patres et domini, Postquam primus parens de patria libertatis in locum miserabilis seruitutis—Ff. 312rb–315rb. [Deposition of St. Benedict.] Repeats W-105. Type 0. Written in the margin, next to the thema, is "Frome," the name of the preacher?

W-161. Ego quasi vitis fructificaui, Ecclesiastici 14 [Ecclus. 24:23]. Reuerendi patres, Que, qualis, et quanta sit beatissima Virgo cuius concepcionem hodie celebramus—Ff. 315rb–317ra. [Conception of BVM.] Repeats W-106. Type 0.

W-162. Iesus faciebat signa, Iohannis 6° [John 6:2]. Solent signa triplici de causa dari aut fieri, videlicet supereminencia et potestate—F. 317ra–vb. Type 0.

W-163. Ecce nunc dies salutis, 2ª Ad Corinthios [2 Cor. 6:2]. Karissimi, Istud verbum veraciter vobis prolatum supponit quod perdidistis optimum diligibile—Ff. 317vb–318vb. [1 Lent?] Also A-47. Type B1.

W-164. Psallite Deo qui ascendit, Psalmo lx7° [Ps. 67:34]. Karissimi, Musica seu melodia adeo est naturalis secundum Boecium—Ff. 318vb–319vb. Type 0.

W-165. [Regressi sunt in Ierusalem (Luke 24:33)] Reuerendi domini, Vos intelligetis secundum quod dicunt clerici quod Ierusalem accipitur multipliciter in sacra scriptura—Ff. 319vb–320va. [Easter Monday.] Type B1.

W-166. Exaltaui lignum humile, Ezechielis 27 [Ezek. 17:24]. Reuerendi patres et domini, Cum secundum Apostolum 2ª Ad Corinthios, 3° capitulo, infirma nature nostre condicio—F. 320va-b, incomplete. [In praise of BVM.] Type 0.

W-167. Induite vos armatura, Ad Ephesios vi capitulo, et in epistola dominice iam instantis [Eph. 6:11]. Reuerendi domini patresque conscripti, Quamdiu in valle miserie simus—Ff. 333–335. [21 after Trinity.] Type 0.

X

Worcester, Cathedral Library, MS F.126

Parchment. 294 leaves. Dimensions: 355 × 240 mm; written space 295 × 200. Collation: medieval foliation, which counts several leaves that were subsequently excised: I¹² (1–12), II¹² (13–23, leaf 24 excised), III⁸ (25–32), IV¹² (33–44), V¹² (45–56), VI¹² (57–68, leaves 62–63 wanting), VII¹² (69–80, leaves 73–76 wanting), VIII¹² (81–92), IX¹² (93–104), X¹² (105–116), XI¹² (117–128), XII¹² (129–140, leaves 131–138 wanting), XIII¹² (141–152, leaves 151–152 excised), XIV¹² (153–164), XV¹² (165–169, 180–186, i.e., no folios numbered 170–179), XVI¹² (187–198, leaf 198 excised), XVII¹² (199–210, leaf 199 excised), XVIII¹² (211–222), XIX¹² (223–234), XX¹² (235–246), XXI¹² (247–258), XXII¹² (259–270), XXIII¹² (271–282), XXIV¹² (283–294), XXV¹² (295–306), XXVI¹² (309[!]–320), XXVII⁵ (307–308, 321–323). Written in two columns of an average of fifty–five lines, in several Anglicana hands with Secretary features, of the late fourteenth and early fifteenth century. Secundo folio: *tam letaliter.*

Bound in wooden boards, which show clasp marks. "Liber Beate Marie Wygornie" is written on f. 69, top.

The volume contains nearly 330 sermons, which are followed by a table that gives their occasion, thema, and folio reference (ff. 307–308);

the table misses at least two sermons. On ff. 19ra–23rb appears the *Confessio Magistri et Fratris Iohannis Tyssyngtone de ordine minorum* (ed. W. W. Shirley, *Fasciculi zizanniorum,* Rolls Series 1858, pp. 133–80); and on ff. 309ra–323rb is a copy of *Liber VI Decretalium* sent by Boniface VIII to Oxford.

Most of the sermons are in Latin only; but the pieces listed here have English material.

X-01. Benedictus qui venit in nomine Domini [Matt. 21:9, etc.]. Karissimi, Humana natura in primo parente per peccatum quasi infecta—Ff. 12ra–13ra. [The table lists this sermon for 1 Advent, but internal references are to Palm Sunday.] Type C marginal.

X-02. Benedictus qui venit, etc., vbi prius [Matt. 21:9, etc.]. Karissimi, Celum, terra, mundus totus, angeli, demones—Ff. 27ra–28ra. [1 Advent.] Type B2.

***X-03.** Extrema gaudii luctus occupat, Prouerbiorum 14 [Prov. 14:13]. Karissimi, Ista verba que nunc dixi in latinis possunt sic dici in Anglico: Worliche blysse . . . Quia si consideremus gaudium—Ff. 29rb–31rb, incomplete? [Palm Sunday.] Type C.

X-04. Venit tibi, idest veniet tibi, Mathei 21, et in ewangelio huius prime dominice [Matt. 21:5]. Karissime [!], Scitis quod duo sunt motiua—F. 34rb–va. [1 Advent.] Type B1.

X-05. Et in terra pax hominibus [Luke 2:14]. Sicud dicunt isti clerici qui varia instituta inspexerunt—Ff. 71va–72vb. [Christmas Vigil.] Type A.

X-06. Illi soli seruies, Mathei 4° [Matt. 4:10]. Quatuor sunt secundum beatum Bernardum quibus seruimus—Ff. 103rb–104rb. [Lent.] Type B1.

X-07. Dic vt lapides isti panes fiant [Matt. 4:3]. Secundum omnes doctores quanto diucius viuimus, tanto peior est mundus—Ff. 106ra–107vb. [Lent.] Type C minimal.

X-08. Dum tempus habemus operemur bonum, Galatharum [Gal. 6:10]. Omnia tempus habent, et est tempus laborandi et tempus quiescendi—Ff. 108ra–109ra. [Lent.] Type A.

X-09. Ecce nunc tempus, 2ª Ad Corinthios [2 Cor. 6:2]. Ecce nunc tempus idoneum—F. 111ra–va. [Lent.] Type A.

X-10. Quomodo stabit regnum [Luke 11:18]. Reuerendi, Scitis quod terra sterilis fructum non facit—Ff. 111vb–112ra. [3 Lent.] Type A.

X-11. Vt quid dereliquisti me, Mathei [Matt. 27:47]. Reuerendi, Multi cotidie ad predicaciones veniunt set paruum perficiunt—F. 116ra–vb. [Palm Sunday.] Type B2.

X-12. Eamus et moriamur cum illo, Iohannis 11 [John 11:16]. Ieronimus *Contra Iovinianum* tangit libro primo quamdam historiam—F. 117ra–vb. [Good Friday.] Type B2.

X-13. Cum dilexisset suos qui erant in mundo, in finem dilexit eos [John 13:1]. In hoc euangelio duo principaliter tanguntur: Christi caritas—Ff. 118va–119rb. [Maundy Thursday.] Type A.

X-14. Rex mutauit habitum suum et ingressus est bellum, 2 Regum 22 [1 Kings 22:30]. Solent reges quando procedunt—F. 130ra–vb, incomplete. [Good Friday.] Type A.

X-15. Viderunt reuolutum lapidem, Mathei xxviii [Matt. 28:17]. Karissimi, Omnium auctorum vnanimis sentencia in hoc concordat quod quando diucius mundus durat—Ff. 145rb–146ra. [Easter season.] Type C minimal.

X-16. Sedet a dextris Dei, Marci vltimo [Mark 16:19]. Wlgariter dicitur: "Cum poteris quod vis, probat accio tua quid sis. Wan þou"—Ff. 147vb–148vb. [Easter season (tabula), Ascension (internal references).] Type C marginal.

X-17. Seruus nunciauit, Luce 14, et in ewangelio dominicali [Luke 14:21]. Primo inducatur qualiter iuxta diuersa officia diuersa nomina inponit Deus seruis suis—F. 186rb–vb. [St. John.] Type C marginal. If the sermon was for the feast of St. John (tabula) and on 2 after Trinity (rubric), it could have been given in 1324, 1403, or 1408.

X-18. Pax vobis [John 20:19]. Karissimi, Gigas gemine (?) mediator Dei et hominum, homo Iesus Christus pro nobis miseris peccatoribus mortem subiit—F. 192rb–va. [1 after Easter.] Type B1.

X-19. Redde racionem, Luce 16 [Luke 16:2]. Karissimi mei, Dicit Plato in *Timeo* bene post principium sic: "Cum, inquid, omnibus mos sit et quasi quedam religio"—Ff. 192va–194ra. [9 after Trinity.] Type B2.

X-20. Fiet vnum ouile et vnus pastor, Iohannis 10 [John 10:16]. Karissimi, Ysaie 53: "Omnes quasi oues errauimus . . ." Certe, karissimi, pro tanto dicitur—Ff. 194ra–195ra. [2 after Easter.] Type B2.

X-21. Transfiguratus est, Mathei 17 [Matt. 17:2]. Per verba preassumpta intelligo tres figuraciones—Ff. 207rb–208rb. [St. Augustine.] Type A.

X-22. Ego sum pastor bonus [John 10:11, etc.]. Karissimi, Videmus quod nec clerici nec laici erubescunt habere pannos dissutos—F. 209rb–va. [St. Thomas (of Canterbury?)]. Type A.

X-23. Hoc est signum federis, Genesis [Gen. 9:12]. Quando dilecti recedunt, inuicem solent aliquod preciosum donarium relinquere—Ff. 247ra–249va. [Corpus Christi.] Type A.

Z

Arras, Bibliothèque Municipale, MS 184 (254)

Parchment and paper. i (excised) + 227 leaves. Dimensions: 290 × 220, written space 223/232 × ca. 162. Collation: I^{12} (modern ff. 1–10, leaves 1 and 12 excised), II^{12} (ff. 11–21, leaf 12 excised), III^{12} (ff. 22–32, leaf 12 excised), IV^{12} (ff. 33–44), V^{12} (ff. 45–55, leaf 1 excised), VI^{12} (ff. 56–67), VII^{12} (ff. 68–79), VIII^{12} (ff. 80–88, leaves 4–6 excised), IX^{12} (ff. 89–99, leaf 12 wanting), X^{14} (ff. 100-112, leaf 14 excised), XI^{12} (ff. 113–124), XII^{12} (ff. 125–136), XIII^{12} (ff. 137–148), XIV^{12} (ff. 149–160), XV^{12} (ff. 161–171, leaf 7 excised), XVI^{12} (ff. 172–183), XVII^{12} (ff. 184–194, leaf 12 excised), XVIII^{12} (ff. 195–206), XIX^{12} (ff. 207–216, leaves 6–7 excised), XX^{12} (ff. 217–227, one leaf wanting). The quires are consistently constructed of paper, with parchment bifolia on the outside and in the center. Most of the missing leaves have clearly been cut out, with the cuts often penetrating through one or even more paper leaves. Medieval foliation, which was entered before individual leaves, the original second quire (medieval ff. 13–24), and at least one quire at the end were lost. Written in two columns, in one hand of xv^1; the ink varies from black to light brown. Enlarged capitals in red, some with flourishes. Secundo folio: *siue sapiencia* (modern f. 1).

The volume has sustained damp or water damage, affecting the paper leaves, many of which are crumbling at their lower outside corner. On the inside of the front cover it bears the mark "n.° [space] art. 61" and is hence thought to have come from the Abbaye de Mont–Saint–Eloi (*Catalogue géneral . . .* 1872, 109–10); but see the cautionary note by J. Quicherat, ibid., 7. A sixteenth- or seventeenth-century hand wrote "Sermones Johannis Broniard [!] fratris dominicani" on f. 1, top. Perhaps the same hand wrote on modern f. 2, "Procur. R. a P. Prou. a S. Clar. 2° Mur' Pro. 1650." The manuscript was noticed by Friend 1957.

Medieval binding: vellum on paper. Written on the spine is "Io. Bromiar Sermones" (at top, written horizontally), "Joh. Bromyard" (written vertically), both in the same hand. Written at the bottom is a large P.2., apparently over an older B.4.

Contents (in modern foliation):

120ra–126va	Sermon 43.
126va–133ra	Notes, with some English.
133rb–134va	Sermon 44.
134va–135ra	Note.
135rb–va	Sermon 45.
135va–136rb	Notes.
136rb–137vb	Sermon 46.
137vb–138rb	Notes.
138rb–vb	Sermon 47.
138vb–140ra	Notes.
140ra–141ra	Sermon 48.
141ra–143rb	Notes.
143va–152rb	William of Auvergne, *Tractatus de confessione*: "Con-uertimini ad me in toto corde . . . et non vestimenta ves-tra. Non mirum est, fratres, si seruus rogat dominum—qui custodit vestimenta sua ne nudus ambulet." Bloom-field 0988.
152rb–162vb	*Speculum sacerdotis:* "Sanctus Edwardus rex et con-fessor in extremitate vite—dignus planus est morte qui tibi Domine Iesu recusat viuere. Amen. Explicit visio et exhortacio sancti Edwardi regis et confessoris, et vocatur spiculum sacerdotis." Bloomfield 5269.
162vb–166ra	Origen, *Omelia de beata Maria Magdalena:* "Maria stabat ad monumentum foris plorans, etc. Audiuimus Mariam ad monumentum foris stantem—et hec dixi michi. Cui sit honor et gloria in secula seculorum. Amen."
166ra–b	Note: "Tenet Deus hominem et homo Deum tenet. Primo penitentem vt eleuet."
166va	Note on seven sacraments.
166va–170va	Sermons 49–51.
170va	Excerpt from Wallensis super psalterium.
170vb–174vb	Sermon 52–54.
174vb–175rb	Note on Redde.
175rb–179ra	Sermons 55–57.
179ra–180vb	Treatise on the Annunciation: "Missus est angelus Ga-briel a Deo in ciuitatem . . . Dominus apparuit in flam-ma ignis—dirigere non possimus etc."

181ra–190ra   Odo of Cheriton, *Fabulae:* "Legitur in libro Ruth, Proicite de manipulis vestris—vt periculum suum minime intueatur." See Welter 1927, 128 note.

190rb–194vb   *Miracula beate Virginis:* "In villa que dicitur Castellum Radulphi duo scurri alleatores—et tunicam supra capud" (incomplete).

195ra–225vb   Nicholas de Hanapis, *Liber de exemplis sacre scripture.* Prologue: "Tanta pollet excellencia predicacionis officium." Ch. 1: "Precepit Dominus Ade dicens Genesis 2." Text ends 225ra, followed by table of topics, to 225vb. Bloomfield 1006 (?); Welter 1927, 230.

226ra–227ra   *Meditacio sancti Bernardi:* "Qvis dabit capiti meo aquam . . . O vos filie Ierusalem sponte dilecte Dei."

227rb–vb   *Meditacio beati Bernardi:* "Quis me consolabit" (incomplete).

The sermons are as follows:

Z-01. *Sermo 1, de passione Christi.* [Corruit in platea veritas [Isa. 59:14]. [Thema and *initium* missing; the text begins in the division:] siue sapiencia quod modo extincta et reprobata—Ff. 1ra–4rb, acephalous. Passion. Also in Oxford Trinity College 42, ff. 65–73. Type C minimal. Preacher: Henry Chambron, as indicated in the colophon: "Explicit sermo Magistri Henrici Chambron predicatus Oxon' Anno Domini MCCC82. Cuius anime, etc." (f. 4rb).

Z-02. *Sermo 2, quomodo est orare pro mortuis.* Mortuus viuet, Iohannis xi [John 11:25]. Reuerendi, Secundum sentenciam beati Anselmi in *De cura circa mortuos agenda,* inter omnia opera—Ff. 4rb–5va. Type 0.

Z-03. *Sermo 3, de nomine Iesu.* Iesus, Mathei 4to [Matt. 4:1 etc.]. Tria mouent me istud thema accipere: dede, nede, and spede—Ff. 5va–7vb. Also in H-01. Type B1.

Z-04. Petite et dabitur vobis, Luce 11 [Luke 11:9]. Secundum Wallensem *De penitencia,* volens orare et aliquid a Deo petere debet seipsum diligenter considerare—Ff. 7vb–9vb, incomplete? Also in Cambridge, Jesus College MS 13, art. vi, ff. 104–107v. Type 0. The Latin text ends, "Sequitur quid Christus docuit orare, quia Pater Noster," and is at once followed by an English (supposedly Wycliffite) tract on the Lord's Prayer and another on the Creed; see contents listed above. In Jesus College 13, sermon Z-04 ends as it does here but is not followed by the English tracts.

Z-05. *In die pasche.* Dicunt eum viuere, Luce 24, et in ewangelio hodierno [Luke 24:23]. Karissimi, Ista verba dicebantur a quodam discipulo Christi nomine Cleophas—Ff. 15rb–17rb. Easter [Monday]. Type A.

Z-06. *In dedicacione ecclesie.* In domo tua oportet me manere, Luce 19 [Luke 19:5]. Scribitur 2 Paralipomenon 6 de prima ecclesia, templo scilicet Ierusalem—Ff. 17rb–19rb. Dedication of a church. Also in Cambridge, Jesus College MS 13, art. vi, ff. 107v–110v. Type 0.

Z-07. Penitenciam agite, Mathei 3°, et pro themate hodierno [Matt. 3:2; cf. 4:17]. Karissimi, Quod totum hoc sacrum tempus quadragesime est specialiter dedicatum hominibus—Ff. 22va–28rb. [Lent.] Type 0.

Z-08. Rex fecit grande conuiuium pueris suis, Hester 1 [Esther 1:3]. Notandum quod opus mirabile, nobile, et subtile cuius operarius eciam penitus [*read* est peritus?] solent queri tres questiones—Ff. 28rb–30ra. Type 0.

Z-09. Sanctus, sanctus, sanctus, Apocalipsis 4 [Rev. 4:8]. Nota secundum Ysidorum quod sanctus dicitur quasi sine terra—F. 30ra–va. The text ends, "Fac finem si vis." Type 0.

Z-10. Sequebatur eum multitudo magna [John 6:2]. Pro antethemate dicatur historia euangelii cum ista moralizacione: Mare Galilee signat mundum istum—Ff. 31rb–34va. Type 0.

Z-11. Obsecro vos tanquam aduenas et peregrinos abstinere vos a carnalibus desideriis, prima Petri 2° capitulo, et in epistula hodierna [1 Pet. 2:11]. Karissimi mei, Cum vita cuiuslibet Christiani peregrinacio quedam versus Ierusalem sit—Ff. 34va–b, 36ra–vb. [3 after Easter.] Type A.

Z-12. Hec est autem vita eterna, vt cognoscant te solum verum Deum et quem misisti, Iesum Christum, Iohannis 8° [John 17:3]. Cum diabolus, qui est capitalis hominis inimicus, laboret fortiter—Ff. 36vb–37vb, 35, 38ra–b. Type 0. At end, "Iste sermo fuit predicatus a domino Roberto Lychelade bacalaurio in artibus Oxon', quem scripsit et dixit quod omnia verba in eo scripta sunt vera, pro quo fuit bannitus per monachos i° die mensis octobr' anno domini MCCCxv^to [!]" (f. 38rb).

Z-13. Hoc facite in meam commemoracionem, Luce 22 [Luke 22:19]. Reuerendi domini, Sicut patet ex processu sancti Ricardi *De sacramentis noui legis*—Ff. 38rb–39vb, 42ra. [Easter.] Type 0.

Z-14. Surge et commede [1 Kings 19:5]. Dicit Gregorius in *Morum* quod qui Deo loqui desiderat de nulla re confidere debet nisi de gracia Dei—Ff. 42ra–vb, 40ra–41rb. [Easter.] Also in H-07. Type B1.

Z-15. Inimici mei animam meam circumdederunt, Psalmo 16, et pro themate hodierno [Ps. 16:9]. þe help of Crist of wam is all wyt . . . Leue cristen sovlus, experiens schewit and teches us al day—Ff. 41rb–vb, 43ra–45ra. Type D.

Z-16. Clausa est ianua, Mathei 25 [Matt. 25:10]. Sicut legitur in quadam historia quam ostendit nobis Virgilius—Ff. 45ra–49rb. Type A.

Z-17. Per triennium nocte et die non cessaui cum lacrimis monens vnumquemque vestrum, et nunc commendo vos Deo et verbo gracie ipsius qui potens est edificare et dare hereditatem in sanctificacionibus. Argentum aut et aurum nullius concupiui, sicut ipsi scitis, Actuum 20°, etc. Ibidem notate: Vocauit nos Deus, 1 Thessalonicensium 4 [Acts 20:31–34 and 1 Thess. 4:7]. Amici, Processus huius breuis collacionis siue est notandum siue intelligendum quod sicut est vocacio—Ff. 49rb–50vb. Type 0.

Z-18. Qui facit voluntatem patris mei qui in celis est, Mathei 7 [Matt. 7:21]. Karissimi, In hoc euangelio precipit nos Saluator cauere et vitare consilium falsorum prophetarum—Ff. 50vb–51rb. Type 0.

*Z-19. Christus passus est pro nobis vobis reliquens exemplum vt sequamini, Petri 2° capitulo [1 Pet. 2:21]. Anglice sic: Crist in hys passioun reliquit exemplum . . . Quamuis hec verba—Ff. 51vb–61va. [Good Friday.] Also H-25, S-01, and W-006. Type C.

Z-20. Qvare rubeum est indumentum tuum, Ysaie 2 [Isa. 63:2]. Secundum sentenciam doctorum hec fuit questio angelorum in die ascensionis Domini, et erit questio iudicandorum—Ff. 61va–68va. Also in A-35, S-19, and Cambridge University Library Ee.6.27, ff. 73–84v; and a shorter version in S-20. Type B1. Z-20 is the only complete copy of this sermon. The sermon is possibly an accidental combination of two different developments of the same thema or, in its second half, of a very confusing structure.

Z-21. Verbum caro factum est [John 1:14]. Primo queritur quando, cur, et vbi—Ff. 68va–69rb, incomplete? [Christmas; refers to the first responsorium of the first nocturn for Christmas Day.] Type 0.

Z-22. Dominus noster Iesus Christus, eternus eterni Dei patris filius, de sacratissimo sinu Dei eterne [!] patris descendit—Ff. 69rb–72rb, incomplete. Type 0. Robert Grosseteste's sermon 14, preached at the council of Lyon in 1250. Written in the margin by the thema is "Sermo episcopi [Lin]coln' missus [ad] papam [?] crostet'."

Z-23. Remittuntur tibi peccata tua, Luce 7, et in euangelio hodierno [Luke 7:48]. In quibus verbis intelligitur primo illud quod causa est cuiuslibet doloris—Ff. 72rb–73ra, incomplete. Type 0.

Z-24. *In festo omnium sanctorum.* Merces vestra copiosa est in celis, Mathei 5 [Matt. 5:12]. Sicut legitur in euangelio Matthei 4, Christus Iesus ante passionem suam circuibat totam Galileam—Ff. 73rb–76ra. All Saints. Also H-10. Type A.

Z-25. *Dominica quinquagesime.* Iesu fili David, miserere mei. Luce

18 capitulo, et in euangelio hodierno [Luke 18:38]. Karissimi, Legitur in primo libro Regum capitulo 11 quod viri Rabes—Ff. 76rb–78rb. Quinquagesima. Repeated as the protheme of Z-29. Type 0.

Z-26. *In die pasche.* Surrexit Dominus vere, Luce 24 [Luke 24:34]. Karissimi, Sicut medicina corporalis si fuerit conueniens complexioni recipientis multociens cum bona gubernacione est causa salutis—Ff. 78va–80vb. Easter. Also in H-08. Type 0.

Z-27. *Dominica in passione.* Qvi est ex Deo, verba Dei audit, Iohannis 8 [John 8:47]. Karissimi, Sicut dicit Ianuencis, ista dominica vocatur dominica in passione—Ff. 80vb–82ra. Passion Sunday. Type C minimal.

Z-28. *In die palmarum siue in die parascheues.* Hoc sentite in vobis quod in Christo Iesu, Philephensium 2º [Phil. 2:5]. Karissimi, Officium Ecclesie hodie reducit ad memoriam nostram diram Christi passionem— Ff. 82ra–84vb. Palm Sunday or Good Friday. Type A.

Z-29. *In die pentecostes.* Ille vos docebit omnia, Iohannis 14, et in euangelio hodierno [John 14:26]. Karissimi, Legitur in primo libro Regum, capitulo 11, quod viri Rabes—Ff. 84vb–86rb. Pentecost. The protheme repeats Z-25. Type A.

Z-30. *Dominica 14ª post trinitatem.* Surge et vade, quia fides tua saluum te fecit, Luce 17 [Luke 17:19]. Karissimi, Sicut legitur in euangelio hodierno, factum est dum erat Iesus in Ierusalem—Ff. 86rb–87va. 14 after Trinity. Type 0.

Z-31. *Dominica 15 post trinitatem.* Nemo potest duobus dominis seruire, Matthei 6 [Matt. 6:24]. Karissimi, In hoc euangelio monet nos Saluator noster specialiter de tria [!]—Ff. 87va–90vb. 15 after Trinity. Type A.

Z-32. *Dominica xvi.* Deus visitauit plebem suam, Luce 7º [Luke 7:16]. Karissimi, Sicut legitur in euangelio hodierno Christus Iesus transiens in ciuitatem Naym—Ff. 90vb–92vb. 16 after Trinity. Type 0.

Z-33. *Dominica 4 post trinitatem.* Estote misericordes sicut et pater vester misericors est, Luce vi [Luke 6:36]. Karissimi, Experimentum docet quod si filius regis vel [?] domini eiectus esset de terra—Ff. 92vb–94va. 4 after Trinity. Type 0.

Z-34. *Dominica 18.* Diliges Dominum Deum tuum, Matthei 22 [Matt. 22:37]. Karissimi, Sicut legitur in historia scolastica, tres erant secte inter Iudeos—Ff. 94va–96ra. 18 after Trinity. Type 0.

Z-35. *Dominica xxi.* Rogabat eum vt descenderet et sanaret filium eius [John 4:47]. Karissimi, Siquis vellet in terra guerre pugnare contra iminicos—Ff. 96ra–99rb. 21 after Trinity. Type 0. Written before the thema, in the rubric, is "Iesu mercy quod T [?]."

Z-36. *In die sancti Iohannis Baptiste.* Iohannes est nomen eius, Luce primo [Luke 1:63]. Karissimi, Sicut videtis quilibet homo componitur ex duobus, scilicet ex corpore et anima—Ff. 99rb–100va. St. John the Baptist. Type 0. The same *initium* occurs in Z-49.

Z-37. *Dominica prima quadragesime.* Ductus est Iesus in desertum a spiritu vt temptaretur a diabolo, Mathei 4° [Matt. 4:1]. Karissimi, Duccio ista in desertum qua Iesus ducebatur a Spiritu Sancto—Ff. 100va–103va. 1 Lent. Type 0.

Z-38. *Dominica 2ª quadragesime.* Miserere mei, fili David, filia mea a demonio male vexatur, Mathei 15 [Matt. 15:22]. Karissimi, Sicut legitur in euangelio, Christus Iesus Saluator noster existens in terra Genasareth—F. 103va–b, incomplete. 2 Lent. Type 0. The text ends after the division, with the reference "in sermone precedenti, etc."

Z-39. *Dominica 3ª quadragesime.* Locutus est mutus, Luce xi° [Luke 11:14]. Karissimi, Sicut experimentum docet, vox hominis muti per magnam distanciam faciliter non auditur—Ff. 103vb–106vb. 3 Lent. Type C minimal.

Z-40. *In die pasce post prandium.* Estote solliciti vt custodiatis, Iosue 23 [Josh. 23:6]. Karissimi, Sicut legitur Exodi xvi, quando Moyses eduxit filios per desertum—Ff. 106vb–109vb. Easter Sunday after the midday meal. Type A. For sermons on Sunday afternoons, see Owst 1926, 356–57.

Z-41. *In aduentu.* Abiciamus ergo opera tenebrarum et induamur arma lucis, Romanos xiii, et in epistula hodierna [Rom. 13:12]. Karissimi, In aduentu magni regis uel principis homines qui ipsum recipient—Ff. 110ra–112vb. Advent. Type B1.

Z-42. Milicia siue temptacio est vita hominis super terram, Iob 7 [Job 7:1]. Duo genera sunt militum, scilicet spiritualium et corporalium—F. 113ra–va, incomplete. Type 0.

Z-43. *In die parasceue.* Hic est Iesus rex, Mathei 27 [Matt. 27:37]. Scitis quoniam pauper et indigens qui haberet magnum negocium et viagium faciendum—Ff. 120ra–126va, incomplete. Good Friday. Also in Cambridge, Jesus College MS 13, art. vi, ff. 100v–104. Type C minimal.

Z-44. *Dominica 1ª quadragesime.* Hortamur vos ne in vacuum graciam Dei recipiatis [2 Cor. 6:2]. Nota quod tripliciter in uacuum vas recipit aliquid—Ff. 133rb–134va, incomplete? 1 Lent. Type B1.

Z-45. *Dominica iii quadragesime.* Omne regnum in seipsum diuisum desolabitur, Luce xi [Luke 11:17]. Moraliter quilibet suum corpus possidet quasi regnum—F. 135rb–va, incomplete. 3 Lent. Type 0.

Z-46. *Dominica iiii quadragesime.* Est puer vnus hic qui habet quinque panes, etc., Iohannis 5 [John 6:9]. Puer iste potest dici Christus propter tria—Ff. 136rb–137vb. 4 Lent. Type 0.

Z-47. Vivus est sermo Dei et efficax, etc., Hebreorum q[uarto] [Heb. 4:12]. Audistis, karissimi, quod frequenter incitaui vos ad libenter audiendum verbum Dei—F. 138rb–vb, incomplete. Type 0.

Z-48. *In die lune post pascha.* Mane nobiscum, Domine, Luce 24 [Luke 24:29]. Reuerendi, Propter peccatum primi parentis expulsi fuimus a propria terra—Ff. 140ra–141ra. Easter Monday. Type C minimal.

Z-49. *Dominica 3ª post octauam epiphanie.* Et ecce leprosus veniens adorabat eum dicens, Domine, si vis, potes me mundare, Matthei 8 et in euangelio hodierno [Matt. 8:2]. Karissimi, Sicut videtis quilibet homo componitur ex duobus, scilicet ex corpore et anima—Ff. 166va–168ra. 3 [or 4?] after Octave of Epiphany. Type 0. See Z-36.

Z-50. *In purificacione beate Marie Virginis.* Nunc dimittis seruum tuum, Domine, secundum verbum tuum in pace, Luce 2º capitulo, et in euangelio hodierno [Luke 2:29]. Karissimi, Sicut bene nostis, mos modernorum talis est quod mortuo aliquo nobili nobilior et eius sanguini propinquior faciet primo oblacionem—Ff. 168ra–169vb. Purification of BVM. Type 0.

Z-51. *Dominica 19.* Surge, tolle lectum tuum, et vade in domum tuam, Mathei 9 [Matt. 9:6]. Karissimi, Postquam Iesus ostendisset plura miracula in terra Gerasenorum—Ff. 169vb–170va. 19 after Trinity. Type 0.

Z-52. Confitemini, Iacobi 5 [James 5:16]. Nota quod quadruplex est [confessio] ab hominibus facta—Ff. 170vb–171va. Type 0.

Z-53. Facite vobis amicos de Mammona iniquitatis [Luke 16:9]. Mammona Sira lingua diuicias sonat et dicitur mammona iniquitatis—Ff. 171va–172va. Type 0.

Z-54. Psallite Domino qui ascendit, Psalmo 67 [Ps. 67:34]. Dicit Boicius quod vir b[ene] [dispositus?] et sanus audiens suauem melodiam naturaliter gaudet—Ff. 172va–174vb. Type A.

Z-55. Confitemini Domino quoniam bonus, quoniam in seculum misericordia eius, in spalmo [!] [Ps. 105:1]. Tria noscuntur precipue pertinere ad prelatum siue confessorem—Ff. 175rb–176va. Type 0.

Z-56. Probet seipsum homo et sic de pane illo edat, Corinthiorum xi [1 Cor. 11:28]. Karissimi, Debetis in principio orare . . . Sicut scitis bene, ceteri cibi corporales sunt probandi—Ff. 176va–177vb. [Easter.] Type 0.

Z-57. Sanguis Christi emundauit consciencias nostras, Ad Hebreos 9 [Heb. 9:14]. Christus pro sua magna passione quam sustinuit pro toto genere humano—Ff. 177vb–179ra. Type 0.

APPENDIX B

Sermon S-07, *Amore langueo*

This sermon is known to be extant in four copies: B-088, D-1, S-07, and T-6. All four show the corruptions typical of late-medieval copying and a varying amount of correction. In this appendix, I present a semicritical text that is based on one manuscript and slightly emended. The emendations I have introduced, which are printed in square brackets, are required by grammar and sense and are supported by variants that appear in the other witnesses. The base is manuscript S; it has the smallest number of individual readings (146; cf. 173 in B, 290 in D, and 563 in T) and has undergone some, though by no means perfect, correction both in the text and in the margins. The textual apparatus provided is limited to the readings of S that have been emended. Superscript numbers in the text and the respective variant readings concern the single word before the superscript number. Where more text than a single word is affected, I give the text with a square bracket in the apparatus. When a variant note is given, the readings of all four manuscripts are recorded, either silently, if they agree with the reading of the text, or as specified by the manuscript sigla. Material that appears in the margin in the manuscript is enclosed in angle brackets; material that appears between lines is reproduced within slashes. I do not distinguish whether readings are in the hand that wrote the text or in that of a corrector. I have, however, recorded all variant readings that affect the English material, to give a full picture of the amount and kind of variation in the English elements one encounters in a macaronic sermon that has been preserved in several manuscripts. Manuscript D frequently renders English words and phrases that are part of the divisions (i.e., *b* elements) in Latin, though here and there this rendition is in turn supplemented with an interlinear gloss in English, which therefore returns to what I take to be the original English.

The sermon *Amore langueo* has the following structure.

1. Preview of the materia sermonis (2–42)
2. Protheme:
   Today is a day of bliss and of sorrow (44–86)
   Seven signs of love shown on Friday (87–124)
   Prayer (124–26)
3. Introduction of thema: Narrative of knight and unfaithful lady (127–85)
4. Division: Seven signs of languishing love (186–206)
5. Development:
   (a) Loss of strength
       Seven torments; figura of Daniel in the lions' den (207–366)
   (b) Sighing
       Seven insults; figura of Pharaoh's dream (367–480)
   (c) Solitude
       Seven kinds of people who persecuted Christ; figura of seven Canaanite nations (481–571)
   (d) Thought of the beloved
       Seven miracles, i.e., portents of the passion; figura of the seven angels from Revelation (572–657)
   (e) Sweet speech
       Seven words on the cross; figura of God's words on the seven days of creation (658–718)
   (f) Suffering hardships
       Seven wounds; figura of the healing of leprosy (719–50)
   (g) Gifts
       Seven sacraments; no figura (751–69)

Oxford, Balliol College, MS 149, ff. 31–38v (S-07).

Amore langueo, Canticorum 2 capitulo.

Prolatiue[1] potest dici sic. Karissimi, sicut manifeste vide[tis],[2] in isto themate non sunt nisi tantum duo verba, et in vtroque verbo sunt tantum tres sillabe. A tribus igitur sillabis huius verbi "langueo" accipio tria nomina. A prima enim sillaba, scilicet "lan," accipio languedo; a secunda sillaba, scilicet "gue," accipio guerra; et a tercia sillaba, scilicet "o," accipio hora. Et tunc habemus ista tria nomina substantiua langue[d]o,[3] guerra, et hora. Eodem modo a tribus sillabis huius nominis "amore" accipiantur tria nomina adiectiua ab eisdem sillabis. A prima enim sil-

10 laba, scilicet "a," accipitur amarissimum; a secunda, scilicet "mo," mortalissimum; et a tercia, scilicet "re," reprobissimum. Et tunc habemus ista tria adiectiua, scilicet amarissimum, mortalissimum < et reprobissimum >. Coniu[n]gatur[4] ergo primum adiectiuum cum primo substantiuo et secundum cum secundo et tercium cum tercio, et dicatur sic: Langueo quia modo instat languedo amarissima; \et/ langueo quia instat < guerra mortalissima; et langueo quia instat > hora reprobissima. Vnde propter ista tria dicit nobis hodie Christus: *Amore langueo*.

Et pro certo langu[et][5] amore legis, [amore regis,][6] et amore gregis. Igitur clamat Christus "scicio," et si non verbo amore langueo. Et quare?

20 Quia modo instat languedo amarissima, et hoc quia lex confunditur. Instat eciam guerra mortalissima, et hoc quia rex occiditur. Instat eciam hora reprobissima, et hoc quia grex dispergitur. "Set hec est hora vestra et potestas tenebrarum," Luce 22. Vnde in persona Christi sic languentis dicit sponsus, Canticorum 2: "Adiuro vos, filie Ierusalem, vt < cum > inueneritis dilectum meum nuncietis michi, quia *amore langueo*."

Est aduertendum, carissimi, quod languentes ex amore per septem signa manifeste cognoscuntur. Nam tales corporaliter extenuantur, mentaliter alienantur, ab hominibus sequestrantur; fit de dilecto frequens recordacio, fit cum dilecto dilectissima confabulacio, fit grata tollerancia

30 aduersorum, et habundans donacio siue collacio donariorum. Reuera,

---

1. *corrected from* probatiue S; *Mynors reads* primo latine, *which is possible;* prolatiue BD; probatiue T.
2. videntes S.
3. langueo S.
4. coniugatur S.
5. languent S.
6. amore regis] *om.* S.

Translation

I languish with love, Song of Solomon, chapter 2.[1]

By way of a preview,[2] we may say as follows. Dearly beloved, as you clearly see, in this thema are but two words, and in each word are but three syllables. From the three syllables of the verb *langueo,* I derive three nouns: from the first syllable, *lan,* I derive *languedo,* "languishing"; from the second, *gue,* I derive *guerra,* "war"; and from the third, *o,* I derive *hora,* "hour." As a result, we have the nouns "languishing," "war," and "hour." In the same way, from the three syllables of the noun *amore* may be derived three adjectives: *amarissimum,* "bitterest," from the first, that is, *a; mortalissimum,* "deadliest," from the second, that is, *mo*; and *reprobissimum,* "vilest," from the third, that is, *re.* As a result, we get the three adjectives "bitterest," "deadliest," and "vilest." Now we join the first adjective to the first noun, the second to the second, and the third to the third, and we can say: I languish, for now is the bitterest languishing; I languish, for now is the deadliest war; and I languish, for now is the vilest hour. And for these three reasons, Christ says to us today, *I languish with love.*

And certainly he languishes with love for the law, the king, and the flock; hence Christ exclaims, "I thirst," even if he does not literally say, "I languish with love." And why so? Because now is the bitterest languishing, for the law is overturned. Now is the deadliest war, for the king is being killed. And now is the vilest hour, for the flock is being scattered. "But this is your hour and the power of darkness," Luke 22.[3] Hence, in speaking like Christ, who thus languishes, the lover of Canticles 2 says, "I charge you, daughters of Jerusalem, to tell me when you find my beloved, for I languish with love."[4]

We should notice, dearly beloved, that those who languish with love can be easily recognized by seven signs. They are weakened in their

---

1. Song of Sol. 2:5.
2. I have accepted the reading *prolatiue* and consider this section to be a preview to the sermon proper. It furnishes a complex division of the thema *ab intra,* followed by a second division *ab extra.* It is possible to read the first word as *primo Latine,* as was suggested by Sir Roger Mynors for S. In that case, the present sermon would parallel the pattern found in L-1, where a more sophisticated division of the thema that is spoken only in Latin and destined for a clerical audience is followed by a second division and its development that is to be preached in English or with English elements to, presumably, a lay audience. See the discussion in chapter 4.
3. Luke 22:53.
4. Song of Sol. 5:8.

carissimi, cuncta[7] ista septem signa hodierna die in Christo patuerunt
manifeste. Nam primo fuit Christus corporaliter extenuatus, et hoc per
septem tormenta dolorosa. Secundo fuit quasi mentaliter alienatus, et
hoc per septem obpropria ignomin\i/osa. Tercio fuit Christus [fraterna][8]
dileccione[9] separatus,[10] et hoc per persecutorum septem genera. Quarto
Christus dilecte [viscerose][11] recordabatur, et hoc per septem mirabilia
hodie ostensa. Quinto suauiter [*f. 31v*] confabulatur, et hoc probant in
cruce semptem eius verba. Sexto Christus gratanter tollerauit aduersa,
et hoc patet per septem corporis[12] vulnera. Septimo habundanter contulit
40   donaria, scilicet septem sacramenta noue legis. Vnde propter omnia ista
iam dicta Christus potest hodierna die dicere veraciter, *Amore langueo.*
Et hec materia sermonis.
    Anthethema "Amore langueo."
    Carissimi mei, michi videtur quod racionabiliter possum dicere quod
ista dies est[13] **a blisful day** et[14] est **a carful**[15] **day.** Est dies bene[di]cta[16] quia
vnum de maioribus gaudiis quod vnquam accidit in isto die accidit hu-
mano generi, quia genus humanum fuit ed[u]ctum[17] de seruagio et iste qui
fuit ʒral factus fuit **free.** Et quod ista dies fuit benedicta inter omnes que
vnquam fuerunt, probat beatus Gregorius dicens, "Quid nobis profuisset
50   quod Christus fuit natus nisi nos redimisset?" quasi dicat, nichil. Ex quo
ergo tantum gaudium isto die accidit generi humano, possumus dicere
cum Psalmista, "Hec dies quam fecit Dominus," etc. Iste dies similiter
est **sorfful,** quia vnum **of þe rewfullyste**[18] **and of þe sorffullest**[19] que
vnquam accidit isto die accidit, quia hodierna die iste qui fuit innocens et
sine macula peccati fuit irracionabiliter et falso modo interfectus et sicut
agnus in dolore vitam finiuit, et [ita impletur][20] illud quod ipse dicit per
prophetam in Psalmo: "Defecit in dolore vita mea," etc.

---

7. *exp.* S, *but present in* BDT.
8. *corr. from* ferrea B; ferrea SD; fere T.
9. *corr. to* delectacione D.
10. superatus B.
11. viciose SDT.
12. *add.* in S; *add.* sui D.
13. ys BT.
14. and T.
15. sorwful BDT.
16. benecta S.
17. edictum S; liberatum D.
18. sorwfullyst BT.
19. and . . . sorffullest] and of the rewfullyst dedys B; *add.* \thyngys/ D; *om.* T.
20. ita impletur] *om.* SD.

bodies, become alienated in their minds, and are shut off from other people; they often think of their beloved, talk most lovingly with their beloved, suffer hardships gladly, and give abundant gifts. Indeed, dearly beloved, all these seven signs have manifestly appeared in Christ on this day. For first Christ was weakened in his body, through seven painful torments. Next, he was, so to speak, alienated in his mind, through seven shameful insults. Third, he was separated from fraternal love, through seven kinds of persecutors. Fourth, he remembered his beloved intimately, through seven miracles which he showed today. Fifth, he spoke sweetly, through his seven words on the cross. Sixth, he glady suffered hardships, through the seven wounds in his body. And seventh, he gave abundant gifts, namely, the seven sacraments of the New Law. Because of all these things I have just listed, Christ can truly say today, *I languish with love*. And this is the matter of our sermon.

The protheme for *Amore langueo*.

Dearly beloved, I think I can rightly say that this is **a blissful day** and **a sorrowful day**. It is a blissful day because on it occurred one of the greatest joys that ever happened to the human race, for mankind was led out of servitude, and he who was **a slave** became **free**. That this day was blessed among all that ever have been is proven by blessed Gregory when he says, "What would we have gained by Christ's birth if he had not redeemed us?"[5] as if to say, nothing. Since such great joy came to mankind on this day, we can say with the Psalmist, "This is the day the Lord has made," etc.[6] Likewise, this is a **sorrowful day** because one **of the most pitiful and sorrowful things** that have ever happened occurred on it, for today, he who was innocent and without stain of sin was unreasonably and falsely killed and ended his life in pain like a lamb; and thus is fulfilled what he himself said through the prophet in a psalm: "My life has ended in pain," etc.[7]

---

5. Cf. Ambrose *In Lucam* 2.41 (*CC* 14:49).
6. Ps. 117:24.
7. Ps. 30:11.

My lyue y hynde²¹ in sorwe and wo²²
Man to hyme²³ from ys fo.

60   Si ergo nos sicut homines grati cogitauerimus ex vna parte quantum
     gaudium per Christum lucrati sumus, tenemu[r]²⁴ eum intente diligere;
     et si cogitauerimus ex alia parte materiam doloris, tenemur languere. Et
     ista sunt illa duo verba que dixi vobis in principio, et sunt scripta in
     libro amoris: *Amore langueo*. Angelice: **Y morne fore loue**.²⁵
         Et possunt ista verba esse verba Christi hodierna die ad genus hu-
     manum, et e conuerso generis humani ad Christum. Nam Christus poterit
     hodie veraciter dicere generi humano *"Amore langueo,"* quasi diceret:

     Y morne for loue þou may se,
     þat makide²⁶ me deye²⁷ for þe.

70   Ista eciam verba possunt esse verba generis humani ad Christum sponsum
     suum, quia quilibet nostrum tenetur hodie dicere Christo *"Amore lan-*
     gueo" quasi diceret:

     For loue of Iesu, my swete herte,
     Y morne²⁸ and seke wyþ teres smert.

     Nam ista benedicta passio Christi isto die trahere debet lacrimas de
     oculis et singultus de corde cuiuslibet boni Christiani²⁹ < sicud testatur
     beatus Augustinus sic loquens de passione Christi > : "Memoria passionis
     tue, o bone Iesu, lacrimas allicit, oculos confundit, faciem inmutat, et
     cor dulcorat."

---

21. y hynde] ys bownde B; y end D.
22. My . . . wo] and yn my lyf y had snowe and wo T.
23. brynghe B; bye DT.
24. tenemus S.
25. Angelice . . . loue] *om.* BT.
26. makyth BT; made D.
27. to dye B; drery D; dye T.
28. loue T.
29. *add.* de S, *evidently from original* de memoria istius benedicte passionis loquitur
beatus Augustinus sic *(thus BDT), omitted by eyeskip and supplied by the marginal*
sentence.

My life I end in sorrow and woe,
To rescue mankind from its foe.

If we therefore, like grateful people, think on the one hand how much joy we have gained through Christ, we must love him intently; and if, on the other hand, we think about his pain, we must languish. And these are the two words I told you in the beginning, and they are written in the Book of Love: *amore langueo.* In English: **"I mourn for love."**

These words can be considered as Christ's words spoken today to mankind, and conversely they can be considered as mankind's words to Christ. For Christ could truly say to mankind today "I languish with love," as if he were saying:

I mourn for love, as thou canst see,
That made me die because of thee.

And these words can be considered as being spoken by mankind to Christ, its spouse, for each one of us is held to say to Christ today, "I languish with love," as if to say:

For Jesus' love, my sweetheart dear,
I mourn and sigh with painful tear.

For the blessed passion Christ suffered on this day should draw tears from the eyes and sighs from the heart of every good Christian, as Augustine witnesses when he speaks of Christ's passion: "The memory of your passion, oh good Christ, draws tears, clouds the eyes, distorts the face, and sweetens the heart."

80   þe[30] **mynde of** þy[31] **swet passion, Iesu,**[32]
        teres it telles,
        <eyen>[33] **it bolleȝ,**
        my vesage it wetes,
        and my hert it swetes.[34]

Et ideo sicut dicit idem Augustinus, "semper fit tibi fixus in mente qui pro te semel fuit fixus in cruce."

Carissimi, debetis intelligere \quod/ septem signa **of loue and of mornyng**[35] inuenimus in sacra scriptura que isto die acciderunt generi humano. Et aliqua eorum sunt signa intenti amoris, et alia maximi
90 langoris. Primum sig[num][36] fuit magni amoris. Nam isto die, scilicet feria sexta, primus homo, scilicet Adam, fuit creatus. Sicut enim habetur ex scriptura, Deus enim fecit mundum totum et quicquid est in eo in sex diebus. Et p[rimo][37] fecit celum et terram, set in sexto die, scilicet vltimo, creauit hominem, et sicut dies Veneris est dies [*f. 32*] sextus [ebdomade],[38] patet ergo, etc. Et istud fuit signum amoris, quia non creauit hominem ad similitudinem alicuius animalis set ad similitudinem propriam. Ergo isto die ostendit homini maximum amorem. Secundum signum fuit similiter signum amoris, quia isto die collocauit hominem in paradiso deliciarum. Nam sicut doctores dicunt, Adam non fuit creatus
100 in paradiso set in agro Damascene, et postquam Deus fecit eum, tran[s]tulit[39] eum in paradisum, vbi eum regem constituit; et hoc fuit signum amoris. Tercium fuit signum **of gret mornyng,**[40] quia isto die Adam legem preuaricatus est, quia eodem die quo fuit positus in paradiso, eodem die fecit contra preceptum Domini et comedit de ligno. Propter quam tran\s/grescionem omnes fuimus perditi, et ideo omnes tenemur dolere. Quartum signum fuit signum magni langoris, quia isto

---

30. þe . . . swetes] *om.* D.
31. the T.
32. *om.* T.
33. *marg. for* ene; *om.* D; myn eyes B; eyes T.
34. it swetes] swetyth B; filleth yn swetnesse T.
35. of . . . mornyng] amoris et meroris D.
36. sig S.
37. et primo] et post SD; in primo BT.
38. abdomede S.
39. trantulit S.
40. of gret mornyng] magni meroris D.

The memory of thy sweet passion, Jesus,
   it draws tears,
   makes eyes run over,
   bedews my face,
   and sweetens my heart.[8]

And as Augustine further says, "Let him always be fastened in your mind who was once fastened for you on the cross."

Dearly beloved, you should know that in Holy Scripture we find seven signs **of love and of mourning** that on this day happened to mankind. Some of them are signs of intense love, others of the greatest suffering. The first sign was one of great love. For on this day, namely, Friday, the first human being, Adam, was created. As we find from Holy Scripture, God made the whole world and all that is in it in six days. First he made heaven and earth, but on the sixth day, that is, the last, he created man; and since Friday is the sixth day of the week, it is clear, and so on.[9] And this was a sign of love, for God did not create man in the likeness of some animal but in his own likeness. Thus God has, on this day, shown man the greatest love. The second sign was likewise one of love, for on this day he placed man in the garden of delights. As the teachers tell us, Adam was not created in paradise but in the field of Damascus, and after God had made him, he transferred him to paradise, where he made him king; and this was a sign of love. The third sign was one **of great mourning,** for on this day Adam broke the law, because on the same day that he was placed into paradise, he acted against God's commandment and ate from the tree. For that transgression we all were lost, and thus it behooves all of us to mourn. The fourth sign was one of great pain, for on this day man was wretchedly driven from paradise, because as our teachers tell us, Adam was in paradise

---

8. Both the Latin sentence and its rhymed Englishing are devotional commonplaces in medieval sermons, lyrics, and elsewhere; see Wenzel 1978, 128, 131.

9. I.e., that man was created on Friday.

die fuit homo de paradiso miserabiliter fugatus, quia sicut dicunt doctores, Adam non fuit in paradiso nisi per sex horas vnius diei. Sexta
autem peccauit, et venit angelus cum gladio versatili et effugauit eum
110 de paradiso. Et illa eadem hora qua Adam fugatus [est][41] de <para-
diso>, scilicet hora sexta, Christus moriebatur in cruce. Quintum signum fuit similiter magni langoris, quia isto die homo fuit adiudicatus
multiplici miserie, quia ille qui fuit dominus paradisi et semper debuit
vixisse sine aliqua molestia vel angustia, si stetisset, set propter suam
inobedienciam fuit adiudicatus vt hic in mundo viueret in labore et
tribulacione. Sextum signum fuit signum amoris, quia isto die Dei Filius
factus est homo. Nam sicut dicunt doctores, hodie angelus Gabriel venit
ad Mariam et nunciauit ei quod Dei Filius ex ea nasceretur, qui et genus
humanum redimeret. Septimum \et/ vltimum signum inter alia fuit ma-
120 xime dileccionis, quia isto die Christus Dei Filius per mortem suam in
cruce nos redemit et Patri suo reconsiliauit, etc. Ista, karissimi, sunt
septem signa languoris et amoris que isto die acciderunt generi humano.
Vnde si de istis \intime/ cogitemus sicut tenemur, videtur michi quod
quilibet nostrum potest racionabiliter dicere *Amore langueo*. In principio
ergo, vt nobis concedat graciam suam, offeramus Christo in ligno pen-
denti et matri summe dolenti Pater Noster et Aue Maria.

Amore langueo. Narratur quod erat quidam miles in armis strenuissimus et ex nobili sanguine procreatus. Iste habuit vxorem pulcherimam
que propter suam pulcritudinem a diuersis amabatur; tandem amore
130 alterius allecta dominum proprium repudiauit et sibi adhesit, et sic diu
cum illo in peccato miserabiliter vixit. Tandem autem domina predicta
recognoscens miseriam suam et ingratitudinem, iniuriam, et offensam
erga dominum suum vehementer doluit et beneuolenciam domini sui
multum desiderauit nec tamen ausa fuit ad eum accedere personaliter,
set misit sibi literam pro reconsiliacione sua, et cum litera misit pulcrum
donum. Tenor litere erat talis:

Quem fugi diligo, quem dilexi fugio,
Quem fugi peniteo, penitendo resilio.

Donum enim quod misit erat cor totaliter ex auro, et ex illo corde
140 cressebat **trelow** cum quatuor foliis. In primo enim folio scribebatur

---

41. *om.* S; fuit T.

for no more than six hours of one day. In the sixth hour, he sinned, and the angel came with his flashing sword and drove him from the garden. And in the same hour as Adam was driven from paradise, that is, the sixth, Christ died on the cross. The fifth sign was likewise one of great pain, for on this day man was sentenced to manifold wetchedness or distress, for he who was the lord of paradise and should have always lived without adversity or need if he had remained firm in righteousness, was, because of his disobedience, sentenced to live in this world in hardship and tribulation. The sixth sign was a sign of love, for on this day the Son of God became man. As our teachers say, on this day the angel Gabriel came to Mary and announced to her that the Son of God would be born of her, he who would redeem mankind. Finally, the seventh and last sign was one of the greatest love, for on this day Christ, the Son of God, redeemed us through his death on the cross and reconciled us to his Father. These, dearly beloved, are the seven signs of mourning and of love that on this day happened to mankind. If we reflect on them inwardly as we should, it seems to me that everyone of us can rightly say "I languish with love." To begin with, then, in order that Christ may give us his grace, let us offer to him who hung on the cross, and to his mother in her supreme pain, an Our Father and Hail Mary.

I languish with love. A story has it[10] that there was a knight, strong in arms and sprung from a noble line. He had a most beautiful wife, who for her beauty was loved by many different men. At last, drawn by another man's love, she left her own lord and stayed with the other, and thus she lived in wretched sin with him for a long time. But at last this lady recognized her wretchedness and the ingratitude, hurt, and offense she was bringing to her husband, and she grieved violently and much desired her lord's good will. But she did not dare go to him in person and instead sent him a letter asking for his forgiveness, and with the letter she sent a beautiful gift. The message of the letter was as follows:

**I love whom I fled, I flee whom I loved,
My flight I regret, in regret I return.**

And the gift she sent him was a heart made entirely of gold, from which grew a **trewlove** with four leaves. On the first leaf was written "I languish

---

10. See Tubach 3866 and Wenzel 1986, 235–38.

"Amore langueo," in secundo "Langore pereo," in tercio sic: "Pereundo spero," in quarto sic: "Sperando reuiuisco." Anglice:

For loue Y morne.[42]
Y peris al for þi sake.
Y hop[43] **þy grace.**
Mi liue[44] **ys**[45] **on thi face.**[46]

Et isto modo [*f. 32v*] per suam humilitatem et per donum magnum quod misit sibi reconsiliata est domino suo.

Spiritualiter per istum militem nobilem intelligo Christum, qui est ex
150 nobili genere procreatus, quia Dei Filius. Strenuissimus eciam fuit, sicut patuit hodierna die in bello contra diabolum. Et ecce qualiter mirabiliter iste miles fuit armatus vt procederet ad bellum: Primo enim habuit suum **actoun,** suum corpus mundum /vel nudum/; et pro suo **ha < u > berk**[47] quod est **ful of holes**[48] habuit corpus suum plenum vulneribus. Pro galea habuit coronam spineam capiti inpressam, et pro cirothecis de **plate** habuit duos clauos fixos in manibus. Pro calcaribus habuit clauum fixum in pedibus. Pro /e/quo habuit crucem super quam pependit. Pro scuto opposuit latus suum. Et processit sic contra inimicum cum lancea non in manu set **stykand in his side.**[49] Isto modo fuit Christus mirabiliter
160 armatus isto die pugnando contra diabolum. Et tamen cum ista armatura eum vicit et de eius potestate eripuit. Ergo iste miles est Christus. < Domina > anima humana, que pulcra dici potest quia ad imaginem Dei formata et Christo in baptismo desponsata. Set timeo michi quod multi nostrum sicut ista domina fecit dilectum sponsum nostrum repudiauimus, diuersimode allecti per mundum, carnem, et diabolum. Quid ergo facies, peccator, qui ita ingratus fuisti sponso tuo Christo? Certe non restat nisi vt cum domina ista peniteas in corde et recognoscas humiliter ingratitudinem tuam. Mittas ergo sibi donum et literam scribe. Donum

---

42. Y morne] *om.* T.
43. *add.* al yn B; *add.* yn T.
44. loue T.
45. *add.* all D.
46. on thi face] in thy swete face that thou will me take T. S *adds an expanded version of the four lines marginally:* < For loue I morne and sorowe make, for mornige Y perische for þi sake, Though Y perysche Y hope þi grace, My lyue my hope ys in þi face. >
47. *add.* <haburicium> S; *add.* /lorica/ D; habuticum T.
48. ful of holes] plenum foraminibus D.
49. stykand . . . side] in suo latere infixus /stikand/ D.

with love," on the second "With languishing I perish," on the third "In perishing I hope," and on the fourth "In hoping I revive." In English:

For love I mourn.
I perish for your sake.
I hope for your grace.
My life is in your face.

And thus, for her humility and the great gift she sent him, she became reconciled with her lord.

Spiritually speaking, by this noble knight I understand Christ, who was born of a noble lineage, since he was the Son of God. And behold how marvellously this knight was armed for battle: first, for his **coat** he had his clean or naked body; for his **hauberk full of holes** he had his body full of wounds; for a helmet he had a crown of thorns pressed into his head; for gloves of **steel** he had two nails piercing his hands; for spurs he had a nail piercing his feet; for a horse he had the cross on which he hung; for a shield he offered his side. And thus he rode against his enemy, with a lance not in his hand but **sticking in his side**. In this fashion Christ was marvellously armed for the battle against the devil he undertook on this day. And yet he overcame him with this armament and freed us from his power. This knight, then, is Christ. His lady is man's soul, who can be said to be beautiful because she was formed in God's image and married to Christ in baptism. But I fear that many among us leave our beloved spouse just as that lady did, being drawn away from him in various ways through the world, the flesh, and the devil. What then will you do, O sinner, who have been so ungrateful to your spouse, Christ? Surely, nothing else but to mourn in your heart with that lady and in humility to acknowledge your ingratitude. Therefore, send him a gift and write him a letter. That gift

ergo illud erit cor tuum et non cor aureum, quia bonorum nostrorum
170　non eget. Et oportet \quod/ de corde isto procedat vnum **trewloue:**
itaque diligas eum ex toto corde et perseueranter, quia diligere eum hodie
et cras derelinquere nichil valet. Quatuor folia istius fidelis amoris[50] sunt
dileccio Dei super omnia, dileccio proximi, dileccio animi siue anime
tue, et dileccio inimici. Tenor litere quam sibi mittes erit que superius
dixi: "Quem fugi diligo," scilicet dulcissimum sponsum meum **that**[51] **Y**
forsoke to [s]ew[52] **synne.** "Quem dilexi fugio," scilicet diabolum cui
adhesi et cui seruiui quamdiu fui in peccato. "Quem fugi peniteo,"
scilicet illum qui est dulcis et salus anime mee valde peniteo [et per][53]
penitenciam spero graciam et veniam, quia "facies tua, dulcissima spon-
180　sa, plena est graciarum." Ex quo ergo, bone Iesu, es ita curialis quod
me vis recipere ad graciam tuam, teneor te diligere; quia deliqui contra
te, ingratus fui, teneor doiere \et/ languere. Et illud est verbum quod
dixi in principio, *Amore langueo.*

For[54] **loue of Iesu that is mi hert,**
Y morne and[55] **sike wiþ teres smert.**

Carissimi, debetis intelligere quod omnis amor non est amor languens,
set amor intensus dicitur amor languens, scilicet quando homo aliquam
rem ita diligit quod non cogitat de aliquo alio quam de illa re, nec aliquem
saporem habet nec dilec\ta/cionem nisi tantum in illa. Et talem amorem
190　Christus habuit erga nos, sicut bene ostendit hodierna die. Ergo e conuerso
talem amorem erga eum debemus habere. Loquendo ergo de isto amore
languenti, videtur michi quod septem signa inuenio manifeste per que
possumus cognoscere hominem qui languet ex amore, et sunt ista septem:

He[56] **lesus**[57] **is myth and waxit**[58] **wan.**
He syket as a [*f. 33*] **sorful man.**

---

50. *add.* \trewluff/ D.
51. that . . . synne] *om.* D.
52. to sew] torew S; onely for T.
53. et per] *om.* S.
54. *add.* the T.
55. y T.
56. he . . . loue-mornyng] *in top margin, the first two lines lost* D.
57. lost B.
58. *add.* al BT.

will be your own heart, not one of gold, for he does not need our goods. And from the heart a **trewlove** must come forth; you must love him with your whole heart and with perseverance, for to love him today and to leave him tomorrow is worthless. The four leaves of this trewlove are the love of God above all things, the love of your neighbor, the love for your own soul, and the love of your enemy. The message in the letter you must send him will be as I said earlier: "I love whom I fled," namely, my most sweet spouse **whom I forsook to follow sin.** "I flee whom I loved," namely, the devil, with whom I stayed and whom I served as long as I was in sin. "My flight I regret," that is, I am sorry that I abandoned him who is sweet and the salvation of my soul. And through penance I hope for his grace and forgiveness, for "your face, my sweetest spouse, is full of graces."[11] Since you, O good Jesus, are so courteous that you will take me back to your grace, I am held to love you; and since I have sinned against you and been ungrateful, I am held to mourn in pain. And this is what I said in the beginning: *I languish with love.*

> **For Jesus' love, my sweetheart dear,**
> **I mourn and sigh with painful tear.**

Dearly beloved, you should understand that not every love is a languishing love, but only intense love is said to be languishing, that is, when someone loves something so much that he thinks of nothing else beside it, nor has any taste or delight except for it alone. Such love did Christ have for us, as he clearly shows today. Hence we must in return have the same love for him. Speaking of such languishing love, it seems to me that I find seven clear signs by which we can recognize a man who languishes in love. They are:

> **He loses his strength and grows wan.**
> **He sighs like a sorrowful man.**

---

11. Esther 15:17.

Alone [he][59] **drawes fro compenye.**
And euer he[60] **herkenes**[61] **one**[62] **ys drurie.**
Louelyche he spekis to his herte.
For hym he suffrus[63] **peynis smert.**
200   **<þorow**[64] **tokenes of ȝyftes ȝyuynge**
He[65] **schewet >**[66] **in hert loue-mornyng.**[67]

Ista sunt septem signa per que possimus cognoscere qui languet \ex/ amore, et omnia ista signa in Christo hodie fue\r/unt inuenta. Nam primo fuit totaliter extenuatus, et illud [probant][68] manifeste et [ostendunt][69] septem tormenta dolorosa que sustinuit pro amore nostro. Et sic de aliis, sicut patet superius. Ergo Christus potuit dicere *Amore langueo,* etc.

Primum ergo signum per quod possimus cognoscere hominem qui languet ex amore est quod amittit fortitudinem corporalem et debilis efficitur et discoloratur. Et sic fuit Christus hodie, vt ostendunt et probant 210 septem tormenta, etc. Et fuerunt septem:

Blod-[s]wetyng.[70]
Hard byndyng.
Gret traualyng.
Smert[71] **betyng.**
Long wakyng.
Croys-beryng.[72]
Scherp prikyng.

Primum tormentum fuit sanguinis sudacio. Et videtur michi quod

---

59. hem S.

60. *om.* T.

61. syghys D.

62. afftyr B; of T.

63. For hym he suffrus] for he has sufferyd D; for that suffred T.

64. þorow . . . ȝyuynge] *om.* BT—*evidently the listing of seven items in four rhyming quatrains puzzled some scribes;* thurgh tokynys gret of gyftys gyfyng D.

65. He schewet] I swete BT; vnto hys swete D.

66. *add.* wet S, *a remainder of the original text erased and replaced by the marginal addition.*

67. for mornyng T.

68. probat ST.

69. ostedant S; ostendit T.

70. wetyng S.

71. hard D.

72. þe crosberyng BT; *add.* and D.

He withdraws from company to be alone.
He always listens for his lover.
He speaks lovingly to his sweetheart.
For her he suffers bitter pain.
Through tokens of gift giving
He shows in heart love mourning.

These are the seven signs by which we can tell a person who languishes from love, and all of them were on this day found in Christ. For first he was totally weakened, and this is openly proven and shown by the seven painful torments he suffered for our love. And thus likewise with respect to the other signs I mentioned earlier. Therefore, Christ could say, *I languish with love,* etc.

The first sign by which we can recognize a man who languishes with love is that he loses his bodily strength and becomes weak and discolored. This happened to Christ today, as his seven torments show and prove. Those seven were: **blood-sweating, hard binding, being dragged around, bitter beating, long waking, the cross-bearing, and sharp piercing.**

The first torment was his sweating blood. I think it is no wonder that

mirum non est quod sanguinis sudacio fecit eum debilem corporaliter
220 [et][73] discoloratum, quia si homo multum sudaret aquam, que est naturalis sudacio, adhuc multum debilitat eum et discolarat. Multo magis
si homo sudauit sanguinem, etc. Set modo sicut habetur ex euuangelio,
Christus heri post cenam intrauit ortum quendam cum discipulis suis et
ibi illis relictis solus in quodam loco secreto orauit ad Patrem dicens:
"Pater, si possibile est," etc. "Tamen non mea voluntas," etc., quasi
diceret, si proficuum fuerit generi humano quod ego paciar, paratus sum
vilissimam mortem subire pro eius amore. Et sicut dicitur, ita fuit anxi-
atus et corporaliter mortem timuit quod "factus est sudor eius sicut gutte
sanguinis," etc. Quod autem sanguinem sudauit per racionem potest
230 aliqualiter probari. Nam sicut dicunt medici, sudor prouenit naturaliter
ex superfluitate humorum qui sunt in corpore hominis. Set Christus
nullam superfluitatem habuit, quia sicut anima eius erat munda sine
aliqua macula peccati, sic corpus eius sine aliqua feditate corporali, quia
secundum Ambrosium corpus non fuit de putredine sicut corpus nostrum
set de purissimis guttis sanguinis que erant in corpore matris eius. Ex
quo ergo non habuit in corpore superfluitatem humorum, oportuit eum
omnino sudare sanguinem, et per consequens pena eius fuit grauior et
magis eum debilitauit. Hoc est ergo primum tormentum, sanguinis sudacio. Set quare voluit Christus sic sudare sanguinem? Quia secundum
240 doctores vt daret exemplum quod carnem et sanguinem tuum in bonis
operibus penitencie expenderes, quia "omnis Christi accio nostra fuit
instruccio."

Secundum tormentum dura ligacio.[74] De isto habetur in passione.
Nam cum Iudas tradidisset dominum suum, non audebat accedere vt
eum caperet, set habiit ad principes sacerdotum et peciit homines ar-
matos, quibus acceptis iuit ad ortum in quo erat Iesus, quia sciebat eum
illum locum frequentare. Illis vero cum armis intrantibus et clamantibus,
"Vbi est traditor falsus?" processit eis Christus obuiam dicens, "Quem
queritis?" Illis vero respondentibus, "Iesum Nazarenum," intulit Chris-
250 tus, "Ego sum." Et statim abierunt retorsum et ceciderunt ad terram.
Hoc idem eciam secundo [*f. 33v*] fecerunt. Tandem resumptis viribus
venerunt ad eum et Iudas primus accessit et osculatus est eum. Et illud
fuit miserum osculum, per quod impletur homicidium. Statim autem

---

73. *om.* S.
74. *add.* <anglice hard bindynge> S.

sweating blood weakened him bodily and made him lose color, because when a man sweats a lot of water, which is natural perspiration, he grows very weak and discolored. Much more so if a man sweats blood. But as the gospel has it, yesterday after his supper, Christ went into a garden with his disciples and, having left them there, prayed in solitude to the Father, saying: "Father, if it is possible," etc., "but not my will but yours," etc.,[12] as if he were saying: if it should be useful to mankind that I suffer, I am ready to endure the most shameful death for mankind's sake. And as it is reported, he became so troubled and afraid of his bodily death that "his sweat became like drops of blood," etc.[13] That he sweated blood can be explained in some rational way. For as the physicians tell us, sweat comes naturally from the overabundance of bodily humors. But Christ had no such overabundance, for just as his soul was pure without any stain of sin, so his body was without any bodily impurity, because according to Ambrose, his body was not made from corruption, as our body is, but from the absolutely pure drops of blood that were in the body of his mother.[14] Since he, therefore, did not have any overabundance of humors in his body, of necessity he had to sweat blood, and as a result his suffering was more grievous and weakened him more. This, then, is his first torment, sweating blood. But why did Christ thus want to sweat blood? According to our teachers, to give an example that you should spend your own flesh and blood in good works of penance, because "every action of Christ was for our instruction."[15]

The second torment was his hard binding. Of this we hear in the passion.[16] For after Judas had betrayed his lord, he did not dare go near him to capture him, but instead went to the high priests and asked for armed men. With them he went to the garden where Jesus was, for he knew that Jesus was often there. As they entered with their weapons and shouted, "Where is that false traitor?" Christ went toward them and said, "Whom do you seek?" But when they answered, "Jesus of Nazareth," Christ replied, "I am the one." And at once they drew back and fell to the ground. They did the same a second time. Finally they gathered their strength again and came up to him, and Judas approached

---

12. Matt. 26:39 and Luke 22:42.
13. Luke 22:24.
14. This statement is elsewhere attributed to Bernard.
15. A commonplace of medieval devotional literature, attributed to various authorities.
16. John 18:1–7.

manus iniecerunt in eum et ligauerunt eum sicut furem, manus a tergo
et ita dure sicut dicit quidam doctor quod sanguis pro violencia de digitis
perfluxit. Et quare voluit Christus sic ligari? Certe, secundum doctores,
vt nos de vinculis peccatorum solueret. Et ideo consulo, si fueris ligatus
aliquo peccato, vt cum Christo agas ad solucionem tuam, \ne/ in fine
dicatur \illud/ Mathei, "Ligatis manibus et pedibus proicite," etc.

260   Tercium tormentum fuit **gret trauayle**.[75] Nam secundum < ew >an-
gelium fuit ductus circumquaque de loco ad locum sicut latro. Et ad sex
loca fuit specialiter ductus, quia primo ad domum Anne sacerdotis,
deinde ad domum Cayphe pontificis, deinde ad Pilatum, et de eo ad
Herodem, et de Herode iterum reductus est ad Pilatum, et vltimo[76] ad
montem Caluarie, vbi crucifixus est. Et sicut narrat Damascenus in
prologo, dum Iesus sic circumquaque ducebatur per plateas ciuitatis,
posuerunt cordam maximam circa collum suum in signum quod fuit
dampnatus ad suspendendum. Mulieres vero et paruuli proiecerunt super
eum lutum, lapides, [et][77] huiusmodi. Maria mater eius sequebatur eum
270   dilacerans crines dicens, "Fili, quare michi non loqueris?" Et ista pena
fuit sibi maior omni morte, scilicet quod filius suus sic tractabatur et
quod sibi \non/ loquebatur. Et quare Christus sic voluit vexari? Certe,
vt daret nobis exemplum quod corpus nostrum vexaremus in operibus
penitencie, etc.

Quartum tormentum fuit dura flagellacio,[78] et propter duas raciones
fuit flagellatus. Vna fuit quod Romani a Iudeis conducti eum interfece-
runt, et [mos][79] fuit apud eos quod nullus mortem acciperet nisi prius
flagellaretur. Alia racio fuit quia Pilatus vidit quod Iudei omnino voluerunt vt interficeretur. Ipse enim voluit eum liberasse, quia nullam cau-
280   sam mortis inuenit in eo, set non audebat, et \ideo/ iussit flagellari vsque
ad sanguinis effusionem, et sic Iudei eius sanguine saciati mortem illius
vlterius non desiderarent. Ministri eius accipientes eum ligauerunt eum
ad columpnam et durissime verberauerunt eum, et adhuc, sicut dicit
Magister Istoriarum, remanent vestigia sanguinis in illa columpna, que
est Rome. Et sicut vnus doctor dicit, Christus [fuit flagellatus][80] talibus

---

75. gret trauayle] magna laboratio BD; grete trauyllyng T.
76. *add.* reductus est S.
77. *om.* S.
78. *add.* < anglice smart betyng > S.
79. mors S.
80. fuit flagellatus] *om.* S.

in front of them and kissed him. That was a wretched kiss, by which murder was committed. The others at once laid hand on him and bound him like a thief, his hands in back and so tightly that, as some teacher says, for that pressure his blood flowed out of his fingers. And why did Christ want to be thus bound? Certainly, as the teachers say, so that he might release us from the bonds of our sins. Therefore I suggest that if you are bound by some sin, you negotiate with Christ for your release, lest in the end those words in Matthew be said of you, "Tie his hands and feet and throw him," etc.[17]

The third torment was his **being dragged around**. According to the gospel, Christ was led from place to place like a thief. In particular he was led to six different places: first to the house of Annas the high priest, then to the house of Caiaphas the priest, then to Pilate, and from there to Herod, and from Herod again back to Pilate, and lastly to Mount Calvary, where he was crucified. And as John Damascenus reports in his prologue, as Jesus was thus being led about the city squares, they put a large rope around his neck as a sign that he was condemned to be hanged. But the women and children threw mud and stones and such at him. Mary, his mother, followed him, tearing her hair and saying, "O son, why do you not speak to me?" And this pain was greater than death itself, namely, that her son was thus being dragged about and did not speak to her. And why did Christ want to be thus tortured? Certainly so that he might give us an example that we should torture our body with the works of penance, etc.

The fourth torment was his bitter scourging. He was scourged for two reasons. One was that the Romans were led by the Jews to kill him, and it was their custom that no one would be punished with death without being scourged. The other reason was that Pilate noticed that the Jews absolutely wanted Jesus to be killed. He wished to free him, for he found no cause for death in him, but he did not dare to do so; and therefore he had him scourged to the blood, so that the Jews, satisfied with his blood, might no longer desire his death. Pilate's servants took Jesus and tied him to a column and beat him bitterly, and to this day, as the Master of the Histories tells us, the traces of his blood remain visible on that column, which is in Rome.[18] As one teacher declares, Christ was

---

17. Matt. 22:13.

18. Peter Comestor, *Historia scholastica,* In evangelia 167 (*PL* 198:1628). The column, supposedly, has been in the church of Santa Prassede since 1228.

flagellis que habebant vncos \idest nodos/ in fine, tali modo factos vt in percuciendo carnem rumperent et pecies carnis secum traherent. Narrat vnus doctor quod vnus de flagellantibus Christum habuit nomen Manchus, eo quod vnam manum aridam et incuruatam [habuit],[81] quem
290   euangelium nominat Malcus, cuius auriculam Petrus absidit. In flagellando cum vna manu gutte sanguinis s[al]tabant[82] de corpore Christi super manus eius arridam, et statim sanata est illa manus. Ille vero propter miraculum non cessauit flagellare Christum, set forcius quam prius deseuit in Christum, quia tunc cum vtraque manu ipsum flagellauit. Et quare Christus voluit sic [*f. 34*] flagellari? Certe, \vt/ daret tibi exemplum quod corpus tuum per disciplinas et \per/ ali\a/s penas castigares.

Quintum tormentum fuit diutina vigilacio,[83] quia tempore illo quo fuit captus, scilicet heri, vsque ad mortem nullam requiem corporalem
300   permiserunt eum habere set continue fecerunt eum vigilare, nunc trahendo, nunc percusciendo et aliis diuersis modis infestando. Et sicut dixit quidam doctor, quando voluit dormiuisse, extraxerunt pilos de capite et eciam de barba sua, vt eum excitarent a sompno. Et quare voluit Christus sic continue vigilare? Certe, vt tu vigilares spiritualiter contra temptacionem diaboli, quia ipse nunquam dormit. "Vigilate ergo et orate, ne intretis in temptacionem," etc.

Sextum tormentum [fuit][84] crucis baiulacio,[85] quia sicut habetur ex euangelio, quando Christus fuit dampnatus vt suspenderetur in cruce, posuerunt crucem super dorsum eius et fecerunt eum portare crucem.
310   Narratur in *Euangelio Nazareorum* quod quando Beata Virgo audiuit quod filius suus fuit morti adiudicatus et ductus per ciuitatem ad locum Caluarie, sequebatur eum vt cum eo colloquium haberet. Set nullo modo potuit propter pressuram circa eum. Cogitauit ergo intra se: "Pre\ce/-dam eum ad montem Caluarie et stando supra montem videbo eum." Iuit ergo per semitam et venit ad montem, et ibi expectauit. Cum ergo venisset < Iesus > et Virgo eum vidisset a longe ita vulneratum, pre dolore cordis statim cecidit ad terram. Et hoc videns Iesus similiter cecidit. Quod videntes ministri eum ducentes angariauerunt Symonem Cireneum

---

81. *om.* S; habebat B.
82. stabant S; cadebant B; stillabat T.
83. *add.* < anglice longwakyng > S.
84. *om.* S.
85. *add.* < croys berynge > S.

scourged with the kind of scourge that has barbs at the end, made to tear the flesh in scourging and rip out pieces of flesh. Some teacher reports that one of those who scourged Christ was called Mancus, because one of his hands was paralytic and crippled; the gospel calls him Malcus, the one whose ear Peter cut off.[19] As he was scourging Jesus with one hand, drops of blood sprang from Christ's body on his crippled hand, and it was healed at once. But despite this miracle, he did not stop scourging Christ but raged more fiercely against him, for now he scourged him with both hands. And why did Christ want to be thus scourged? Surely to give you an example that you should chastize your body with disciplines and other works of penance.

The fifth torment was his long waking, for from the time he was captured, that is, yesterday, until his death, they allowed him no bodily rest but constantly kept him awake, now drawing him, now striking him and molesting him in various other ways. And as some teacher says, when Jesus wanted to sleep, they pulled hairs out of his head and beard, so that they would rouse him from sleep. And why did Christ want to stay awake so continuously? Surely so that you might spiritually be awake against the devil's temptation, for the devil never sleeps. "Wake and pray, that you may not enter into temptation," etc.[20]

The sixth torment was his carrying the cross, for as the gospel declares, when Christ was condemned to be hung on the cross, they put a cross on his back and made him carry it. The *Nazarite Gospel* tells us that when the Blessed Virgin heard that her son was sentenced to die and led through the city to Calvary, she followed him that she might speak to him. But she could do this in no way because of the crowd around him. Then she thought to herself: "I will go before him to Mount Calvary, and standing on the hill, I will see him." So she went by that way and came to the hill and there waited for him. And when Jesus came and the Virgin saw him from afar so much wounded, she at once fell to the ground for heartache. And when Jesus saw that, he too fell down.[21] As the servants who were leading him saw that, they forced Simon of Cyrene, who was passing by that way, to carry his cross. They did not do this out of reverence but because of his lack of strength.

---

19. John 18:10.
20. Matt. 26:41.
21. Apocrypha 1:164; cf. Ludolf of Saxony 2.62 (1495, 616a).

transeuntem per viam illam vt crucem eius tolleret. Et istud non fecerunt
320   sibi causa reuerencie, set causa inpotencie. Quare voluit Christus crucem
portare? Certe, vt daret tibi exemplum vt tu portares crucem penitencie.
Set consulo quod non portes sicut Symon fecit, scilicet inuitus—ideo non
legimus in ewangelio eum saluatum—set portes sicut Christus fecit, voluntarie, et tunc erit Deo **to**[86] **qweme**[87] et tibi **notful to soul.**

Septimum tormentum **scharp prykyng.**[88] Nam sicut habetur in euangelio, milites Romani eum crucifixerunt, et quia voluerunt fuisse cito
liberati de eo, festinauerunt cum eo ad locum vbi moreretur. Iesus vero,
quia fuit valde debilis ex sanguinis effusione et ex diuersis tormentis,
non potuit bene incedere, et ideo fecerunt sibi quadruplicem violenciam
330   vt festinanter iret, scilicet trahendo, pungendo, pellendo, et percuciendo.[89] Et [quare][90] voluit Christus sic **ben**[91] **yprykkyde**[92] **and hastid** in
itinere suo? Certe, vt tibi \daret/ exemplum vt tu festinares spiritualiter
corrigere vitam \et/ vt pungeres in corde [per][93] contricionem. Et propter
ista septem tormenta potest Christus querelare et dicere cum Psalmista,
"Miser factus et curuatus sum," etc.

Y am disseset[94] **and al for-schende,**[95]
Sori[96] **and sykande**[97] **and alle to-rent.**

[*f. 34v*] De \istis/ septem tormentis[98] que Christus hodie pertulit
habemus figuram in sacra scriptura. Nam Daniele habetur < Danielis
340   XIIII > quod Babilonii propter inuidiam quam habuerunt erga eum
propter suam sanctitatem accusauerunt falso apud regem, sic quod fuit
morti condempnatus. Acceperunt ergo eum et posuerunt in lacu leonum,
vbi fuerunt septem leones vt Danielem interficerent et deuorarent. Set

---

86. to(1) ... soul] conueniens et placabile T.
87. to qweme] queme B; queme ad placitum D.
88. scharp prykkyng] aspera confixio \prykkyng or naylyng or brodyng/ D.
89. *add.* \compellyd with portyng and drawyng/ D.
90. *om.* S.
91. ben ... hastid] esse stimulatus \prykkyd/ et festinatus D.
92. pryckyng T.
93. *om.* S.
94. mysseyn D.
95. to-schend D.
96. sore B.
97. syke B.
98. De ... tormentis] of þys tormentis B.

Why did Christ want to carry the cross? Surely so that you might not carry your cross as Simon did, unwillingly—hence we do not read in the gospel that he was saved—but rather as Christ did, of his free will. Then it will be **pleasing to** God and **useful for** your **soul**.

The seventh torment was the **sharp piercing**. For as the gospel reports, the Roman soldiers crucified him, and since they wanted to be rid of him soon, they hurried with him to the place where he was to die. But because Jesus was very weak from the loss of blood and various torments, he could not walk well, and so they inflicted four kinds of violence on him so that he might go quickly, namely, by drawing, stabbing, pushing, and striking him. And why did Christ want **to be** thus **pricked and hastened** on his way? Surely to give you an example that you might spiritually hasten to correct your life and be pricked in your heart by contrition. And on account of these seven torments Christ may well complain and say with the Psalmist, "I have become wretched and a cripple," etc.[22]

I am diseased and all forlorn,
Sorry and sighing, to pieces torn.

These seven torments that Christ suffered this day were foreshadowed in Scripture. For in the Book of Daniel we find that out of the envy that the Babylonians had for Daniel because of his saintliness, they falsely accused him before the king, so that he was condemned to death. They took and put him into the lions' den, where there were seven lions to

---

22. Ps. 37:7.

tamen per miraculum Dei euasit. Per Danielem prophetam intelligo
Christum, in quo pre ceteris fuit spiritus prophecie. Et de propheta
loquitur in antiqua lege ad litteram: "Prophetam suscitabo vobis de
fratribus vestris; ipsum audietis." Iste propheta false fuit accusatus a
Babiloniis, idest a Iudeis falsis, et per eorum suggestionem malam morti
adiud[i]catus.[99] Set qui fuerunt septem leones ordinati ad eum deuoran-
350   dum et interfi[ci]endum?[100] Certe, septem tormenta iam dicta, que fuerunt ordinata vt eum traherent ad mortem. Leo est rex animalium, et
ideo ab omnibus animalibus timetur. Set inter omnia que magis timemus
sunt tormenta et in presenti et in futuro. Christus autem non solum
sustinuit vnum tormentum set omnia ista septem. Ergo mirum non est
si eum trahebant ad mortem.

Ista ergo septem sunt tormenta que Christus sustinuit hodie que eum
corporaliter debilitauerunt <et faciem eius benedictam discoloraue-
runt>. Set quia omnia ista sustinuit pro salute nostra et vt nobis exemplum daret, et ideo facies sibi oracionem et rogabis quod tormenta
360   que sustinuit habeant effectum in anima tua, etc., et dicas sic:

> **Lorde þat[101] suffrydist harde turment[102]**
> **And on[103] \the/ rode were[104] alle to-rent,**
> **Let me suffri wo and pyne,**
> **þat Y may be on \of/ þine.**

Primum ergo signum amoris languentis est quod ille qui sic languet **lesis
is myth and waxis wan.**[105]

Secundum signum est quod[106] **he[107] syket as a sorful[108] man.** Et illud
signum ostendit Christus hodie, et hoc probant septem opprobria ig-
nomin[i]osa[109] que sustinuit hodie pro amore nostro. Primum fuit quod

---

99. adiudcatus S.

100. interfiendum S.

101. þu D.

102. tormentis B.

103. in D.

104. was BDT.

105. lesis . . . wan] amittit vim suam et pallet \lesyth hys myȝth and wexit wan/ D.

106. þat B.

107. he . . . man] ipse suspirat quasi homo dolorosus \he syghys as a sorofull man/ D;
he that sykes a sorowfull man T.

108. sory B.

109. ignominosa S.

kill and devour Daniel. But through a miracle of God, he escaped.[23] By the prophet Daniel I understand Christ, in whom was the spirit of prophecy before all others. And the Old Testament says literally about a prophet: "I will raise you a prophet from among your brothers; listen to him."[24] This prophet was falsely accused by the Babylonians, that is, the false Jews, and through their evil suggestion sentenced to death. But who were the seven lions set to devour and kill him? Surely the seven torments we have discussed, which were ordained to draw Jesus to death. The lion is the king of animals and hence is feared by all the beasts. But among the things we fear most are torments, both now and in the future. Christ suffered not only one torment but all these seven. Therefore it is no wonder that these drew him to his death.

These are the seven torments that Christ suffered this day, which weakened him in body and discolored his blessed face. But as he endured all this for our salvation and for the example he wanted to give us, pray to him and ask him that the torments he suffered may have their effect in your soul, and say thus:

Lord, thou suffer'dst hard torment,
On the cross to pieces rent.
Let me suffer woe and pine,
That I may be one of thine.

Thus, the first sign of languishing love is that he who thus languishes **loses his strength and grows wan**.

The second sign is that **he sighs like a sorrowful man**. Christ showed this sign on this day; and this is proven by the seven shameful insults he suffered this day for our love. The first was that the Jews held the worst thief in higher esteem than him. Behold what an insult this was:

---

23. Dan. 6.
24. Deut. 18:18.

370 plus de pessimo latrone quam de eo <re> putauerunt. Et aduerte quantum opprobrium: vnus fortis latro homicida, qui fuit incarceratus propter
sua scelera, preponitur Christo Filio Dei et de eo magis reputabatur,
nam pecierunt quod latro dimitteretur libere abire <et> quod Christus
innocens crucifigeretur, sicut patet ex euangelio quando Pilatus quesiuit
ab eis vtrum vellent petere pro Barabam vel pro Christo, etc. Et quare
Christus sic voluit despici et inhonorari? Certe, vt daret nobis exemplum
quod de mundi honoribus non curaremus, quia honores aliquando ducunt
ad perdicionem, et e conuerso opprobrium hic in isto mundo ducit ad
gaudium, sicut de omnibus Christi electis <patet>, etc.

380 Secundum opprobrium fuit quod totam cohortem congregauerunt vt
eum despicerent. Nam isto tempore, scilicet contra Pascha, totus populus
patrie ad ciuitatem venerat vt Deo in templo in illa solempnitate im-
molaret. Et ideo Iudei volentes \eum/ despicere quantum scirent,[110] omnem populum: mulieres, paruulos, et ribaldos, congregauerunt vt omnes
vnanimiter clamarent super eum et despicerent. Et certe, [*f. 35*] magis
opprobrium est despici a multis quam a paucis. Set in hiis omnibus
Christus paciencer se habuit, quia eis non respondit. Et hoc certe vt
nobis daret exemplum quod quando homines nos despicerent, paciencer
sustineremus libenter pro amore illius, etc.

390 Tercium opprobrium fuit quod eum coram toto populo nudauerunt,
sicut habetur ex ewangelio. [Ter][111] eum nudauerunt hodie, primo scilicet
quando debuit ligari ad columpnam et flagellari. Tunc eum nudauerunt
et sic flagellauerunt ita quod sanguis per totum corpus emanauerat. Et
tunc induerunt eum mantello rubeo et accipientes coronam spineam
compresserunt capiti suo et genuflectentes salutabant eum dicentes,
"Aue, rex Iudeorum." Et postquam sibi sic illuserant, iterum illum
nudauerunt extrahentes mantellum et vestibus suis eum induerunt. Et
sicut dicit quidam doctor, sanguis illius fuit infrigidatus et mantellus
carni conclutinatus sicut <patet> de vulnere cui apponitur lintheum,
400 et ideo in extrahendo mantellum totam pellem suam que remanserat in
clamide a corpore extraxerunt. Tercia vice fuit nudatus coram populo
quando debuit suspendi super crucem. Nam ita nudus ibi pendebat sicut
de matre fuit natus. Set sicut Ieronimus dicit, mater siue vna de Mariis
que eum sequebantur accepit velum de capite suo et pependit circa secreta

---

110. *add.* scilicet SD.
111. <Iudei> *corr. from* rei S; *om.* BD.

a murderer and thief, in prison for his misdeeds, is placed ahead of Christ, the Son of God, and held in higher repute, because they asked that the thief be allowed to go free and that the innocent Christ be crucified, as is shown by the gospel when Pilate asked them whether they wanted to ask for Barabbas or for Christ, etc.[25] And why did Christ want to be thus despised and dishonored? Surely that he might give us an example not to care for worldly honors, for honors sometimes lead to perdition, while, conversely, insult in this world leads to joy, as is shown in all of Christ's elect, etc.

The second insult was that they gathered the entire cohort to scorn him. For at this time, namely, about Easter, all the people of the country had come to the city to bring sacrifices to God in the temple on this solemn feast. And thus the Jews, wanting to put as much scorn on him as they could, gathered all the people—women, children, and the riffraff—so that all might cry out at him and scorn him. Surely, it is a greater insult to be scorned by many than by a few. But in all this, Christ acted patiently, for he did not reply to them. And he acted this way, surely, to give us an example of suffering patiently and willingly for his love when people scorn us, etc.

The third insult, as we find in the gospel, was that they undressed him in front of all the people. Three times they undressed him on this day. First, when he was to be tied to the column and scourged. Then they undressed him and scourged him so that his blood flowed over his whole body. After that they put a red cloak on him, took a crown of thorns and pressed it on his head, and greeted him on bent knees, saying, "Hail, king of the Jews."[26] After they had thus mocked him, they took the cloak off again and put on his own clothes. And as one teacher says, his blood had congealed and the cloak become glued to his flesh, as it happens with a wound on which one puts a bandage, and therefore by taking off this cloak, they tore off all his skin that clung to the cloth. Then he was undressed in front of the people a third time when he was to be crucified. For he hung on it as naked as he was at birth. But as Jerome says, his mother or one of the Marys that followed him took the veil from her head and dressed it around Christ's private parts.[27] Poor and naked he came into the world, and in the same way he left it.

---

25. Matt. 27:15–23.
26. Matt. 27:29.
27. Cf. Ludolf of Saxony 2.63 (1495, 620a).

corporis < Christi >. Pauper ergo et nudus venit in mundum, et eodem modo exiuit.

Quartum opprobrium fuit quod eum vestibus derisoriis induerunt, et sicut patet ex euangelio inuenio eum dupplici veste derisoria vestitum. Induerunt eum scilicet mantello et tunica. Primo mantello rubeo, de quo
410 superius, et iste fuit vestis derisionis quia, sicut dicit quidam doctor, in illo mantello fuerunt scripture cum literis [continentibus][112] omnes malediciones Legis, in signum quod ille fuit maledictus a Deo, et a Lege, et ab omni populo. Secunda tunica alba fuit, in signum derisionis, qua fecit eum indui rex Herodes, quia fatuum eum reputauit. Et quare voluit ista duo vestimenta Christus portare? Certe, vt nos portaremus in corde mantellum **of holines**[113] et in anima tunicam **of clenes,**[114] etc.

Quintum opprobrium fuit quod in faciem spuerunt. "Heu," dicit Bernardus, "illa facies que fuit clarior sole et dulcior melle, in quam dilectantur angeli prospicere, modo totaliter est cooperta et fedata sputis
420 Iudeorum in signum derisionis et despeccionis." Set quare sic conspuebant in faciem eius benedictam? Et respondit quidam doctor quod facies eius fuit ita gloriosa et delectabilis aspectui quod cuicumque diligenter intuenti eam videbatur ita delectabilis et amabilis quod naturaliter trahebatur eum diligere. In quam faciem benedictam multi intente respicientes non habuerunt voluntatem in aliquo sibi nocere set ad eum diligendum. Quod videntes illi qui magis sibi inuidebant, in eum spuerunt et lutum in faciem proiecerunt vt horribilis appareret. Et ex hoc animarentur omnes ad eum interficiendum. Et quare Christus voluit quod facies sua sic federetur sputis Iudeorum quod sic fetet? Certe, vt tu
430 vanam gloriam de pulcritudine non haberes, quia qui te fecit pulcrum potuit te fecisse leprosum, etc.

Sextum opprobrium fuit quod tradiderunt sibi arundinem in manu, et propter istam causam inposuerunt sibi quod ipse [*f. 35v*] dixerat se esse regem, ad quem pertinent regalia, scilicet corona et septrum. Set prius coronauerunt eum, scilicet corona spinea, postmodum autem tradiderunt sibi arundinem pro ceptro, in signum quod sicut arundo est vacua interius, sic ipse fuit vacuus sine regno. Cum ista arundine percusserunt eum et in capite depresserunt coronam, sicut dicitur in euangelio. Ista arundo

---

112. *om.* SD.
113. of holines] sanctitatis D.
114. of clenes] puritatis D.

The fourth insult was that they clothed him in garments of derision. As is shown by the gospel, I find him clothed with a twofold garment of derision, for they put on him a cloak and a tunic. First a red cloak, of which I spoke earlier, and this was a garment of derision because, as some teacher says, on this garment were written all the curses of the Law, as a sign that he was cursed by God, by the Law, and by the whole people. The other garment was a white tunic as a sign of derision, which Herod had put on him because he thought Jesus was a fool. And why did Christ want to wear these two garments? Surely so that we might wear the cloak **of holiness** in our heart and the tunic **of purity** in our soul, etc.

The fifth insult was that they spat in his face. "Alas," says St. Bernard, "that face that was brighter than the sun and sweeter than honey, which the angels rejoiced to behold, now it is wholly covered and dirtied with the spittle of the Jews, as a sign of derision and mockery."[28] But why did they thus spit in his blessed face? A certain teacher replies that his face was so glorious and delightful to look at that it caused in whoever looked at him diligently such delight and affection that it naturally drew him to love Jesus. Many who looked intently into that blessed face had no desire to harm him but only to love him. When those who hated him most saw this, they spat at him and threw dirt in his face that it might look horrible. And by doing this all were encouraged to kill him. Why did Christ want his face to be so dirtied with the spittle of the Jews that it stank so much? Surely so that you might not derive any vainglory from your own beauty, because he who made you beautiful could have made you a leper, etc.

The sixth insult was that they put a reed in his hand, and they did so because he had said he was a king. Since a king is characterized by such regal attributes as crown and scepter, they first crowned him, namely, with a crown of thorns, and afterward they gave him a reed as a scepter, to indicate that, just as a reed is hollow inside, he himself was hollow and without kingdom. With this reed they struck him and pressed his crown on his head, as the gospel says.[29] This reed was a fool's

---

28. Another meditative commonplace.
29. Matt. 27:29–30.

fuit **babel**[115] fatui, in signum quod eum et opera sua fatua reputaue-
440 runt, etc.

Septimum [opprobrium][116] fuit quod faciem eius velauerunt. Nam
sicut habetur ex euangelio, velauerunt faciem eius et percusserunt ad
modum illius ludi qui vocatur **a-bobete**,[117] dicentes sibi: "Prophetiza quis
est qui te percussit." Set Christus nichil respondit.

Narratur quod erat quidam paruulus inter [eos][118] quando sic illu-
debant sibi et vt dicitur erat filius Pilati. Iste intente respiciens in dul-
cissimam faciem Christi in tantum aspiciebat et conpaciebatur de
illusione sua quod libentissime voluit fuisse percussus pro eo et eum
liberasse si potuisset. Videns autem semel quod quidam male percuteret,
450 prosiliit contra ictum vt illum recip[er]et.[119] Percuciens vero ita dure
percussit quod puer cecidit ad terram et mortuus est. Istam vindictam
audiens Pilatus ex tunc voluit Christum liberasse, ne maiorem vindictam
in seipso reciperet. Set Christus noluit suam passionem inpediri. Be-
nedixit puerum, et reuixit.

Ista ergo sunt septem opprobria que Christus hodie pro amore nostro
sistinuit, propter quem potest dicere cum Psalmista, "Quoniam propter
te sustinui obpprobrium," etc.

For þe, man, Y suffre[120] **schame,**
Wo and peyne and gret[121] **blame.**

460 De istis septem opprobriis habemus aliqualem figuram Genesis 41. Dicitur enim ibi quod Pharao rex Egipti habuit quoddam sompnum, in quo
videbatur sibi quod videbat segetem crescere et spice septem pululabant
in culmo vno pleno et formoso. Postea vidit aliud bladum crescere sicut
prius viderat. Iterum septem spice pululabant in culmo vno, set ille spice
fuerunt **hungry** et fede aspectui. Et tamen ille fede deuorabant et de-
struebant priorem pulcritudinem. Per **cornwaxand**[122] intelligo Christum,

---

115. pegina \idest babyl/ B; *om.* D.
116. signum SD.
117. a-bobbyd B; abacuk D; a-bobet T.
118. quos S.
119. recipet S.
120. Y suffre] y suffred BD; suffre T.
121. mekyll D.
122. cornwarnyng B; grani crescenciam \cornwaxyng/ D; cornewaxyng T.

scepter, indicating that they thought he and his works were foolish, etc.

The seventh insult was that they veiled his face. As we have it from the gospel, "they veiled his face and struck him," as in that game called **"abobbed,"** saying to him, "Prophesy who it is that has struck you."[30] But Christ said nothing in reply.

It is reported that there was a child among them when they mocked him thus, and, as is reported, this was Pilate's son. He was looking intently into Christ's sweet face and watched and felt so sorry for this mocking that he would gladly have been struck in Jesus' stead if possible. At one point, when he saw someone striking very hard, he sprang forward against that stroke to stop it. But the man who was striking did so with such force that the child fell to the ground and was dead. When Pilate heard this act of punishment, from that moment on he wanted to set Christ free to avoid an even greater vengeance. But Christ did not want to have his suffering halted. He blessed the child, and he revived.

These, then, are the seven insults that Christ suffered this day for our love, for which we can say with the Psalmist, "For your sake I suffered insult," etc.[31]

For you, O man, I suffer shame,
Wo and pain and bitter blame.

We find a biblical figura for these seven insults in Genesis 41. There it is said that Pharaoh, the king of Egypt, once had a dream, in which he seemed to see a stalk grow, and seven ears grew at its top that were full and beautiful. After that he saw another stalk grow like the earlier one. Again seven ears grew at its top, but these were **emaciated** and looked ugly. And then the ugly ears devoured and destroyed the former beautiful ones.[32] By **this growing grain** I understand Christ, who in the gospel likens himself to a grain;[33] for just as our body is nourished and fed by grain, so our soul is nourished by Christ's grace and the living bread of his blessed body. But that grain of Pharaoh's dream had seven ears, by which I understand the seven gifts of the Holy Spirit. These

---

30. Luke 22–64.
31. Ps. 68:8.
32. Gen. 41:1–7.
33. John 12:24 or Matt. 13:31, etc.

qui se comparat in euangelio grano; sicut [enim corpus nutritur et
pascitur de grano, sic][123] anima de gracia Christi et de pane viuo sui
benedicti corporis. Set illud granum habuit septem spicas, per quas
470   intelligo septem dona Spiritus Sancti, que fuerunt in Christo plus quam
in aliquo alio. Merito ergo pulcher et gloriosus tam corpore quam anima.
Set[124] que deuorauerunt priores? Certe opprobria hodie sibi illata, que
deuorauerunt et destruccerunt totam pulcritudinem sui corporis. Nam
Ysaias prophetauerat de eo \quod/ magis similis fuit leproso quam
homini. Vt ista ergo obprobria cedant nobis ad salutem anime, facies
sibi istam oracionem:

> **Lorde, blessed[125] be þi name.**
> **For me þou suffred dispite and schame.**
> **As[126] þou art ful of grace,**
> 480   **The to serue gyfe me space.**

Tertium signum amoris languentis est quod qui languet ex amore se
subtrahit a societate, quia nulla est sibi societas nisi tantum illius quem
sic amat. Isto modo Christus **ys alone**,[127] quia nullus cum eo remansit,
immo "discipuli eo relicto omnes fug\i/erunt." \Nec/ eciam tunc perfecte cre- [*f. 36*] diderunt in eum, quia resurreccionem eius non sper-
abant, nisi tantum Beata Virgo, in qua stetit fides Ecclesie per illud
triduum. Quod autem sic fuit **pylt alone**[128] a cordibus hominum, \hoc/
probant et ostendunt septem genera hominum qui illum persequebantur.
Primi fuerunt Iudei in eum spuando. Nam sicut habetur in euangelio,
490   Christus eos honorauerat plus quam omnes gentes quia carnem de eis
assumpserat, et tamen illi eum magis odebant. Nam die ac nocte cogi-
tabant qualiter eum poterant capere in opere et sermone. Et nota hic
exemplum qualiter adduxerunt ad eum callide mulierem deprehensam in
adulterio, et de malicia eorum, etc. Secundi fuerunt pontifices conspi-
rantes. Nam inter omnes homines illi magis ei invidebant, et hoc quia
multos conuertebat ad fidem et sic perdiderunt honores et oblaciones,

---

123. enim . . . sic] *om.* ST *(longer om.)*; omnia B.
124. *add.* sunt septem alie spice percusse erugine \anglice myldew/ D.
125. yblessed BD.
126. for as D.
127. ys alone] was hymsylf alone B; \pilt alone/ D; ys hymself alone T.
128. pylt alone] alone B; put alone T.

were in Christ more than in anyone else, and he therefore was rightly full of beauty and glory in body and soul. But what are the ones that ate up the earlier ears? Surely the insults Christ suffered this day, which devoured and destroyed all the beauty of his body. For Isaiah prophesied of him that he was more like a leper than a man.[34] That these insults may be for the salvation of our soul, pray to him as follows:

Blessed, O Lord, may be thy name,
For me thou suffere'dst scorn and shame.
As thou art full of grace,
To serve thee give me time and space.

The third sign of languishing love is that he who languishes for love withdraws from company, for there can be no companionship for him except that of his beloved. In this way Christ **was alone**, for no one remained with him, even "his disciples abandoned him and fled."[35] At that time they did not yet fully believe in him, for they did not expect him to rise from the dead, all except the Blessed Virgin, in whom the Church's faith stood alive during those three days. That Jesus was thus **cast out** from men's hearts is proven and shown by seven kinds of people who persecuted him. The first were the Jews who spat at him. As the gospel tells us, Christ had brought them greater honor than any other nation, because he was born of them, and yet they hated him most severely. Day and night they plotted how they might catch him in word or deed. Consider here, for instance, how they cunningly brought a woman taken in adultery to him, and with what mischief, etc.[36] The second group were the high priests in their conspiracy. They among all people hated him most, because he turned many to the faith, whereby they lost their honors and incomes, etc. As a result they took counsel and said, "If we leave him alone, all the people will believe him, and then the Romans will come," etc.[37] But one of them, the high priest Caiaphas, said, "It is better that one man should die," etc.[38] The third group were those false witnesses. For when the Jews saw that they could

---

34. Isa. 53:4.
35. Matt. 26:56.
36. John 8:3–11.
37. John 11:48.
38. John 11:50.

etc. Et ideo simul consilium acceperunt dicentes, "Si dimiserimus eum, omnes homines credent in eum et venient Romani," etc. Vnus vero illorum, Cayphas pontifex, dixit: "Expedit quod vnus homo moriatur,"
500   etc. Tercii fuerunt falsi testes. Videntes en[i]m[129] Iudei quod non potuerunt [eum][130] condemnare ad mortem sine causa, conduxerunt falsos testes vt testimonium perhiberent contra eum. Set ipsi venientes coram iudice, vnus affirmauit, alius negauit. Et ideo dicit euangelium, "Non erat conueniens testimonium eorum." Set absit quod sint aliqui falsi testes, etc. Quartus fuit Iudas traditor, qui eum tradidit pro triginta argen[teis].[131] Et quar\re/ eum sic vendidit? Causa fuit ista, sicut tangit Grisostimus. Christus autem ante passionem suam intrauit domum Symonis, vbi accessit ad eum Magdalena portans in pixide vnguentum istud quod "venundari poterat plus quam trecentis denariis et dari pau-
510   peribus." Set < sicut > habetur ex\e/uangelio, illud non dixit quia voluit quod pauperes habuissent illam pecuniam set quia fur erat et latro et multum cupidus et ea que dabantur Christo et discipulis furabatur. Vnde de d[ecem][132] denariis semper vnum denarium furabatur, et decima pars trecentorum denariorum faciunt triginta denarii, et quia ibi tunc perdiderat triginta denarios, voluit eos recuperare, et ideo vendidit magistrum suum pro triginta denariis. Set tamen postea penituit de mercacione sua, "et proiectis argenteis in templo abiit et laqueo se suspendit." Et sicut dicit Ieronimus in Glosa super illo Psalmo "Deus laudem," plus Iudas displ[i]cuit[133] Christo in desperando et se suspendendo quam eum
520   tradendo et vendendo. Set absit quod modo sint aliqui proditores, etc. Quintus fuit Herodes, qui eum remisit ad Pilatum indutum alba tunica. Stans enim Christus coram Pilato quesiuit de qua patria esset, et cum audisset quod de Galilea esset, scilicet de potestate Herodis, volens sibi placere quia inimici erant, misit eum ligatum ad Herodem. Herodes vero multum gaudebat eum videre, quia multa mirabilia audiebat de eo. Vnde sperabat aliquod mirabile de eo videre. Set cum Christus accusaretur coram eo, nichil respondit. Quod videns Herodes putauit eum fatuum, et ideo in signum fatuitatis induit eum veste alba et remisit \eum/ ad Pilatum. Et propter istam causam facti sunt amici Herodes et Pilatus,

---

129. enm S; autem T.
130. *om.* S.
131. argententeis S.
132. dimus S; decimis D; BT *have a different sentence.*
133. displcuit S.

not condemn him to death without cause, they brought false witnesses together that these might testify against him. But when these came before the judge, one affirmed one thing, and another denied it. Hence the gospel says, "Their testimony was conflicting."[39] Far be it from us that there be false witnesses, etc.! The fourth kind was Judas, his betrayer, who betrayed him for thirty pieces of silver. Why did he sell him thus? As Chrysostom explains it,[40] the cause was as follows. Before his passion, Christ came to the house of Simon, where Magdalene approached him carrying in a vessel ointment that "could have been sold for more than three hundred denarii and given to the poor."[41] But as we find from the gospel, Judas did not say this so that the poor might have that money but because "he was a thief"[42] and very greedy, and he used to steal what was given to Christ and his disciples. Of ten denarii, he always stole one, and the tenth part of three hundred denarii amounts to thirty; so, because he on that occasion lost thirty denarii, he wanted to retrieve them and therefore sold his master for thirty denarii. But afterward he repented of this deal, "and throwing the silver coins down in the temple, he went and hanged himself."[43] Jerome says in his gloss on the Psalm "God, be not silent in my praise" that Judas offended Christ more in his despair and suicide than in his betrayal and selling him.[44] Far be it from us that there be any traitors, etc.! The fifth kind was Herod, who sent him back to Pilate dressed in a white tunic. When Christ stood before Pilate, the latter asked him what country he was from, and when he heard he was from Galilee, that is, from the realm of Herod, he wanted to please Herod (for they were enemies) and sent Jesus to him in fetters. Herod was very pleased to see him, for he had heard many marvellous things about him and thus expected to see a miracle. But as Christ was being accused before him, he said nothing in reply. When Herod perceived this, he thought Jesus was a fool, and as a sign of foolishness, he had him dressed in a white tunic and sent back to Pilate.

---

39. Mark 14:58.

40. A common explanation of the thirty denarii; see Peter Comestor, *Historia scholastica,* In evangelia 168 (*PL* 198:1614); or Ludolf of Saxony 2.52 (1495, 544).

41. Mark 14:5.

42. John 12:6.

43. Matt. 27:5.

44. Ps. 108; in his commentary on this psalm, Jerome mentions Judas, but not in the terms quoted here. But see Peter Comestor, *Historia scholastica,* In evangelia 162 (*PL* 198:1625), with the same reference to Jerome.

530 etc. Sextus fuit Pilatus, falsus iudex. Nam [*f. 36v*] cum sciret eum
     innocentem et quod per inuidiam tradidissent eum seu accusassent, et
     ipsemet dixisset, "Nullam causam mortis inuenio in eo," adhuc tamen
     nolens Iudeis displicere concessit eis peticionem eorum et condempnauit
     innocentem. Set absit quod sint aliqui falsi iudices qui ex odio, fauore,
     et amore falsum iudicium proferant. Vere tales si sint, peiores sunt Pilato,
     etc. Septimi fuerunt milites spoliantes, et apparet quod fuerunt ribaldi,
     quia Christus non habuit nisi pannos simplices et exiles. Et cum illi
     diuiserunt vestimenta sua, sinderunt[134] illa in partes, tunicam vero in-
     consutilem non diuiserunt set sortem miserunt quis haberet, etc. Ista
540 ergo sunt septem genera hominum que hodie persequebantur Christum,
     <quorum timore omnes discipuli eius et illi quos conuertebat ad fidem
     dereliquerunt eum>. Propter quod Christus querelando potest dicere
     cum propheta: "Ego sum vermis et non homo," etc.

>   **Y am a worme and no[135] man,[136]**
>   **Out-castyng of alle[137] men.**

     "Omnes videntes me," etc.
     De istis septem generibus hominum Christum persequencium habemus
     figuram. Nam legimus in Exodo quod quando populus exiuit de Egipto vt
     irent ad terram promissionis, inuenerunt gentes septem contra eos pug-
550 nantes, scilicet Eueum et Amoreum, etc. Contra eos pugnauerunt filii Is-
     rael antequam potuerunt vincere. Tandem tamen per auxilium [Dei][138]
     habuerunt de eis victoriam. Per filios Israel intelligo Christum, qui fuit de
     filiis Israel quando de eis natus fuit. Israel eciam interpretatur videns
     Deum, et semper Christus clare videt Deum. Set iste exiuit de Egipto ad
     terram promisionis, de terra scilicet huius mundi ad terram vite. De quo
     loquitur Psalmista: "Credo videre bona Domini in terra," etc.

>   **In þe[139] londe of liue Y hop[140] to se**
>   **Ioy[141] and blisse þat euer schal be.**

---

134. *add.*\diuiserunt/ S; sciderunt BT.
135. noght a D.
136. *add.* schame and D.
137. al B; *om.* D.
138. *om.* SDT.
139. *om.* D.
140. trow D.
141. þe ioye D.

And for that reason Herod and Pilate became friends, etc. The sixth kind was Pilate, the false judge. Though he knew Jesus to be innocent, and that they were handing him over and accusing him out of envy, and though he himself stated, "I find no cause of death in him," he still did not want to displease the Jews, but granted their petition and condemned Jesus in his innocence. Far be it from us that there be any false judges who out of hatred, favor, or love give a wrong judgment! If there are any such, they are worse than Pilate, etc. The seventh group are the soldiers who despoiled Jesus. They appear to have been riffraff, for Christ had only simple and scanty clothing. When they divided his clothes, they cut them in parts, but his seamless robe they did not divide among them but cast lots over, to see who should have it, etc. These, then, are the seven kinds of people who on this day persecuted Christ. Out of fear of them, all of Christ's disciples and those he had brought to the faith abandoned him. For that reason Christ could complain and say with the prophet: "I am a worm and not a man," etc.[45]

I am a worm and not a man,
From all mankind placed under ban

"All who see me," etc.[46]

For these seven kinds of people who persecuted Christ we have a biblical figura in Exodus, where we read that, when the people left Egypt to go to the Promised Land, they encountered seven nations fighting against them: the Hivites and Amorites, and so forth.[47] The children of Israel fought against them before they could overcome them, but at last, through God's help, they gained the victory. By the children of Israel I understand Christ, who was one of them because he was born of them; also, Israel means "seeing God," and Christ always had a clear sight of God. And he went out of Egypt to the Promised Land, that is, from the land of this world to the land of life. Of him the Psalmist says, "I believe I shall see the goodness of the Lord in the land," etc.[48]

In the land of life I hope to see
Joy and bliss that ever shall be.

---

45. Ps. 21:7.
46. Ps. 21:8.
47. Exod. 3:8, etc.
48. Ps. 26:13.

Set antequam istam benedictam terram potuit lucrari, inuenit septem
560 gentes que eum persequebantur. Istis tamen tandem victis per magnas
tribulaciones et angustias lucratus est celum, quod dicitur terra vite. Si
ergo voluerimus ad eum venire, oportet nos tribulaciones sustinere sicut
omnes electi eius fecerunt. Et quia istas angustias sustinuit pro nobis,
rogabis eum vt [det][142] tibi voluntatem et graciam vt alia valias pro eius
amore sustinere, et dices sic:

Lorde þat suffredist[143] **peynes stronge**
Of[144] **thyn <enemys>**[145] **al with wronge,**
Iesu þat didist[146] **one þe tre,**
Let me suffre sum p\e/yne[147] **for þe.**

570 <Et istud est tercium signum, quod ille qui languet ex amore trahit se
alone[148] **from compone.**
Quartum signum est> **that he euer**[149] **herkenet aftir hys druri.** Et
illud signum ostendit Christus hodie. Nam intime cogitauit de genere
humano quod fuit suum **drury**[150] quod dilexit plus quam totum mundum.
Et illud probant et ostendunt manifeste septem mirabilia que Christus
ostendit hodie ad <attrahendum>[151] durum cor hominis ad eum diligendum et de eo cogitandum. Primum mirabile fuit terre motus, quia
sicut dicit euangelium, in morte eius terra tremuit. Et aduerte quia fuit
illud valde mirabile, nam inter omnia elementa que Deus fecit, terra in
580 se est magis **sad** et stabilis,[152] et[153] quia est fundamentum omnium et
omnia supportat; set in morte Saluatoris facta est [*f. 37*] instabilis et
cepit tremere et deficere in cordibus omnium hominum, sicut dicunt
doctores, in tantum quod illi qui fuerunt principales cum eo et magis

---

142. *om.* S.
143. sufferd D.
144. Of . . . wronge] for me y-wys al with wrong T.
145. thyn enemys] þe iewes B.
146. dyed D.
147. sum peyne] sumwhat B.
148. all D.
149. that he euer] *add.* \he/ S; istud euer B; ille semper D; Christus autem semper T.
150. *om.* T.
151. *marg.* S *with* al', *to replace* mouendum; trahendum B; attrahendum DT.
152. et stabilis] and stabill T.
153. *evidently a clause has disappeared at this point without leaving a trace in the four surviving texts, to the effect that "terra interpretatur fides."*

But before he could reach that blessed land, he encountered seven nations that persecuted him. When he had overcome these through great tribulations and sufferings, he gained heaven, which is called the land of life. Therefore, if we want to come to him, we must endure tribulations as all his elect have done. And because he endured those sufferings for us, you must ask him for the will and grace to be able to suffer others for his love; and so say to him:

Lord who suffer'dst pains so strong
From thine enemies with wrong,
Jesus who diedst on the tree,
Let me share thy pains with thee.

And this is the third sign, that he who languishes for love withdraws **in solitude from company.**

The fourth sign is **that he always listened for his paramour.** Christ showed this sign on this day, for he thought inwardly of humankind, who was his **paramour,** whom he loved more than the whole world. This is proven and shown openly by seven miracles that Christ showed today to draw man's hard heart to love him and to think of him. The first was the earthquake, for as the gospel says, at his death the earth quaked.[49] Notice that this was very wonderful, for of all the elements that God created, the earth is by nature the **heaviest** and most stable, [and it signifies the faith] because it is the foundation of all things and

---

49. Matt. 27:51.

eum dilexerunt, de eius resureccione dubitauerunt. Et hoc patet quia
reuersi sunt ad piscacionem suam. Ex quo ergo, karissimi, terra sic
tremuit, ostendendo signum doloris in morte Saluatoris, multo magis
debet homo ostendere dolorem hodie pro eius morte, etc. Secundum
mirabile fuit quod sol perdidit lumen suum. Nam sicut dicunt doctores,
sol illa die ita clare lucebat sicut vnquam fecit, set in morte Christi
590   perdidit lumen suum totaliter, in tantum quod nullus potuit videre alium.
Et illud non tantum in illo loco set per totum mundum facte sunt tenebre,
sicut dicit euangelium. Origenes [tamen dicit][154] quod tenebre iste facte
sunt per vniuersam Iudeam et non alibi. Set magis credo euangelio, in
quo innuitur per vniuersum orbem facte sunt. Quod autem ista tene-
brositas facta fuit per vniuersum orbem potest probari per < Dyonisium >[155] in epistula sua *Ad Policarpum,* et eciam per illud quod Magister
Hystor[iarum][156] [ponit][157] de eodem Dionisio Ariapagia apud Athenas,
etc. Nota in hystoria Actuum Apostolorum. Ex quo ergo, karissimi, sol
amisit lumen suum contra naturam et quasi condolebat creatori suo,
600   multo magis debemus nos, pro quibus est mortuus et non pro sole, etc.
Istud ergo fuit secundum mirabile, quod sol **lest is lyth**.[158] Tercium mirabile fuit quod infernus **lesed is myth,**[159] quia ex eo mortuo in cruce
anima cum diuinitate descendebat ad lymbum et infernum spoliauit, illos
secum educendo qui expectabant redempcionem suam. Videtur michi
quod \infernus/ **mad**[160] < **knowlachyng** >[161] hodie quod Christus fuit
verus Deus, quia isto die **he ȝelde hym creande**[162] et dedit sibi homagium
in signum quod fuit dominus celi, terre, et inferni, etc. Quartum mirabile
fuit quod velum templi cissum est. Debetis intelligere quod in templo
Salamonis erat quoddam velum preciosum valde interius ante sancta
610   sanctorum, scilicet ante altare infra magnum; quod velum nulli intrare
licebat nisi sacerdoti, scilicet summo pontifici legis, et hoc vt offerret
ibi sacrificium Deo pro peccatis populi. Illud autem velum tempore

---

154. tamen dicit] vnde S; vnde dicere B; tamen dicit *corr. from* vnde dicitur D; bene
dicit cum dicit T.
155. diabolum *in text*, Dyonisium *marg.* S.
156. hystore S.
157. *om.* SD; dicit T.
158. sol . . . lyth] sol scilicet amisit claritatem suam D; that the sonn lest his liȝt T.
159. lesed is myth] amisit potestatem \myght/ suam D.
160. man B; *longer om.* DT.
161. *marg., apparently to replace* chauwlangyng S.
162. he . . . creande] *longer om.* DT.

supports them all. But at the Savior's death, faith became destabilized and began to tremble and to lose its strength in the hearts of all men, as the teachers say, to the point that those who were his chief friends and loved him most became doubtful of his resurrection. This is shown by the fact that they returned to their occupation as fishermen. Because the earth quaked in this way and showed its grief for the dying Savior, dearly beloved, man should even more show his grief for Christ's death today, etc. The second miracle was that the sun lost its light. As the teachers say, on that day the sun shone as brightly as it ever did, but when Christ died it lost its brightness completely, so that no one could see anyone else. This not only happened in that place but "darkness fell over the whole world," as the gospel says.[50] But Origen declares that that darkness fell over all Judea and nowhere else. But I prefer to believe the gospel, which indicates that darkness fell over the whole earth. That this darkness indeed occurred in the whole world can be proven by Dionysius in his *Letter to Polycarp* and by what the Master of Histories quotes from the same Dionysius the Areopagite of Athens. You can find this in the section on the Acts of the Apostles.[51] Since therefore, dearly beloved, the sun lost its brightness against the course of nature and, so to speak, mourned for its maker, we should all the more do the same, as he died for us and not for the sun, etc. This then was the second miracle, that the sun **lost its light**. The third miracle was that hell **lost its might,** because after Christ died on the cross, his soul in its divinity descended to hell and despoiled it, drawing with it those who were waiting for their redemption. It seems to me that on this day hell **acknowledged** that Christ was true God, for today **it surrendered** and paid him homage, as a sign that he was the lord of heaven, earth, and hell, etc. The fourth miracle was that the veil of the temple tore. You should understand that in Solomon's temple there was a precious veil before the Holiest of Holies, that is, in front of the high altar. No one was allowed to pass this veil except the priest, that is, the high priest of the Law, and that for the purpose of bringing God a sacrifice in that place for the sins of the

50. Matt. 27:45.
51. Peter Comestor, *Historia scholastica,* In evangelia 175 (*PL* 198:1631), with references to Dionysius and Origen.

mort[is][163] Christi ruptum est totaliter, in signum sicut dicunt doctores
quod tunc lex antiqua cessauit, quod significabatur per illud velum, et
lex Christi tunc incepit. Aliqui tamen dicunt [quod][164] erant duo vela in
templo, vnum interius et aliud exterius, et quod vtrumque velum scissum
est, etc. Quintum mirabile fuit quod petre cisse sunt, quia sicut [dicit][165]
euangelium, tempore mortis Christi petre **to-borstoun** et saxa **to-clouen**.
Et adhuc \dicunt/ peregrini qui ibi fuerrunt quod adhuc apparent cissure
620   saxorum qui illo tempore erant **to-cleuen**.[166] "Heu ergo," dicit [Bernar-
dus],[167] "quod durissime petre **to-borstoun**[168] in signum doloris Christi,
et cor peccatorum factum de carne non potest cindi ad penitenciam et
ad dolendum pro morte sui Saluatoris!" Sextum mirabile fuit quod
sepulcra mortuorum per seipsos apperiebantur et mortua corpora reui-
xerunt et surrexerunt. <Septimum mirabile fuit quod illi qui surrexe-
runt>[169] a mortuis venerunt in ciuitatem Ierusalem et apparuerunt multis
sicut homines viuentes, scilicet post resurreccionem Christi testificati sunt
de Christo quod Dei Filius erat et a mortuis resurexisset, sicut habetur
in *Euangelio Nazariorum*. Multi eorum narrauerunt quomodo Christus
630   decendit [*f. 37v*] ad limbum, et illi qui erant ibi vehementer gaudebant
in aduentu eius, et demones horribiliter vlulabant et lamantabantur, et
alia multa mirabilia narrabant. Ex quo ergo Christus ostendit tot mirabilia hodie vt alliceret corda nostra ad eum diligendum, [tenemur][170] sibi
regraciari et dicere cum Psalmista: "Cantate Domino canticum nouum."

Syng we[171] **a new song**
For hym þat[172] **dyed for vs wyþe wrong,**
For þis <**day**> **wondris**[173] **he wroth,**

---

163. morte S.
164. *om.* S.
165. *om.* S.
166. scisse \aut clouyn/ D.
167. *om.* S *but* Bernardus *marg.*
168. *om.* T.
169. Septimum . . . surrexerunt] *marked to be inserted (wrongly) after the following* multis S.
170. *om.* S.
171. ȝe B; to owre lorde D.
172. hym þat] þat he D.
173. wonder B.

people. That veil was completely rent at the time of Christ's death, as a sign, as our teachers say, that at that moment, the Old Law, which is indicated by that veil, ceased, and the Law of Christ began. But some say that there were two veils in the temple, one inside, the other outside, and that both were rent, etc. The fifth miracle was that the rocks burst open, for as the gospel says, at the time of Christ's death the rocks **burst open** and boulders **were split**.[52] Modern pilgrims who have been there say that the traces of rocks that were **split** at that time can still be seen. "Alas," says Bernard, "that the hardest rocks **burst open** in sign of Christ's suffering, while the heart of a sinner, made of flesh, cannot be rent in penance and grief at its Savior's death!"[53] The sixth miracle was that the tombs of the dead opened by themselves and the bodies of the dead came back to life and rose up. The seventh miracle was that those who rose up from the dead came into the city of Jerusalem and appeared to many like living beings, that is to say, after Christ's resurrection, they bore witness that Christ was the Son of God and rose from the dead, as we find in the *Gospel of the Nazarites*.[54] Many of them told how Christ descended to hell, and those who were there rejoiced greatly in his coming, while the devils howled and lamented horribly; and they reported many other marvellous things. Because, therefore, Christ showed so many miracles on this day that he might draw our hearts to his love, we are held to thank him and to say with the Psalmist, "Sing to the Lord a new song."[55]

Sing we therefore a new song
For him who dies for us with wrong.
For this, wonders he has wrought,

---

52. Matt. 27:51.
53. A commonplace; cf. Ludolf of Saxony 2.64 (1495, 640b).
54. Again quoted by Peter Comestor, *Historia scholastica,* In evangelia 178 (*PL* 198:1633).
55. Ps. 95.1, etc.

On þe rod[174] **þare**[175] **he vs bouth <with his blode>.**[176]

640   De istis septem mirabilibus habemus signum in scriptura. Legimus in
Apocalipsi qualiter Deus ostendit beato Iohanni multa mirabilia, et inter
alia ostendit ei septem angelos stantes cum septem tubis, et buccinauerunt
cum tubis suis vnus post alium, et ad quodlibet **trompe blowyng** accidit
vnum mirabile magnum, que pertranseo propter breuitatem diei. Per
angelos ad presens intelligo Christum regem angelorum. Iste fuit "angelus magni consilii," de quo Ysaias. Angelus interpretatur missus, et
ideo Christus potest dici angelus quia missus fuit a Patre in mundum
vt nos redimeret. Iste autem septem tube que **blowen**[177] sunt ista septem
mirabilia que Christus ostendit hodie in cruce, \et/ ad ostendendum
650   quod fuit verus Deus, \et/ ad alliciendum cor nostrum ad eum diligendum et in eum credendum. Vt ergo ille qui ostendit homini \tanta/
mirabilia ostendat aliquod mirabile in anima tua conuertendo te a peccatis \et/ ad mundam vitam, facias sibi hanc oracionem et dices:

Lord[178] **þat schewdest**[179] **<wundres> gret,**
<Qwan þou scholdes þi liff lete,>[180]
Schilde þou me,[181] **\Lord,/**[182] **fro schame and synne**
And bryng me[183] **to þi blis**[184] **that þou arte ynne.**[185]

Quintum signum languentis amoris[186] est quod qui languet ex amore
pulcre \et/ suauiter loquitur suo dilecto. Et istud signum ostendit Chris-
660   tus hodie, quod probant in cruce eius septem verba. Primum verbum
fuit quod orauit pro suis crucifixoribus dicendo, "Pater, dimitte eis, quia

---

174. On þe rod] *om.* T.

175. þat D.

176. with his blode] *om.* BDT.

177. que blowen] blowyng T.

178. Lord . . . gret] a lord þat schedde þi blode so rede D.

179. showest T.

180. qwan . . . lete] *to replace* thi lyue þou scholdist to lete *marked vacat* S; whan \þy/
lyf \þou/ schuldyst lete B; and losyd þi lyff for owre mysdede D; *om.* T.

181. þou me] vs *corr. from* me *exp.* D; me T.

182. *om.* BDT.

183. vus D.

184. þi blis] þat \ioye/ B; blys DT.

185. that . . . ynne] þer þou dwellys in D; *om.* T.

186. *add.* <anglice: louely he spekus to his erte> S.

On the cross where we were bought.

There is a figura for these seven miracles in Scripture. In Revelation we read that God showed St. John many marvels, and among them, he showed him seven angels with seven trumpets, which they blew one after another, and at each **trumpet blow** a great marvel occurred,[56] which I will bypass because of the shortness of time. For the moment, by these angels I understand Christ, the king of angels. He was "an angel of great counsel," of whom Isaiah speaks.[57] The word *angel* means "sent"; therefore Christ can be called an angel because he was sent by the Father into the world to redeem us. The seven trumpets that **blew** are the seven miracles Christ wrought today on the cross, both to show that he was true God and to draw our heart to love him and to believe in him. That he who has wrought so many miracles for mankind may work a miracle in your soul by converting you from sins and to a pure life, make this prayer to him and say:

Lord who show'dst such wonders great
When thou this life didst vacate,
Shield me, Lord, from shame and sin
And bring me to the bliss that thou art in.

The fifth sign of languishing love is that he who languishes with love speaks to his beloved with beauty and sweetness. Christ showed this sign this day, as is proven by his seven words on the cross. The first was that he prayed for those who crucified him, saying, "Father, forgive them, for they do not know what they are doing," etc.[58] Because of this prayer, as Jerome says, three thousand onlookers were converted to believe in Christ,[59] and the gospel indicates this where it says, "Returning," that is, to the faith, "they struck their breasts,"[60] as a sign that they were sorry for their deed and now believed that he was the savior of the world. And it was right that God should hear the prayer of his son,

---

56. Rev. 8:6–11:19.
57. Perhaps Isa. 11:2?
58. Luke 23:34.
59. Cf. Ludolf of Saxony 2.63 (1495, 629a); the connection was already made by Bede in his commentary on Luke 23 (*CC* 120:403), but without the number 3000.
60. Luke 23:47.

nessiunt quid faciunt," etc. Propter quam oracionem, sicut dicit Ieronimus, tria milia de circumstantibus conuersi fuerunt ad fidem Christi, et
illud innuit euangelium cum dicit: "Reuertentes," ad fidem, "percucie-
bant pectora" sua in signum quod penituerunt de facto suo et reputa-
uerunt eum saluatorem mundi. Et iustum erat quod Deus exaudiret
oracionem filii sui, ex quo exaudiuit oraciones peccatorum. Orauit eciam
pro persequentibus, vt nobis daret exemplum diligendi inimicos et pro
eis orandi, etc. Secundum verbum fuit magne confortacionis peccato-
670 ribus, quia dedit latroni paradisum. Nam sicut habetur ex euangelio,
< Christus pendebat inter duos latrones, et > ipse \qui/ pendebat ad
dextram suam dixit ei, "Memento mei, Domine," etc. Statim Christus
respondit ei, "Hodie mecum eris in paradiso." Ecce pro modico lucratus
est paradisum. Et ideo non est desperandum quantumcumque mali fue-
rimus si conuerti < voluerimus, etc. Tercium verbum fuit verbum doloris,
scilicet quando dixit > matri sue, "Mulier, ecce filius tuus." Non dixit
"Mater, ecce," etc., set "Mulier," quia secundum Ancelmum et Bernardum si tunc eam "matrem" vocasset, pre dolore continuo conspirasset
\nisi/ miraculose preseruata fuisset. Quartum verbum fuit verbum que-
680 rimonie quando dixit Patri, "Deus meus, vt quid dereliquisti me." Non
conquerebatur Patri quod eum totaliter dereliquerat, set quod quasi videbatur astantibus quasi derelictus a Patre [*f. 38*] in hoc quod permisit
eum tot penas et obprobria sustinere. Vel aliter secundum Origenem:
Christus conquerebatur Patri quia preuidebat ingratitudinem multorum
qui \non/ curarent de sua passione nec per eam forent saluati, quia
passio sua benedicta sufficit [pro][187] toto mundo, immo pro mille mundis.
Conquerebatur de tam horribili passione pro qua tamen ita pauci erant
saluandi. Quintum verbum erat verbum **rewful and blisful,**[188] quando
dicebat, "Scicio." Fuit verbum dolorosum quia totaliter fuit < desicca-
690 tus > ita quod nec sanguis nec aliquod aliud in corpore remanserat propter
tormenta que sustinuerat. Et ideo sciciebat. Set illi maledicti optu\le/-
runt ei **eysel [and] gall**[189] vt biberet. Set cum modicum gustasset, noluit
bibere. Dolorosum ergo fuit quod regi innocenti dabatur talis potus. Set
quantum ad nos fuit verbum gaudiosum, quia secundum Bernardum non
dixit tantum "cicio" pro citi corporali set magis pro citi spirituali. Quid

---

187. *om.* S.
188. and blisful] *om.* BT.
189. eysel and gall] eysel gall S; actum et fel D.

because he heard the prayer of sinners. Christ also prayed for his per-secutors to give us an example to love our enemies and to pray for them, etc. His second word on the cross was one of great comfort to sinners, for it gave a thief paradise. As we find in the gospel, Christ was hanging between two thieves, and the one on his right said to him, "Lord, remember me," etc. Christ at once replied, "Today you shall be in paradise with me."[61] Behold for how little he gained paradise. Therefore we must not despair, however evil we have been, if we will return, etc. The third word was one of pain, namely, when Christ said to his mother, "Woman, behold your son." He did not say "Mother, behold," but "Woman," for according to Anselm and Bernard, if at that point he had called her "mother," she would have at once died for grief unless she had been miraculously strengthened.[62] The fourth word was one of complaint, when he said to the Father, "My God, why have you forsaken me." He was not complaining to the Father that he had completely abandoned him, but that he appeared to those around him to be, as it were, abandoned by his Father, because he allowed him to suffer so many pains and insults. Origen has a different explanation: Christ complained to his Father because he foresaw the ingratitude of many people who would pay no attention to his passion nor be saved by it, because his blessed passion is sufficient for the whole world, indeed for a thousand worlds.[63] Christ complained that only so few were to be saved by his horrible passion. The fifth word, when he said, "I thirst," was both **sorrowful and blissful**.[64] It was a word of grief since he was so completely dried out that because of the torments he had suffered, neither blood nor anything else remained in his body; hence he was thirsty. His cursed tormentors offered him **vinegar and gall** to drink. But when he had tasted a little, he would not drink it. Thus it was grievous that this innocent king was given such a potion. But with respect to ourselves, this was a joyful word, for according to Bernard, Jesus said, "I thirst," not just because of his bodily thirst but even more so because of his spiritual thirst. Why do you thirst, Lord? And he replies: "I thirst for the salvation of souls."[65] O Lord, would that this thirst lasted until you had drunk

---

61. Luke 23:42–43.
62. A medieval commonplace attributed to various fathers.
63. Cf. Ludolf of Saxony 2.63 (1495, 633b).
64. John 19:27.
65. Cf. Bernard *Meditatio in passionem et resurrectionem Domini* 3.6 (*PL* 188:744); taken into Ludolf of Saxony 2.63 (1495, 635a).

ergo citis, Domine? Et respondet: "Scicio salutem animarum." Vtinam
ergo, Domine, ista citis tıŏi duret quousque omnia peccata biberes, etc.
Sextum verbum fuit illud: "Consummatum est"; scilicet, ostendit que
dicta fuerant de aduentu meo in mundum et de passione mea pro genere
700   humano per prophetas iam consum\mata/ sunt. Et ideo non restat nisi
vt spiritum tradam, etc. Et sic inclinato capite emisit spiritum, eadem
scilicet die et hora qua Adam fuit expulsus de paradiso.

De istis septem verbis possumus habere figuram in scriptura. Legimus
enim Genesis 1 capitulo in pr\i/ncipio, quando Deus fecit mundum,
fecit illum in sex diebus, et septimo die requieuit. Et in operando n[on][190]
dixit nisi sex verba curta, et statim facta sunt omnia. Ita[que][191] pro toto
mundo fuit isto die quando Christus debuit emere genus humanum pen-
dendo super crucem. Ibi enim loquebatur sex verba of[192] **merci and of
pite,** et septimum verbum fuit of[193] **loue and**[194] **charite,** quia non solum
710   **he betauȝte**[195] spiritum in manus Patris set animas omnium nostrum pro
quibus moriebatur. Et statim cum illud verbum dixisset, emisit spiritum
et requiescebat, scilicet corpus in sepulcro vsque ad diem Pasche, quando
surrexit a mortuis. Vt ergo ista verba dulcia que ibi loquebatur habere
valeant aliquem effectum in animabus nostris, facias sibi hanc oracionem:

Lorde Iesu[196] **that**[197] **arte so swete,**
Wiþ alle my herte Y the grete.
Swete hert, my loue-longyng,
Gyffe me[198] **grace and**[199] **thi blissyng.**

Sextum signum[200] est quod ille qui languet ex amore libenter sustinet
720   duras penas pro dilecto suo. Et illud signum ostendit hodie Christus,
quod probant manifeste septem vulnera que hodie sustinuit in septem

---

190. nam S.
191. ita quod DST; ita B.
192. of . . . pite] misericordie et pietatis D.
193. of . . . charite] amoris et caritatis D.
194. *add.* of T.
195. be-toke BT.
196. *add.* Cryst BT.
197. þou BDT.
198. *add.* þi D.
199. of B.
200. *add.* <anglice: for hym he suffres peynus smerte> S.

every sin, etc. The sixth word was "It is fulfilled,"[66] that is, he showed "that all was fulfilled that had been said by the prophets about my coming into the world and my suffering for mankind. And thus nothing remained except that I render my spirit," etc. Then, "bending his head, he gave up his spirit,"[67] on the same day and in the same hour that Adam was expelled from paradise.

We have a figura for these seven words in scripture, in the beginning of Genesis, chapter 1, where we read that when God created the world, he did so in six days, and on the seventh he rested. And in doing this work, he said only six short words, and at once all things came into being.[68] What happened with respect to the whole world also happened today when Christ was to redeem mankind by hanging on the cross. For there he spoke six words **of mercy and pity,** and the seventh word was **of love and charity,** for **he commended** not only his own spirit into the Father's hands but also the souls of all of us for whom he died. And as soon as he had spoken this word, he gave up his spirit and rested, that is to say, his body rested in the tomb until Easter Day, when he rose from the dead. That these sweet words that he spoke there may have some effect in our souls, say this prayer:

Jesus, Lord, who art so sweet,
Thee with all my heart I greet.
Sweetheart, my love-longing,
Give me thy grace and thy blessing.

The sixth sign is that he who languishes with love willingly endures hard sufferings for his lover. Christ showed this sign today, which is openly proven by the seven wounds he sustained in seven places of his

---

66. John 19:30.
67. John 19:30.
68. Gen. 1.

partibus sui corporis benedicti. Nam in capite fuit vulneratus per coronam spineam, in latere per lanceam, in duabus manibus per clau[o]s,[201]
in duobus pedibus per clauum vnum, \et/ in toto corpore per flagella.
Ista sunt septem vulnera que in septem partibus corporis sustinuit. De
quibus vulneribus sanguinem effudit pro salute animarum nostrarum.
De istis septem possumus habere figuram, quia legimus in antiqua
[lege][202] quod si homo apparet leprosus, si deberet mundari, deberet
venire ante sacerdotem et portare secum [*f. 38v*] duos passeres viuos.
730 Vnus permittebatur volare in agrum et alter interficiebatur, et sacerdos
accipiet in vase [sanguinem][203] ipsius ad hoc preparato, et de vna parte
illius sanguinis fecit sacrificium Deo et de alia parte aspersit leprosum
sepcies, et sic mundabatur. Isto modo erat ex parte ista. Nam totum genus
humanum ex peccato primi parentis infectum lepra fuit peccati. Lepra
enim est morbus infectiuus. Sic peccatum Ade transiuit de eo ad omnes
de semine suo. Leprosi enim eiciuntur a communi habitacione hominum;
non enim permittuntur habitare inter homines in ciuitatibus vel villis set
extra. Sic nec homo dignus fuit habitare in ciuitate superna nec in societate angelorum propter peccatum suum. Quod videns amicus noster, Dei
740 Filius, condoluit miserie nostre, et vt nos mundaret optulit semetipsum in
cruce pro nobis, et de illo benedicto sanguine qui decurrebat de septem
partibus corporis sui nos aspersit, et eciam sacrificium Deo optulit. Et sic
nos a lepra peccati mundauit et ad ciuitatem supernam reuocauit, etc. Vt
ergo ista benedicta vulnera que pro nobis pertulit nos mund[e]nt[204] ab
omni inquinamento peccati et mundas custodiat animas nostras et tandem ad regna celorum perducat, facies sibi istam oracionem:

Lorde[205] þat schaddest[206] thi swete[207] blode
For me sinful on[208] þe rode,
For thy blisful[209] woundes seuene

---

201. claues ST.
202. *om.* ST.
203. *om.* S.
204. mundant S.
205. *om.* T.
206. schedde D.
207. thi swete] þyn owen B; þi T.
208. For . . . on] for synful men vpon B; for synfull man on T.
209. blessed T.

blessed body. For he was wounded in his head by the crown of thorns, in his side by the spear, in his two hands by the nails, in his two feet by another nail, and in his whole body by the scourges. These are the seven wounds he sustained in seven places of his body. From these wounds, he shed his blood for the salvation of our souls. Of these seven we may find a *figura* in the Old Testament, where we read that when a person appeared to be infected with leprosy and was to be purified, he was to come before the priest and bring two live birds with him. One bird was allowed to fly off into the field, and the other was killed. Then the priest put its blood in a vessel prepared for this purpose; one part of this blood he offered to God, and the other he sprinkled seven times over the leper, and so he was healed.[69] The same happened in Christ's passion. For by the sin of our first father, all mankind was infected with the leprosy of sin—leprosy is an infectious disease, and thus Adam's sin passed from him to all born of his seed. Now, lepers are cast out from the common society of men; they are not allowed to live together with other people in cities or villages but must reside outside. In the same way, man was not worthy to dwell in the city of heaven or together with the angels, on account of his sin. When our friend, the Son of God, saw this, he had pity for our wretchedness, and to cleanse us, he offered himself on the cross for us. He sprinkled us with the blessed blood that flowed down from the seven places in his body and likewise made of it a sacrifice to God. Thus he cleansed us from the leprosy of sin and called us back to the city of heaven, etc. That these blessed wounds he sustained for us may cleanse us from all stain of sin and keep our souls pure, and that in the end he may bring us to heaven, say this prayer to him:

Lord who sheddest thy sweet blood
For this sinner on the rood,
For these blessed wounds all seven

---

69. Lev. 14:1–7.

750   **Granth to²¹⁰ me thi²¹¹ blis of heuene. Amen.²¹²**

Septimum signum languentis amoris est quod iste qui languet ex amore
libenter dona magna dat dilecto suo. Et illud signum ostendit Christus
hodie, quod probant septem dona que Christus hodie contulit humano
generi, videlicet septem sacramenta noue legis, que sunt baptissmum,
confirmacio, etc. Nam sicut dicunt doctores, ista sacramenta habuerunt
effectum de passione sua benedicta et de illo benedicto sanguine quem
effudit de latere suo. Ibi enim fluxit aqua per [quam]²¹³ abluimur et
sanguis per quem redempti sumus.

De istis septem donis siue sacramentis hodie collatis possumus habere
760   figuram de septem donis Spiritus Sancti, de quibus loquitur Ysaias propheta. Set pertranseo propter breuitatem temporis et facio finem. Vt
ergo ista sacramenta pro salute animarum nostrarum ordinata munde
nos custodiant in hac vita et tandem venire valeamus ad illud gaudium
ad quod hodierna die sumus redempti per Christi sanguinem benedictum,
facimus sibi hanc oracionem:

> **Lorde þat lete oute²¹⁴ blode²¹⁵ of þi side,**
> **Watur and blode þat sprede²¹⁶ wide,**
> **Iesu that were²¹⁷ to man so kynde,**
> **Grant vs þi²¹⁸ blisse wythoute ende.**

770   Ad quam nos perducat qui sine fine viuit et regnat. Amen.

---

210. *om.* BD; thou T.
211. þe BDT.
212. *om.* BD.
213. aquam S.
214. lete oute] scheddest BT.
215. þe blode B; *om.* D.
216. þat sprede] þat sprad ful B; þat spred so D; hit spredde ful T.
217. was DT.
218. euer D.

Bring me to thy bliss in heaven. Amen

The seventh sign of languishing love is that he who languishes with love gives gladly great gifts to his lover. Christ showed this sign this day, as is proven by the seven gifts he conferred today on mankind, that is, the seven sacraments of the New Law, namely, baptism, confirmation, and the rest. As our teachers say, these sacraments received their efficacy from his blessed passion and the blessed blood that he shed from his side. From there flowed water, by which we are washed, and blood, by which we are redeemed.

We have a figura of these seven gifts or sacraments that were given today in the seven gifts of the Holy Spirit that Isaiah speaks of.[70] But I pass on because time is short, and thus I come to the end. That these sacraments, which have been ordained for the salvation of our souls, may keep us pure in this life and at last let us come to that joy for which we have been redeemed on this day through Christ's blessed blood, let us say this prayer:

Lord, who let blood out of your side,
Water and blood that spread so wide,
Jesus, who were to us so kind,
Grant us thy bliss that has no end.

May he let us come to that bliss, he who lives and reigns without end. Amen.

---

70. Isa. 11:2–3.

Sermon O-07, *De celo querebant*

Oxford, Bodleian Library, MS Bodley 649, ff. 40v–48 (O-07).

This and the following sermon have been preserved in unique copies. I present their texts with emendations that are required to make sense; these are enclosed in square brackets, and the rejected manuscript readings appear in the notes. Slashes and angle brackets are used as in the edition of *Amore langueo*.

O-07 has the following structure.

Protheme:
> The vineyard of the Lord is England; it was once flourishing but now, due to neglect by its rulers, has suffered severe damage, especially from the Lollards. A combination of justice and mercy is required (1–115).

Prayer (116–32).

Division:
> A triple division of the thema, as to who sought, what they sought, and from what heaven they sought, with *combinatio partium* (133–54).

Part 1:
> The disciples sad in darkness sought the light of life-giving and holy teaching, from the heaven that is painted with stars and planets brightly shining (155–391).
>
> Subdivision: In the heaven of the Church are
>> (a) the sun of parish priests (167–253),
>> (b) the moon of the merchants (254–321),
>> (c) the planet Mercury of victuallers (322–391).

Part 2:

Wretches wrapped in sickness sought the influence of healing medicine, from the heaven that is clear as the crystal rising out of the
rock (392–502).

Subdivision: The two remedies established by God to cleanse the
heaven of the soul are

(a) the water of contrition (433–69),

(b) the brightness of confession (470–502).

Part 3:

Prisoners afflicted with sadness sought a token of deliverance and
mercy, from the highest heaven where there is gracious comfort and
blissful dwelling (503–602).

Connexio partium, on the basis of Deut. 1:10–11, and closing formula
(603–16).

De celo querebant, Luce XI et in euangelio hodierno.

Gracia **and comfort** benedicte Trinitatis intercessione Beate Domine Christi matris et omnium sanctorum in summo palacio celi sit nobiscum nunc et semper. Amen.

Venerandi domini, verba que sumpsi pro themate scribuntur in euangelio istius diei et tantum sonant in lingua materna: [*f. 41*] **þai soȝt fro heuonn.**

Domini, specialis vinea patris celestis quam Christus suus filius nutriuit et diu custodiuit est et per virtutem Spiritus Sancti [*blank*] fidem
10 **and goode beleue** est nostrum fertile regnum. Deus de sua misericordia istud seruet, quia recte vt in materiali vinea, si vites sint fertiles **and likinge,** rami invtiles absciduntur in tempore, alii fertiles **ar prouynyd and nurchid furd,** \et/ pro fractura **þai ar raisid vp** et vnita[1] **to stif stacus,** sic in nostra spirituali vinea, regno scilicet, si vites, idest magni domini spirituales et temporales, erunt fertiles et referent fructus honoris Deo et proficui regno, oportet vt abscidas omnes ram[o]s[2] **vnthrifti,** ramos superbie et gule, extorcionis et auaricie, et omnes ramos mortalis peccati. **þes nedith most be cutte away** si vites debeant vigere, quia vbicumque aliquod istorum crescit, humor gracie qui esset **chef fode** vitis
20 totaliter destruitur. Virtu[tem][3] que esset **in þe cop and springe huut** in flores et fructus attrahunt in terram; cordialem amorem quem homo haberet in Deo suo, contemplacionem, altam deuocionem quam haberet in anima versus ipsum, mortalia peccata **dun fro him and beset hit on fleschly lustis, on vanitis and falsnes** istius mundi, sic quod sit vitis **neuer so plentiuus, be þou neuer so virtuous ne so holi in lyuynge, ȝif it haponn** aliquem istorum ramorum crescere super istam, vertit ipsam in lubruscam et sterilescere facit a virtutibus. Ideo in isto sacro tempore abscindite istos execratos ramos. Nunc est tempus scindendi spirituales vites, **to puttyn away** omnia peccata. Ideo [non solum][4] **gouernors** set omnes
30 homines **repe[n]te[5]** de vestris viciis et corde conteramini et confitemini vestris spiritualibus patribus. Accipite acutum cultellum penitencie in manibus vestris **and cuttes of** omnes ramos peccati. Non vnus relinquatur.

Set quia **vncrafti cutters [cutte][6]** sepe **away** bonos ramos cum m[a]lis,[7]

---

1. *or* vinta, *for* vincta.
2. ramas.
3. virtus.
4. solum non.
5. repete.
6. *blank*.
7. molis.

Translation

They sought from heaven, Luke 11, and in today's gospel.[1]

The grace **and comfort** of the blessed Trinity, through the intercession of the Blessed Lady, the mother of Christ, and of all the saints in the high palace of heaven, be with us now and always. Amen.

Worshipful sirs, the words I have taken as my thema are written in the gospel of this day and sound thus in our mother tongue: "**They sought from heaven.**"

Sirs, the special vineyard of the heavenly father, which Christ, his son, has nourished and guarded for a long time and through the power of the Holy Spirit, faith **and good belief,** is our fertile realm—may God in his mercy keep it. For right as in a material vineyard, if the vines are to be fertile **and pleasing,** useless branches are cut off in time, other fertile ones **are propagated and nursed along,** and to protect them against breaking, **they are raised up** and tied **to strong staves,** so in our spiritual vineyard, that is, in our realm, if the vines—that is, the great lords spiritual and temporal—are to be fertile and bring fruit to the honor of God and the profit of the realm, it is necessary that one cut off all **useless** branches, the branches of pride and gluttony, of extortion and avarice, and all the branches of deadly sin. **These must needs be cut away** if the vines are to grow strong, for wherever any of these grow, the sap of grace, which ought to be **the chief food** of the vine, is totally destroyed. They draw the sap that ought to be **in the top and spring forth** into blossoms and fruit, to earth. Deadly sins draw the heart's love that man should have for his God, contemplation, and the high devotion man should have in his soul toward God **away from him and set it on carnal pleasures, on the vanities and falseness** of this world, so that, be the vine **ever so fruitful, be you ever so virtuous or so holy in living, if it happens** that any of these branches grows on the vine, it turns it into deadwood and makes it sterile in virtues. Hence, in this holy season, cut off these cursed branches! Now is the time to prune the spiritual vines, **to put away** all sins. Therefore, not only you **governors** but all men, **repent** of your vices, be contrite of heart, and confess to your spiritual fathers. Take the sharp knife of penance into your hands **and cut off** all branches of sin. Not a single one should be left.

But since **unskillful cutters** often **cut away** good branches with the

---

1. Luke 11:16, from the gospel for the third Sunday of Lent.

ideo duo **sufferen** ramos ostendam vobis qui necessario **most be lel sprin-gynge** super quemlibet vitem. Isti duo rami sunt iusticia et misericordia. þes **most grow** super vites spirituales, dominos regni. þes **be nedful** cuilibet habenti **rule and gouernail** super alios. Primo ramus iusticie debet oriri super vitem Domini. Iste ramus non potest flecti **ne be crocud,** set **it most grow** riȝt **furthe.** Isti domini debent ponere iusticiam in
40 execucione et iudicare cuilibet iuste. Non debent flecti [fauore][8] uel **fren-chip** pro precibus nec donis nec **croke awey** a recta via iusticie pro inuidia aut odio, set **trulich** iudicare cuilibet, pauperi sicut diuiti, inimicis sicut amicis. Sic debent gubernatores **boþe in comyng and doo punchynge** subditorum suorum. Ad hoc debent [*blank*]. Non sufficit committere aliis suam potestatem et dimittere, quia sepius per negligenciam et [in]iusti-ciam,[9] sepius per auariciam falsorum ministrorum populus opprimitur, [*blank*] deperit, et [*f. 41v*] rectum in curuum vertitur.

Figuram huius lego in sacra scriptura Exodi 7. Ibi lego quod Aaron **gouernour** filiorum Israel habuit virgam per quam fecit plura mirabilia.
50 Quamdiu tenebat illam in manibus propriis, fuit recta sicut deberet, set statim si a manibus propriis proiecit, mutauit suam similitudinem, **it wax crokut** et vertebatur in serpentem. Ista mirabilis virga nichil aliud est nisi equus ramus iusticie, iusta potestas quam domini haberent **in her rule and gouernail.** Quamdiu prelati et domini temporales habuerunt istam virgam in propriis manibus, **it was ful riȝt and heuen.** Quamdiu ipsimet habuerunt oculum ad religionem et custodiam legum, tamdiu fuit **incres** virtutis et bone vite inter āccī'cas.[10] Vulgus tunc non opprimebatur iniuriis et ex-torcionibus, nullus false [*blank*], non **wron[g]fullich**[11] perdidit suam ter-ram. Set quid aliquis **cleymed,** si fuit iustum titulum, sine mora fuit sibi
60 liberatum. Set plures **gouernouris** iam in diebus vtriusque status proie-cerunt istam virgam extra manus proprias. Plures istorum ordinarunt tot substitutos **and baile errantis** quod ramus iusticie vertitur in serpen-tem, quia **go me to men** Ecclesie ad omnem gradum et reperies quod conuersacio et vita non est similis vite antiquorum patrum. Vulgus sic est **stunge and inuenemed** istis serpentibus, falsis ministris iuris, quod

---

8. fouere.
9. iusticiam.
10. *I fail to make sense of this word and reading; perhaps it reflects an original form of* communitas.
11. wronfullich.

bad, I will show you two **outstanding** branches that of necessity **must faithfully grow forth** on any vine. These two branches are justice and mercy. **These must grow** on the spiritual vines, the lords of the realm. **These are necessary** to anyone who has **rule and governance** over others. First, the branch of justice must issue forth on the vine of the Lord. This branch cannot be bent **or crooked, but it must grow forth straight.** These lords must put justice into action and judge everyone justly. They must not be bent by favor or **friendship,** for prayers or gifts, nor **veer** from the right way of justice through envy or hatred, but must judge **in truth** anyone, poor as well as rich, enemies as well as friends. Thus must rulers **be in coming and punish** their subjects. For this they must [*blank*]. It is not enough to make over their power to others and leave it, for often the people are oppressed through negligence and injustice or through the avarice of false servants and thus come to ruin; and what is right becomes crooked.

I find a figura of this in Holy Scripture, Exodus 7. There I read that Aaron, the **governor** of the children of Israel, had a rod with which he performed many miracles. As long as he held it in his own hands, it was straight as it ought to be; but as soon as he cast it from his hands, it changed its shape, **it became crooked** and turned into a serpent.[2] This miraculous rod is nothing else than the straight branch of justice, the just power that lords should have **in their rule and governance.** As long as prelates and temporal lords held this rod in their own hands, **it was very straight and even.** As long as they had their eyes on religion and the keeping of the laws, there was **increase** of virtue and the good life among the [?]. The common people were then not oppressed by injuries and extortions; no one was falsely [accused] or lost his land **wrongfully.** But whatever anyone **claimed,** if he had a just title, it was rendered to him without delay. But nowadays many **governors** of both estates have cast this rod from their hands. Many of them have appointed so many substitutes **and itinerant bailiffs** that the branch of justice becomes a serpent, for if you **go to men** of the Church at any level, you will find their morals and life are not like the life of the fathers of old. The common people are so **stung and poisoned** by these serpents, these false

---

2. Exod. 7:8–12.

ipsi **ar wobego**. Nunc þai **be caried**[12] ad scannum regium, nunc þai **ar
hurlet into marchessy,** et quamuis sint **worth** viginti uel quadraginta
libris antequam v[e]nerint[13] in illorum custodiam, isti **cautelis and wiles
schull bringe** talem **wryt of** Nichil Habet super capita illorum quod non
70   relinquitur eis vnus denarius. Et certe þis [is][14] **gret ruthe.** Ideo qui estis
hic et habetis **gouernail** aliorum, pro amore Dei habeatis oculum ad
istam **mischef** [et capite][15] virgam iusticie in manus proprias. Si subditi
vestri delinquant, **set to hond,** vosmet **doth correccioun** super illos, et
punite debite secundum iura.

Set quia secundum doctores crudelis punicio sine misericordia cicius
dicetur rigor quam iusticia, ideo necessario ramus misericordie deb[et][16]
eciam crescere super vitem. Domini **gouernouris most** eciam **be merciful
in punchyng.** Oportet ipsos attendere quod **of stakis and stodis** qui
deberent stare in ista vinea quedam sunt **smoþe and liȝtlich wul boo,**
80   quedam sunt **so stif and so ful of warris** quod homo **schal to-cleue hom**
cicius quam planare. Quidam subditi sunt humiles **and buxum,** et de
facili volunt corigi; quidam sunt **as stiburne** et duri cordis quod mallent
frangi quam flecti. Et tamen si discrete agatur cum eis, sunt adeo **nitli**[17]
vinee sicut maxime flexibiles. Ideo qui vult bene seruare istam vineam,
oportet vt sapienter nectat istos duos ramos adinuicem. Discrete[18] in suis
correccionibus misceat misericordiam cum iusticia, non semper punire
secundum vltimum rigorem set secundum condicionem persone, secundum oportunitatem temporis et loci discrete mensurare suam punicionem,
vt vbi videt asperitate[m][19] iusticie non valere, tempte[t][20] mi[t]iciem[21]
90   misericordie. Hec est voluntas Dei, quod quilibet gu- *[f. 42]* bernator
faceret sicut testatur Micheas, Michee VI, vbi sic: "Hoc est quod Dominus querit a te, facere iusticiam et diligere misericordiam."

Set bene nouistis quod **be** vitis **neuer so likinge** in [*blank*], rami **neuer
so fair ne so lusti,** ex quo est gracilis et fere nullius fortitudinis, nisi

---

12. *add.* an *canc?*
13. vnerint.
14. *om.*
15. *blank.*
16. debent.
17. *the manuscript seems to read* nit'i.
18. *written twice.*
19. asperitate.
20. temptem.
21. milliciem.

servants of the law, that they **are woebegone**. Now **they are taken** to the king's bench, now **they are hurled into jail,** and though they may be **worth** twenty or forty pounds before they come into their custody, these **tricks and stratagems shall bring** such a **writ of** Nihil Habet on their heads that not a single penny is left them. And surely **this is a great pity**. Therefore, you who are here and have **the governance** of others, for the love of God have your eye on this **mischief** and hold the rod of justice in your hands. If your subjects commit a crime, **exert yourselves,** you yourselves **bring correction** on them, and punish them fittingly according to the laws.

But since according to the doctors harsh punishment without mercy will be called rigor rather than justice, it is therefore necessary that the branch of mercy, too, should grow on the vine. The lord **governors must** also **be merciful in punishing**. They should take notice that **of the stakes and supports** that should stand in this vineyard, some are **smooth and will easily bend,** others are **so stiff and so full of obstinacy** that a man **will split them** sooner than straighten them out. Some subjects are humble **and obedient** and will be easily corrected; others are **so stubborn** and hard-hearted that they would rather break than bend. And yet, if one deals discreetly with them, they are just as **profitable** as the most flexible vines. Therefore, whoever wants to keep this vineyard well, it behooves him to tie these two branches wisely together. He should discreetly mix mercy with justice in his corrections, not always punish after the utmost rigor but after the state of the person, and assess his punishment according to the condition of time and place, so that where he sees that harsh justice does not avail, he will try mild mercy. This is God's will, that every ruler should do as Micah testifies in Micah 6 when he says: "This is what God asks of you, to do justice and to love mercy."[3]

But you know well that, **be** the vine **ever so pleasant,** the branches **ever so fair or so cheerful,** because it is delicate and has practically no

---

3. Mic. 6:8.

supportentur **railis,** cito possunt **be blow doun and broke.** þes **railis** nichil aliud sunt nisi comunitas regni, populus qui est sub gubernacione dominorum, quos oportet fundari in humilitate, pati **wyt[out]**[22] **grangynge and grennynge** superiorum correcciones si delinquant, þai **most obey to her gouernouris** in omnibus licitis et supportare vites domini corpore

100 **and catel.** Quamdiu vites domini **and railis** comunitatis fuerunt vincti adinuicem in caritate, nullus ventus nec **blast** inimicorum, nulla tempestas guerre aut bellorum potuit ipsos **ouerþrow.** Tunc vinea nostri regni fuit **plentiuous and likinge,** sic **plentiuous** quod vinea Vasconie nullius erat reputacionis, Mons Ros nec Mons Vernal [*blank*] **bere not to purpose** huius. Forte vitis lollardie **and of þe rene stemyth wild and barayn.** Fuit **so likinge** quod rami nostri honoris **spreddonn** totum mundum. Omnes Christiani reges timebant nos et loquebantur de nostris victoriis et fortitudine. Set certe, vtrum vites sint in defectu uel **railis,** nescio. Nostra vinea multum peioratur infra paucos annos. Non fuit adeo sterilis et

110 pauper sicut iam est. Paucos dies iam inuent' [?], quid pro **scharpe schowris** infra, quid pro **stronge stormus** extra, plures vites domini **ar ouerþrow** sicut nouistis, þe **trusti stakis** comunitatis **stond ful þynne,** et maturi **grapis** nostri honoris sunt pauci uel nulli. Sic þis florens vinea **faded** indies quod nisi Christus de sua misericordia apponat manum et iuuet nos, **it is liclich to forfare and turne in** heremum.

Ideo þe **best red** quod scio: **make we oure mone** ad Christum, custodem nostre vinee, deprecantes quod velit habere oculum ad opus manuum suarum, quod velit misereri nobis. Clamemus ad ipsum corditer cum propheta **and say:** "Domine virtutum, conuertere, respic[e][23] de celo,

120 vide et visita vineam istam, et perfice eam quam plantauit dextera tua," in Psalmo. Isto modo specialis vinea Dei, filii Israel, quando fuerunt capti ab inimicis et **put in seruage and þraldom,** videntes quod super terram fuit nisi **care and soroo,** et quod omnis gracia venit de celo sursum, **help and [succur],**[24] precibus [*blank*] querebant de celo, sicut dixi in principio. Et ex [quo][25] ipsi qui fuerunt Iudei et nisi vmbra ad Christianos **fonden** precibus quem querebant **and wer releuid** de sua miseria, si nos qui sumus Christiani et maxime specialis vinea Dei [conuertamus][26] **vus**

---

22. wyt [*blank*].
23. respicere.
24. sintur.
25. *om.*
26. counne [*blank*].

strength, unless they be supported **by rails,** they can **be blown down and broken. These rails** are nothing else than the community of the realm, the common people who are under the rule of the lords, who must be rooted in humility, suffer **without groaning and gnashing of teeth** against the correction by their superiors if they have done wrong; **they must obey their governors** in everything that is lawful and support the vines of their lord with their body **and goods.** As long as the vines of the lord **and the rails** of the community were tied together in charity, no wind or **blast** from our enemies, no storm of war or battles could **overthrow** them. Then was the vineyard of our kingdom **wealthy and pleasant,** so **wealthy** that the vineyard of Gascony was of no repute, Mount Rose and Mount Vernal **bore no comparison to** this. Perchance the vine of **Lollardy and of the realm stood wild and barren.** It was **so attractive** that the branches of our honor **overspread** all the world. All Christian kings feared us and spoke of our victories and strength. But certainly, I do not know whether it is the vines that are defective or **the rails.** Our vineyard has become much worse within few years. It did not use to be as sterile and poor as it now is. Within a few days [?], what with **sharp showers** within, what with **strong storms** without, many vines of the Lord **have been overthrown,** as you know. **The trusted stakes** of the community **stand very thin,** and the ripe **grapes** of our honor are few or none. Thus, **this** flourishing vineyard **has been fading** for so long that, if Christ in his mercy does not lay his hand on it and help us, **it is likely to perish and turn into** a desert.

Hence **the best counsel** I know is that **we make our lament** to Christ, the keeper of our vineyard, and pray that he would keep his eye on the work of his hands, that he would have pity on us. Let us call to him from our hearts with the prophet **and say,** as in the psalm: "Lord of virtues, turn to us, look down from heaven, behold and visit this vineyard, and perfect it as your right hand has planted it."[4] In this way, the children of Israel, that special vineyard of God, when they were taken prisoners by their enemies and **put in bondage and servitude** and saw that on earth there is nothing but **care and sorrow,** and that every grace comes from heaven above, they *sought from heaven* **help and succor** by their prayers, as I said in the beginning. And since those who were Jews and but a foreshadowing of Christians **sought** with their prayers the one they were seeking **and were relieved** of their misery—if we, who are Christians and

---

4. Ps. 79:15–16.

of hour misdedes et depricemur Deum pro misericordia **and help, doutles**
vult misereri nobis **and send vs comfort** de celo secundum quod queri-
130   mus. Ideo in principio huius sermonis preces effundamus ad celi impera-
torem, Christum nostrum, precando ipsum de misericordia **and comfort**
in isto etc.

[*f. 42v*] *De celo querebant,* etc., vbi prius. Domini, hic potestis racionabiliter petere tres questiones: **Ho souȝt,** quid þai souȝt, et—ex quo
sunt septem celi, vt sanctus Thomas dicit 2° *Sentenciarum*—a quo celo
querebant. Ad primum, cum queritis qui querebant, respondeo et dico
quod **disciplis drery in derkenes, wrecchis wrappid in seknes, and prisoners pined with heuynes.** Ad secundum, quid querebant, dico quod
lithe lyfful techinge and holi influens of heldful remedie and a tokon of
140   **deliueraunce and merci.** Ad tercium, a quo celo querebant, dico quod
a celo þat is **payntid with sterres and planetis briȝt schynyng,** de celo
þat is **cler as þe cristal on þe clif springing,** et de summo celo vbi est
gracius comfort and blisful abidinge.

Pro connexione istorum membrorum adinuicem et processu nostri
sermonis dico primo quod

—**disciplis drery in derknes souȝt liȝt of lifful techinge and holi,** de celo
þat is **payntid with sterres and planetis briȝt schynynge.**
—**Wrecchis wrappid in sekenes souȝt influens [of]**[27] **helful remedie,** de
celo þat is **cler as þe cristal on þe clif springinge.**
150   —**And prisoners pined with heuynes souȝt a tokonn of delyueraunce and**
mercy, de summo celo vbi est **gracius comfort and blisful abidinge.**

Et sic triplex genus h[ominum][28] **lakkinge hof liȝt wisdom, pyned [in]**[29]
animo, **and oppressid** diabolica seruitute, contricione cordis **and sorooful**
sykinge succur *querebant de celo,* vt in principio.

Dixi primo, etc. Vt magnus clericus Lincolniensis dicit in suis *Dictis,*
dicto 168, per illud **briȝt schynynge** celum quod clerici vocant celum
stellatum possumus bene intelligere Ecclesiam, que recte vt celum semper
mouetur super duos polos, fidem et spem, **arayid** septem stellis septem
sacramentorum, **and piȝt ful** fixis stellis omnium aliarum virtutum. Iam

27. *om.*
28. h.
29. *blank.*

most especially God's vineyard, turn back **from our misdeeds** and pray God for mercy **and help, doubtless** he will have mercy on us **and send us comfort** from heaven according to what we ask. Thus, in the beginning of this sermon, let us pour forth our prayers to the emperor of heaven, our Christ, asking him for mercy **and comfort** in this, etc.

They sought from heaven, etc., as above. Lords, here you can reasonably ask three questions: **Who sought,** what **they sought,** and—because there are seven heavens, as St. Thomas says in his commentary on the second book of the *Sentences*[5]—from which heaven they sought. With regard to the first point, as you are asking who sought, I answer and say that those were **the disciples sad in darkness, wretches wrapped in sickness, and prisoners afflicted with sadness.** With regard to the second point, what they were seeking, I say that it was **light of life-giving teaching, and holy influence of healing medicine, and a token of deliverance and mercy.** With regard to the third, from which heaven they were seeking, I say from the heaven **that is painted with stars and planets brightly shining,** from the heaven **that is as clear as crystal rising out of the rock,** and from the highest heaven, where there is **gracious comfort and blisful dwelling.**

In combining these members with each other, and for the development of our sermon, I say first: **the disciples sad in darkness sought light of life-giving and holy teaching,** from the heaven **that is paintid with stars and planets brightly shining; wretches wrapped in sickness sought the influence of healing medicine,** from the heaven **that is clear as the crystal rising out of the rock; and prisoners afflicted with sadness sought a token of deliverance and mercy,** from the highest heaven where there is **gracious comfort and blisful dwelling.** And thus, mankind in three different aspects—**lacking the light of wisdom, afflicted** in their minds, **and oppressed** by their bondage to the devil—*sought from heaven* **succor,** in their contrition of heart **and mournful sighing,** as I said in the beginning.

First I said, etc. As the great scholar Grosseteste says in his *Sayings,* item 168,[6] by that **brightly shining** heaven that clerics call the starred sky, we can understand the Church, which just like the heavens always moves on two poles, faith and hope, **arrayed** with the seven stars of the seven sacraments, **and set full** of fixed stars of all the other virtues. It now sheds its light on the earth of the human soul by **preaching and teaching.** There it now causes it, through the influence of its example, to sprout with virtues and to bring forth the fruits of a good life. In

---

5. Aquinas *Commentum in Sententias* 2.14.4 (1852–73, 6:508).
6. Probably *Dictum* 137 of Robert Grosseteste; see Thomson 1940, 231.

160   diffundit suum lumen in terram humane anime per **prechinge and techinge**. Ibidem iam per influenciam exempli facit illam germinare virtutibus
et fructus producere bone vite. In isto lucido celo Ecclesie **is** corpus
perfectum þe **nurchinge sunne** curatorum **with his bemis al brennynge**.
In isto est eciam mater **and succur** noctis, þe **variand mone** diuitum **in
briȝtnes al schynynge**. Et in isto celo est planeta **ful briȝt** Mercurius, **of
smale vitrileris ful besy in meuynge**.

     Prima res intellecta in celo Ecclesie est corpus perfectum, þe **nurchinge**
sol curatorum **with his bemis al brennyng**. Ex quo magnus philosophus
Eraclitus vocat solem fontem celestis luminis, et Plato in *Thimeo* dicit
170   quod regulat cursus omnium aliorum planetarum, racionabiliter possum
huic comparare prelatos, curatos, et **men** Ecclesie, qui pre omnibus aliis
statibus **most schyne** in firmamento Ecclesie **in holy lyuynge**, in contemplacione Dei versus seipsos et prebere lumen omnibus aliis per bonum
exemplum et predicacionem verbi Dei. Et sicut materialis sol mensurat
met[a]s[30] [*f. 43*] aliarum planetarum, sic debent ipsi facere. Si quis erret
in his beleue—quod absit—, excedat limites fidei suscepte in baptismate,
uel offendat contra iura Ecclesie, ad illos pertinet corrigere **and redresse**
tales defectus, omnes errores et hereses destruere, **and informyn him**
iterum **in þe sad beleue**.

180   Iste sol curatorum fulgebat olim **ful briȝt** in celo Ecclesie, quia sicut
materialis sol **goth** suum cursum per omnia duodecim signa in zodiaco,
qui est circulus in firmamento, dare lumen toti mundo, sic spiritualis sol
curatorum et doctorum olim mouebatur continue in circulo zodiaci. Vt
auctor *De spera* dicit, cap[i]t[31] suum nomen ab isto termino greco *zoe,*
quod interpretatur vita. Quid melius potest comparari huic circulo vite
quam fides, que viuificat animam humanam et est vera vita cuiuslibet
Christiani, secundum quod Apostolus dicit Ad Hebreos X: "Iustus autem
ex fide viuit"? Istum circulum vite Christus protraxit ipsemet in firmamento Ecclesie. Et sicut latomus faciendo circulum capit **a cumpas, set**
190   vnam partem firmiter in vno puncto, **and drawþe toþer party al abowte**,
sic quando Christus noster geometer fuit in hoc mundo, habuit **a crafti
cumpas made of twey partes**, de benedicta deitate et humanitate **knyt**

---

30. metus.
31. caput.

this shining heaven of the Church **is** the perfect body of **the nourishing sun** of parish priests, **all afire with its beams**. In it is also the mother **and succor** of the night, **the changing moon** of the rich **all shining in brightness**. And in this heaven is a planet **full bright**, Mercury, **of small victuallers who are full busy in action**.

The first thing that is understood in the heaven of the Church is a perfect body, **the nourishing** sun of parish priests, **all afire with its beams**. Because the great philosopher Heraclitus calls the sun the fountain of heavenly light,[7] and Plato in his *Timaeus* says that it regulates the course of all other planets,[8] I can reasonably compare to it the prelates, curates, and **men** of the Church, who **must shine** in the firmament of the Church before all other estates **in holy living**, in the contemplation of God with respect to themselves, and must give light to all others by their good example and by preaching the word of God. And as the material sun sets the courses of the other planets, so must these do likewise. If anyone wanders astray **in his belief**—may it never happen—if he goes beyond the limits of the faith he has received in baptism or offends against the laws of the Church, it behooves churchmen to correct **and repair** such defects, to destroy all errors and heresies, **and to teach him** again **in the true belief**.

This sun of parish priests was once shining **very brightly** in the heaven of the Church, for as the material sun **runs** its course through all twelve signs of the zodiac, which is a circle in the firmament, to give light to the whole world, so the spiritual sun of the priests used to move continually in the circle of the zodiac. As the author of *De sphaera* says, the zodiac takes its name from the Greek word *zoe*, which means "life."[9] What can be better likened to this circle of life than faith, which gives life to man's soul and is the true life of every Christian, according to what the Apostle says in his Letter to the Hebrews 10: "The just man lives out of faith"?[10] This circle of life Christ himself traced in the firmament of the Church. As a builder, when he traces a circle, takes **a compass, sets** one leg firmly in a point, **and draws the other leg all around**, so when Christ, our draftsman, was in this world, he had **a skillful compass made of two legs**, of the blessed deity and his human nature **knit together in one person**. One part of this **compass**, namely

---

7. Bartholomaeus Anglicus 8.28 (1485) speaks of the sun as "fons tocius luminis" but does not mention Heraclitus.

8. Probably Plato *Timaeus* 39C. The idea occurs in Bartholomaeus Anglicus 8.28 (1485), where "Plato in Thimeo" is also quoted.

9. Joannes de Sacro Bosco, *Sphaera mundi* (Venice, 1478), chapter 2.

10. Heb. 10:38.

togedur in o persone. Vnam partem huius **cumpas,** scilicet benedictam
deitatem, **he set** perfecte in vno puncto beatitudinis. **þis was piʒt so sadlich
in þis** puncto quod nulla miseria huius mundi, **no sikenes ne mischef myʒt
hit touche ne meue.** Altera parte istius **cumpas,** sua humanitate, **he drow**
þis circulum vite. **þis parti he drow aboute** in hoc mundo **in muche woo,
payn, and trauail.** Herwith **he grauyd** in hoc seculo omnia duodecim signa
zodiaci, omnes duodecim articulos fidei, quia quando suscepit carnem et

200 sanguinem ex Beata Virgine, domina sancta Maria, **he grauid** in isto circulo
signum virginis, **þe signe of þe maiden, þe article** sue pure incarnacionis.
Quando ponebatur in cruce et obtulit **up** sanguinem cordis sui patri suo
pro redempcione generis humani, sculpsit in illo signum tauri, **þe signe
of þe bole,** articulum sue acerbe passionis, **and scylfullich** offerendo seipsum sculpsit signum tauri, quia comuniter in veteri lege tauri offerebantur
in sacrificiis. Tercia die resurgens a mortuis **he grauid** in illo signum leonis,
þe signe of þe lionn, articulum sue gloriose resurreccionis. Et racionabiliter
isto tempore sculpsit signum leonis, quia sicut Izodorus dicit 12 *Ethimologiarum,* sicut catulus leonis nouiter **welpit** iacet tribus diebus sine

210 vita et erigitur ad vitam per **roringe noyse** antiqui leonis, sic Christus, leo
de tribu Iuda, iacuit mortuus, secundum comunem modum loquendi doctorum, tribus diebus in suo sepulcro, et tercia die virtute deitatis, que est
þe almyʒti vox Patris, suum corpus et anima reuiuebantur **and rose fro
deth to lyue. In schewyng** sui terribilis vultus custodibus sui sepulcri, **he
purtrid** in illo circulo signum [*f. 43v*] archi[tenen]tis,[32] **þe signe of þe
archir,** articulum terribilis iudicii, quia ista acuta sagitta sagittatur damp-
natis: "Ite maledicti in ignem eternam," etc. Ista acuta verba Christus
habebit in die iudicii dampnandis, **"Goth fro me, ʒe curset men,** in eternum
ignem inferni qui ordinabatur ab inicio mundi diabol[o][33] et eius minis-

220 tris." Ista verba erunt acuciora aliqua sagitta uel **egge tol on hyrt.** Grauabit
ipsos milesies plus quam si essent milesies milesies **schote þorue þe bodi.**
    Domini, longum esset stare in quolibet istorum duodecim. Ideo, vt
bene potest capi ex euangelio, nullum est signum in zodiaco, nullus est
articulus fidei, quin ipsum uel docuit uel exemplauit uel opere compleuit
sua beata humanitate. Et postquam diu laborauit grauiter **in grauynge**
istorum signorum, istorum articulorum, **to performe** istum circulum vite,
ascendit in celum cum deitate et humanitate vnitis ad eundem punctum

---

32. archi'tis.
33. diabola.

his blessed divine nature, **he placed** perfectly in the centerpoint of his blessedness. **This was set so firmly in this** point that no misery of this world, **no sickness or misfortune, could touch or move it.** With the other leg of the **compass,** his human nature, **he drew this** circle of life. **This leg he drew around** in this world **in much woe, pain, and travail. With it he engraved** in this world all twelve signs of the zodiac, all twelve articles of the faith. For when he took flesh and blood from the Blessed Virgin, Our Lady St. Mary, **he engraved** in this circle the sign of Virgo, **the sign of the maiden, the article** of his pure incarnation. When he was put on the cross and offered **up** the blood of his heart to his father for the redemption of mankind, he carved in it the sign of Taurus, **the sign of the bull,** the article of his bitter passion. **And reasonably** did he carve the sign of Taurus by offering himself, for in the Old Law bulls are commonly offered in sacrifice. By rising from the dead on the third day, **he engraved** in that circle the sign of Leo, **the sign of the lion,** the article of his glorious resurrection. And reasonably did he at that time carve the sign of Leo, for as Isidore says in book 12 of the *Etymologies,*[11] as the lion cub recently **born** lies for three days without life and is then raised to life by **the roaring sound** of the old lion, thus Christ, the lion of the tribe of Judah, lay dead for three days in his sepulcher, as our teachers commonly say, and on the third day, by virtue of his godhead, which is **the almighty** voice of the Father, his body and soul came to life again **and rose from death to life. In showing** his awesome face to the keepers at his grave, **he portrayed** in that circle the sign of Sagittarius, **the sign of the archer,** the article of his terrible judgment, for with this sharp arrow he pierces the damned: "Go, cursed ones, into the eternal fire," etc.[12] These sharp words Christ will have for the damned on judgment day, "**Go from me, you cursed men,** into the eternal fire of hell, which has been ordained from the beginning of the world for the devil and his ministers." These words will be sharper than any arrow or **cutting edge in one's heart.** It will pierce them a thousand times more than if they were a thousand thousand times **shot through the body.**

My lords, it would be too long to linger on each of these twelve. Therefore, as it can be well understood from the gospel, there is no sign in the zodiac, no article of faith, which Christ did not teach or give an example of or fulfill in deed in his blessed humanity. And after he worked long and hard **in engraving** these signs, these articles, **to make** this circle

---

11. Isidore *Etym.* 12.2.5.
12. Matt. 25:41.

beatitudinis a quo venit, **and in þis styynge vp** sculpsit signum libre, þe
signe of þe weyt, articulum **of his ioyful ascencion,** quia in ista contra
230   inordinatum **lust of Adam is gilte he weyyt** coram Patre suo acerbas
penas [quas]³⁴ sustinuit et meritum sue passionis. Fuit causa magna quod
per virtutem istius **he paysid vp** omnem maliciam peccati et ap[e]ruit³⁵
celi ianuas toto humano generi **with gret trauail.**

Quando iste circulus vite fuit sic perfectus **and set** in firmamento
Ecclesie, sol sanctorum doctorum **with gret trauail in prechinge, in writ-
inge and disputinge** contra hereticos mouebantur sub illo **and went** suum
cursum, non solum per vnum uel duo signa, set per omnia duodecim,
per omnes articulos fidei, **and al** dare nobis lumen, firmare nos in fide.
Et semper in scriptis, in predicacionibus seruabant se infra limite istius
240   circuli, **þai neuer erred ne wauerid** in fide, set steterunt firmiter in þe
beleue. Set plures iam in diebus qui pretendunt se verum solem Ecclesie
contra naturam solis excedunt limitem circuli vite. Plures, vt heretici
lollardi, errant vt dicitur in fide et faciunt alios errare sua peruersa
doctrina. Isti despiciunt sacramenta Ecclesie **and heltful customis** quos
apostoli ordinauerunt in illa inspiracione Spiritus Sancti. Isti ex proprio
capite predicant contrarium et inficiunt populum. Ideo vos qui essetis
verus sol Ecclesie et habetis curam animarum, caueatis de istis **mester
men,** non detis credenciam suis pictis verbis, fundetis vosmet in fide,
kepe ȝow infra istum circulum, et informatis parochianos vestros in solida
250   fide. Si sic feceritis, Deo placebitis, proficietis vobismet, et multum hono-
rabitis celum Ecclesie. Hoc testatur Sapiens, Ecclesiastici XLIII, vbi sic:
"Species celi in visione glorie, sol in aspectu annuncians in exitu" [*remainder of line blank*].

Secundum intellectum in celo Ecclesie est mater et **succur** noctis, þe
variant mone diuitum, **in briȝtnes al schyning.** Quid melius potest comparari quam grandi diuites istius seculi, quorum diuicie et honores
[*blank*] et varie sicut luna? [*f. 44*] Nunc crescunt **and wex** per magnum
besines and trauail, nunc þai **wansyn o þin perlos** suorum bonorum
robbyn and brennyn. Ista luna est numquam **stabul** nec **stidfast,** quia
260   sicut cotidie **is sen** ad oculum, nunc dominus nunc seruus, nunc miles
nunc garcio, nunc diues nunc mendicus. Et non obstante instabilitate
istius lune, fuit quondam proficuus planeta et necessarius, quia postquam

---

34. *om.*
35. aparuit.

of life, he ascended to heaven with his divine and human natures united, to the same center point of bliss from which he had come, **and in this rising** he carved the sign of Libra, **the sign of the scales**, the article **of his joyful ascension**, for in it **he weighed** against the disorderly **lust of Adam's guilt**, before his Father, the bitter pains he suffered and the merit of his passion. This was a great event, that in virtue of this **he balanced** all the malice of sin and opened the gates of heaven for all mankind **with his great suffering.**

When this circle of life was thus established **and set** into the firmament of the Church, the sun of our holy doctors, **with great travail in preaching, in writing, and in disputing** against heretics, moved beneath it **and went** their course, not only through one or two signs but through all twelve, through all the articles of faith, **and all** to give us light, to strengthen us in faith. And all the time, in their writing and their preaching, they kept themselves within the boundaries of this circle, **they never wandered astray or wavered** in the faith but stood firm **in their belief.** But many nowadays who act as if they were the true sun of the Church go beyond the boundary of the circle of life against the nature of the sun. Many, such as the Lollard heretics, go astray so to speak in the faith and cause others to go astray by their perverse teaching. They despise the sacraments of the Church **and the healthy customs** that the apostles ordained in it by inspiration of the Holy Spirit. Out of their own heads, they preach what is contrary and infect the people. Therefore, you who should be the true sun of the Church and have the cure of souls, beware of these **kind of people**, give no credence to their painted words, root yourselves firmly in the faith, **keep yourselves** within this circle, and teach your parishioners in solid faith. If you do thus, you will please God, earn reward for yourselves, and give much honor to the heaven of the Church. The wise man testifies to this when he says in Ecclesiasticus 43: "The beauty of heaven in a glorious vision, the sun when it appears showing forth in its rising."[13]

The second thing understood in the heaven of the Church is the mother and **succor** of the night, **the changing moon** of the rich, **shining in brightness.** What is more like it than the powerful rich people of this world, whose riches and positions are changeable like the moon? Now they grow **and wax** through much **busyness and labor**; now **they wane through the perilous theft and burning** of their goods. This moon is never **stable** or **steadfast,** for as **is seen** daily to our eye, [a man is] now a lord then a

---

13. Ecclus. 43:1.

receperat lumen fidei a sole Ecclesie, postquam apostoli instruxerant
diuites quomodo viuerent, dimiserunt radios elemosine, pietatis, et com-
passionis in terram pauperum. Deuocio istorum fuit tanta quod quidam
dederunt aurum, quidam iocalia, quidam vendiderunt terras et redditus
ad sustenendum Christianam plebem, vt patet in Actibus Apostolorum.
Illo tempore fuit pulcher planeta et proficuus. Set **a,** Domine Deus,
quomodo est iam in diebus? Certe, perdidit multum lumen. Deuocio
270   multum remittitur, elemosina fere obliuiscitur. Timeo quod intrauit caput
uel caudam draconis et est in eclipsi. Vt autores astronomie dicunt quod
materialis luna in celo habet duos circulos in quibus moueretur, vnus est
equans, **an euene circle,** alter deferens, idest **beringe aboute.** Iste circulus
deferens scindit et diuidit circulum equantem in duobus locis, et figura
tocius diuisionis vocatur draco, quia est lata in medio et arta versus
fines. Et si luna in suo cursu intret þe **diparting** punctum ex parte australi,
qui vocatur caput draconis, uel punctum ex parte boriali, qui vocatur
cauda draconis, **be it neuer so cler ne so briȝt,** per antea cadit in eclipsim
et deperdit suum lumen. Moraliter: nostra luna in firmamento Ecclesie
280   habet duos circulos, corpus et animam. Anima est equans circulus istius
lune. Non potest mori, **it is endeles** sicut circulus, et equaliter distat a
terra ex omni parte. Non fuit de limo terre, nec fetido **filth,** set est purus
spiritus sine corrupcione, factus **euene** secundum similitudinem Dei. Alter circulus deferens est corpus quod defert animam **aboute** hic super
terram. Homo bene potest dici circulus, quia fuit de terra, cum postquam
intrauerit mundum numquam [quiescit][36] set continue mouetur **in care
and soroo** usque reueniat ad punctum a quo venit, in tempus quo
v[er]tatur[37] in terram et in corrupcionem. Iste circulus corporis diuidit
circulum anime in duobus locis, quia impedit intellectum et racionem a
290   summo amore, summa contemplacione Dei, et per fragilitatem suam
trahit voluntatem ad consensum mortalis peccati. Et vere figura et causa
istius tocius diuisionis, **boþe** retraxionis cordialis amoris a Deo et con-
sensus ad mortale peccatum, bene potest vocari draco, þe draco auaricie,
quia vt Apostolus dicit Ad Thimoteum VI^{to}, "radix omnium malorum
est cupiditas." Iste est execratus draco qui deuorat totum mundum et
numquam saciatur. Et vt Solinus refert *De mirabilibus mundi,* recte vt
verus draco est sitibundus aut parum dormit et habet maximum venenum

36. *om.*
37. vtatur.

servant, now a knight then a stable boy, now rich then a beggar. Yet notwithstanding the instability of this moon, at one time it was a beneficial and necessary planet, for after it had received the light of faith from the sun of the Church, after the apostles had taught the rich how they should live, they sent forth their rays of alms, of piety, and of compassion into the land of the poor. Their devotion was so great that some gave gold, others precious objects, others sold their lands and gave the profit to sustain the Christian people, as is seen in the Acts of the Apostles.[14] In that time this was a fair and beneficial planet. But **ah**, Lord God, how is it nowadays? It surely has lost much light. Devotion is much abandoned, almsgiving is almost forgotten. I fear the moon has entered the head or tail of the dragon and is in an eclipse. As the writers on astronomy say,[15] the material moon in the sky has two orbits in which it moves. One is the equant, **an even circle**; the other is inclined, that is **swinging through** it. The latter circle intersects the equant circle in two places, and the figure of the entire intersection is called Dragon, because it is wide in the middle and narrow toward the ends. Now, when the moon on its course enters **the intersecting** point in the southern part, which is called "the head of the dragon," or else the point in the northern part, which is called "the tail of the dragon," **however clear or bright it may be**, it first goes into an eclipse and loses its light. Morally speaking, our moon in the firmament of the Church has two orbits, the body and the soul. The soul is the equant circle of this moon. It cannot die, **it is endless** as a circle, and it is at every point equidistant from the earth. It was not made from the dust of the earth or from stinking **dirt**, but is pure spirit without corruption, created **even** in the likeness of God. The other orb, the inclined one, is the body, which carries the soul **about** here on earth. Man can well be called an orb, for he was made of earth, and after he enters the world, he is never at rest but moves **in care and sorrow** until he returns to the point from which he came, until he turns to earth and corruption. This orb of the body intersects the orb of the soul in two places, for it cuts off man's intellect and reason from its highest love, the contemplation of God, and through its weakness draws man's will to consent to deadly sin. Truly, the figure and cause of this intersection, **both** of the withdrawal of heartfelt love from God and consent to deadly sin, can well be called Draco, **the** dragon of avarice, for as the Apostle says in his Letter to

---

14. Acts 2:45, 4:43, etc.

15. See for instance Gerardus Cremonensis, *Theorica planetarum* (Venice, 1478). For an explanation with diagrams, see Price 1955, 103–4.

in cauda, sic est de isto dracone auaricie. Isti iuuenes qui intelliguntur
per draconis caput, quando receperint saporem in isto peccato, incipiunt
300 arescere et sitire. Tantum siciunt pro auro et bonis istius seculi quod
quidam exponunt se **in auenture** sue vite [*f. 44v*], **suffere mani mischeuis,**
plura pericula in mari, in terra. In diebus sic tormentantur **in tene** et
labore quod in noctibus non habent requiem, habent **dremes** sufficienter
and mony brok slep. Set maximum venenum est in cauda. Isti senes,
qui intelliguntur per caudam, sunt adeo **snarid and rotid** in auaricia quod
si deperdant bona sua per **brennynge, robbing,** uel aliqua alia infortunia,
adeo dolent quod quidam infirmantur, quidam moriuntur, quidam des-
perant et transiunt ad infernum. Iste est periculosus draco **and a ve-**
nemus. Deus pro sua misericordia seruet iuuenes et senes ab isto! Iste
310 draco **hath clippid** plures homines iam in diebus, sicut timeo. Luna nostra
intrauit eius caput uel caudam et est in eclipsi, **las lith** elemosine et
pietatis. Quam iam est nunquam fuit. Nullus habet iam oculum **to naked**
ne to nedy, infirmo nec pauperi, set vt Apostolus ait Ad Philippences,
"Omnes querunt que sua sunt." Non sic, domini, set toto nisu fugite
istum **venemus** draconem auaricie, quia certe **he is** verus **gide** ad desperacionem, recta via ad dampnacionem. Ideo qui essetis confortans luna
pauperum, iam in isto sacro tempore demittite radios elemosine, habeatis
ruth and pite on ʒour euencristonn, visitetis vinculatos et infirmatos, diui-
dite bona que Deus contulit vobis cum vestris pauperibus proximis. Si sic
320 feceritis opera misericordie, habebitis incrementum bonorum, et sicut
propheta ait, eritis **cler and briʒt** sicut luna perfecta in celo.

Tercium intellectum in celo Ecclesie est planeta **ful briʒt** Mercurius
of smal vitril[er]is[38] **ful besi in meuynge.** Possuntne victuarii comparari planete Mercurio? Et racionabiliter, propter duas causas. Sicut
[B]artholomeus[39] dicit *De proprietatibus rerum,* iste planeta est velox **in**
meuyng et disponit hominem ad eloquenciam **and to gay speking.** Et
propter istas duas causas Ouidius primo *De transformatis* [describit ipsum
cum alis][40] in pedibus et fistula ad os. Istas duas proprieta[te]s[41] artifices
et vitularii **most nedes** habere. Primo þai **most** esse veloces in motu et
330 habere alas in pedibus, þai **most bestere hem and besy hem aboute** in

---

38. vitrilis.
39. Lartholomeus.
40. scribit ipsum causa alis.
41. proprietas.

Timothy 4, "the root of all evil is cupidity."[16] This is the cursed dragon who devours the whole world and is never satisfied. And as Solinus reports in *De mirabilibus mundi*,[17] just as a real dragon is thirsty, sleeps little, and has much poison in his tail, so it is with the dragon of avarice. Young people, who are understood by the dragon's head, when they get some taste for this sin, begin to grow dry and thirsty. They thirst so much for gold and the goods of this world that some expose themselves **in danger** of their life, **they suffer many hazards,** many dangers on sea and land. By day they are so tormented **in worry** and labor that at night they cannot sleep, they have **dreams** aplenty **and many a broken sleep.** But the worst poison is in the dragon's tail. Old people, who are understood by the tail, are so **snared and rooted** in avarice that, should they lose their goods through **fire, theft,** or any other mishap, they mourn so much that some of them become sick, others die, and yet others despair and go to hell. This is a dangerous dragon **and a poisonous one.** May God in his mercy keep young and old from it! This dragon **has intersected** many people nowadays, as I fear. Our moon has entered its head or tail and is in eclipse, it **has lost the light** of almsgiving and piety. The way things are now, they have never been before. Nobody has an eye **for the naked and needy,** the sick and the poor, but as the Apostle says To the Philippians, "All seek their own profit."[18] Do not let it be thus, sirs, but with all your power flee this **venemous** dragon of avarice, for surely **he is** a true **guide** to despair, a straight way to damnation. Hence you, who should be the comforting light for the poor, send forth now, in this holy season, the rays of almsgiving, have **mercy and pity on your fellow Christians,** visit prisoners and the sick, share the goods God has given you with your poor neighbors. If you thus do the works of mercy, you will have an increase of riches and, as the prophet says, you will be **clear and bright** as the full moon in the sky.

The third thing understood in the heaven of the Church is the **very bright** planet Mercury, **of small victuallers that are very busy in moving about.** Can victuallers be compared to the planet Mercury? Quite rightly so, and for two reasons. As Bartholomew says in *De proprietatibus rerum,* this planet is swift **in movement** and disposes a person to eloquence **and to fair speech.**[19] For these two reasons, Ovid in book 1 of

---

16. 1 Tim. 6:10.
17. Solinus discusses dragons at 30.15, but not quite in these terms (1958, 132–33).
18. Phil. 2:21.
19. Cf. Bartholomaeus 8.27 (1485).

mundiali occupacione, **swenge** et sudare pro propria sustentacione. Et sicut planeta Mercurius in suo cursu ascendit ad circulum solis, a sole versus circulum planete qui vocatur Mars, sic isti vitularii debent facere. Primo oportet visitare suis lucris, bonis, et **catel** solem **of men** Ecclesie, veraciter **do to hom** decimas, oblaciones, et omnia alia debita. Ab istis oportet vt transiant **to** Mars milicie et temporalium dominorum, quia **boþe clergie and chiualrie most be sustened** per illos. **þe[i]**[42] **most** habere eciam fistulam ad os. Ista nichil aliud est nisi veritas in empcione et vendicione. Istam habuerunt vitularii antiquitus. In ista fecerunt **meryle**

340   melodiam. Et quid creditis **þai pipid**? Certe nichil aliud est nisi planum tenorem [*f. 45*] veritatis. Sicut fuit in corde, ita eloqueba[n]tur.[43] Non fuit cautela nec decepcio in verbo nec actu, set sicut potuerunt **hwt** sua bona et replere, sic emerunt et vendiderunt. Ista fuit **glad mynstracy** et vtilis. Set nostri vitularii iam in diebus **pipin al amys.** Plures illorum tantum studerunt pro **werblis of flateryng and flurchinge** verbis, **þai ha pipid,** tam diu fistularunt [triplum][44] falsiter quod nesciunt medium. Tenor veritatis totaliter obliuiscitur. Et sicut musici s[ci]unt,[45] quando tenor cantus deficit, totus cantus est **vncertayn,** sic ex quo nostri vitularii carent veritate, verba illorum sunt adeo incerta et instabilia quod nullus habet

350   saporem **in her talkinge,** nullus confidit in eis. Et non sufficit pluribus illorum false decipere proximos suos, set **in meyntenynge** sue falsitatis in aggrauacionem sui peccati capiunt nomen Dei in vanum, dilacerant membra Christi, et false se periurant. Hoc non est vnus uel duo, set fere omnes homines, mas et femina, senes et iuuen[e]s.[46] Tantum vsitatur quod non habent inde conscienciam, non reputatur pro peccato. Attendite, pro amore Dei, quantam vindictam Christus sumpsit pro isto peccato.

    Legi tarde quod vnus **ansyent** miles **and wel trauelid** habuit s[er]uum[47] vocatum Gilam. Ille vtebatur multum iurare per benedictos oculos Christi saluatoris nostri, et sepe periurauit. Hac consuetudine vtebatur **muche**

360   **of his liue.** Tandem Christus venit ad ipsum recte sicut fuit **peyned** in cruce, vulneribus sanguine perfusis, et ipsum sequebatur diabolus cum

---

42. ʒe.
43. eloquebatur. *But the reading* eloquebatur *may have been intended, as a nonclassical passive form: "it was spoken forth."*
44. tripliter.
45. sunt.
46. iuuens.
47. suum.

Metamorphoses describes him as having wings on his feet and a flute at his mouth.[20] These two properties workmen and victuallers **must needs** have. First **they must** be swift in their motion and have wings on their feet, **they must bestir themselves and busy themselves** in worldly activity, **slave** and sweat for their own livelihood. And as the planet Mercury in its course rises to the orbit of the sun, from the sun to the orbit of the planet called Mars, so must these victuallers do likewise. First they must visit with their profit, goods, and **chattel** the sun **of the men** of the Church and faithfully **bring them** tithes, oblations, and everything else they owe. Then they must go beyond these **to** the Mars of knighthood and temporal lords, for **both clergy and knighthood must be supported** by them. **They must** also have a flute at their mouth. This is nothing else than truth in buying and selling. The victuallers of old had that. With it they **merrily** made music. And what do you think **they piped?** Certainly nothing other than the plain tenor of truth. As it was in their hearts, so they spoke it. There was no trick or deceit in word or deed, but as they could **hawk** their goods and replenish them, so they bought and sold them. That was a **happy minstralcy** and a useful one. But our victuallers today **pipe all amiss.** Many of them have been trying so hard with **warbling sounds of flattery and embellishing** words, **they have piped,** they have so long played a false treble that they do not know the middle voice. The tenor of truth is totally forgotten. As musicians know, when the tenor line of a song falters, the whole song becomes **uncertain;** just so, because our victuallers lack truth, their words are so uncertain and unstable that no one has any pleasure **in their talk,** no one puts any trust in them. And for many of them it is not sufficient to falsely deceive their neighbors, but **in maintaining** their falsehood, they aggravate their sin by taking God's name in vain, tearing apart Christ's limbs, and falsely perjuring themselves. This is not just one or two people but nearly everybody, men and women, old and young. This practice is so much in use that they have no conscience about it, it is not considered a sin. Listen, for the love of God, what revenge Christ took for that sin.

I have read recently that an **ancient** knight, **a well-traveled one,** had a servant named Gilam. He used to swear a lot by the blessed eyes of Christ, our Savior, and often foreswore himself. He used that custom **much of his life.** Finally Christ came to him, looking exactly as when he was **tormented** on the cross, with his wounds streaming with blood,

---

20. Ovid *Met.* 1.671, 677.

furca ferrea, niger vt **pich.** Cui Christus austero vultu et terribili dixit
ista verba: "Istas acerbas penas, ista **bledinge** vulnera sustinui pro isto
homine. Pro isto caput meum **was al toprickid,** corpus meum **al tobetonn
and rent,** et cor **clef o too.** Quid vltra debui sibi facere quam vendere
vitam meam et effundere sanguinem cordis mei ad ostendendum sibi **loue
and kindnes?** E[x][48] quo ipse pro amore michi reddit odium, pro omnibus
beneficiis ingratitudinem, et false periura[ui]t[49] se per oculos meos, vade
tu, erue sibi oculos, et occide eum cum tua furca." Ille diabolus ad
370 preceptum Dei accessit ad illum **woful creature,** eruit sibi ambos oculos,
penetrauit eius cor cum furca, **and reuyd him** de ista vita. Filius autem
militis, qui multum dilexerat [seruum per annos],[50] sicut iacuit cum patre
hab[ui]t[51] de hoc plenam visionem et pre timore **he braide** extra sompnum
suum et clamauit: "Heu, pater, heu, Gilam vester seruus est mortuus,"
et retulit sibi totum processum quare et quomodo accidebatur. Miles
attonitus surrexit, secum sumpsit seruos suos, et transiuit ad cameram
eius. Recte vt suus filius retulit inuenit ambos oculos erutos et ipsum
iacentem mortuum, nigrum vt pix.

Attendite, [*f. 45v*] magni iuratores, qui[52] **rend lith fro lith** in benedicto
380 corpore Christi et cotidie periuratis vos. Capiatis hic exemplum, caueatis
per illum, cessate a maledicta consuetudine iuracionis et omnis fallacie,
resumite veritatem, sit ista tenor vestri cantus, tocius vestre loquele. Si
isto modo sequamini proprietates istius planete Mercurii, eritis vtilis
planeta Ecclesie. **ȝoure minstralsy** erit **lusty** Deo et h[ominibus],[53] quia
vt Esdras dicit, 2° Esdre, veritas est magna et forcior pre omnibus. Omnis
terra veritatem inuocat, celum et ipsam benedicit. Set pro tanto quod
sol plurium curatorum diu fuit **ouercaste** nube false doctrine, luna diuitum fuit in eclipsi auaricie, et planeta Mercurius **of smale vitreliris** diu
latuit in **myst** fallacie—et quando docti perdiderint lumen, necessario
390 laici[54] **must leue in derkenes**—, igitur simplex populus in terra, **disciplis
vncunnynge,** lumen *querebant de celo,* sicut dixi in principio.

Dixi[55] secundo principaliter quod **wrecchis wrappid in sekenes** quere-

---

48. et.
49. periurant(?).
50. suum per anna.
51. habent.
52. *add.* p't.
53. h.
54. *add.* conu (?), *perhaps beginning of* conuenit.
55. <Secundum principale>.

and after him came the devil with an iron fork, black as **pitch**. To the devil, Christ, with severe and terrifying face, said these words: "I have suffered these bitter pains, these **bleeding** wounds for this man. For him my head **was all pierced**, my body **all beaten and torn to pieces**, and my heart **split in two**. What more could I do for him than sell my life and shed the blood of my heart to show him **love and kindness**? Because he has returned hatred for my love, ingratitude for all my good deeds, and has perjured himself by my eyes, you go ahead, rip out his eyes, and kill him with your fork." The devil approached that **woeful creature** at God's behest, ripped out both his eyes, pierced his heart with his fork, **and snatched him** from this life. The knight's son, who had much loved this servant for a long time, had a full vision of the event as he was lying with his father, and in a fright **he started** out of his sleep and shouted, "Alas, father, alas, your servant Gilam is dead," and he told him the whole occurrence, why and how it happened. The knight rose in astonishment, took his servants with him, and went to the servant's chamber. Just as his son had told him, he found both eyes ripped out and the man himself lying dead, black as pitch.

Attend, you great swearers, who rend **limb from limb** in Christ's blessed body and daily perjure yourselves. Take an example from this. Take heed through this man. Let go of your cursed habit of swearing and every deceit. Take truth back to yourselves. Let it be the tenor of your song, of all your talking. If you follow the properties of the planet Mercury, you will be a useful planet for the Church. **Your minstralcy** will be **pleasing** to God and men, for as Esdra says, in 2 Esdra, truth is great and stronger than all else. All the earth calls on truth, and heaven blesses it. But because the sun of many priests has long been **overcast** with the cloud of false doctrine, the moon of the wealthy has been in the eclipse of avarice, and the planet Mercury **of small victuallers** has long been hidden in **the mist** of falsehood—and when the learned lose their light, the laity of necessity **must live in darkness**—therefore the simple people on earth, **the unlearned disciples,** *sought* light *from heaven,* as I said in the beginning.

For the second principal part, I said that **wretches wrapped in sickness**

bant influenciam sal[ubr]ioris⁵⁶ remedii de celo, quod est **cler as þe cristal on þe clif springing**. Vt [Bartholomeus]⁵⁷ dicit *De proprietatibus rerum,* libro VIII, istud clarum celum vt cristallus quod doctores vocant celum cristallinum est **clene and cler,** in se recipit lumen a celo superiori, **and sent it donn** in celum inferius. Quid melius potest comparari huic celo quam anima humana, que vt doctores dicunt in paradiso fuit **cler** in omnibus naturalibus virtutibus et pura **fro al filth** viciorum et peccati.

400   Illa recepit lumen originalis iusticie a summo celo, **fro Goddis hye maieste.** Quem adeo perfecte illuminabit celum anime humane quod superior pars racionis ardebat [uiriliter]⁵⁸ in contemplacione Dei et inferior obediebat superiori, corpus anime; omnia fuerant vn[i]ta⁵⁹ in vnitate et concordia. Et tam fecunde anima diffudit illud lumen in corpus quod per virtutem illius, si homo non peccasset, preseruatum fuisset ab omni miseria, a morte et omni corupcione. Voluntas, memoria, et intellectus fuerunt adeo **perfite and ful of bewte** quod omnipotens Pater celi misit **donn** suam virtuosam potenciam in memoriam, Filius **parfith wisdom** in intellectum, et Spiritus Sanctus graciosam bonitatem in liberam

410   [volun]tatem.⁶⁰ Isto modo benedicta Trinitas ornauit celum anime humane et fecit illud perfectam imaginem et similitudinem sue deitatis. Set prodolor, prius parens noster, Adam, instigacione diaboli deformauit ymaginem Dei. Sic polluit celum anime humane cum actuali et originali peccato quod omnes patriarche et prophete in veteri lege non potuerunt purgare. Pluries temptarunt, set modicum profuit. Enos, Enoch, et Noe in lege nature ceperunt aquam et sanguinem bestiarum in sacrificiis, **lauyd on sore, wesche fast, it wold not away.** Postea venerunt Abraam et Moyses cum sua lege, et videntes quod peccatum noluit **away** locione, inuenerunt nouam subtilitatem: ceperunt acutam silicem circum[cisi]-

420   onis,⁶¹ **herwid þai schrapud and scrapid fast, it wold not be.** Peccatum fuit adeo **clunge** anime humane quod nulla aqua, nulla ars potuit repellere, in tempus quo Christus rex celi ex misericordia, pietate, et compassione morie[ba]tur⁶² in cruce et respersit aqua et sanguine [*f. 46*]

---

56. salioris.
57. *blank.*
58. nigriter.
59. vnuta.
60. bonitatem.
61. circumfo'is.
62. morietur.

sought the influence of a healing remedy from heaven, which is **as clear as the crystal growing out of the rock**. As Bartholomew says in book 8 of *De proprietatibus rerum*, that heaven that is clear as crystal, which the teachers call the crystalline heaven, is **clean and clear**; it receives light from the higher heaven into itself **and sends it down** to the lower heaven.[21] What can be better compared to that heaven than the human soul, which, as the teachers say, was **clear** in paradise in all natural virtues and pure **from all filth** of vices and sin? It received the light of original justice from the highest heaven, **from God's high majesty**. The latter illuminated the heaven of man's soul so perfectly that the higher part of reason burned vigorously in contemplating God, and the lower part obeyed the higher, the body the soul; all things were at one in unity and concord. And the soul shed that light so fruitfully into the body that, if man had not sinned, he would through its virtue have been kept free from all misery, from death and all corruption. His will, memory, and intellect were so **perfect and full of beauty** that the almighty Father of heaven sent **down** his virtuous power into the memory, the Son his **perfect wisdom** into the intellect, and the Holy Spirit his gracious goodness into the free will. In this way the Blessed Trinity adorned the heaven of man's soul and made it the perfect image and likeness of its divinity. But alas, our forefather Adam, through the instigation of the devil, deformed the image of God. He so stained the heaven of man's soul with actual and original sin that all patriarchs and prophets in the Old Testament could not purify it. They tried many times, but it helped little. Enos, Enoch, and Noah, under the law of nature, took water and the blood of animals in sacrifice, **poured it on their stain, washed it keenly— it would not go away**. Later came Abraham and Moses with their law, and seeing that sin would not go **away** through washing, they invented a new trick: they took the sharp flint of circumcision, **scraped and scratched fast with it—it would not go away**. Sin **clung** so much to man's soul that no water, no human rite could repel it, until the time that Christ, the king of heaven, died on the cross out of mercy, pity, and

---

21. Bartholomaeus 8.3 (1485).

qui emanarunt de illius vulneribus. Iste liquor fuit adeo preciosus,⁶³ **so violent** [et]⁶⁴ corrosiue quod **it frete away** þe **hold rust** originalis peccati, lauit **away** þe **filth** actualium viciorum, et reformauit imaginem deitatis. Postquam Christus isto modo purgauerat celum anime, videns quod per fragilitatem corporis annexi anime potest faciliter returpari et deformari, recte sicut in celo superiori, celo scilicet cristallino, est aqua et eminens

430 claritas, sic in remedium contra ista in celo anime humane ordinauit ista duo: aquam contricionis **to wasche away al filth** peccati **and vnclennes,** et **briȝtnes** clare confessionis **to receyue** lumen gracie et bonitatis.

Primum remedium contra vicia in celo anime humane est aqua contricionis, etc. Ex quo nullus homo, [nec]⁶⁵ senex nec iuuenis, est purus a peccato, uel deturpatur fumo superbie et inuidie uel fimo luxurie uel gule, oþer mortali peccto uel venali, necesse est cuilibet habere istam aquam contricionis **and repentouns.** Set quis velit esse **a crafty lauandur** et lauare **awey** omnes maculas peccati, oportet adiscere suam artem a rege Ezechia. Iste rex, vt lego IIII Regum XX, **fel seke** in puncto mortis.

440 Dum sic iacuit, propheta Esaias venit ad eum et dixit: "Dispone pro domo tua et familia, quia morieris et non viues." Statim rex conuertit faciem suam ad parietem et fleuit adeo **sore** et amare quod Deus placatus remisit prophetam dicentem hec verba: "Audiui oracionem et vidi lacrimas tuas, et pro contricione quam habuisti in corde tuo liberabo te **of** þi **maledy** et custodiam te a cunctis inimicis." Iste rex spiritualiter nichil aliud est nisi h[ominis]⁶⁶ libera voluntas, que secundum Philosophum est suppremus gubernator in regno anime. þis rex **failith craft** quando desiderat aliquid contra legem Dei, set **he falth seke** in puncto mortis quando post longam deliberacionem, quando post longam cogitacionem

450 bene nouit quod offendit Deum et tunc delectatur in suo peccato. Dum est in isto statu, propheta, idest consciencia, que semper murmurat contra peccatum, venit ad eum, **wissid and warneth him of his missededes,** et dicit, "Dispone pro domo tua, corpore et anima, quia morieris et non viues." Et certe si ille rex velit curari a sua infirmitate, **he most** conuertere faciem suam ad parietem sicut Ezechias et flere amare. Quid est iste murus, creditis? Nichil aliud nisi peccata mortalia per prius perpetrata, quia sicut murus diuidit vnam domum ab alia, sic mortale peccatum

63. *add.* adeo, *apparently exp.*
64. in.
65. est.
66. h.

compassion and sprinkled it with the water and blood that flowed from his wounds. That liquor was so precious, **so violent** and corrosive, that **it ate away the old rust** of original sin, washed **away the filth** of actual sins, and restored the divine image. After Christ had in this fashion purified the heaven of the soul, seeing that because of the body's frailty attached to it the soul could easily become stained and deformed again, he established in the heaven of man's soul two things as remedies, just as in the higher heaven, that is, the crystalline heaven, there are water and an outstanding brightness: he established the water of contrition **to wash away all filth** of sin **and uncleanness**, and the **brightness** of clear confession **to receive** the light of grace and goodness.

The first remedy against vices in the heaven of man's soul is the water of contrition, etc. Because no man, neither old nor young, is pure from sin, but each is stained with the fumes of pride and envy or the dung of lechery or gluttony, **or** by deadly or venial sin, it is necessary for all to have this water of contrition **and repentance**. But whoever wishes to be **a skillful launderer** and wash **away** all stains of sin must learn his art from King Hezekiah. As I read in 2 Kings 20, this king **fell sick** to the point of death. As he was thus lying, the prophet Isaiah came to him and said: "Dispose your house and family, for you shall die and not live." At once the king turned his face to the wall and wept so **heavily** and bitterly that God was appeased and sent his prophet back, saying these words: "I have heard your prayer and seen your tears, and for the contrition you have had in your heart, I will free you **of your illness** and keep you safe from all enemies."[22] This king is nothing else than man's free will, which according to the Philosopher is the highest ruler in the kingdom of the soul. **This** king **lacks skill** when he desires anything against God's law, but **he falls sick** unto death when, after long deliberation and reflection, he knows well that he has offended God and yet delights in his sin. When he is in this state, the prophet, that is, his conscience, which always murmurs against sin, comes to him, **alerts and warns him of his misdeeds**, and says: "Dispose your house," body and soul, "for you will die and not live." And certainly, if this king wishes to be healed of his sickness, **he must** turn his face to the wall as did Hezekiah and weep bitterly. What is this wall, you think? Nothing other than the deadly sins formerly committed, for as a wall separates one house from another, so mortal sin separates man from

---

22. 2 Kings 20:1–6.

diuidit h[ominem][67] a Deo et Deum ab [anima][68] humana. Ad istum
murum oportet quemlibet habentem liberam voluntatem suam conuertere
460 faciem, intime cogitare quam grauiter offendit Deum suum, quas penas
meruit pro suo peccato, et quam turpiter polluit celum sue anime quod
Christus consecrauit suo precioso sanguine. Isto modo, si aliquis vestrum
sit in mortali peccato (quod absit), vertite vos ad istum murum et flete
amare, non solum oculo corporali **as faytors do** set oculo spirituali,
corde **with[in].**[69] Capiatis aquam contricionis, aspergite cum ista celum
anime vestre, et lauetis **away al filth** mortalis peccati. Si modo isto
feceritis, Deus seruabit vos a spiritualibus inimicis et sana[bit][70] adeo
graciusliche de vestro **malady** quod poteritis dicere cum propheta: "Misit
de celo et liberauit me," in Psalmo.
470 [*f. 46v*] Secundum[71] remedium contra peccatum in celo anime humane
est **briȝtnes** clare confessionis, etc. Ista confessio oris est necessaria cuilibet volenti saluari, quia ut Magister *Sentenciarum* dicit libro 4 sub
auctoritate Iacobi apostoli et Augustini, nemo potest ingredi paradisum
nec potest peruenire ad gaudium celi nisi confiteatur suo patri spirituali
si a[s]sit[72] facultas. Set ex quo tot sancti doctores plenarie determinarunt
quod oris confessio est necessaria cuilibet habenti discrecionem et loquelam, et sine illa non potest saluari, quomodo sunt isti lollardi **so bold**
predicare contrarium? Quomodo possunt inuenire in eorum cordibus
informare Christi populum quod non debent confiteri suis curatis?
480 Caueatis ab eis, quia certe doctrina est verum venenum, recta via ad
infernum. Et nunc in isto sacro tempore, si sitis **diffowlit** mortali peccato,
si perdidistis lumen gracie et virtutis, capiatis exemplum de pauone in
natura. Pauo, vt Vincencius refert in *Speculo naturali,* est pulcra auis
plena coloribus diuersis. Tantum in die delectatur in suis coloribus quod
nocte quando se non videt incipit gemere et clamare, credens se perdidisse
totam suam **bewte.** Ista pulcra auis plena diuersis coloribus est **mankinde,**
que secundum Gregorium habet **lyuing** cum arboribus, **feling** cum bestiis,
et intelligere cum angelis. Ista est pulcra auis quia fuit ad similitudinem
Dei. Ista deperdit colores gracie et virtutis statim vt cadit in noctem uel

---

67. h.
68. omnia.
69. w't inf'd (?).
70. sanare.
71. secundum *marg.*
72. absit.

God and God from man's soul. Whoever has free will must turn his face to this wall and reflect intimately how seriously he has offended his God, what punishment he has deserved for his guilt, and how vilely he has stained the heaven of his soul, which Christ has consecrated with his precious blood. In this way, if any of you is in deadly sin—may you be far from it!—turn to this wall and weep bitterly, not only with your bodily eye **as hypocrites do** but with your spiritual eye, with your heart **within**. Take the water of contrition, sprinkle it on the heaven of your soul, and wash **away all filth** of deadly sin. If you proceed in this fashion, God will keep you from your spiritual enemies and heal you so **graciously** of your **illness** that you can say with the prophet: "He has sent from heaven and delivered me."[23]

The other remedy against sin in the heaven of man's soul is the **brightness** of a clear confession, etc. This confession of mouth is necessary to anyone who wishes to be saved, for as Peter Lombard says in book 4, following the authority of the apostle James and Augustine, no one can enter paradise or come to the joy of heaven unless he confesses to his spiritual father if he has the opportunity.[24] But because so many holy teachers have fully proven that confession of mouth is necessary to everyone who has discretion and speech, and that without it he cannot be saved, how then are these Lollards **so bold** to preach the opposite? How can they find it in their hearts to teach the people of Christ that they must not confess to their parish priests? Beware of them, for certainly their doctrine is true poison, a straight way to hell. And now, in this holy season, if you are **defiled** with mortal sin, if you have lost the light of grace and virtue, take an example from nature, in the peacock. As Vincent reports in his *Speculum naturale,* the peacock is a bird full of divers colors. By day he delights so much in his colors that at night, when he does not see himself, he begins to sigh and shout, believing that he has lost all his **beauty**.[25] This beautiful bird full of divers colors is **mankind**, which according to Gregory shares **life** with the trees, **sensation** with animals, and intelligence with the angels.[26] It is a beautiful bird because it was created in the likeness of God. It lost its colors of grace and virtue as soon as it fell into the night or darkness

23. Ps. 56:4.
24. Cf. Lombard *Sent* 4.17.3 (2:348–50).
25. Vincent *Speculum naturale* 16.122 (1624, 1: cols. 1223–24).
26. Gregory *Homiliae in Evangelia* 2.29.2 (*PL* 76:1214).

490 tenebras mortalis peccati. Set si velis recuperare tuam antiquam speciem, oportet vt lugeas et clames recte sicut pauo. **þou most** primo penitere de tuis malefactis et conteri corde. Et hoc non sufficit, set oportet eciam vt clames. Vade ad ipsum qui habet curam anime tue, ne moreris de die in diem, ne defferas in terminum vite, set in isto sacro tempore vade ad **þi gostliche fadur,** clama in aure eius **þi mysleuynge, tel him** omnia tua peccata, **and take þi penaunce** pro illis. Si sic feceritis, Deus seruabit vos ab omnibus spiritualibus inimicis et sanabit vos adeo perfecte de vestra **maledy** quod poterit bene dici de quolibet vestrum: "Confessio eius super celum." Set quia omnis spiritualis salus in terra humani cor-
500 poris venit a celo anime, et omnes partes corporis diu languebant **in soroo and sekenes,** igitur miseri pro **sekenes sy[k]ing**[73] **helth** *querebant de celo,* sicut dixi in principio.

Dixi tercio quod **prisoners pynid with heuynes** querebant signum **of deliueraunce and mercy** de summo celo, vbi est **gracius comfort and blisful abidinge.** Licet mirabilis stella que vocatur comata, fulgur, et tonitruum ducant hominem in cognicionem potencie et sciencie Dei, nullum signum in celo ita directe ducit in cognicionem sue **myknes** et misericordiesicut [iris].[74] In cuius signum quando totum genus humanum exceptis octo personis destruebantur pro peccato in Noe flumine, om-
510 nipotens Deus habuit pietatem et compassionem super relictos **and in comfort** tocius humani generis promisit eis quod numquam voluit eos destruere postea per aquas et magna flumina. In euidens signum istius pacti et federis, vt sacra scriptura testatur Genesis IX, erexit iridem suam in nubes celi, vt quando homo [*f. 47*] istam videret, recordaretur federis quod Deus pepigit inter Deum et hominem, et confideret in eius mise-ricordia. Ideo, domini, quando respeximus istam iridem deberemus mul-tum iocundari et gaudere, quia est signum bonitatis et misericordie Dei. Moraliter ista aqua magna est flumen peccati in quo genus humanum fuit submersum et dampnatum. A tempore quo Adam peccauit in tempus
520 natiuitatis Christi aque peccati sic crescebant, **þe wawis wex so hye** quod **was þer neuer** mons tam altus, numquam fuit in toto isto tempore mas uel femina **so holi ne so parfite in leuynge** quin **he was ouerflow** isto flumine peccati. Tandem misericordiarum pater videns quod genus hu-manum **went al towrake and schuld ha ben lost** in isto flumine peccati,

---

73. syhing.
74. *blank.*

of mortal sin. But if you wish to recover your ancient beauty, you must mourn and cry just like the peacock. First **you must** repent your evil deeds and have heartfelt contrition. And this is not enough, but you must also cry out. Go to the one who has the cure of your soul. Do not delay from day to day, do not postpone until the end of your life, but go to **your spiritual father** in this holy season, cry into his ear **your misliving, tell him** all your sins, **and receive your penance** for them. If you do this, God will keep you from all spiritual enemies and heal you so perfectly of your **illness** that one can say of each of you, "His confession is above the heaven."[27] But because all spiritual well-being in the land of man's body comes from the heaven of his soul, and because all parts of the body languished for a long time **in sorrow and sickness**, the wretches in their **sickness seeking a remedy** *sought from heaven,* as I said in the beginning.

For the third part, I said that **prisoners afflicted with sadness** sought a sign **of deliverance and mercy** from the highest heaven, where there is **gracious comfort and blisful dwelling**. Even if that marvelous star called comet, or else lightning, or thunder could lead a man to recognize the power and knowledge of God, no sign in heaven leads him so directly to recognize his **meekness** and mercy as the rainbow. After the whole human race with the exception of eight persons was destroyed for its sin by Noah's flood, almighty God had pity and compassion over those left **and as a comfort** for all mankind promised them in this sign that he would never afterward destroy them through water and mighty floods. As an open sign of the pact and covenant, as Holy Scripture testifies in Genesis 9,[28] he set his rainbow in the clouds of heaven, so that whenever anyone saw it, he might remember the covenant God had plighted between himself and man and might trust in his mercy. Therefore, sirs, whenever we see this rainbow, we ought to rejoice much and make joy, for it is a sign of God's goodness and mercy. Morally speaking, this great water is the flood of sin in which mankind was submerged and condemned. From the time that Adam sinned to the time of Christ's birth, the waters of sin grew, **the waves climbed so high** that **there was never** a mountain so high, there was never in that whole time a man or woman **so holy or so perfect in living** but **he was washed over** by this flood of sin. At the last, as the father of mercies saw that mankind **was going to be shipwrecked and should have been lost** in this flood of sin,

---

27. Ps. 148:14.
28. Gen. 9:13.

habuit magnam compassionem de illis, et de infinita sua bonitate misit
de celo suum proprium Filium, secundam personam in Trinitate, qui
moriebatur in cruce in die Parasceues, effudit sanguinem cordis sui pro
nostro **sake, and of his endles mercy** fecit istud pactum nobiscum: "Qui
crediderit et baptizatus fuerit saluus erit," Marci XVI. In signum euidens
530   istius federis erexit iridem suam, i[dest][75] gloriosos sanctos humani generis, martires, virgines, et confessores, in summum celum quod vocatur
empireum. Et secundum quod merita fuerunt maiora hic in via, sic
remunerat eos ibi, erigit eos superius et superius in ordinibus angelorum.

    Set possuntne sancti comparari iridi? Eciam racionabiliter, quia sicut
Philosophus dicit 3 *Metheororum,* recte vt [in][76] iride sunt tres colores
qui reddant ipsam delectabilem humano visui, sic in ista spirituali iride,
nostris sanctis, sunt tres colores beatitudinis. Primus color in materiali
iride est rubeus. Iste est ardens amor, quem sancti in supprema ierarchia
angelorum habent in Deo suo. Isti sunt ascessores Dei semper morantes
540   in eius [*blank*]. Sunt [ita] propinqui eius **briȝt** maiestati quod radii deitatis tangunt eorum liberam voluntatem et faciunt ibi tantum ignem
dileccionis quod numquam potest extingui; numquam cessant a contemplacione benedicte Trinitatis, set semper ardent in perfecto amore et clara
visione sue graciose deitatis. Medius color in materiali iride est viridis,
qui designat **mirth and solace**. Ista est perfecta securitas quam sancti in
media ierarchia habent de sua beatitudine, quia sicut viredo pre aliis
coloribus est delectabilis oculo et confortat visum, sic quando isti sancti
vident þe **briȝt godhed** et cognoscunt quod sunt securi, de ista beatitudine
multum gaudent. Et non mirum, quia secundum Augustinum XIII *De*
550   *Trinitate* securitas est maxima pars beatitudinis illorum. Infimus color
in materiali iride est **a pale** terrestris color. Iste conuenit sanctis \in/
infima ierarchia angelorum, quia ex quo intellectus istorum non est ita
clarus nec recipiunt tantum lumen a deitate sicut alii superiores, gaudium
eorum est minus, color beatitudinis eorum est pallidus respectu aliorum.
Et licet alii sint superiores in beatitudine et habeant maius perfectum
gaudium quam isti, non est **strif** nec lis inter ipsos, non est superbia in
superiori nec inuidia in inferiori, set quilibet letus de gaudio alterius **and
ioyful** in suo proprio, quia gaudium minimi est adeo magnum quod
omnes clerici terre nesciunt magnitudinem referre.

---

75. in.
76. *om.*

he had great compassion for them, and out of his infinite goodness, he
sent his own son from heaven, the second person in the Holy Trinity,
who died on the cross on Good Friday, shed the blood of his heart for
our **sake, and out of his endless mercy** made this covenant with us:
"Whoever believes and is baptized will be saved," Mark 16.[29] As an
open sign of this covenant, he set his rainbow, that is, the glorious saints
of mankind, the martyrs, virgins, and confessors, in the highest heaven,
which is called the empyrean. And according to the greatness of their
merits here on their way, he rewards them there and places them higher
and higher in the orders of angels.

But can the saints be compared to the rainbow? Yes, indeed, for as
the Philosopher says in book 3 of his *Meteorologica,* just as there are
three colors in the rainbow that make it delightful to human sight,[30] so
there are three colors of blessedness in this spiritual rainbow, our saints.
The first color in the material rainbow is red. That is the fervent love
that the saints, in the highest order of angels, have for their God. They
sit next to God and always live in his [presence]. They are so close to
his **bright** majesty that the divine rays touch their free will and make
there such a great fire of love that it can never be quenched; they never
cease from contemplating the blessed Trinity, but always burn in the
perfect love and the clear vision of its gracious godhead. The color in
the middle of the material rainbow is green, which signifies **mirth and
solace.** This is the perfect certainty that the saints in the middle of the
heavenly hierarchy have of their bliss, for just as green, before the other
colors, is pleasing to the eye and soothes the sight, so, when these saints
see **the bright godhead** and understand that they are secure, they have
great joy of this bliss. And this is no wonder, for according to Augustine
in book 13 of *De Trinitate,* security is the greatest part of their bliss.[31]
The lowest color in the material rainbow is **a pale** earthen one. This fits
the saints in the lowest rank of the angels, for because their intellect is
not as clear and because they do not receive as much light from the
godhead as the other, higher ones, their joy is less, the colors of their
bliss is pale in comparison with that of the others. Yet although the
others are higher in bliss and have a more perfect joy than these, there
is no **strife** or contest between them, there is no pride in the higher group
or envy in the lower, but each is happy at the joy of the other **and joyful**

---

29. Mark 16:16.
30. Aristotle *Meteor* 3.2 (371b–372a).
31. Augustine *De Trinitate* 13.7.10 (*CC* 50A:394).

560 Ista[m][77] **blisful reynbow** Christus erexit in summum celum omnium,
vt quociens eam videret haberet memoriam sui federis et [*f. 47v*] mise-
re[re]tur[78] humano generi. Ideo tu qui diu fuisti **prisoner** diaboli et iacuisti
vinctum in mortali peccato, quantumcumque peccasti, licet iacuisti in
isto per totam vitam, **be** peccatum tuum **neuer so gret ne so greuous**,
numquam cadas in desperacionem, **lift vp** tuum oculum ad istam **blessid**
iridem, fige tuam spem et cor super illos sanctos, **and beseche hom of
help. And dowtles** si ita feceris **and be** in voluntate dimittendi peccatum
tuum, habebis veniam et misericordiam. Et hic refero vobis pulcram
fabulam.

570 Legi tarde quod fuit quidam Normandie vocatus Geruaise. Ille fuit
magnus fur, homicida, **a dislauy man** \de/ suo corpore **and a vicius man
with all. þis** vitam duxit ʒeris **and dayes**, numquam se dedit bonitati nec
deuocioni, excepto quod prope vbi manebat fuit capella **bild** in honore
omnium sanctorum; et cotidie pretereundo dixit, "Omnes sancti, orate
pro me." Tandem iste homo cecidit in magnam etatem, et sicut iacuit
in lecto suo, incepit recordare de sua mala vita et dixit: "**Alas**, victum
non habeo, etas **is fal** super me quod non possum laborare **ne bestere
me abowte** vt olim. Tant[o][79] sum exosus patrie quod si fuero captus
suspendar uel perdam caput meum. **And alas** quod vmquam fui natus.

580 Offendi Deum meum adeo grauiter quod **trulich** credo dampnari." Et in
ista cogitacione, [t]am[80] diabolica temptacione quam sua pe[n]ali[81] **sorue,
þes woful wrecche fel in dispair.** Et sicut ibat ad mergendum se, preteribat
capellam et non dixit oracionem suam. Statim Petrus apostolus clamauit
dixitque: "Geruais, quo vadis, quare non dicis oracionem vt solebas?"
Ipse vero attonitus perstitit. "Geruais," dixit apostolus, "**þou hast mony
day made þi deuocioun** nobis **and trust** in precibus nostris, **and trulich**
iam in maxima necessitate non eris deceptus. Reuertere, confitere, et
emenda vitam tuam, et societas mea et ego exorabimus patrem misericordiarum pro te, **and trulich** habebis misericordiam." Ille reuertebatur,

590 **schrof him,** et emendauit vitam, et precibus omnium sanctorum fecit
letum finem. Attendite quo laque[o][82] ille fuerat captus, quamdiu fuit

---

77. ista.
78. miseretur.
79. tante.
80. quam.
81. pelali.
82. laque.

in its own, for the joy of the lowest is so great that all the scholars on earth cannot describe it.

Christ set this **blessed rainbow** in the highest heaven of all so that, whenever he looked at it, he would remember his covenant and have mercy on mankind. Therefore you, who have long been a **prisoner** of the devil and lain bound in mortal sin, however much you have sinned, even if you have lain in it for your whole life, **be** your sin **ever so great or so grievous**, do not ever fall into despair; **lift up** your eye to that **blessed** rainbow, set your hope and heart on those saints, **and beseech them of help. And doubtless,** if you do so **and are** willing to leave your sin, you will have forgiveness and mercy. And here I tell you a beautiful story.

I read the other day that there was someone in Normandy by the name of Gervais. He was a great thief, a murderer, **a dissolute man** in his body **and a vicious man withal. This** life he led **for years and days;** he never engaged in any good deed or devotion, except that close to where he stayed there was a chapel **built** in honor of all the saints, and each day as he went by, he said, "All you saints, pray for me." In the end this man declined into great age, and as he lay in his bed, he began to remember his evil life and said: "**Alas,** I have no livelihood, age **has fallen** on me so that I cannot work **or be busy** as formerly. I am banished from my country so that, if I were to be caught, I would be hanged or lose my head. **And alas** that I was ever born. I have offended my God so grievously that I **truly** believe to be damned." And with this thought, both through the devil's temptation and through his own painful **sorrow, this woeful wretch fell into despair.** And as he was going to drown himself, he came by the chapel and did not say his prayer. At once the apostle Peter cried out and said: "Gervais, where are you going? Why don't you say your prayer as usual?" He stopped dumbfounded. "Gervais," the apostle said, "**you have many days made your devotion** to us **and trusted** in our prayers, **and truly,** now in your greatest need, you will not be deceived. Turn back, confess, and amend your life, and my fellows and I will beseech the father of mercies for you, **and truly** you will have mercy." He turned back, **shrove himself,** and amended his life, and through the prayers of all the saints, he had a happy end. Behold with what a fetter he had been bound,

prisoner diaboli, et quam graciose fuit deliberatus. **Takis** þis ad cor, **print** þis in mente vestra, et in quocumque **heuynes and soroo** sitis, **lokit vp** ad istam iridem, **set** vestram spem super illos sanctos, quia ad preces illorum "aperiet Dominus thesaurum suum, optimum celum, et det pluuiam terre tue," Deuteronomii XXVIII.

Hoc percipientes **prisoners** antiquitus quod omnis **gracius comfort** venit signum misericordie **and releuynge,** *querebant de celo* sicut dixi in principio. Et ex quo fuerunt liberati de sua seruitute per **trust** et bonam
600 spem ad istos sanctos, vos qui estis in aliqua seruitute diaboli in mortali peccato numquam cadatis in desperacionem, **lokith vp** super[83] istam iridem et confidite **olliche** in Dei misericordia.

Si ita feceritis, verificabitur de vobis illud Deuteronomii primo: "Estis sicut stelle celi. Dominus Deus addat ad hunc numerum multa milia et benedicat vobis." "Estis sicut stelle celi," **ȝe beth as veri sterris**—in celo Ecclesie, sol curatorum, luna diuitum, et planeta Mercurius **of smale vitrel[er]is,**[84] pro primo principali. "Dominus Deus addat ad hunc numerum multa milia," Deus **ichet and in-** [*f. 48*] **cresced** multa milia virtutum—in celo anime vestre ad numerum contricionis et confessionis,
610 pro secundo. "Et benedicat vobis" omnipotens Deus, **ȝif ȝow alle** suam benediccionem a summo celo—con[ce]dat[85] **alle prisoners**[86] veniam et misericordiam de suis peccatis, pro tercio. Istam misericordiam et benediccionem concedat vobis sum[m]us[87] pontifex celi, Christus Iesus, qui sacrauit celum Ecclesie et celum anime suo precioso sanguine, et in vna deitate cum Patre et Spiritu Sancto regnat **in** þe **empire** summi celi. Amen. Quod Io S.

---

83. *written twice.*
84. vitrelis.
85. condat.
86. prisonerers.
87. sumus.

how long he was a **prisoner** of the devil, and how graciously he was freed. **Take this** to heart, **print this** in your mind, and in whatever **heaviness and sorrow** you may be, **look up** to that rainbow, **set** your hope in those saints, for at their prayers, "the Lord will open his treasure, the highest heaven, and give rain to your land," Deuteronomy 28.[32]

When **prisoners** of old perceived that all **gracious comfort** was coming, *they sought from heaven* the sign of mercy **and relief**, as I said in the beginning. And because they were delivered out of their servitude through their **trust** and good hope in these saints, you, who are in any servitude of the devil in mortal sin, do not fall into despair, **look up** on that rainbow, and trust **wholly** in God's mercy.

If you do so, the verse of Deuteronomy 1 will come true of you: "You are like the stars of heaven. May the Lord God add to that number many thousand and bless you."[33] "You are like the stars of heaven," **you are like true stars**—in the heaven of the Church, you are the sun of the clergy, the moon of the rich, and the planet Mercury **of small victuallers**, according to my first principal part. "May the Lord God add to this number many thousand," may God **add and increase** many thousand virtues—in the heaven of your soul to the number of contrition and confession, according to my second part. "And may" almighty God "bless you," **give you all** his blessing from the highest heaven—may he concede **to all prisoners** forgiveness and mercy of their sins, according to my third part. May this mercy and blessing be given to you by the high priest of heaven, Jesus Christ, who consecrated the heaven of the Church and the heaven of your soul with his precious blood, and who reigns as one God with the Father and the Holy Spirit **in the empire** of the highest heaven. Amen. So said John S.

---

32. Deut. 28:12.
33. Deut. 1:10–11.

Sermon W-154, *Quem teipsum facis*

Worcester Cathedral, MS F.10, ff. 289rb–291va (W-154).

W-154 has the following structure:

Protheme:

> The words of the thema apply to man's fall from dignity into sin. The preacher would have liked to treat of man's dignity and his sin, but he bypasses these topics as of now (1–17). (The original protheme, see lines 512–81, has been replaced with a shorter text as edited.)

Prayer: 17–22.

Division:

> Man is led to sin by the falseness of the world, the subtleness of the devil, and the frailty of his own nature (23–32).

Part 1:

> Worldly acclaim and prosperity are transitory. Example of Christ. Debate between Well and Woe, about which of them is the greater. That either can come after the other is shown in a biblical figura (the angelic guard at the entrance of Eden), authoritative quotation (Gregory), and example (falcon and hen). Hence it is folly to trust in the world: exemplum of a man chased by a unicorn (33–232).

Part 2:

> The devil tempts us with his subtlety. Like a physician, he recommends bitter medicine as sweet. His suggestions when we want to do good works. Example of two merchants selling trifles and charity (233–391).

Part 3:

> Pride makes us forget our human frailty. It also is the cause of

false doctrines in the contemporary church, especially (a) that one must not pray to any saint, and (b) that one should not give tithes or (c) pay heed to the priest's excommunication. Arguments against (a); a warning exemplum against (b) and (c) (392–498).

Summary, recapitulation, and concluding formula: 499–511.

Quem teipsum facis? Iohannis viii capitulo, et in ewangelio hodierno.

Ista verba primitus recitata sunt scripta in ewangelio hodierno, et
sunt tantum dicere in anglicis ad vestrum intellectum.

Domini,[1] si consideracionem habere vellemus ad statum, gradum, et
dignitatem in quibus omnipotens Deus ex sua interminabili gracia et
bonitate posuit genus humanum in suo principio, et ex alia parte si
aduertere voluerimus ad **wrechedenes, myschef,** et indignitatem in que
homo ipse ex propria stulticia per peccatum se involuit, racionabiliter
cum admiracione et dolore possunt recitari verba que sumpsi in predi-
10 cacionem: Miser homo, *quem teipsum facis*? vt in principio dixeram.

Et[2] proposui declarasse in parte statum \et/ gradum in quibus omnipotens Deus hominem fecit in principio, et miseriam et **myschef** in
quas homo se precipitauit, quali et honori per suam passionem restaurauit
nos, et quali **vnhoornes** nos inducimus post recepcionem sacramenti
baptismi per peccatum. Set quoniam nollem vos diu tardare et hec materia meo iudicio melius potest omitti quam intendo Dei gracia tangere
posterius, ideo preterio ab illa. Set antequam vlterius progrediamur,
secundum venerabilem et necessariam consuetudinem Ecclesie eleuemus
corda Deo omnipotenti deprecando quod immittat talem graciam inter
20 nos ad presens quod hoc opus cui innitimur possit sic principiari et finiri
quod sit sibi placitum et exspediens ac meritorium tam vobis quam michi.
In qua deprecacione, etc.

[*f. 289va*] Secundum catholicorum doctorum sentenciam tria sunt
inter cetera que hominem inducunt in peccati miseriam. Primum est
instabilis iste mundus et sua falsitas; secundum diaboli subtilitas; et
tercium humana fragilitas. Habendo tunc respectum ad statum in quo
consistit dum est in gracia, et similiter ad **vnhornes** ad quam se inducit
per peccatum, secundum processum quem prius dixi cuilibet deturpanti
se per peccatum non renuendo instabilis mundi falsitatem, non fugiendo
30 diaboli subtilitatem, non videndo nec cognoscendo propriam fragilitatem, illi possum dicere pro quolibet horum trium: Miser homo, *quem
facis teipsum?*

Dico[3] primo et principaliter quod cuilibet homini qui per instabilem
istum mundum est tractus peccato, qui non renuit eius falsitatem, illi

---

1. < Introduccio > .

2. Et . . . deprecacione etc.] *in bottom margin, marked for insertion, to replace the
longer protheme referred to and written in the body of the text, here reproduced below.*

3. < Primum principale. >

Translation

Whom do you make yourself to be? John 8, and in the gospel for today.[1]

The words just recited are written in today's gospel, and are, for your understanding, in English as follows.

My Lords, if we consider the state, degree, and dignity in which almighty God out of his limitless grace and goodness put mankind in the beginning, and if on the other hand we pay attention to the **wretchedness, misery,** and unworthiness into which man by his own stupidity got himself through sin, we may rightly say, with both admiration and mourning, the words I selected for my sermon—Wretched man, *whom do you make yourself to be?*—as I said in the beginning.

I had planned to describe in part the state and degree in which God in the beginning placed man, as well as the wretchedness and **misery** into which man hurled himself, and further to what honor God restored us through his passion as well as what **corruption** we let ourselves fall into through sin after we have received baptism. But as I would not detain you too long, and because, in my judgment, this matter can be easily omitted as I plan with God's grace to touch on it later, I bypass it for now. But before going further, let us, after the venerable and necessary custom of the Church, lift our hearts to God almighty and pray that he send us the grace now that the work we tend to may be begun and finished in such a way as to be pleasing to him and helpful and meritorious to you and me. In this prayer, etc.

According to the thought of our Catholic teachers, there are three things among others that lead people to the wretchedness of sin. The first is this unstable world and its deceit; the second, the devil's subtleness; and the third, human frailty. If we then consider man's state while he was in grace, and likewise the **vileness** into which he falls through sin, following the argument that I outlined earlier, I can thus say to anyone who defiles himself through sin when he does not reject the deceit of this unstable world, or flee the devil's subtleness, or see and understand his own frailty, these words that apply to all three: Wretched man, *whom do you make yourself to be?*

First, and for my first principal part, I say that I can apply the words selected in the beginning—Wretched man, *whom do you make yourself*

---

1. John 8:53, from the gospel for Passion Sunday.

possum dicere verba que sumpsi in principio: Miser homo, quem es tu
te\ipsum/ faciens? Domini, si vellemus et sciremus cordialiter attendere
et vti recto ingenio et discrecione que nobis Deus contulit, mundi falsitas
et instabilitas sunt ita publice nobis ostense ad oculum quod quilibet
homo tam doctus quam illiteratus posset ea videre pariterque cognoscere
40   si vellet. Numquid non publice quasi cotidie videmus quod vbi mundus
est maxime florens **and gay** in aliqua persona qui habet vt apparet
mundum ad votum, dum **chyryfeyr** suum durat credit se ita securum
et portat se **so brag** in dampnum suorum proximorum acsi mundus
perdidisset suam naturam et semper staret in eodem statu? Set istud
non potest esse, quia mundus wlt sequi cursum et naturam, que sunt
variari et non in vno statu permanere. Mundus enim dicitur quasi undique motus, et credatis firmiter quod ita fuit, est, et erit, et non aliter.
<Scrutemur> scripturam sacram, tam nouum testamentum quam ve-
tus, legamus cronicas, et inveniemus quod in omni statu et gradu mundus
50   habuit et seruauit suum cursum. Et credatis quod nos non sumus me-
liores quam patres nostri, nec diebus nostris pro nobis mutabit naturam.
Videamus Christum saluatorem nostrum, quem vno die et tempore
populi eum voluissent rapuisse et fecisse regem, vt patet Iohannis 6°
capitulo; similiter, sicud ewangelium Iohannis \5/ quod lectum fuit
in Ecclesia hodie ad septimanam mencionem facit, multitudo magna
[*f. 289vb*] tam in mari quam in terra \sequebatur eum/ propter signa
que faciebat. Set quid, creditis quod ista prosperitas fuit permanens et
stabilis? Non, pro certo, set sicud ewangelium hodiernum facit mencionem, tulerunt lapides et eum voluissent lapidasse, et quia tunc non
60   potuerunt complere maliciam quam conceperant erga eum, quando habuerunt tempus conueniencius post implere suum malum velle. \Et/
quando peregissent sibi maxima **vylenyes and dyssputes** vmquam facta
alicui creature, imposuerunt sibi mortem turpissimam et horribilissi-
mam. De istis **shame and vylenye** quas Christo intulerunt ipsemet loquitur per prophetam Ieremiam Trenorum 3 capitulo, vbi dicit: "Factus
sum in derisum non vni homini set omni populo." Et si sic tunc vertebatur mundus cum ipso qui fuit verus Deus et homo, non mireris tu
quisquis sis si ostendat in te aliqualiter de cursu suo subtrahendo a te

to be—to any person who is drawn to sin by this unstable world and does not reject its deceit. My lords, if we wanted to pay intimate attention and knew how to do so and use the rightmindedness and discretion that God has given us, the world's deceit and instability are so openly shown to our sight that any human being, whether learned or illiterate, could see and recognize them if he wanted to. Do we not see it openly and, as it were, every day that, when the world is most flourishing **and cheerful** in someone who has, as it seems, the world at his will, as long as his **cherry fair** lasts, he thinks he is so secure and bears himself **so arrogantly** over his neighbors' misfortunes as if the world had lost its characteristic and were always stable and lasting. But it cannot be so, for the world will follow its course and nature, to change and never to remain the same. For *mundus,* "the world," is thus called as if it were *motus undique,* "whirled everywhere,"[2] and you must firmly believe that it has always been, is, and will be so and not otherwise. Let us investigate Holy Writ, both Old and New Testament; let us read histories; and we shall find that in every estate and rank, the world has held and kept its course. And you may well believe that we are no better than our forebears, nor will nature change its course for us in our time. Look at Christ, our Savior: On one day, at one moment, the people wanted to carry him off and make him a king, as is reported in John 6[3]; similarly, as the gospel of John 5 that was read in the church a week ago mentions, a large crowd followed him on water and on land because of the signs he was working.[4] But do you think this natural success lasted and stood firm? No, to be sure, but as today's gospel mentions, they took stones and wanted to kill him;[5] and as they could not carry out their malice against him at that point, they were going to have their evil will on him later at a more convenient time. And after showing him the greatest **vileness and despite** ever done to a creature, they imposed the most shameful and horrible death on him. Of this **shame and villainy** that they inflicted on Christ, he himself speaks through the prophet Jeremiah in Lamentations 3, where he says: "I have become a mockery," not to one person alone, but "to all the people."[6] Hence, if the world dealt

---

2. The etymology derives from Isidore *Etym.* 13.1.1, though the use of *undique* is later. My translation seeks to imitate the wordplay that is involved.

3. John 6:15.

4. John 6:2, in the gospel lection for 4 Lent.

5. John 8:59.

6. Lam. 3:14.

wele et prossperitatem qui fuit ita audax tot magisteria sibi vsurpare in
70   Filio Dei et suo auctore. Non confidas tunc in mundana prossperitate
si tibi arrideat, nec ponas cor tuum nimis alte in desspiciendo et op-
primendo pauperes proximos, quoniam licet sis in alto statu vel gradu
et habeas mundi **wele at wylle,** nescis quam cito per casum tuum **wele**
debet elabere et eris involutus vndique cum **woo.** Et quod hoc sit verum
et euidens ita fore volo ostendere.

Quidam doctor—et dicitur quod est dominus Lincolniensis in quodam
tractatu suo—habet istum conceptum quod quondam fuit magna dis-
cordia inter **Wele and Woo,** que illarum haberet alciorem manum et
magis moraretur inter homines. Et quelibet earum fecit raciones pro
80   parte sua. Et primo **Wele** dixit isto modo pro parte sua: "Deus, inquit,
in principio sequestrauit me et te, et me ordinauit secum esse in celo et
cum omnibus quos ille dilexit et ipsi eum; et te ordinauit sequestrari ab
illo et ab omnibus quos ipse dilexit et ipsi eum et posuit esse in infernum,
ibidem exspectare <solum> cum ipsis qui sibi fuerunt contrarii. Set
inter omnes creaturas Deus habet et habuit specialem dileccionem ad
hominem. Ergo voluit te sequestrari ab illis et me cum illis iugiter permanere." Tunc respondit Dolor et dixit: "In principio Deus ordinauerat
hominem fuisse in eterna quiete et **wele** et dedit ei eleccionem vtrum
vellet permanere in **wele** vel recedere et ponere se **to woo.** Tunc homo
90   spontanee te dimisit et elegit me. Set per legem et racionem, si homo
sit positus in eleccione duorum, tale quod eligit habebit. Ex quo tunc
homo elegit **wo,** et Deus deputauit similiter hominem **to woo** post peccatum, secundum testimonium scripture in principio, ergo," dixit **Woo,**
"ego habebo alciorem manum et principatum inter homines." Tunc respondit **Wele** et dixit: "Licet ita sit," dixit, "quod homo imprudenter
dimisit me et elegit te, tamen Christus passionem acerbam sustinuit ad
restaurandum hominem iterum **to wele fro wo,** sicud ipsemet dicit Apocalipsis: 'Iam non erit amplius neque luctus neque clamor, set nec vllus
<dolor>'; et causam subdit: 'Ecce, noua facio omnia,' Apocalipsis xxi.
100   Ergo tunc Christus passus fuit ad ammouendum **woo** ab homine, et
passio Christi non potest esse frustrata. Per racionem ego debeo prin-
cipari inter homines secundum exigenciam passionis Christi, et tu eris
expulsa." Tunc respondit **Woo** [et]⁴ dixit: "Christus per passionem suam
non adquisiuit aliquid homini quod esset causa dampnacionis hominis

---

4. non.

in this fashion with the one who was true God and man, do not be astonished, whoever you are, if it shows its course to some extent in you as well by taking your **wellbeing** and prosperity away from you, after it lorded it so brashly over the Son of God, its own maker. Therefore, do not trust in worldly prosperity when it smiles on you or set your heart too high by despising and oppressing your poor neighbors; for even if you stand in high estate and degree and have the world's **wealth at your will**, reflect on how soon your **wealth** must dwindle when you fall and how you then become wrapped in **woe** on all sides. This is true and evident, as I will show you.

A certain teacher—said to be Grosseteste—in a treatise of his presents this conceit: There was once a great strife between **Well and Woe**, as to which of them had the upper hand and was more revered among men. Each of them gave reasons in her favor. First **Well** spoke as follows for herself: "In the beginning, God separated me and you; he ordained me to be with him in heaven, and with all whom he loved and who loved him; but you he ordered to be separated from him and from all whom he loved and who loved him, and he placed you in hell, where you were to wait with those who were against him. But among all creatures, God loves and loved mankind especially. Therefore he wanted you to be separated from them, and me to dwell with them forever." Then Woe replied and said: "In the beginning, God had ordained that man should remain in eternal rest and **wellbeing**, and he gave him the choice whether he wanted to remain in **wellbeing** or else depart and stay **with Woe**. At that point mankind freely left you and chose me. Now, according to law and reason, once mankind was given the choice between two things, he would get what he chose. Because man therefore chose **Woe**, God similarly assigned him **to Woe** after his sin, as Scripture in the beginning testifies. *Ergo*," said **Woe**, "I have the upper hand and first place among men." Then **Well** answered and said: "It may well be the case that man imprudently left me and chose you. Yet Christ suffered most bitter pains to restore man **to Well from Woe**, as he himself says in Revelation: 'There will be no more sorrow and weeping, nor any pain.' And he adds the reason for this: 'Behold, I make all things new,' in Revelation 21.[7] Therefore, Christ suffered to remove **Woe** from man, and his passion must not be made void. Thus it is reasonable that I hold the first place

---

7. Rev. 21:4–5.

et occasio ammissionis gaudii celestis. Set tu, **Wele,** sepius per tuam
falsitatem promittis homini plura et non potes nec imples promissa, et
sic plures ad confidenciam trahis per quam sunt decepti et sunt audaciores
Deum offendere per peccatum et retrahere se a via bone vite." Post
longam ergo dissputacionem ad sedandum litem concordate sunt in hunc
110   modum, scilicet quod vna illarum veniret post aliam, [*f. 290ra*] ita scilicet
quod post **Wele** veniret **Woo** et econtra. Et ita **rest** fuit et erit audacter.

Et istius concordie veritas numquam magis practizata fuit quam in
diebus nostris de corporali prossperitate et dolore. Et quod post corporale
wele venit sempiternus dolor [*caret, perhaps with insertion in top margin,
partially cropped?*] euidens est, et possum istud ostendere figura, auctoritate, et exemplo. Primo figura sic. Legimus in scriptura Genesis 3°
capitulo quod postquam primus noster parens eiectus fuerat de paradiso,
omnipotens Deus oposuit in introitu paradisi inter hominem et eius
introitum custodiam angelicam que vocatur Cherubyn, et gladium flam-
120   meum atque versatilem, ita quod homo non posset habere ingressum
nisi per illa. Istam historiam pertractat venerabilis clericus Magister
Sentenciarum libro 2°, distinccione <29>, capitulo 5°, vbi habet per
hunc modum: "Cherubyn tantum est dicere sicud plenitudo sciencie, que
est caritas, quia 'plenitudo legis est dileccio,' Ad Romanos 13° capitulo.
Gladius vero ille qui est flammeus et versatilis, pene temporales sunt,
qu[e]⁵ sunt flammee, et versatiles quia pungitiue, acute, et volubiles,
nunc super, nunc subtus. Ita igitur ad custodiam ingressus paradisi positi
sunt quia non reditur ad paradisum nisi per cherubyn, scilicet caritatem
et dileccionem, et per gladium versatilem et flammeum, scilicet tolle-
130   ranciam temporalium passionum." Hinc tunc potestis videre quod sicud
scriptura bene intellecta commemorat, nullus potest venire ad gaudium
nisi per tolleranciam passionum.

Et hoc idem ostenditur auctoritate sic. Sanctus doctor Gregorius in
Omelia communi vnius virginis sic ait: "Nemo potest hic gaudere cum
seculo et in celo regnare cum Domino." Set antequam progrediamur

---

5. qui.

among men as a logical consequence of Christ's passion, and you will be expelled." To which **Woe** replied and said: "Through his passion Christ did not gain anything for man that would be the cause of his damnation and his loss of heavenly joy. But you, **Well,** through your deceit, often promise man many things that you cannot give, thereby seducing many to trust in you, by which they are deceived and become so much bolder to offend against God through sin and to withdraw from the way of the good life." After a long debate, they agreed to settle their conflict in this way: each of them would follow the other, so that after **Well** would come **Woe,** and the reverse. And thus there was **rest,** and it will remain so without disturbance.

The impact of this agreement concerning material wellbeing and suffering has never been felt more than in our days. That material **wellbeing** is followed by eternal woe is obvious; I can demonstrate this with a biblical figura, authorities, and examples. First with a biblical figura. We read in Scripture, Genesis 3, that after our forefather was cast out of paradise, almighty God placed an angelic guard at the entrance of paradise, to keep man from entering it. This was called Cherubim and had a flashing sword of fire, so that man could not reenter except in passing by them.[8] A venerable cleric, the Master of the *Sentences,* discusses the passage in book 2, distinction 29, chapter 5, where he says as follows: "*Cherubim* means as much as the fullness of knowledge, which is charity, for 'the fulfilling of the law is love,' Romans 13.[9] The flashing sword of fire are temporal sufferings, which are flashing and of fire because they sting bitterly, and they are quivering, now above, now below. They are placed at the entrance of paradise because one cannot return to paradise except by passing Cherubim, that is charity and love, and by passing the flashing sword of fire, that is, suffering temporal pains."[10] From this you see that, as Scripture tells us when it is rightly understood, no one can come to eternal joy except through suffering pains.

The same can be shown with an authoritative quotation as follows. The holy teacher Gregory says in his *Homily for One Virgin*: "No one can rejoice here with the world and in heaven reign with God."[11] But

8. Gen. 3:24.
9. Rom. 13:10.
10. Lombard *Sent* 2.29.5 (1:495).
11. Gregory *Homiliae in Evangelia* 1.11.4 [sic] (*PL* 76:1117).

debetis intelligere quod non est de intellectu scripture primitus recitate
nec de intencione sancti doctoris Gregorii quod omnes qui habent
mundanum[6] **ese, welþe, and prossperite** in istius mundi in magna parte
status, non possunt habere post hunc **welþe** et gaudium \and here wel/
140   in celo, set solum illi qui veniunt ad divicias temporales, **welþe**, et honores
per falsa media \et/ iniuridica, et quando ea habuerint postponunt pro
cura et dileccione illorum amorem Dei[7] et sunt onerosi proximis per
oppressiones et extorsiones que nunc nimis abundant diebus, quod maius
dampnum est. Tales qui decipiendo adquirunt divicias vel extorsiones et
consimilia, faciunt directe contra preceptum diuinum datum in lege veteri
et noua, sicud patet per doctores et ewangelium, Luce 6º capitulo, vbi
expresse precipitur sic: "Prout wltis vt faciant vobis homines, et vos
facite illis." Set certum est quod nullus <talis> contentaretur si alius
ab ipso per talia media recitata raperet bona illius et nollet quod sibi
150   alius ita faceret. Igitur secundum iura diuina et preceptum non deberet
ita facere proximo. De talibus vere verificabitur quod post gaudium venit
luctus.

Et hoc volo ostendere vobis per exemplum sicud prius promisi. Quoniam erit de illis qui ita lucrantur mundanos honores et **wele** et aliis qui
viuunt pacifice in paupertate, dolore, et **woo** mundi sicud est secundum
conceptum doctoris Holcote in lectura super librum Sapiencie de generosis auibus, scilicet **goshaukes, sperhawkes**, et talibus generosis
fowles. Ita fuit eciam de caponibus, gallinis, et ceteris domesticis **fowles**.
Scitis bene dum tales generose aues viuunt et sunt **sounde**, custodiuntur
160   satis sollicite et care et ponuntur circa dominum prope in aulis super
perticas, et habent sub se cirothecas pro offensione **of hure talouns**; et
si dominus spaciatus fuerit, [*f. 290rb*] ex specialitate secum portantur
et multa diligencia, sicud plures cognoscuntur, in eorum custodia est
adibenda. Set galline et capones dum viuunt, quando ambulant in domi-
bus officiorum, extra eiciuntur gardinum <et sterquilinium> et sequestrantur omnino ab aula et nullus est curatus cum custodia illorum.
Set tamen adueniente morte aues ille que fuerunt ita **tendurly** et sollicite
custodite sunt ab aula ad sterquilinium proiecte, gallina vero seu capo

---

6. *add.* \abundanciam diviciarum in quibus/.

7. *perhaps to be inserted here:* <in tantum quod est de eis sicud pluribus generosis
damicellis que quando perdunt virginitatem et cirothecas, magis dolent de cirothecarum
amissione quam virginitatis. Sic illi plus dolent de amissione rei temporalis quam Domini
Dei sui>, *in bottom margin.*

before I go on, you must understand that neither the just-quoted passage nor St. Gregory means to say that none who have worldly **ease, wealth, and prosperity** in a large part of their life in this world can, after this **wealth,** also have joy **and their wealth** in heaven. These authorities speak only of those who come to their temporal possessions, **wealth,** and honors through false and illegal means, and who, when they have attained them, put the love of God in second place because of their worry and love for their goods, and who are a burden on their neighbors through their oppression and extortion, which are rampant these days, which is a great disaster. People who acquire their wealth by deceit, extortion, or similar ways act directly against God's law that was given in both the Old and the New Testament, as is shown by our teachers and by the gospel, in Luke 6, where the explicit commandment is given: "Do as you wish that others do to you," etc.[12] Now, it is clear that none of these people would be happy if someone else took his goods in any of the ways I have mentioned; he would not want that someone else acted toward him in this way. Therefore, according to divine law and commandment, he should not do the same to his neighbor either. Of such people it is true that after joy comes woe.

And finally I will show you the truth of this also by an example, as I promised earlier. People who gain worldly honors and **wealth** in this way, and conversely others who live peacefully in poverty, pain, and **woe** in this world, will be just like noble **birds,** such as **goshawks, sparrowhawks,** and the like on one hand, and roosters, hens, and other domestic **fowl** on the other, according to a comparison drawn by Holcot in a lecture on the Book of Wisdom.[13] As you know well, as long as such noble birds live and are **well,** they are kept with care and love and held nearby in halls on perches, and they have gloves underneath to protect people **from their talons;** and when the lord goes for a walk, they are carried along, and, as many know, much care is spent on their keeping. Hens and roosters, on the other hand, while they are alive, if they walk through the dwelling of the administrators, they are chased out to the garden and dungheap and totally barred from the hall, and no one takes care of them. But when death comes, the birds that were kept so **tenderly** and with care are thrown out of the hall on the dungheap, whereas a

---

12. Luke 6:31.
13. Holcot, lectura 64C (1494).

est multum **made of** et per ministerium seruiencium domini est ducta
170 ad presenciam domini in magno gaudio sui et omnium suorum. Sic est
de istis qui decipiuntur per falsitatem mundi et ponunt cor suum in
gaudio eius, sicud sunt excellentes diuites, **marketbeters, and iurers,** qui
preferuntur aliis in foro et ecclesia, et vbicumque veniunt pascuntur et
custodiuntur nimis laute dum viuunt. Set in fine proiecti erunt in sterquilinium inferni, sequestrati a consorcio Domini celi ibi sine fine cruciari
et fetere; vbi isti pauperes et simplices, de quibus nemo considerauit,
per ministerium seruiencium, idest sanctorum angelorum, in aulam celi
<introducentur> ibidem continue cum gaudio Domini et beatorum
spirituum coregnaturi. Quilibet talis qui talem facit mutacionem potest
180 dicere illudaga dessperabilis." Ieremie 15 capitulo: "Factus est dolor meus
perpetuus et plaga dessperabilis."

Iudicet tunc vnusquisque in seipso numquid non sit magna stulticia
pro modico gaudio vel prosperitate et irracionabili voto quod quis habet
ad habendum temporalia que parum durabunt, que eciam necessario scit
cessare et nescit quam cito, et pro hiis facere se natiuum eterne dampn-
acioni. Plurimi nostrum sciunt quod mundus est instabilis et quod eius
prossperitas **faduþ and falluþ** sicud flos. Et si aliquis loquatur cum eis
de eius instabilitate, ipsi primo volunt loqui de eius **vnstabulnes** et volunt
dicere quod mundus est falsus et cotidie decipit plures. Set pro tota sua
190 pulcra loquela non sunt aliqui qui magis sunt **þral** mundo et magis
nituntur piscare et sollicitari se pro eius habenda prossperitate quam
ipsi. De quibus omnibus dici possunt \verba/ Christi que scribuntur in
ewangelio Matthei 23: "Dicunt set non faciunt."

Stulticiam talium et **onwyt** volo vobis ostendere per exemplum. Est
enim de talibus sicud de quodam de quo refert Wallensis in *Commu-
niloquio,* quasi in fine. Vnicornus, sicud dicit clericus ille, est animal
habens vnum cornu in fronte, et est tam ferox et acutum quod nec
inermis nec armatus ei potest resistere. Accidit tunc in certo tempore
quod quidam homo obuiauit isti periculoso animali, et videns illud sub-
200 traxit se, et animal subsequebatur. Ille timens bestiam insequentem as-

hen or a rooster is much **made of** and, through the ministrations of the lord's servants, brought into the lord's presence to his and his family's great joy. It goes in the same way with people who are deceived by the world's falseness and place their heart in its joy—wealthy men, **people who hang around the market, and jurors**; they are given preference to others in court and church, and wherever they appear they are fed and kept splendidly as long as they live. But in the end, they are thrown out on the dungheap of hell and blocked from the company of the lord of heaven, to suffer and rot there without end. On the other hand, the poor and simple, whom no one has thought of much, will be led into the high hall of heaven by the ministration of its servants, that is, the angels, and there they will reign forever in the joy of the Lord and his blessed spirits. Whoever comes to such a bad end can well say with Jeremiah 15: "My grief has become eternal and my wound without hope."[14]

Let everyone therefore judge for himself whether it is not a great folly, for the sake of a little joy or prosperity and the fulfillment of an unreasonable desire, to spend so much care on acquiring worldly goods that last so little, which we know must end, but do not know how soon, and for which one makes oneself a candidate for eternal damnation. Many among us know that the world is unstable and that its prosperity **fades and falls away** like a flower. And if one were to speak to them about the world's instability, they are the first to speak of its **unstableness**, and they will say the world is false and daily betrays many people. Yet inspite of all their nice talk, no one is a greater **slave** to the world than they are and tries to fish and strain for the world's prosperity more than they do. Of these people one can say Christ's words from the gospel of Matthew 23: "They do not practice what they preach."[15]

I will demonstrate for you their stupidity and **lack of understanding** in an example. They are like a man of whom John of Wales tells a story in his *Communiloquium*, near the end.[16] As that cleric says, the unicorn is an animal that has one horn on its forehead, and this is so fierce and sharp that no one can resist it, whether he is unarmed or armed. It happened some time that a man encountered this dangerous animal, and when he saw it, he drew back and the animal pursued him. As the man

---

14. Jer. 15:18.
15. Matt. 23:4.
16. John of Wales 7.1.2 (1489). The story "Man chased by a unicorn" is used widely in medieval literature; see Tubach 5022.

cendit arborem et resspiciens retro vidit vnicornem proximum promtum
ad ipsum <occidendum>. Asspexit subtus se et vidit duas bestias, albam
et nigram, radicem arboris super quam sedebat corrodentes. Resspexit
a latere vno et vidit draconem promtum vt ipsum devoraret. Ex alia
parte vidit ignem accensum vt ipsum combureret. In hiis periculis constitutus vidit inter ramos arboris pendencia rubeum pomum et modicum
mellis. Que sibi arripuit et oblitus est tocius periculi, et tamdiu in istis
delectabatur donec radices arboris per illa duo animalia fuerunt corrosa
et arbor cecidit cum illo qui supersedit. Quem vnicornus interfecit, draco
210   deuorauit, et ignis consumpsit.

Per istum hominem intelligere possum quemlibet deditum ex toto
corde amori gaudii et prossperitatis mundane. Vnicornus insequens est
mors, qui non habet nisi vnum cornu, cum quo non parcit nec regi nec
principi, domino nec militi, nec alicui alteri in quocumque sit gradu
constitutus. Arbor quam ascendit est mundus. Pomum et mel signant
wele, worshup, et gloriam mundi. Draco paratus eum deuorare est diabolus; ignis, pena infernalis; duo bestie alba et nigra, dies et nox, que
continue minuunt terminum vite humane. Iste homo fugiens mortem
ascendit in mundum, quod est dicere posuit suam confidenciam super
220   iuventa etate et fortitudine, per que credit se satis securum. [*f. 290va*]
Tandem per casum memoratus sui et status in quo est intuetur, licet
ficte, quod per istas duas bestias vita imminuitur et finis instat. Videt
eciam et percipit per predicatores verbi Dei quod peccatores tales in fine
diabolus deuorabit et ipsos in ignem infernalem proiciet. Inter illa pericula <in arbore, scilicet> in mundo, mel et pomum vidit pendencia,
scilicet **worshup and wele,** et ponit totum ingenium et consideracionem
super illa. Quid accidit tunc? Subito antequam sciuerit arbor cadit, **myȝt**
et fortitudo, <**bewte and**> **wele** cadit ab ipso, mors interficit ipsum,
diabolus propter peccatum deuorat et mittit in ignem eternum eternaliter
230   cruciandum. Cuilibet tali sic obliuiscenti sui modo consideranti fluxum,
falsitatem, et instabilitatem mundi possum dicere **what euer he be:** Miser
homo, *quem facis te?*

Secundo[8] principaliter dixi quod cuilibet moto peccato per temptacionem diaboli qui non fugit eius **suttelte,** ipsi possum dicere: Miser
homo, *quem facis te?* De subtilitate illius loquitur scriptura Genesis 3°
capitulo, vbi habetur: "Serpens erat callidior cunctis animantibus que

---

8. <Secundum principale.>

was afraid of the animal that followed him, he climbed into a tree, and when he looked back, he saw the unicorn close and ready to kill him. Then he looked straight down and saw two animals, one white, the other black, gnawing at the root of the tree he was on. He looked to one side and saw a dragon set to devour him. And on the other side he saw a fire kindled to burn him. In these precarious circumstances, he noticed a red apple and a little honey hanging among the tree branches. These he caught hold of and forgot about all the danger, and he took his delight in them until the tree roots were gnawed through by the two animals and the tree fell to the ground with him. Then the unicorn killed him, the dragon ate him up, and the fire burnt him to ashes.

By this man we may understand anyone who gives himself whole-heartedly to the love of worldly joy and prosperity. The pursuing unicorn is death, who has but one horn, which spares neither king nor prince nor lord nor soldier nor anyone else of whatever rank. The tree that he climbs is the world. The apple and honey signify the **wealth, worship,** and glory of the world. The dragon that is ready to devour him is the devil; the fire, eternal pain; the white and black animals, day and night, which constantly bring us closer to the end of life. In fleeing death, this man climbs up into the world, which is to say he puts his trust in his youth and strength, thinking he is secure in them. When at last by chance he becomes conscious of his nature and condition, he sees, as it were, that his life is being gnawed at by those two animals and his end is near. He also sees and understands, through the preachers of God's word, that in the end the devil will devour such sinners and cast them in the fire of hell. In these dangerous circumstances he notices that on that tree, that is the world, hang an apple and some honey, that is **worship and wellbeing,** and he directs his whole mind and attention to them. What happens then? Suddenly, before he knows it, the tree falls down, his **might** and strength, **beauty and wellbeing** fall away from him, death kills him, and the devil devours him for his sin and casts him into the eternal fire to be tortured forever. To anyone, **whoever he may be,** who thus forgets himself by not reflecting on the rushing course of the world, its deceit and instability, I can say: Wretched man, *whom do you make yourself to be?*

For the second principal part, I said: to anyone who is moved to sin through the temptation of the devil and does not flee his **subtleness,** I can say, Wretched man, *whom do you make yourself to be?* Of the devil's subtleness Scripture says, in Genesis 3: "The serpent was more cunning

fecerat Deus.'' Iste serpens diabolus ab inicio fuit inimicus generis humani, et ex invidia quam habet ad hominem semper nititur viis et modis
trahere hominem ad peccatum ne homo ascenderet ad gaudium vnde
240   ipse cecidit. In ista temptacione et traccione ad peccatum vtitur multa
subtilitate et pluribus **slexus and wyles,** et inter alias subtilitates quas
habet, habet modum faciendi quem habet medicus qui wlt dare infirmo
acerbam medicinam: multum coloribus pulcris commendat medicinam
antequam receperit, set in recepcione monet ut non masticet set statim
degluciat ne eius amaritudine percepta eam reiceret. Sic facit diabolus
peccatori quando eum temptat ad peccandum: colorat medicinam valde
subtiliter et dicit quod est valde salubre suo corpori et monet quod
festinanter recipiat, dicens <quasi sibi> verba que scribuntur in ewangelio Iohannis xiii capitulo: "Quod facis, fac cicius." Et non wlt quod
250   peccator deliberet nec examinet de amaritudine peccatum sequente. Set
pro Deo, si <homo> conetur facere bonum factum, tunc ita multum
sicud procurauit festinanciam in malum, ita multum tardat exitum boni
operis.
    Exsperiencia huius sufficiens esset probacio, set quia plurimorum in-
genia sunt curta et et [!] **slydur,**[9] ideo magis volo stare in ostensione
istius subtilitatis et artificii. Pluries contingit quod si aliquis sit in proposito malefaciendi, vtputa facere malum factum proximo, eum spoliare,
vel percutere, vel occidere, istud factum est sine consilio et coniecturacione periculi, nisi fuerit tale consilium per quod malum suum propo-
260   situm possit promoueri. Que causa credatis firmiter medicus ille infelix
diabolus est in proximo et agitat illum valde. Set si sit motus spiritu Dei
facere aliquod bonum opus, omnia pericula excogitabilia erunt quesita.
Tunc wlt petere consilium, et si vnus contradicat licet sex vel septem
dent consilium <in contrarium>, ipsum wlt audire, quia est commune
dictum quod modica res potest impedire. Set in malo proposito si vnus
det consilium faciendi et alii viginti oppositum, ipse vnus reputabitur
amicus et alii inimici. Ista \est/ phisica diaboli. Et ideo cauete, domini,
bene consulo, quia ille subtilis creuit medicus et docet artem medicine.

---

9. *apparently, corr. from* shydur.

than the other animals God had made."[17] This serpent, the devil, was from the beginning mankind's enemy, and out of envy that he has to man, he always tries by whatever ways and means to draw man to sin, so that man may not rise to the joy from which the devil had fallen. To thus tempt and draw man to sin, he uses much subtleness and many **tricks and wiles,** and among others of his tricks, he uses the one a physician employs when he wants to give a sick person bitter medicine: he recommends it with much praise before the sick person takes it, but when he takes it, he warns him not to chew it but rather to swallow it at once so that he may not taste its bitterness and hence spit it out. The devil acts in the same fashion with a sinner when he tempts him to sin. He praises his medicine with great subtleness and says it is very healthy for his body and encourages him to take it quickly, as it were with the words written in the gospel of John, chapter 13: "What you do, do it quickly."[18] He does not want the sinner to ponder or reflect on the bitterness that follows sin. But by God, if a man tries to do some good, then the devil slows him down in carrying out the good work and suggests that there are many dangers ahead, just as much as he had pushed him to be quick to do evil.

Experience should be sufficient proof of this, but because many people's thinking is short and **wavering,** I will spend a little more time on showing the devil's subtleness and craft. It often happens that when a man intends to do some evil, such as inflict harm on his neighbor, rob him, strike him, or kill him, he does so without reflection and without weighing the danger; he only thinks how he can carry out his evil plan. Believe me, the cause behind this is that wretched physician, the devil, who is nearby and stirs him mightily. But if such a man is moved by the spirit of God to do something good, he turns his mind to every conceivable danger. Then he will ask for counsel, and if a single person advises him against it, even if six or seven advise the opposite, he will listen to the one, for it is a common saying that a small matter can make a big obstacle. But when, in contrast, he has some evil plan, if a single person counsels him to do it and twenty others advise the opposite, he will hold the one his friend, and the others his enemies. Such is the devil's medicine. Therefore, sirs, beware, I advise you: the evil one has become a physician and teaches the art of medicine.

---

17. Gen. 3:1.
18. John 13:27.

Volumus magis videre de **suggerye** istius medici. Scimus bene quod
270 plures volunt sedere ad vinum et seruiciam et ludere ad alias, audire et
narrare fabulas **of wnþryft and rybawdrie** per maiorem partem diei et
noctis, tamdiu aliquando quod erit facessia que tibia precedet. Et in
talibus actubus homo inveniet in diuersis partibus sine coniecturacione
periculi < vel accepcione **of dropesye or gowte** > societatem sufficientem.
Et vt dicitur, si bene quererentur, homo posset invenire in villa et patria
vicina de huiusmodi duodenam Iacob. Set si talis deberet audire missam,
que vix durat per terciam partem hore, vel sermonem, qui durat per
horam, volunt fatigari, oportet eos surgere et pretendere latera, nunc
spaciari et garrulari, [*f. 290vb*] et nec ipsi volunt audire sermonem nec
280 permittere alios qui vellent si possent pro ipsis. Non dico quod sederetis
ad sermonem per totam diem nec per tres horas vel quatuor. Set per
graciam Dei, domini, sermones non veniunt nisi semel in septimana, et
aliquando nisi semel in termino vel bis. Per vnam horam diei possetis
subtrahere vos a corporalibus et pro salute animarum vestrarum indulgere
predicacioni verbi Dei. Et si sermo fuerit ante nonam, "Per fidem,"
dicunt, "iste longus sermo tuus; esset transire ad prandium quia nocet
multum stomachis hominum < et nature > **to be long fastyng.**" Vere,
domini, iste modus faciendi et dicendi non est ex parte Dei set venit ex
subtilitate diaboli iuncta humane fragilitati. Quia credatis firmiter quod
290 quando diabolus immittit tales cogitatus hominibus, quod natura eorum
et complexio debilitatur per longum auditum verbi Dei ieiunando, eo
quod generantur infirmitates per talia, non facit hoc pro alico bono quod
eveniret hominis complexioni vel nature, set vt sub tali pulcro colore
faceret auditores cicius tediosos de auditu verbi Dei et minus operari
secundum illud. Et ideo cauete, domini, bene.[10]

Et quod non ostendit istam artem ad tenendum hominem in statu
meliori et remouere infirmitates ostendo sic. Dampnat longas staciones
ad sermones, ieiunium, et abstinenciam, set non loquitur de longa ex-
spectacione ad tabernas, de **surfetus** esu et potu, nec excessiua et **ryotus**
300 vigilia, per quas natura hominis multo cicius destruitur, sicud exsperiencia monstrat, et sepius corpus et anima perduntur. Caueatis igitur ab
huiusmodi falsis suggestionibus diaboli, et habeatis mencionem de illis

---

10. *add. a cross and letter* a, *but I find no corresponding marginal insertion.*

Let us look a little more at the **suggestions** of this physician. We know that many people love to sit at wine and beer, to play at dice, and to hear and tell **useless and ribald** tales through most of the day and the night, so long that sometimes their wit outruns their feet.[19] In such actions, one will, in many different places, find sufficient company without thinking about any danger and getting **the dropsy or the gout**. As the saying goes, if one were to seek, one could find a Jacob's dozen of such people in one's town or country. But if such a person were to hear mass, which hardly takes twenty minutes, or a sermon, which lasts an hour, he will get tired, he must get up and stretch himself, he must go for a walk and chat, and such people will neither themselves hear a sermon nor allow others who might want to do so if they could. I am not saying that you should sit at a sermon for a whole day or even three or four hours. But for God's grace, sirs, sermons do not come but once a week, and sometimes not more than once or twice a term. For an hour, you can withdraw from physical activity and for the salvation of your souls attend to the preaching of God's work. And if the sermon comes before noon, they say: "Faith, this sermon is so long; it is time to go to lunch, for **to fast so long** hurts our stomach and goes against nature." Truly, sirs, to act and speak this way does not come from God but from the subtleness of the devil that plays on our human frailty. Believe me, if the devil plants such thoughts into men's minds, namely, that their constitution and health are weakened by listening to God's word for a long time without breakfast so that one gets ill from it, he does not do this out of concern for man's health or nature but rather that, under such a pretense, he might make the audience quickly get bored with listening to God's word and thus live less in accordance with it. Take good heed therefore, sirs.

That the devil does not practice this craft to keep man in good health and out of sickness I will demonstrate as follows. He speaks against long attendance at sermons, fasting, and abstinence, but he says nothing about long visits to the tavern, about **too much** food and drink, about **excessive** night-watches and revels, which ruin a man's health much more easily, as experience shows, and often destroy both body and soul. Be on guard against such false suggestions from the devil, and be advised

---

19. I am unsure what the Latin sentence means; the suggested translation is not in agreement with the Latin syntax.

vt cum diabolus ipsas vobis proposuerit renuatis ipsas. Et secundum
consilium Sapientis Ecclesiastici 3°, "Sic facite ut salvi sitis."

Set magis dampnum est: plures modernis temporibus sunt ita **dullud**
cum istis **wylus** et subtilitatibus quod non uolunt ipsi resistere quando
eos prouocat ad peccatum. Set faciat Christus per dona et data et per
predicatores moneat ipsos ad bonum quod possint habere eternam beati-
tudinem, set ipsi nolunt consentire sic quod ipse potest dicere in se et
310   in persona predicatorum verba que scribuntur Ysaie 26 capitulo: "Mise-
reamur impio et non discet facere iusticiam."

Videtur quod est de Christo, diabolo, et omnibus talibus sicud fuit
de duobus hominibus de quibus legi. Legi quod duo homines venerunt
quondam ad vn[a]m[11] villam foralem vendere suum **ware**. Vnus portauit
calathum in quo fuerat magna multitudo de **trufulus,** et alius alterum
calathum in quo fuit caritas. Isti duo homines inierunt forum et mon-
strauerunt suum **chaffare**. Ille qui habuit **tryfulus** statim eos vendidit
et habuit mercatores sufficientes. Set alius qui habuit caritatem stetit
per totam diem et nullus appreciauit. Tandem ille **sely** homo accepit
320   calathum cum caritate < in colirio [?] > et iuit ad hosspicium, et quando
venit ad hosspicium, subito calathus fuit furatus. Tunc ille pro caritate
multum tristatus transiuit ad maiorem et baliuos querelando quomodo
caritatem adduxit ad villam et fuit furata. Maior, baliui cum satrapis
transierunt de domo in domum caritatem querendo inter burgenses, et
maritus et vxor iuramento affirmarunt quod non fuit ibi per annum
Domini. Tandem ex communi consensu iuerunt ad locum fratrum in
villa vbi susspicabantur eam invenisse, et cum illuc venissent, ibi in-
venerunt calathum, set caritas absens fuit. Nemo reportet me hic, queso,
quod hic reprobacionem venerabilis Ordinis Fratrum dicerem, quoniam
330   vt infra patebit non plus loquar de ipsis quam de monachis et secularibus
sacerdotibus.

Tunc ad propositum. \Ita/ est hiis diebus inter Christum, diabolum,
et plures homines. Diabolus venit in mundum quasi homo in forum,
portat secum magnam multitudinem de [**trufulus**].[12] Qui sunt illi [**trufulus**][13] nisi subtilitates et **wyles** ad trahendum homines peccato? Et statim

---

11. vnum.
12. *a mark resembling a colon with a tail:* :>.
13. *the same mark as in the preceding note.*

against them, so that when the devil presents them to you, you may reject them and, after the advice of Solomon in Ecclesiasticus 3, "do thus that you may be saved."[20]

But it is a great shame: many people in our times are so **dulled** by these **wiles** and subtlenesses that they will not resist when he entices them to sin. Let Christ give them his gifts and, through his preachers, admonish them to do good, so that they may have eternal life—they themselves will not concur. Hence Christ can say, both for himself and in the person of his preachers, the words written in Isaiah 26: "We could have pity on the sinner, but he will not learn to do justice."[21]

It seems to be with Christ, the devil, and all such people as it is with two men about whom I have read the following. Two men once came to a market town to sell their **goods**. One carried a basket with a great amount of **trifles**, and the other a basket in which he had love. These two came to the market and showed their **wares**. The one with the **trifles** quickly sold them and had buyers enough. But the other, who had love, stood all day, and nobody came to purchase. Finally, this **poor** man took his basket with love and went to the inn, and when he got to the inn, his basket was suddenly stolen. In his sorrow for love, he went on to the mayor and the beadles, complaining how he had brought love to the town and how it had been stolen. The mayor and the beadles with their officers went from house to house, looking for love among the citizens, but husband and wife swore with oaths that it had not been there since God knows when. In the end, by common consent, they went to the house of the brethren in that town, where they thought they would have found her, and when they got there, they found the basket but no love. (Let no one report of me, please, that I am saying this in reproach of the venerable order of Friars Minor, because as you will find out later,[22] I am not saying this of them any more than of monks and the secular clergy!)

The meaning of this is as follows: the story shows today's relationship between Christ, the devil, and many people. The devil comes into the world like a man who goes to market and carries a large amount of **trifles**. What are these **trifles** but his tricks and **wiles** to draw men to

---

20. Ecclus. 3:2.
21. Isa. 26:10.
22. See below, translation of lines 353–54.

cum venerint homines, eos accipiunt et in eis delectantur, \et/ quia credunt quod ipsius sle\x/þus non sufficiunt, homines inter se coadunarunt diabolo plures adiutores, sicud sunt inventores istorum **vnþrifty newiettus,** et illos \omnes/ statim suscipiunt. Set quid? Christus venit
340 in forum istius mundi et portauit caritatem, quia sicud ewangelium testatur Luce vi° capitulo, non solum inter amicos verum eciam inter inimicos voluit caritatem haberi, vbi precepit isto modo: [*f. 291ra*] "Diligite inimicos vestros, benefacite hiis qui oderunt vos." Set quid? Ipse stetit in foro istius mundi in magna mora et **dysese,** set pauci attendebant ad emendum istam preciosam rem ab ipso. Quid accidit? Bonus homo ille, Christus, quando exiuit de foro istius mundi dimisit illam in suo hosspicio. Quid fuit suum hosspicium? Certe, sancta Ecclesia, que in principio in omnibus suis membris habuit cor vnum et anima vna. Set quid nunc? Certe, caritas furatur. Quid facit nunc Christus? Certe facit
350 maiores et baliuos ciuitatis Ecclesie, scilicet arciepiscopos, episcopos, et ceteros Ecclesie prelatos et predicatores, querere caritatem. Multa est inquisicio, set absconditur, non invenitur. Quando requisierint eam in communibus locis, oportet diuertere ad fratres. Per istos fratres intelligo omnes qui acceperunt ordines sacros sacerdocii in Ecclesia Dei, qui specialius ceteris tenentur habere caritatem in invicem, quia ipsis pertinet tractare sacramentum benedicti corporis dominici, quod sicud est vnum in multis locis quantumcumque remotis, sic isti continue essent assimilati per vnitatem, vt vbicumque essent vel quantumcumque separati, semper vnum in corde sentirent per dileccionem. Set si queramus nunc, quid ibi
360 inveniemus? Certe in pluribus nisi calathum, qui nichil aliud est nisi signum ordinis sacerdocii; istud remanet, set caritas auolauit. Seculares eciam pretendunt eciam pulcrum calathum, idest nomen Christianitatis, et quidam coniugii, set calathus vacuus est. Et quod sit verum ad oculum patet quoniam plures in ecclesiasticis et secularibus sunt leti audire de aduersitate proximorum, parati eos posteriorare et de illis mala loqui, et quanto virtuosiores sint, tanto cicius eis detrahent. Omnes tales modum contrarium habent caritati, et eos assimilari possum medico equino.

sin? As soon as people come, they accept them and delight in them, and because they think that his **tricks** are not enough, they give the devil many helpers, such as the inventors of these **useless new fashions**; and they receive all those at once. What then? Christ came to the market of this world and carried love, for as the gospel witnesses in Luke 6, he wanted love to be not only among friends but among enemies, when he commanded: "Love your enemies, do good to those who hate you."[23] Then what? He stood in the market of this world for a long time and with **discomfort,** but few paid attention to purchase that precious object from him. What happened then? When that good man, Christ, departed from the market of this world, he left love in his inn. What was his inn? Surely, holy Church, who at its beginning had one heart and one soul in all its members. And then what happened? Yes, love was stolen. So, what does Christ do now? Well, he establishes mayors and bailiffs in the city of the Church, that is to say, archbishops, bishops, and other prelates and preachers, to seek love. They seek intently, but love is hidden; she cannot be found. After looking for her in all the common places, it remained for them to go to the brethren. By these brethren I understand all who have received holy orders of priesthood in God's Church. They especially among all others ought to have love for each other, for it is their task to handle the sacrament of the blessed body of the Lord— just as that is one in many places, however distant from each other, so these priests should always be bound in unity, so that wherever they may be, and however distant from each other, they should always feel the same in their hearts through love. But if we look now, what shall we find there? Indeed, in many of them only the basket, which is nothing but the sign of their priestly order; it remains, but love has flown away. Seculars, too, and some married people show forth a beautiful basket, that is, the name of Christianity, but their basket is empty. That this is true is plain to our eyes, for many among both clergy and laypersons are glad to hear of their neighbors' misfortune, ready to push them down and to speak ill of them; and the more virtuous these neighbors are, the more willingly they slander them. All these live in opposition to love, and I can liken them to the horseleech.[24]

---

23. Luke 6:27.
24. The usual Latin name for this animal is *sanguisuga*. Clearly the *medicus equinus* used by this sermon writer is a calque of English *horseleech.*

Est condicio illius animalis quod si homo venerit in aqua, statim
vult **streyne** illum per tibiam \vel/ per aliud membrum, set in sua
370   **streynyng** non extrahit aliquem sanguinem nisi corruptum et impurum.
Sic huiusmodi detractores qui nunc vigent nimis diebus, si inciderint in
communicacionem de alico, nolunt recitare aliquid de eo nisi sit malum.
Et si tale quid sciuerint, recitabitur cum clamosa voce, et iste modus
faciendi facit plures habere malos conceptus de proximis et est causa
quare <caritas> est absconsa. In antiquis temporibus lego quod pena
illius vicii fuit excisio lingue, et si ista pena esset iam obseruata, credo
quod sunt quidam mercatores in patria qui male venderent suum **ware,**
et quidam ecclesiastici male dicerent suas matutinas. Set dum ista caritas
fuerit absens, sumus in incerta via versus celum et indirecta, quia ipsa
380   secundum sentenciam doctorum est radix et fundamentum omnium
virtutum, et alie virtutes quasi rami. Et ideo licet habuerimus fidem
solidam et demus plura pro Dei amore et cetera bona opera exerceremus,
non essent nobis meritoria versus vitam eternam. Hoc testatur propheta
Osee ix capitulo: "Exsiccata est radix; fructum nequaquam facient."
Hec est res quam diabolus cum omnibus subtilitatibus maxime nititur
euacuare a nobis et maxime est **looþ** homines ipsam habere. Quia vbi
est caritas, ibi est Deus, quia Deus est caritas; et vbi est Deus, ibi
diabolus nullum introitum habere potest. Qui hanc habet est Dei filius,
et qui non, est filius diaboli. Qui tunc istam per aliquam instigacionem
390   diaboli vel subtilitatem perdit in se vel frangit inter proximos, illi possum
dicere, **be bond or fre**: Miser homo, *quem facis te?*

Tercio[14] principaliter dixi quod cuilibet exaltanti se per superbiam,
obliuiscen\ti/ proprie fragilitatis, ipsi possum dicere, in quocumque
statu fuerit vel gradu: Miser, *quem facis te?* Si consideremus statum
generis humani, reperiemus quod non est aliquod genus animalium quod
in principio est tam impotens et tam **nedy** sicud est homo <si es rex,
princeps, vel alius> quando primo venit in mundum, quia non est
aliquod animal quod non scit per suam [*f. 291rb*] naturam se adiuuare,
\homine/ solo excepto. Et in suo victu pro alico quod habet ex se est
400   ita pauper vel pauperior omnibus animantibus, quia sua sustinencia est
ab piscibus, auibus, et bestiis, vestura sua **and aray** venit a bestiis, sic
quod illud quod homo habet de se in omni statu de se est valde nudum.

---

14. <Tercium principale.>

This animal's nature is to **stick** to a man's leg or any other limb when he steps into a body of water, but in this **sticking**, the leech draws only corrupt and impure blood. In the same way, these slanderers who prosper so much these days, when they start speaking of someone, will say nothing of him but evil. And what they know will be said in a loud voice, and this behavior causes many people to have a bad opinion of their neighbors and is the reason why love is hidden away. I read that in ancient times the punishment for this vice was to have one's tongue cut out. If this punishment were still being used, I believe some merchants in our country would hardly be able to sell their **wares,** and some clerics would hardly be able to say their office. But as long as this love is wanting, we are on an uncertain and crooked way to heaven, for according to our teachers, love is the root and foundation of all virtues, and the other virtues are its branches. Even if we have a solid faith and give much for the love of God and do the other good works, these would not merit us eternal life. The prophet Hosea witnesses this in chapter 9: "Their root is dried up, they will bring no fruit whatever."[25] This is the one thing that the devil tries with all his tricks to take from us, and that he is most **loath** for people to have. For where there is love, there is God, because God is love; and where God is, the devil can find no entrance. He who has love is God's child, and he who does not is a child of the devil. So, whoever loses love in himself through any instigation or subtleness of the devil or destroys it among his neighbors, to him I can say, **whether he is a bondsman or free**: Wretched man, *whom do you make yourself to be?*

For my third principal part, I said that to anyone who exalts himself in pride and forgets his own frailty, in whatever estate or rank he might be, I can say, Wretch, *whom do you make yourself to be?* If we consider the condition of the human race, we shall find that no other species is so feeble and **needy** in its beginning as man when he first comes into the world, whether you are a king or prince or someone else, for there is no animal that does not know by nature how to help itself, except only man. Further, in gaining his livelihood, in so far as it comes from himself, he is as poor and poorer than all living things, for his food comes from fish, birds, and beasts, his clothing **and array** from animals, so that what he has of his own, in whatever estate, is very scant. And

---

25. Hos. 9:16.

Et finis, nisi bene fecerit (et \non/ potest homo nisi per graciam), miserabilior est omni, quia ipsa cum moriuntur, post mortem penam non senciunt, vbi alii male viuentes ad penam transiunt infernalem. Ex quo tunc homo est **so vnhelply** sibi in principio, et continuat in suo victu solum per succursum bestiarum, et pena erit tam grandis in exitu quem necesse est attingere, magna stulticia est homini se extollere acsi esset securus de permanencia hic et omnia que habet essent de propriis.

410 Set quod dolendum est, nunc in omni statu et gradu contingit invenire plures qui obliuiscentes sui inicii, progressionis, et finis non attendunt ad Deum nec ad bonum hominem, similes anguille que, cum capud et cauda fuerint abscisa, medium facit multiplicem mocionem. Sic isti quando capitis sui et caude, idest inicii et finis, priuantur agnicione, medium, idest conuersacio quam habent in corpore, est in multiplici mocione peccat[i],[15] et tamen mortuum est aut proximum morti, quia sicud mortuus et sepultus caret communione et societate, ita sepultus in peccatis beneficiis militantis et societate triumphantis caret. Et illi qui sic mouentur, quia obliuiscuntur < sui inicii et finis >, sunt, fuerunt,

420 et erunt causa multiplicis perturbacionis in mundo. Que, rogo, est causa tantarum guerrarum inter nacionem et nacionem, regnum et regnum, patriam et patriam, et dissencion[u]m[16] inter proximum et proximum, et—quod est contra naturam—cognacionem et cognacionem? Certe, causa vna et precipua \est/ quod quidam constituebantur in tam alta superbia quod eis apparebat quod quando ipsi mouerentur, totus mundus vacillaret. Et alii in parte sua fuerunt in eadem altitudine et sicud duo grandes non potuerunt nodari in uno sacco, et sic venit **care and sorw** ad terram.

    Que eciam est causa istius **vnþryfty and rownyng** doctrine que creuit

430 iam in Ecclesia et specialiter in isto regno? Certe, superba presumpcio et vanae gloria quam habuerunt fundatores istorum errorum < et illi similiter qui continuant in illis >, susspicando quod ingenium illorum excederet omnes ante illos. Set quid, per Deum? < De se > "dicentes se enim esse sapientes stulti facti sunt," Ad Romanos, 1° capitulo. Horum superbia ad tantum creuit quod postposuerunt omnes constituciones et consuetudines in Ecclesia Dei que fuerunt facte et ordinate per delibe-racionem et discrecionem sanctorum patrum precedencium. [Hi][17] pre-

---

15. peccatis.
16. dissencionem.
17. .h.

in the end, unless man has done good deeds (and these he cannot do except by grace), he is more wretched than all other creatures, for when these die, they do not feel any pain after death, whereas many men who have led an evil life go to the pain of hell. Because man is then **so helpless** in his beginning and continues the course of his life only with the help of animals, and because in the end (which he must come to), his suffering will be so great, it is very foolish for him to exalt himself as if he were certain of permanence here and as if all the things he possessed were his own. But it is to be lamented that one can nowadays find so many people in every estate and rank who forget their beginning, their course of life, and their end and pay no attention to God or to man's good. Like the eel, which, after its head and tail have been cut off, still wiggles a lot with its middle part, so it is with such people. When they have lost knowledge of their head and tail, that is, their beginning and end, their middle part still moves about a good deal in sin, and yet it is dead or close to death, for just as a person who is dead and buried has no further companionship, so one who is buried in sin is separated from the benefits of the Church on earth and the companionship of the Church in heaven. And people who thus move about because they forget their beginning and end are, have been, and will be the cause of much confusion in this world. For what, I ask, is the cause of so many wars between nations, kingdoms, and countries, and of strife between neighbors and—what is clearly against nature— relatives? Surely, the one and foremost cause is that some stand so high in pride that when they move, they think the whole world shakes. Others on their part stand just as high, and two great ones cannot fit in the same bag; hence **care and sorrow** come into the world.

And what is the cause of this **useless and whispered** doctrine that has recently grown in the Church, and specially in our realm? Surely it is the proud presumption and vainglory of those who started these errors and of those who continue to hold them in the belief that their own ingenuity surpasses that of all who have lived before them. What then, by God? "By declaring themselves wise, they have become fools," Romans 1.[26] Their pride has grown so much that they leave behind all constitutions and customs of God's Church that were established and ordained through the deliberation and discretion of the holy fathers

---

26. Rom. 1:22.

dicant inter cetera quod non debemus orare ad aliquem sanctum, non
daremus decimas curatis, et si curatus excommunicacionis sentenciam
440   < dederit pro eisdem >, docent de illa non curare. Ista doctrina est falsa,
et Dei amore caueatis de illa. Et nisi vos caueritis, certe multum estis
culpandi pre ceteris, quia audacter dicere volo quod post Oxon', Cam-
brug, et Londoun non est aliqua ciuitas se\u/ villa in regno que habet
plures bonos sermones quam hec ciuitas, Deus eam saluet. Ex quo tunc
habetis tot bonos sermones per quos potestis scire que est voluntas Dei,
si feceritis contrarium, multo plus ceteris estis culpandi. Et sic eritis
prout dominus ille in ewangelio sic dicit: "Seruus \qui cognouit/ voluntatem domini sui et non \fecit secundum voluntatem eius/ plagis va-
pulabit multis," Luce xii capitulo. Et vere, prelati Ecclesie < et ministri
450   qui occupant iurisdiccionis locum sub ipsis > multum sunt culpabiles,
qui ipsos permittunt predicare, quia illis incu[m]bit[18] tales corrigere. In
antiquis temporibus prelati fecerunt contra huiusmodi diuersos libros et
habuerunt magnam diligenciam in eneruacionem ipsorum. Set certe nunc
diebus de pluribus possum dicere verba que scribuntur Psalmo 37: "Factus sum sicud homo non audiens et non < habens > in ore suo redar-
guiciones." Set si esset tantum lucrum in hiis sicud in probacione
testamentorum vel correxcione fornicacionis < vel adulterii >, vellent sine
mora [*f. 291va*] partem interponere.

Set ad materias respondendum de quibus prius tetigi, sciendum quod
460   ad primam materiam volo respondere, quoad duas alias volo narrare
vobis quomodo accidit de vno qui quondam eiusdem \fuit/ opinionis,
per quod cum gracia \Dei/ agitati eritis ad illas falsas opiniones fu-
giendum. Quantum[19] ad primum: Principalis racio quam audiui vel legi
est hec. Deus, dicunt, est magis misericors quam est aliquis sanctus
vel sancta que habuit naturam hominis. Ergo, si sibi ostenderimus miseriam nostram, cicius vult audire nostram oracionem. Ergo frustra est
orare ad sanctum. Huic respondeo cum doctore sancto Thoma, *Secunda
secunde,* questione 172, articulo 2° in pede, modo quo respondet ad
questionem qua querit vtrum Deus reuelauit per se vel per angelos me-
470   dios. Vbi allegat dictum Apostoli Ad Romanos 13, vbi dicit, "Omnia
que a Deo sunt, ordinata sunt," et hic ordo, < secundum Dionisium >

---

18. incubit.
19. *marg.* non erat dictum.

before us. They preach, among other things, that we must not pray to any saint, that we should not give tithes to our curates, and that one need not pay attention when a curate pronounces the sentence of excommunication for this error. This doctrine is false; for the love of God, stay away from it. If you do not guard yourselves, you are certainly to be blamed before all others, for I will say boldly that after Oxford, Cambridge, and London, there is no other town or village in the kingdom that hears more good sermons than this city, may God keep it. Because you therefore have so many good sermons through which you can know God's will, if you do the opposite, you deserve more blame than other people. And you will be like the one of whom the Lord says in the gospel: "A servant who knows his master's will and does not act accordingly will be beaten with many stripes."[27] Truly, the prelates and the ministers in their jurisdiction are much to blame if they allow those to preach, for it is their duty to correct them. In times of old, prelates wrote many books against such men and took great care to weaken them. But today I can surely apply to many what is written in Psalm 37: "I have become like a man who does not hear and has no reproof in his mouth."[28] If there only were as much profit in these duties as there is in proving wills or correcting cases of fornication or adultery, they would intervene without delay.

But to deal with the matters I touched on: I will deal with the first by argument, but with regard to the other two, I will tell you what happened to a person who once held such an opinion, which by God's grace will move you to flee these false teachings. About the first, then: The main reason I have heard or read is this. They say that God is more merciful than any of the saints, man or woman, who are only human. Therefore, if we show our misery to God, he will quickly hear our prayer. Hence it is in vain to pray to a saint. To this I answer with St. Thomas in his *Summa theologiae* II–II, question 172, article 2 at the end, in the same way as he responds to the question whether God has revealed anything by himself or through his intermediate angels. Thomas adduces the words of the Apostle Paul in Romans 13: "All that is from God, is ordered."[29] And this order, according to Dionysius in *The Heavenly*

---

27. Luke 12:47.
28. Ps. 37:15.
29. Rom. 13:1.

De celesti ierarchia, capitulo 3°, est quod infima per media dissponat. Nunc media inter nos et Deum sunt <sancta Maria>, angeli, et sancti in celo, quos Deus ordinauit mediare pro nobis, ita quod sit honor et reuerencia illis, sicud dominus terrenus vult honorare illos qui sunt circa illum, et similiter proficuum nostrum, quia quando miseria nostra Deo offertur per bona media sanctorum, cicius habebit remedium quam haberet per se. Et ista est causa quare sancta Ecclesia ordinauit quod cantaremus letaniam, in qua dicimus "Sancta Maria, ora pro nobis.
480 Sancte Petre," etc. Et fecit similiter deuotas oraciones que sunt in vsu in missis et in matutinis in Ecclesia. Ex quo tunc est ordinacio Dei secundum testimonium Apostoli et sancti doctoris Dionisii, et similiter ordinacio Ecclesie, deprecemini ad sanctos vt solito, non obstante illa **vnþryfty** doctrina. Illa doctrina est expresse contra auctoritates omnium doctorum sanctorum et vsum tocius sancte Ecclesi[e][20] Dei, qui vocant sanctam Mariam "aduocatam nostram" et "mediatricem" inter Deum et nos; et similiter contra scripturam sacram, Deuteronomii 17 capitulo, vbi dicit: "Si difficile et ambiguum apud te persspe[x]eris[21] inter sanguinem et sanguinem, causam et causam, ascende ad locum quem elegit
490 Dominus Deus tuus, veniesque ad sacerdotes et queres ab eis veritatem, et facies quantumcumque dixerint qui presunt." Ex quo tunc omnes boni rectores qui fuerunt ante nos et similiter iam sunt hoc ordinauerunt, \sicud/ tenemur per istam sentenciam scripture, sequamur doctrinam illorum et resspuamus istam doctrinam nouam.

Quoad secundam materiam, quod non tenemur soluere decimas nec curare de excommunicacione, vellem ostendere sentenciam doctorum in materia set non audeo morare. Ideo sicud promisi volo dicere vobis quomodo accidit de vno qui tenuit hanc opinionem. Nota narracionem.

Hic poteritis videre quam dire et longe iste fuit punitus quia noluit
500 timere Ecclesiam sicud debuit et soluere decimas. Pro Dei igitur amore, capiatis exemplum ab istis et recusetis istas falsas opiniones in istis et in aliis. Si tunc resspueritis istam falsam doctrinam et custod[ieri]tis[22]

---

20. Ecclesi.
21. persspereris.
22. custodrietis.

Hierarchy, chapter 3, disposes the lower elements through those in the middle.[30] Now, those in the middle between us and God are St. Mary, the angels, and the saints in heaven, whom God has ordained to intervene for us, so that they may receive honor and reverence, as an earthly lord wants to honor those around him, and so that at the same time, we receive some profit, for when our misery is offered to God through the intermediacy of the saints, it will be more readily cured than on its own. This is the reason Holy Church has ordained that we sing the litany, where we say, "St. Mary, pray for us. St. Peter, pray for us," and so on. And the Church likewise established prayers that are used in its masses and matins. Because this is, then, God's ordination according to the testimony of the Apostle and of the holy teacher Dionysius, and similarly the ordinance of the Church, let us pray to the saints as we used to, in spite of that **useless** doctrine. For that teaching is expressly against the authority of all our holy teachers and the custom of the holy Church of God, who call St. Mary "our advocate" and "mediatrix" between God and us; it is also against holy Scripture, which says, in Genesis 17: "If you perceive that there is among you anything difficult or doubtful in the judgment between blood and blood or cause and cause, go up to the place that the Lord your God has chosen; come to the priests and ask them for the truth, and do whatever those who preside will tell you."[31] As all good pastors who have been before us and those who are now living have ordained, and as we are held to do by this sentence in Scripture, let us follow their teaching and totally reject this new doctrine.

With respect to the second matter, namely, that we are not obligated to give tithes or to pay attention to excommunication, I would like to show you what our teachers have said, but I dare not spend more time. Hence, as I have promised, I will tell you what happened to someone who held this opinion. Tell the story.

Here you can see how bitterly and long he was punished because he would not respect the Church as he ought to and give tithes. For the love of God, then, take an example of these things and reject these false opinions in these and other matters. If you reject this false teaching and

---

30. Aquinas *Summa theologiae* 2-2, qu. 172, art. 2, responsio, with the quotations cited here (1852-73, 3:575b).

31. Deut. 17:8-10.

vos infra limites fidei ecclesiastice sicud vos docui in isto principali sine superbia **and presumpcioun**; fugiatis subtilitates diaboli et custodiatis caritatem sicud ostendi in secundo principali sine **enuye and detraccyoun**; et quod sicud docui in principali <primo> non sitis positi [?] nimis auaricie \decepti/ per falsam mundi promissionem, de quolibet vestrum verificabitur illud quod scribitur Genesis 2° capitulo: "Factus est homo in animam viuentem," hic scilicet viuere in gracia et **goodnes**, et in celo
510 eternaliter **in blys and gladnes**. Quo perducat tam vos quam me qui nos redemit suo cruore. Amen.

* * *

The following is the fuller protheme referred to by the preacher (see lines 11–15). It follows after line 10 and is marked *va . . . cat* in the margin, f. 289rb–va.

Quoad primum <quod sicud> clerici sciunt in primo libro scripture fit mencio quod omnipotens Deus ex sua interminabili gracia et bonitate creauit hominem ad ymaginem et similitudinem propriam et posuit eum in statu innocencie et mundicie absque qualicumque culpa vel miseria et quacumque mocione et incitamento ad peccatum infra se. Dedit \sibi/ possessionem in felici ac delicioso loco paradisi, semper ibi fuisse et numquam mortem sensisse nec corporaliter nec spiritualiter, et constituit eum dominum omnium creaturarum corporalium, ita quod quelibet il-
520 larum deseruisset sibi et subiecta fuisset sine rebellione. Iste fuit status et gradus in quo Dominus Deus posuit hominem in principio. Nunc vertamus ad aliam partem et videamus qualem se per peccatum homo fecit ex propria stulticia, cum illo honore ingenti quem Deus dederat <ei in creacione> sine aliquali merito noluit contentari, set per falsam suggestionem diaboli erectus in superbiam appeciit transcendisse limites condicionis sue nature in qua factus fuerat, et cepit esse rebellis et inobediens suo creatori. Propter quam inobedienciam et **mysgouernaunse** iusto Dei iudicio priuatus fuit originali iusticia, per quam habuit posse non mo[r]tuus[23] fuisse nec peccato se subdidisse, et cecidit in necessita-
530 tem peccandi et moriendi, sic quod non est aliquis qui surgit ex eius genere exceptis Christo et eius gloriosa genitrice, qui fuerunt preseruati

---

23. motuus.

stay within the boundaries of the Church's faith without pride **and presumption,** as I told you in this principal part; if you flee the devil's tricks and guard love without **envy and slander,** as I showed in the second principal part; and if, as I showed you in the first principal part, you do not let yourselves be deceived by avarice through the false promise of the world, then of each one of you the words of Genesis 2 will be true: "Man was made a living soul,"[32] namely, to live here in grace and **goodness,** and in heaven forever **in bliss and gladness.** To which may he who has redeemed us in his blood bring both you and me. Amen.

*   *   *

As to the first point, our clerics know that the first book of Scripture mentions that almighty God, out of his endless grace and goodness, created man in his image and likeness and placed him in the state of innocence and purity, without any guilt and misery and any stirring to sin from within him. He gave him possession of the happy and delightful place of paradise, so that he might always be there and might never experience death in either body or spirit, and he made him lord over all bodily creatures, so that each one of them would serve him and be subject to him without rebellion. That was the state and rank in which God placed man in the beginning. Now let us turn to the other side and see what man has made of himself through sin, out of his own stupidity, when he would not be content with that enormous honor God had given him, without his merit, when he created him, and instead, on the false suggestion of the devil, raised his head in pride and desired to transcend the limits of his natural condition in which he was created, and began to rebel and disobey his creator. Because of this disobedience and **misgovernance,** he was, by God's just judgment, deprived of his original righteousness, which gave him the possibility of not dying or being subject to sin, and he fell into the necessity to sin and die, so that there is none of his offspring who rises except Christ and his glorious mother, who were preserved from sin, for all other men inherit sin of necessity in their beginning and fall into the snare of death in their end. Man was also expelled from that delightful and happy place of paradise, where, as I said before, no heat or cold, labor or sickness could have

---

32. Gen. 2:7.

a peccato, quin necesse est eos trahere \peccatum/ in suo exordio et
incidere in nexus \mortis/ in fine. Fuit eciam expulsus de illo delicioso
et felici loco paradisi vbi, sicud predixi, nec estus nec frigus, labor nec
infirmitas ei nocuisse poterant, in hunc miserabilem mundum, vbi est
facilitas cadendi et difficultas standi vel resurgendi, vbi semper molestatur
\quasi/ totum genus humanum cum estu, frigore, labore, vel infirmitate,
de quibus preuie fuit liberrimum. Similiter vbi fuerat constitutus dominus
omium creaturarum sic quod omnia ipsa sine rebellione sibi subiecta
540 fuissent, magna pars illorum non solum non subiecta permanet set plura
ipsorum quasi accipiendo sibi dominium supra hominem, vt exsperiencia
monstrat, diuersis modis ei noc\ent/ et molestiam inferunt. Hic poteritis
videre statum et dignitatem in quibus Deus hominem fecit, et in quas
myscheef and wrechednes homo se per peccatum induxit. < Et in hac
stetit > genus humanum per totum tempus legis nature et legis scripte,
que durarent per milia annorum. Hic fuit **a rewful** et dolorosa mutacio.
Tunc de isto statu hominum poterant < verificari > verba que scribuntur
1º Machabeorum 1º capitulo: "Factus est planctus in Israel."

    Set magis appropinquando et veniendo ad tempus gracie in quo nos
550 modo sumus, videamus quid homo nunc se faciat per peccatum. De
racione sciretis, quia est fides et tota die vobis predicatur, quod quando
humanum genus fuit reductum ad talem miseriam de qua preloquebar
et non potuit se liberasse, Christus Dei Filius venit de felici habitaculo
celi in hunc miserum mundum ad saluandum genus humanum per suam
acerbam passionem, de qua hodie sancta Ecclesia pre ceteris anni temporibus magis specialem incipit facere mencionem. Per quam passionem
quam Christus sustinuit et eius virtutem, ibi sicud [*f. 289va*] fuimus
ante nati filii tenebrarum et ire, et propter peccatum quod traximus in
nascendo a nostris parentibus in fine transiuimus ad infernum, modo
560 per illius passionem et recepcionem sacramentorum Ecclesie, que ex
Christi passione suam sumpserunt virtutem, facti sumus filii lucis et
gracie, connexi sicud membra Ecclesie Christo, qui est capud corporis
Ecclesie per **sennus** fidei, amoris, et dileccionis. Sine esitacione in fine
transitur ad **eendles** gaudium et **blys** celi si post recepcionem sacramenti
baptismi custodierimus nos a peccato implendo promissum quod in baptismo Christo vouebamus. Hic est status in quo iam positi sumus per
adiutorium et graciam Christi. Set tunc si ita sit quod nos post baptismum, sicud dolor est quod multi faciunt, frangamus votum quod voui-
mus nostro saluatori et voluntarie submittamus nos seruituti peccati,
570 statim violenter expellimus a nobis lucem gracie et sumus causa quare

harmed him, and he came into this wretched world, where it is easy for him to fall and hard to stand or rise again, where as it were the whole human race is constantly afflicted by heat, cold, labor, and sickness, of which he was free before. Likewise, whereas he had been set as lord over all creatures so that all would be subject to him without rebellion, now not only are a large part of them not subject but many of them, as it were, take on lordship over man, as experience shows, by causing him harm and trouble in many ways. Thus you can see the state and dignity in which God created man and the **misery and wretchedness** in which man fell through his sin. Man remained in that state through the whole period of natural law and the law of Moses, which lasted thousands of years. This was **a sorrowful** and grievous change. To this state of human beings can be applied the words in 1 Maccabees 1: "There was weeping in Israel."[33]

But as we come to the time of grace in which we now live, let us see what man has made of himself today through sin. You surely know, because it is a matter of our faith and being preached every day, that when mankind was brought to the wretchedness I have spoken of and could not free itself, Christ, the Son of God, came from his blessed dwelling in heaven into this wretched world to save mankind through his bitter passion, which the Church begins today especially to call to mind, more so than at other times of the year. Through the passion that Christ suffered and its effect, though we were born children of darkness and wrath, and though, because of the sin we inherit at birth from our parents, we go to hell in the end, we now have become children of light and grace through his passion and the reception of the sacraments of the Church, which derived their power from Christ's passion. As members of the Church, we are linked to Christ, who is the head of the body of the Church, through the **sinews** of faith, love, and charity. Without doubt, in the end, we shall go to the **endless** joy and **bliss** of heaven if, after receiving the sacrament of baptism, we keep ourselves from sin and fulfill the promise we made to Christ in baptism. This is our current state in which we have been put through the help and grace of Christ. But if it is the case that after baptism we break the promise we made to our Savior, as unfortunately many do, and of our own will subject ourselves to the servitude of sin, we expel at once with force the light

---

33. 1 Macc. 1:26.

bona nostra opera non proficiunt nobis ad vitam eternam, et facimus nos exspertes omnium bonorum que fiunt in Ecclesia sancta Dei et segregamus nos a corpore Ecclesie et Christo, eius capite, et efficimus nos membra diaboli et ipsum capud nostrum, et arripimus iter[24] versus penam eternam inferni. Hic est status miserabilis, in quem quilibet mortaliter peccans se inducit. Non solum tunc Ade, nostro primo parenti, qui fuit causa exilii nostri a paradiso et amissionis glorie, set eciam cuilibet \nunc/ mortaliter peccanti, qui vt ostendi de tam digno statu et gradu in quo est dum est in gracia facit se \ita/ horribilem et **wreched-**

580   **ful** quando cadit in mortale peccatum, cum dolore et admiracione possum dicere verba thematis, *Quem facis teipsum?*

---

24. iter] *add.* versus directe.

of grace from ourselves and become the cause why our good deeds do not help us to eternal life; we lose our share in all the good works done in God's holy Church, cut ourselves off from the body of the Church and Christ, its head, make ourselves members of the devil, with him being our head, and take the way to the eternal pain of hell. This is the wretched state in which everyone who commits mortal sin places himself. Therefore, I can say with grief and admiration the words of the thema not only to Adam, our forefather, who was the cause of our exile from paradise and our loss of glory, but likewise to anyone who commits mortal sin today, who—as I have shown—changes himself from such a worthy state and rank in which he stands while he is in the state of grace, to such a horrible and **wretched one** when he falls into mortal sin: *Whom do you make yourself to be?*

Statistical Table

Sermon	Total Words	English Words	Switches
A-25	2,353	394	49
A-33	2,341	265	40
B-088	7,173	548	70
B-113	3,153	145	41
B-136	4,151	425	85
H-25	13,918	444	66
L-1	17,393	2,114	465
O-01	5,948	212	50
O-02	4,814	214	81
O-03	4,576	244	102
O-04	6,357	1,270	318
O-05	4,887	596	175
O-06	5,679	304	88
O-07	6,605	1,225	379
O-08	5,458	1,220	292
O-09	5,767	705	232
O-10	7,090	965	248
O-11	5,452	765	295
O-12	5,064	362	126
O-13	4,919	383	135
O-14	5,582	556	133
O-16	2,237	141	47
O-17	1,594	135	57
O-18	2,855	588	124
O-22	5,304	682	161
O-23	3,785	438	125
O-24	2,786	157	55
O-25	3,087	900	191
Q-19	3,784	946	221
Q-20	5,302	1,755	391

Sermon	Total Words	English Words	Switches
Q-21	3,738	572	167
Q-22	4,809	705	106
Q-24	6,222	775	193
Q-25	4,454	563	101
Q-42	3,976	579	108
R-12	4,514	364	80
R-14	5,849	914	127
W-068	6,088	138	43
W-072	3,769	128	47
W-102	4,823	244	43
W-152	5,135	273	46
W-154	6,018	160	94
X-03	5,821	1,025	88

Notes:

O-05: Includes the repeated paragraph.

O-16: Incomplete.

O-17: Possibly incomplete.

Q-24: Includes the material of Q-23, which I consider part of Q-24.

Bibliography

Manuscripts Cited

ARRAS
Bibliothèque Municipale, MS 184 (254)
CAMBRIDGE
Gonville and Caius College, MS 356
Jesus College, MS 13
Pembroke College, MS 199
Peterhouse, MS 210
University Library, MS Ii.3.8
University Library, MS Kk.4.24
DUBLIN
Trinity College, MS 277
LONDON
British Library, MS Cotton Titus C.ix
British Library, MS Harley 331
British Library, MS Harley 2250
British Library, MS Harley 7322
British Library, MS Royal 7.E.vi
Lambeth Palace, MS 352
MANCHESTER
John Rylands Library, MS 367
OXFORD
Balliol College, MS 149
Bodleian Library, MS Barlow 24
Bodleian Library, MS Bodley 144
Bodleian Library, MS Bodley 649
Bodleian Library, MS Bodley 859
Bodleian Library, MS Lat.th.d.1
Bodleian Library, MS Laud misc. 296
Bodleian Library, MS Laud misc. 706
Magdalen College, MS 93
New College, MS 88
Trinity College, MS 42

WORCESTER
   Cathedral Library, MS F.10
   Cathedral Library, MS F.126

Printed Sources

Alford, John A. 1992. *Piers Plowman: A Guide to the Quotations*. Binghamton, NY.
Anstey, Henry, ed. 1868. *Munimenta Academica, or Documents Illustrative of Academic Life and Studies at Oxford*. 2 vols. Rolls Series 50. London.
Aquinas, St. Thomas. 1852–73. *Opera omnia*. 25 vols. Parma.
Archer, John R. 1984. "The Preaching of Philip Repingdon, Bishop of Lincoln (1405–1419): A Descriptive Analysis of His Latin Sermons." Ph.d. diss., Graduate Theological Union, Berkeley, CA.
Archibald, Elizabeth. 1992. "Tradition and Innovation in the Macaronic Poetry of Dunbar and Skelton." *MLQ* 53:126–49.
Bartholomaeus Anglicus. 1485. *Liber de proprietatibus rerum*. Strasbourg.
Bataillon, Louis Jacques. 1989. "Sermons rédigés, sermons réportés XIIIe siècle." *Medioevo e Rinascimento* 3:69–86.
Beardsmore, Hugo Baetens. 1986. *Bilingualism: Basic Principles*. 2d ed. San Diego.
Bériou, Nicole. 1978. "La prédication au béguinage de Paris pendant l'année liturgique 1272–1273." *Recherches Augustiniennes* 13:105–229.
———. 1987. *La prédication de Ranulphe de la Houblonnière: Sermons aux clercs et aux simples gens à Paris au xiiie siècle*. 2 vols. Paris.
———. 1992. "Latin and the Vernacular. Some Remarks about Sermons Delivered on Good Friday during the Thirteenth Century." In *Die deutsche Predigt im Mittelalter,* edited by Volker Mertens and Hans–Jochen Schiewer, 268–84. Tübingen.
Blake, N. F., ed. 1964. *The Phoenix*. Manchester.
Boeren, P. C. 1956. *La vie et les oeuvres de Guiard de Laon*. La Haye.
Brinton, Thomas. 1954. *The Sermons of Thomas Brinton, Bishop of Rochester 1373–1389*. Edited by Sister Mary Aquinas Devlin, O.P. Camden Series, 3d ser., vols. 85–86. London.
Brown, Carleton, ed. 1932. *English Lyrics of the Thirteenth Century*. Oxford.
Cambridge University. 1858. *A Catalogue of the Manuscripts Preserved in the Library of the University of Cambridge*. Vol. 3. Cambridge.
Carley, James P. 1985. *The Chronicle of Glastonbury Abbey: An Edition, Translation and Study of John of Glastonbury's* Cronica sive Antiquitates Glastoniensis Ecclesie. Woodbridge.
Catalogue général des manuscrits des Bibliothèques publiques des Départements. 1872. Vol. 4, *Arras-Avranches-Boulogne*. Paris.
Catto, J. I., and Ralph Evans, eds. 1992. *The History of the University of Oxford*. Vol. 2: *Late Medieval Oxford*. Oxford.
Charland, Th.-M. 1936. *Artes praedicandi: Contribution à l'histoire de la rhétorique au Moyen Âge*. Paris.
Chaucer, Geoffrey. 1987. *The Riverside Chaucer*. 3d ed. General editor, Larry D. Benson. Boston.
Cigman, Gloria, ed. 1989. *Lollard Sermons*. Early English Text Society 294. Oxford.

Clanchy, M. T. 1979. *From Memory to Written Record: England 1066–1307.* London.

Coletti, Vittorio. 1983. *Parole dal pulpito: Chiesa e movimenti religiosi tra latino e volgare nell'Italia del medioevo e del Rinascimento.* Casale Monferrato.

Colker, Marvin L. 1991. *Trinity College Library Dublin, Descriptive Catalogue of the Mediaeval and Renaissance Latin Manuscripts.* 2 vols. Aldershot, Hants.

Coxe, H. O. 1973. *Bodleian Library, Quarto Catalogue.* Vol. 2: *Laudian Manuscripts,* reprinted with corrections and additions, etc., by R. W. Hunt. Oxford.

Delcorno, Carlo. 1986. "La diffrazione del testo omiletico. Osservazioni sulle doppie 'reportationes' delle prediche bernardiane." *Lettere italiane* 38:457–77.

Diehl, Patrick S. 1985. *The Medieval European Religious Lyric: An Ars Poetica.* Berkeley, Los Angeles, and London.

Dolan, T. P. 1989. "English and Latin Versions of Fitzralph's Sermons." In *Latin and Vernacular: Studies in Late-Medieval Texts and Manuscripts,* edited by A. J. Minnis, 27–37. Cambridge.

Ebin, Lois. 1979. "Chaucer, Lydgate, and the 'Myrie Tale.'" *Chaucer Review* 13.4:316–36.

Eccles, Mark, ed. 1969. *The Macro Plays.* Early English Text Society 262. London.

Emden, A. B. 1957–59. *A Biographical Register of the University of Oxford to A.D. 1500.* 3 vols. Oxford.

Erb, P. C. 1971. "Vernacular Material for Preaching in MS Cambridge University Library Ii.III.8." *MS* 33:63–84.

Fletcher, Alan J. 1986. "The Sermon Booklets of Friar Nicholas Philip." *MAe* 55:188–202.

————. 1991. "'Magnus predicator et deuotus': A Profile of the Life, Work, and Influence of the Fifteenth-Century Oxford Preacher, John Felton." *MS* 53:125–75.

Floyer, John Kestell. 1906. *Catalogue of Manuscripts Preserved in the Chapter Library of Worcester Cathedral.* Edited and revised by Sidney Graves Hamilton. Oxford.

Forde, Simon. 1989. "Nicholas Hereford's Ascension Day Sermon, 1382." *MS* 51:205–41.

Friend, Albert C. 1957. "The Dangerous Theme of the Pardoner." *MLQ* 18:305–8.

Galbraith, V. H. 1919. "Articles Laid Before the Parliament of 1371." *EHR* 34:579–82.

Gillespie, Vincent. 1989. "*Cura pastoralis in deserto.*" In *De Cella in Seculum: Religious and Secular Life and Devotion in Late Medieval England,* edited by Michael G. Sargent, 161–81. Cambridge.

Greatrex, Joan. 1991. "Benedictine Monk Scholars as Teachers and Preachers in the Later Middle Ages: Evidence from Worcester Cathedral Priory." In *Monastic Studies,* vol. 2, edited by Judith Loades, 213–25. Bangor, Gwynedd.

Greene, Richard Leighton. 1977. *The Early English Carols.* 2d ed. Oxford.

Grisdale, D. M., ed. 1939. *Three Middle English Sermons from the Worcester Chapter Manuscript F.10.* Leeds.

Gumperz, John J. 1982. *Discourse Strategies.* Cambridge.

Gwynn, Aubrey, S.J. 1937. "The Sermon–Diary of Richard Fitzralph, Archbishop of Armagh." *Proceedings of the Royal Irish Academy* 44:C1–57.

Haines, Roy M. 1972. "'Wilde Wittes and Wilfulnes': John Swetstock's Attack on Those 'Poyswunmongeres,' the Lollards." In *Popular Belief and Practice,* Studies in Church History 8, edited by G. J. Cuming and Derek Baker, 143–53. Cambridge.

———. 1975. "Church, Society and Politics in the Early Fifteenth Century as Viewed from an English Pulpit." In *Church, Society and Politics,* Studies in Church History 12, edited by Derek Baker, 143–57. Oxford.

———. 1976. "'Our Master Mariner, Our Sovereign Lord': A Contemporary Preacher's View of King Henry V." *MS* 38:85–96.

———. 1978. *The Church and Politics in Fourteenth-Century England: The Career of Adam Orleton, c. 1275–1345.* Cambridge.

———. 1989. *Ecclesia anglicana: Studies in the English Church of the Later Middle Ages.* Toronto.

Hamers, Josiane F., and Michael H. A. Blanc. 1989. *Bilinguality and Bilingualism.* Cambridge.

Hamesse, Jacqueline. 1986. "*Reportatio* et transmission de textes." In *The Editing of Theological and Philosophical Texts from the Middle Ages,* Studia latina Stockholmensia 30, edited by Monika Asztalos, 11–34. Stockholm.

Holcot, Robert. 1494. *Super libros Sapientiae.* Hagenau. Reprint. Frankfurt/Main, 1974.

Horner, Patrick J., F.S.C. 1975. "An Edition of Five Medieval Sermons from MS Laud Misc. 706." Ph.d. diss., State University of New York at Albany.

———. 1977. "John Paunteley's Sermon at the Funeral of Walter Froucester, Abbot of Gloucester 1412." *ABR* 28:147–66.

———. 1978. "A Sermon on the Anniversary of the Death of Thomas Beauchamp, Earl of Warwick." *Traditio* 34:381–401.

———. 1989. "Benedictines and Preaching in Fifteenth–Century England: The Evidence of Two Bodleian Library Manuscripts." *Revue Bénédictine* 99:313–332.

Horstmann, C., ed. 1881. *Altenglische Legenden.* Neue Folge. Heilbronn.

Hudson, Anne, ed. 1978. *Selections from English Wycliffite Writings.* Cambridge.

———. 1988. *The Premature Reformation: Wycliffite Texts and Lollard History.* Oxford.

Hunt, R. W. 1984. *The Schools and the Cloister: The Life and Writings of Alexander Nequam (1157–1217).* Edited and revised by Margaret Gibson. Oxford.

Isidore. 1911. *Etymologiae.* Edited by W. M. Lindsay. 2 vols. Oxford.

Jacob, E. F. 1933. "*Florida verborum venustas*: Some Early Examples of Euphuism in England." *BJRL* 17:264–90.

James, M. R. 1907. *A Descriptive Catalogue of the Manuscripts in the Library of Gonville and Caius College.* 2 vols. Cambridge.

James, M. R., and Claude Jenkins. 1930–32. *A Descriptive Catalogue of the Manuscripts in the Library of Lambeth Palace.* Cambridge.

Jennings, Margaret. 1975. "Monks and the *artes praedicandi* in the Time of Ranulph Higden." *Revue Bénédictine* 86:119–28.

John of Wales. 1489. *Communiloquium.* Strasbourg. Reprint. Wakefield, England, 1964.

Knight, Ione Kemp. 1967. *Wimbledon's Sermon* Redde rationem villicationis tue: *A Middle English Sermon of the Fourteenth Century.* Pittsburgh, PA.

Koopmans, Jelle, and Paul Verhuyck. 1986. "Quelques sources et parallèles des sermons joyeux français des XVᵉ et XVIᵉ siècles." *Neophilologus* 70:168–84.

Lazzerini, Lucia. 1971. "'Per latinos grossos . . .': Studio sui sermoni mescidati." *Studi di Filologia Italiana* 28:219–339.

Lecoy de la Marche, Albert. 1886. *La Chaire française au Moyen Âge, spécialement au XIIIe siècle, d'après les manuscrits contemporains.* 2d ed. Paris.

Lewis, R. E., N. F. Blake, and A. S. G. Edwards. 1985. *Index of Printed Middle English Prose.* New York and London.

Lindemann, Erika. 1973. "Translation Techniques in William Langland's *Piers Plowman.*" Ph.d. diss., University of North Carolina, Chapel Hill.

Little, A. G. 1943. "A Fifteenth-Century Sermon." In *Franciscan Papers, Lists, and Documents,* 244–56. Manchester.

Longère, Jean. 1983. *La prédication médiévale.* Paris.

Ludolf of Saxony [Landulfus Cartusiensis]. 1495. *In meditationes vitae Christi et super evangeliis totius anni opus divinum.* Brixen.

Madan, Falconer. 1905. *A Summary Catalogue of Western Manuscripts in the Bodleian Library at Oxford.* Vol. 5. Oxford.

Martin, Hervé. 1988. *Le métier de prédicateur en France septentrionale à la fin du Moyen Âge (1350–1520).* Paris.

Martin, Janet. 1982. "Classicism and Style in Latin Literature." In *Renaissance and Renewal in the Twelfth Century,* edited by Robert L. Benson and Giles Constable with Carol D. Lanham, 537–68. Cambridge, MA.

McKisack, May. 1959. *The Fourteenth Century, 1307–1399.* Oxford.

Mendenhall, J. C. 1919. *Aureate Terms: A Study in the Literary Diction of the Fifteenth Century.* Lancaster, PA.

Mom[igliano], A[ttilio]. 1934. "Maccheronica, Letteratura." In *Enciclopedia Italiana di scienze, lettere ed arti,* 21:730. Rome.

Mueller, Janel M. 1984. *The Native Tongue and the Word: Developments in English Prose Style 1380–1580.* Chicago.

Mynors, R. A. B. 1963. *Catalogue of the Manuscripts of Balliol College Oxford.* Oxford.

Newhauser, Richard. 1987. "Latin Texts with Material on the Virtues and Vices in Manuscripts in Hungary: Catalogue I." *Manuscripta* 31:102–15.

Nithardus. 1907. *Historiarum libri IIII.* Edited by Ernestus Müller. Scriptores Germanicarum rerum in usum scholarum. Hanover.

Norton-Smith, John, ed. 1966. *John Lydgate: Poems.* Oxford.

O'Carroll, Maura. 1984. "Two Versions of a Sermon by Richard Fishacre, OP, for the Fourth Sunday of Lent on the Theme *Non enim heres erit filius ancille cum filio libere.*" *AFP* 54:113–41.

O'Malley, J. W. 1979. *Praise and Blame in Renaissance Rome: Rhetoric, Doctrine and Reform in the Sacred Orators of the Papal Court, c. 1450–1521.* Durham, NC.

Owen, Nancy H. 1966. "Thomas Wimbledon's Sermon: 'Redde racionem villicacionis tue.'" *MS* 28:176–97.

Owst, G. R. 1926. *Preaching in Medieval England: An Introduction to Sermon Manuscripts of the Period c. 1350–1450.* Cambridge. Reprint. New York, 1965.

———. 1933. *Literature and Pulpit in Medieval England: A Neglected Chapter in the History of English Letters and of the English People.* Cambridge. Reprint (with additions). Oxford, 1961.

Paccagnella, Ivano. 1973. "Mescidanza e macaronismo: Dall'ibridismo delle prediche all'interferenza delle macaronee." *Giornale Storico della Letteratura Italiana* 159:363–81. Repeated in substance in Paccagnella, *Le macaronee padovane: Tradizione e lingua* (Padova, 1979), chapter 1.

Palmer, Nigel F. 1983. "'Antiquitus depingebatur': The Roman Pictures of Death and Misfortune in the *Ackermann aus Böhmen* and Tkadleček, and in the Writings of the English Classicizing Friars." *DVj* 57:171–239.

Pantin, W. A. 1931–37. *Chapters of the Black Monks.* Camden Series, 3d ser., vols. 45, 47, 54. London.

———. 1933. "A Sermon for a General Chapter." *Downside Review* 51:291–308.

Paoli, U. E. 1959. *Il latino maccheronico.* Firenze.

Parkes, M. B. 1991. "Tachygraphy in the Middle Ages: Writing Techniques Employed for Reportationes of Lectures and Sermons." In M. B. Parkes, *Scribes, Scripts and Readers: Studies in the Communication, Presentation and Dissemination of Medieval Texts,* 19–33. London and Rio Grande. Originally published in *Medioevo e rinascimento* 3 (1989): 159–69.

Pearce, Ernest H. 1916. *The Monks of Westminster: Being a Register of Brethren of the Convent From the Time of the Confessor to the Dissolution.* Cambridge.

Pearsall, Derek. 1970. *John Lydgate.* London.

Pfander, Homer G. 1937. *The Popular Sermon of the Medieval Friar in England.* New York.

Picot, Emile. 1886–88. "Le monologue dramatique dans l'ancien théâtre français." *Romania* 15:358–422; 16:438–542; 17:207–75.

Poplack, Shana. 1980. "Sometimes I'll start a sentence in Spanish y termino en español: Toward a Typology of Code–Switching." *Linguistics* 18:581–618.

Powell, Susan, and Alan J. Fletcher. 1981. "*In die sepulture seu trigintali*: The Late Medieval Funeral and Memorial Sermon." *LSE* 12:195–228.

Price, Derek J., ed. 1955. *The Equatorie of the Planetis.* Cambridge.

Richter, Michael. 1979. *Sprache und Gesellschaft im Mittelalter.* Stuttgart.

Riley, Henry Thomas, ed. 1867. *Gesta Abbatum Monasterii Sancti Albani.* Rolls Series 28, part 4, vols. 1–3. London.

Roberts, Phyllis Barzillay. 1968. *Stephanus de Lingua-Tonante. Studies in the Sermons of Stephen Langton.* Toronto.

Romaine, Suzanne. 1989. *Bilingualism.* Oxford.

Ross, Woodburn O., ed. 1940. *Middle English Sermons, Edited From British Museum MS. Royal 18 B.xxiii.* Early English Text Society 209. London.

Rusconi, Roberto. 1989. "*Reportatio*." *Medioevo e rinascimento* 3:7–36.

Salu, M. B., trans. 1955. *The Ancrene Riwle.* London.

Sankoff, David, and Shana Poplack. 1981. "A Formal Grammar for Code-Switching." *Papers in Linguistics* 14.1:3–46.

Schneemelcher, Wilhelm, ed. 1991. *New Testament Apocrypha.* Translated by R. McL. Wilson. 2 vols. Louisville, KY.

Schneyer, Johannes Baptist. 1969. *Geschichte der katholischen Predigt.* Freiburg im Breisgau.

Searle, Eleanor, ed. 1980. *The Chronicle of Battle Abbey.* Oxford.

Smalley, Beryl. 1960. *English Friars and Antiquity in the Early Fourteenth Century.* Oxford.

Solinus. 1958. *C. Ivlii Solini Collectanea rerum memorabilium.* Edited by Th. Mommsen. Berlin.

Southern, R. W. 1970. *Medieval Humanism*. New York.

Spector, Stephen. 1991. *The N-Town Play: Cotton MS Vespasian D.8*. Early English Text Society, Supplementary Series, 11. London.

Stainer, J. F. R., and C. Stainer. 1901. *Early Bodleian Music: Sacred and Secular Songs*. Edited by Sir John Stainer. 2 vols. London.

Stemmler, Theo. 1975. "More English Texts from MS. Cambridge University Library Ii.III.8." *Anglia* 93:1–16.

Stolt, Birgit. 1964. *Die Sprachmischung in Luthers Tischreden: Studien zum Problem der Zweisprachigkeit*. Acta Universitatis Stockholmensis, Germanistische Forschungen 4. Stockholm.

Swanton, Michael. 1987. *English Literature Before Chaucer*. London and New York.

Thomson, S. Harrison. 1940. *The Writings of Robert Grosseteste, Bishop of Lincoln, 1235–1253*. Cambridge.

Tolkien, J. R. R., ed. 1962. *The English Text of the Ancrene Riwle: Ancrene Wisse, edited from MS. Corpus Christi College Cambridge 402*. Early English Text Society 249. London.

Torres–Alcalá, Antonio. 1984. *Verbi Gratia: Los escritores macarronicos de España*. Madrid.

Vincent of Beauvais. 1624. *Speculum quadruplex*. 4 vols. Douai. Reprint. Graz, 1964–65.

Völker, Paul-Gerhard. 1963. "Die Überlieferungsformen mittelalterlicher deutscher Predigten." *ZfdA* 92:212–27.

Walsh, Katherine. 1981. *A Fourteenth-Century Scholar and Primate: Richard Fitzralph in Oxford, Avignon and Armagh*. Oxford.

Wehrle, William O. 1933. *The Macaronic Hymn Tradition in Medieval English Literature*. Washington.

Welter, J.-Th. 1927. *L'Exemplum dans la littérature religieuse et didactique du Moyen Âge*. Paris. Reprint. New York 1973.

Wenzel, Siegfried. 1974a. "Unrecorded Middle-English Verses." *Anglia* 92:55–78.

———. 1974b. "The Moor Maiden—A Contemporary View." *Speculum* 49:69–74.

———. 1976. "Vices, Virtues, and Popular Preaching." In *Medieval and Renaissance Studies: Proceedings of the Southeastern Institute of Medieval and Renaissance Studies, Summer 1974*, edited by Dale B. J. Randall, 28–54. Durham, NC.

———. 1978. *Verses in Sermons: "Fasciculus Morum" and Its Middle English Poems*. The Mediaeval Academy of America Publications No. 87. Cambridge, MA.

———. 1982. "Macaronic Sermons in Medieval England: Some Observations." Paper presented at the Third International Medieval Sermon Studies Symposium, Oxford, July 7, 1982. Abstract published in Medieval Sermon Studies 1982, *Report* (part of *Medieval Sermon Studies Newsletter* 10, Spring 1982): 3–4.

———. 1983. "A New Occurrence of an English Poem from the Red Book of Ossory." *Notes and Queries*, n.s., 30:105–8.

———. 1985. "Poets, Preachers, and the Plight of Literary Critics." *Speculum* 60:343–63.

———. 1986. *Preachers, Poets, and the Early English Lyric*. Princeton.

————. 1989. "*Somer Game* and Sermon References to a Corpus Christi Play." *MP* 86:274–83.

————. 1993. *Monastic Preaching in the Age of Chaucer*. The Morton W. Bloomfield Lectures on Medieval English Literature, 3. Kalamazoo, MI.

Whiting, Bartlett Jere, and Helen Wescott Whiting. 1968. *Proverbs, Sentences, and Proverbial Phrases from English Writings Mainly Before 1500*. Cambridge, MA.

Wilkins, David. 1737. *Concilia Magnae Britanniae et Hiberniae, AD. 446–1718*. 4 vols. London.

William of Auvergne. 1674. *Opera omnia*. Paris.

Wyclif, John. 1913. *Opera minora*. Edited by J. Loserth. Wyclif Society 21. London.

Young, Patrick. 1944. *Catalogus librorum manuscriptorum bibliothecae Wigorniensis Made in 1622–1623 by Patrick Young*. Edited by Ivor Atkins and Neil R. Ker. Cambridge.

Zumthor, Paul. 1960. "Un problème d'esthétique médiévale: l'utilisation poétique du bilinguisme." *Le Moyen Âge* 66:301–36, 561–94.

Index

357